Terrorists in Our Midst

TERRORISTS IN OUR MIDST

COMBATING FOREIGN-AFFINITY TERRORISM IN AMERICA

Yonah Alexander
Editor

Forewords by M. E. (Spike) Bowman and David G. Reist

Praeger Security International

🔵 PRAEGER

AN IMPRINT OF ABC-CLIO, LLC
Santa Barbara, California • Denver, Colorado • Oxford, England

Library of Congress Cataloging-in-Publication Data

Terrorists in our midst : combating foreign-affinity terrorism in America /
  Yonah Alexander, editor.
   p. cm.
  Includes bibliographical references and index.
  ISBN 978–0–313–37570–5 (hbk. : alk. paper) — ISBN: 978–0–313–37571–2 (ebook)
1. Terrorism—United States—Prevention. 2. Terrorism—Prevention. 3. Transnational crime
—Prevention. I. Alexander, Yonah.
HV6432.T4784 2010
363.325′170973—dc22   2009052372

ISBN: 978–0–313–37570–5
EISBN: 978–0–313–37571–2

14 13 12 11 10   1 2 3 4 5

This book is also available on the World Wide Web as an eBook.
Visit www.abc-clio.com for details.

Praeger
An Imprint of ABC-CLIO, LLC

ABC-CLIO, LLC
130 Cremona Drive, P.O. Box 1911
Santa Barbara, California 93116-1911

This book is printed on acid-free paper ∞

Manufactured in the United States of America

Copyright Acknowledgment

The author and publisher gratefully acknowledge permission to use excerpts from the
following material:

Michael B. Mukasey, "The Spirit of Liberty," *Wall Street Journal*, May 10, 2004, p. A16.
Reprinted with permission from Michael B. Mukasey.

This book is published in cooperation with the Inter-University
Center for Terrorism Studies, administered by the International
Center for Terrorism Studies at the Potomac Institute for Policy Studies
and the Inter-University Center for Legal Studies at the International
Law Institute.

Contents

Foreword

Today writing about terrorism is almost a cottage industry. There is so much literature available on the subject that it is tempting to simply allow new literature to dissolve into the wallpaper. That would be a mistake with respect to *Terrorists in Our Midst*. This book is one product of a great many years of thought and interdisciplinary analytics. Many distinguished individuals, not all represented in this book, studied foreign-affinity terrorism for nearly seven years, guided by three persistent issues:

1. The organizational structure and interior workings of international networks in the United States;
2. The policies and legal framework of the United States that we rely on for protection of both security and democratic values; and
3. The lessons to be learned from past experiences, from which we might be able to discern "best practices."

Unlike most literature about terrorism, *Terrorists in Our Midst* focuses on those among us who would do us harm. It provides a focus on those who would cause harm due to their own demons, those such as a Timothy McVeigh or Ted Kaczynski, but especially on those who are influenced by terrorists from afar. More than that, the panel of experts who contribute to this book offer assessments of policies and practices we have adopted to meet the threat and provide an agenda of best practices. Moreover, unlike most literature of this genre, *Terrorists in Our Midst* is brutally frank in ascribing shortcomings where, logically, the American public has a right to expect better.

One issue common to most terrorism literature is the fact that the world order has not yet settled on a definition of terrorism, which restricts the ability of the nations of the world to find common ground for remedial actions. The reasons for lack of consistency are legion and typified by the types of terrorism we have experienced in our own history. Yonah Alexander provides a catholic reference to terrorism throughout the ages. As does Oliver Revell, Dr. Alexander also points out the uncomfortable fact that we have had experiences, stemming from the Ku Klux Klan to the Murrah building, that would qualify as terrorism but which generally have been treated disparately. He explains that we in the United States did not begin to develop a homeland security approach to terrorism until the 1970s, and even then it was a nascent exercise. Dr. Alexander further points out how difficult it is internationally to hold nations responsible for terrorist acts perpetrated by individuals and even by organized groups.

Raymond Tanter and Stephen Kersting take a novel approach by addressing foreign-affinity terrorism through the medium of three questions:

1. How does it challenge intelligence capabilities;
2. How does the intelligence community respond to the threats; and
3. What changes are needed to make the intelligence community more effective?

Tanter and Kersting focus a great deal of their analysis on institutions, in particular the Federal Bureau of Investigation (FBI). They are quite complimentary in noting that the Bureau very quickly grew a " joint" capability within the United States through the Joint Terrorism Task Force (JTTF) concept and further established and participated in other, similarly constituted centers for joint analysis and investigation.

Tanter and Kersting also note that the Director of National Intelligence (DNI) was charged with instituting an information-sharing process, with growing the National Counterterrorism Center (NCTC), and with overseeing the intelligence community (IC). Despite the efforts of the FBI, and the apparent authority of the DNI, they note that there was substantial knowledge of shortcomings that Congress (and the media) failed to properly address. By comparing the Israeli Knesset and Israeli media with their U.S. counterparts, they conclude the balance and perspective of our own society is sadly wanting, leaving the public in unnecessary peril.

Further contributing to the issues of intelligence, William Lewis squarely focuses the reader on the core principle that intelligence is the most important antiterrorism weapon in the arsenal. Adopting a point of view similar to that of Tanter and Kersting, he sees more blame and finger pointing than proposals for change. He takes the 9/11 Commission to task for consistently pointing out flaws without making serious suggestions for how to improve the situations the Commission uncovered. He notes the wastage of money by the FBI in trying to improve information management. However, his sharpest criticism is reserved for Congress when he predicts that the persistent Congressional modality of reviewing "excesses" will assuredly produce additional acrimony and ill will. Given the current approaches, he believes it may take another decade before the public will again view the IC as credible.

Unlike his co-authors, Oliver Revell provides the insider's view, having served in the FBI for 30 years. As previously noted, he believes it important to recognize that we have had incidences of terrorism stretching well back into our history. From the vantage of a participant, Revell offers his views on social and cultural antecedents for affinity terrorism and comments favorably on both purpose and implementation of the PATRIOT Act.

Bruce Zagaris provides the reader with an uncommonly clear view of the mechanisms we employ to preempt financing for foreign-affinity terrorism in the United States. Bruce notes that these mechanisms apply both to ostensibly legal typologies, such as NGOs that nevertheless fund terrorist purposes, and to illegal typologies, such as cigarette smuggling.

Zagaris provides a good deal of information on the actual mechanisms employed, but laments that they are primarily of U.S. origin only. He notes that we have tried to convince other nations to adopt similar mechanisms, but with mixed success. He singles out HAMAS, in particular, explaining that we continue to have limited success in preempting financing operations that support that organization. More importantly, he points out that stringent application of financial control much stricter than those which other nations employ undermines our own economic security by virtue of creating a climate unfriendly to investment. He concludes that counterterrorism financial enforcement has strict limits of effectiveness—a view that stands ascounterpoint to the positions taken by the last three administrations.

Zagaris also contributes a chapter on border security in which he notes the difficulties of controlling the borders due to the needs of transportation, the gaps in the nonimmigrant visa process, and the arduousness of inspecting containerized cargo. He discusses the difficulties of fortifying border infrastructure and recommends, strongly, that we focus on law and regulation to secure where and what we can—the unspoken caution is not to expect too much. He also cautions that whatever we do can have diplomatic, environmental, legal and ... unintended consequences—another unspoken caution consisting of "look before you leap."

The concluding chapter by Edgar H. Brenner focuses on an aspect of affinity terrorism on which there is very little literature. Brenner notes the importance of civil rights in our culture and how those rights are protected by the rule of law. Importantly, Brenner explains how a misguided sense of civil rights prevented the FBI from transforming efficiently into a primarily intelligence-driven organization due to the erection of an artificial wall between criminal and intelligence personnel and information.

In explaining the tension that civil rights and investigatory issues promoted both in Congress and in the judiciary, Brenner provides a valuable lesson to the reader. It was this tension, he explains, that prevented Congress from doing more to implement solutions to the systemic failings identified by the 9/11 Commission. Worse, however, was the failure of the Foreign Intelligence Surveillance Court (FISC) to understand the law it was supposed to monitor. The FISC exercised very poor judgment in preserving the "wall." The FISC required a warrant to intercept foreign-to-foreign communications simply because the interception occurred in the United States.

Brenner saves his final criticism for the House of Representatives which permitted portions of the very necessary PATRIOT Act to sunset on February 6, 2008, thereby sacrificing security to the artificially created tension between civil liberties and security—a tension created in large part by the privacy lobby and acquiesced to by Congress.

In sum, *Terrorists in Our Midst* breaks both ground and rice bowls. It advances best practices and condemns worst practices. It unhesitatingly highlights the situations when the emperor was wearing no clothes. Unlike most books on terrorism, this one focuses on systemic issues of homeland security and provides the reader with important points of view not easily found in any other single volume.

M. E. (Spike) Bowman
Former Deputy, National Counterintelligence Executive and
Deputy General Counsel
(National Security Law, FBI)

Foreword

Immunity from terrorism is unfortunately long gone. Understanding and combating terrorism—starting with a thorough critical analysis—will allow every country to counter this constantly evolving threat. Most discussions regarding terrorism focus on the traditional—a recap of what has happened and the tactics employed by foreigners. *Terrorists in Our Midst* takes the discussion of affinity terrorism in America to the next intellectual level.

Dr. Yonah Alexander has woven a mosaic of prescient thoughts that defines affinity terrorism—how it has been dealt with to date and most importantly what must be done in the future. He succinctly provides definitional perspectives that serve as the needed foundational piece to understand the contributing factors, state sponsorship, and the future outlook of terrorism, what he defines as super terrorism. Dr. Alexander then transitions to America's homegrown terrorism issues and then directly focuses on affinity terrorism and what counterterrorism strategies have been taken to combat the issue. By focusing on foreign nationals and American citizens alike and looking at terror networks both home and abroad, this work holistically addresses the entire problem. His opening missive magnificently sets the table for the remaining chapters.

The following six chapters dissect what Dr. Alexander has introduced and provide insights that need to be understood by every American. The initial focus is the role intelligence plays and how intelligence has to be analyzed and shared in order to safeguard our nation. The background and detailed analysis superbly illustrate the challenges that have confronted the intelligence community in the past and that will continue to challenge it in the future. The focus on the PATRIOT Act and its implications are especially revealing and are continually stressed throughout the book. The spotlight then transitions to the role of law enforcement, with special focus on efforts pre and post September 11, 2001. This chapter specifically challenges the balance between individual rights and those actions required to protect America. The financial support required to fund affinity terrorism is then detailed. It should come as no surprise that the connection between actions of terrorists and required funding is inexplicably linked. Border security is then analyzed and this chapter debunks some of the conventional myths that exist, while providing keen insights. The final chapter addresses civil rights and foreign intelligence surveillance. The "wall" created between intelligence and law enforcement is poignantly discussed through several very important case analyses. What the PATRIOT Act was supposed to do—permit effective coordination between intelligence gathering and law enforcement to prevent terrorism—did not happen completely under the rigors of legal interpretations. All the aforementioned chapters are critical in their analysis, but most importantly offer solutions required to guide our nation through this labyrinth of defeating terrorism.

National and global security concerns of the twenty-first century and beyond will always require keen academic insights. This work is one of those insights. The threats of tomorrow are rooted in history, but detailed analysis is required in order to cull out the salient points that are germane and those that will endure. *Terrorists in Our Midst* provides the analysis of terrorism and the associated networks both inside and outside America. It is a seminal work addressing what is facing America and should be read by anyone who is addressing these challenges in the future.

David G. Reist
BGen, USMC (Ret)

Preface

Since the dawn of history, fear has been deemed as the most cursed of human passions. Its numerous painful perceptions and emotions have been cited in the annals of civilization through various ominous forms: apprehension, anxiety, awe, despair, alarm, horror, panic, and peril. Indeed, every generation has dreaded and distressed over imminent and potential misfortunes and calamities. These unpredictable or anticipated afflictions were invariably caused by providential fury, nature's ravaging disasters, and man-made political violence in the name of "national interests," as well as "higher principles" of "just" ideologies and theologies.

Expressions of psychological intimidation and physical force in the struggle of power within and among nations in violation of domestic and international law provide the theoretical and practical context for our study, *Terrorists in Our Midst: Combating Foreign-Affinity Terrorism in America*. The resort to tactical and strategic tools of "inhumanity of man to man"—aggravated by hatred, animosities, fanaticism, extremism, and savagery—has been a permanent feature of power politics; although the concept "terrorism," thus far at least, has escaped a universally acceptable definition. Thus, the United Nations, as the prime global security body, has failed for over six decades to overcome differing dispositions of member states and thereby reach a consensus on the meaning of the term, its root causes, and the required remedies to cope effectively with widening conventional and unconventional dangers.

Nevertheless, the brutal reality is that the perpetrators of terrorism—individuals, groups, and state actors—in seeking to achieve avowed political, social, and economic goals have struck intensive fear in the hearts and minds of those communities and nations they consider as "enemies."[1] The unprecedented catastrophe that befell the United States on September 11,

2001, has dramatically demonstrated that 19 al Qaeda suicide operatives, employing "airplane missile" weapons, were successful in bringing, at least temporarily, the only superpower to its knees. In addition to the enormous human and other associated costs,[2] this previously unimaginable scale of attack resulted in extraordinary fear of future threats directed by al Qaeda and other adversaries at home and abroad.

Now, over eight years after the most devastating terrorist assault in history, the key strategic question is whether the United States, unilaterally or in concert with its friends and allies, can successfully confront the terrorist challenge in the twenty-first century in spite of escalating levels of fear and formidable odds.

Addressing this growing concern, President Barack Obama, in his State of the Union speech on January 27, 2010,[3] observed that "throughout our history, no issue has united this country more than our security." Discussing the terrorist threat, the president specifically cited the need for better aviation security and more effective responses to bioterrorism. He also urged securing "all vulnerable nuclear materials around the world ... so that they never fall into the hands of terrorists."

Subsequently, Secretary of State Hillary Rodham Clinton, during an interview with CNN on February 8, 2010, further elaborated that even a nuclear-armed North Korea and Iran do not pose as great of a threat as "the transnational non-state networks, primarily the extremists who are connected—al Qaeda in the Arab Peninsula, al Qaeda in Pakistan and Afghanistan, [and] al Qaeda in the Maghreb [region of North Africa]." Echoing the president's earlier trepidations, Secretary Clinton warned "the biggest nightmare that any of us have is that one of these terrorist member organizations within this syndicate of terror will get their hands on a weapon of mass destruction."

This grim security concern was also shared by senior U.S. intelligence officials. Testifying before the Senate Select Committee on Intelligence on February 2, 2010, Dennis C. Blair, Director of National Intelligence, warned of looming terrorist risks from al Qaeda that "maintains its intent to attack the homeland preferably with large-scale operations that would cause mass casualties, harm the U.S. economy or both."[4] Among the major threats, he mentioned a cyber attack and the likelihood of an attempted terrorist operation in the United States by July 2010.

Other intelligence leaders who appeared with Director Blair at the same Senate hearing[5] agreed with this assessment.[6] Moreover, the prevailing official view is that, despite the fact that al Qaeda has been weakened by numerous American countermeasures in Iraq, Afghanistan, and Pakistan; financial pressures; and eroding popular support in the Muslim world; the jihadist global network continues to pose serious dangers. Several reasons seem to account for reality: al Qaeda's core leadership, headed by Osama bin Laden, is still intact and in pursuit of weapons of mass destruction; low-level and short-term operations mounted by regional affiliates and like-minded groups are expanding; and jihadist ideology preys on local and global grievances and radicalizes more young recruits for future missions in the United States and abroad.

Recently intensified terrorist-related plots in the United States are frightening wake-up calls. The first spectacular attack occurred on November 5, 2009, at one of the largest U.S. military installations in the world: the army's Soldier Readiness Center at Fort Hood, Texas.[7] Major Nidal Malik Hasan, born in Arlington, Virginia, to a Palestinian family, who served at the base as a psychiatrist, allegedly opened fire at his fellow soldiers as they prepared for deployment overseas, killing 13 and wounding 30. The suspect, apprehended by police officers, personifies a self-radicalized jihadist "loner" rather than a "formal" member of al Qaeda or any other terrorist movement.

The second major incident that deeply shook America was the December 25, 2009, failed bombing of Northwest Flight 253, carrying 278 passengers and crew from Amsterdam to Detroit.[8] The alleged attacker, Omar Farouk Abdulmutallab, a Nigerian citizen, found inspiration in al Qaeda's global jihadist ideology. He traveled to Yemen to obtain operational instruction and explosives intended for his mission from al Qaeda in the Arabian Peninsula (AQAP).[9] Claiming responsibility for the Christmas Day failed plot, AQAP in a released statement dated December 28, declared that "the hero Mujahid Martyrdom-seeker ... broke through all modern advanced technological equipment and security barriers in world airports ... but due to Allah's will a malfunction happened which caused only partial detonation rather than a full one." The statement further promised "we will continue on this path, Allah willing, until we reach our goal so that religion is all Allah's."[10]

Disturbingly, these two seemingly unrelated dramatic incidents are linked through the fact that a Yemeni-American cleric, Anwar al-Awlaki born in Las Cruces, New Mexico, who had subsequently relocated to his ancestral homeland to become a key AQAP religious leader, had provided radical inspiration and advice to both Major Hasan and Abdulmutallab. The former suspect attended Dar Al Hijrah Center (a mosque in Falls Church, Virginia) where al-Awlaki served as an Imam, exchanged e-mails, and frequently visited the cleric's Web sites. Similarly, the latter operative also maintained correspondence with al-Awlaki and even met with him in Yemen.[11]

Moreover, not only did al-Awlaki radicalize the alleged perpetrators through jihadist indoctrination, but for several years he also developed a growing following of Americans and other Westerners through his influential English-language Internet and online video activities in support of jihad.[12] Concerns were therefore raised that the cleric's efforts will result in recruiting more "soldiers of Allah" to attack the United States at home and abroad.[13] In light of this potential threat, President Obama reportedly authorized a December 24, 2009, drone attack against al-Awlaki, but the cleric survived the strike.[14]

Indeed, instances of homegrown and foreign-based jihadist indoctrination and violence increased dramatically in 2009. In that year, a total of 54 American defendants had federal terrorism-related charges filed or unsealed against them, thus recording more cases than any other year since 2001. Among some of the contributing factors explaining this emerging trend are Internet recruiting activities, expansion of al Qaeda's operations abroad, shifting tactics developed by the network in response to more effective governmental countermeasures, and intensified terrorism and insurgency efforts in Iraq, Afghanistan, and Pakistan.[15]

There are several recent cases that underscore the nature and scope of the "enemy within" who is imbued with foreign-fidelity assertiveness. For example, Najibullah Zazi, an Afghani immigrant driver from Denver, was charged by a New York Grand Jury on September 24, 2009, with planning to use one or more "weapons of mass-destruction" against New York subways. Zazi underwent terrorist training in Pakistan and contacted other suspected Muslim extremists in the United States. One of his alleged supporters was Ahmad Wais Afzali, the Imam of the al-Bakar mosque in Queens who had also served as a New York Police Department intelligence informant.[16]

Another accused jihadist operative is David Coleman Headley (formerly known as Daod Gilani), an American raised in Pakistan who subsequently moved to Chicago. He has been charged with terrorist scouting missions for the November 2008 Mumbai attack and with conducting surveillance of a nuclear weapons plant in India in the service of Lashkar e-Taiba, the Pakistan affiliate of al Qaeda. Headley was also involved in a plot against the Danish newspaper *Jyllandsposten* that published cartoons of the Prophet Muhammad which offended Muslims around the world in 2005. His collaborator was Tahawwur Hussain, a Pakistani-Canadian businessman who legally resided in Chicago.[17]

Another worrisome instance of indoctrinated Americans willing to join the global al Qaeda network is the group of five Northern Virginia young men (Waqur Khan, Ramy Zamzam, Umar Farooq, Ahmed Minni, and Aman Hassan Yemer) who attended the same neighborhood mosque and traveled to Pakistan in order to join the "Holy War" against U.S. troops in the region. Their plan was aborted when Pakistani police arrested the jihadists.[18]

To be sure, the largest alleged Islamic network since 9/11 was exposed when federal authorities in November 2009 charged eight Americans with recruiting some 20 co-nationals, mostly of Somali background, to join al Qaeda's associated insurgent movement al-Shabab in the Horn of Africa. The concern expressed by U.S. law-enforcement officials was that some of these operatives, in cooperation with radical European fighters, will ultimately target America.[19]

Clearly, the foregoing cases of unpredictable American jihadist "lone wolves" and other extremist co-religionists with close links to al Qaeda and its affiliates mirror only a partially radical challenge to the homeland. A more insidious (and seemingly less short-term) deadly threat is the spike in Internet activity among uncounted multitudes of silent extremists in the United States who might become the next operatives. A recent illustration of such a development is the flurry of electronic chatter among this radical minority of the Muslim community swapping ideas on how to "beat" the security systems within the country.[20]

These manifestations of the growing challenge must, however, be supplemented by other concerns. Consider, for example, the potential danger posed by Hezbollah and Hamas, the two major theologically-nourished terrorist groups supported primarily by Iran and Syria. Their activities in the United States in 2009 raised warning signals. Thus, a federal court in Philadelphia indicted Hassan Hodroj, Dib Hani Harb, and Hassan Antar Karaki —all from Beirut—who had conspired with Moussa Ali Hamdan of Brooklyn to funnel counterfeit money and other illegal cash to Hezbollah. The scheme, involving other collaborators in the United States, also included the buying and shipping of weapons to Hezbollah.[21] Similarly, in 2009, Ghassan Elashi and Shukri Abu Baker, founding members of the Holy Land Foundation for Relief and Development, once the largest Islamic charity in America, were each sentenced to 65 years for providing more than $12 million to Hamas.[22] These incidents suggest that both groups might potentially continue with their activities in the United States simply because of the availability of American supporters.

Yet, regardless of the intense indoctrination of the "jihadist next door"[23] or the scope and impact of terrorist operations mounted by individuals and foreign-affinity groups in the United States and abroad, the Obama administration, following the approach initiated in 2008 by President George W. Bush, is seeking to defuse the theological elements from the strategic lexicon. In fact, the concepts of "Islam," "Islamic," or "Islamist" have not been incorporated in either the "Quadrennial Homeland Security Review" published by the Department of Homeland Security, or the "Quadrennial Defense Review" released by the Department of Defense, both in February 2010.[24] This sensitivity to a religious-based terminology stems from American concern that counterterrorism efforts should not be perceived as a "war" against Islam and the Muslim world. Accordingly, terms such as "radicalism," "extremism," or "violent extremism" have been utilized by the United States to characterize the challenge rather than to attribute religion as a critical component of the problem. As a result, the official U.S. policy is to focus on preventing and deterring terrorism from whatever source.

Obviously, future events will ultimately determine whether the government's reluctance to label the gravest threat to national security in jihadist terms would effectively work or not work. Nevertheless, "knowing the enemy" also requires consideration of homegrown ideological radicalism. Indeed, the largest act of domestic terrorism occurred on April 19, 1995, when a federal building in Oklahoma City was bombed by two American right-wing extremists, killing 168 people, including 19 children, and wounding 674 other victims. Now, nearly 16 years later, ideological extremist expressions of violence are sporadically continuing, and more frequent and spectacular attacks triggered by political, social, and economic disturbances cannot be ruled out.[25]

In light of the multiple and complex security considerations reviewed previously, the following work, *Terrorists in Our Midst: Combating Foreign-Affinity Terrorism in America*, which was initially undertaken in the aftermath of 9/11, focuses primarily on two key aspects of the challenge. The first aspect is assessing the role of American citizens and permanent residents who consider themselves members of a distinct national "diaspora," or belonging to a broader global ethnic, racial, or religious community, whose loyalties lie with radical "foreign-affinity" strategic objectives sanctified by extremism and violence. The second aspect is the experience of the intelligence community, law enforcement agencies, and other relevant bodies in coping with homegrown terrorism while preserving the American value system.

To put it differently, we are dealing with several questions in our study: How did foreign terrorist organizations exploit American human and material resources to perpetrate attacks domestically and internationally? What lessons can be drawn from the successes and failures of countermeasures directed against foreign-affinity terrorism through local, state, and federal structures? Finally, are there any specific recommendations that can be effective in bringing the "enemy next door" challenge to a manageable level within America?

In an effort to consider these and related questions, this volume is organized into seven chapters, each of which offers a particular perspective. The first chapter provides a general overview of the terrorism challenge confronting the United States. The role of intelligence in combating foreign-affinity terrorism is analyzed in the next two chapters. Chapter 4 focuses on the experiences and roles of the law enforcement agencies. The three chapters that follow concentrate on financial matters, border security, and civil liberties issues. A postscript section updating the findings of the study that was completed in fall 2009 is included, along with preliminary conclusions and a brief suggested strategic agenda to combat foreign-affinity terrorism.

Finally, some acknowledgments are in order. This volume, like other similar multi-authored works, is a product created by a team of academics and practitioners. My friends and colleagues—Raymond Tanter, Stephen Kersting, William H. Lewis, Oliver (Buck) Revell, Bruce Zagaris, and Edgar

H. Brenner—have shown intellectual and professional commitments as well as unending patience and dedication. Without their superb cooperation, our study could not have been completed. Deep appreciation is also due to both M. E. (Spike) Bowman and David G. Reist, BGen, USMC(Ret) who have written most insightful forewords in spite of a very tight schedule. Many other individuals, such as R. James Woolsey (former Director, CIA) and Ambassador L. Paul Bremer (former Coordinator for Counterterrorism, U.S. Department of State), have also provided valuable guidance to the study.

Our research work has also benefited from the continuing support of our core three academic institutions: the Inter-University Center for Terrorism Studies (a consortium of universities and think tanks in some 40 countries); the International Center for Terrorism Studies at the Potomac Institute for Policy Studies (Arlington, Virginia); and the Inter-University Center for Legal Studies at the International Law Institute (Washington, D.C.). The encouragement and logistical assistance provided by Michael S. Swetnam, Chairman and CEO of the Potomac Institute is greatly appreciated. Likewise, Edgar H. Brenner, in his capacity as co-director of the IUCLS deserves our gratitude for his legal guidance on the project. Also, Professor Herbert Levine's important contribution is acknowledged. He reviewed several drafts of the study and made valuable suggestions.

Indeed, the above core institutions, as well as other private and public bodies in the United States and abroad, have facilitated many meetings, seminars, and conferences, focusing on the interdisciplinary perspectives of the foreign-affinity terrorism challenge. My colleagues and I owe them our thanks for their important cross-fertilization contributions in the work. Thanks are also due to the winter 2010 team of young researchers which assisted in the production of the study, particularly in the preparation of the extensive index. This group consisted of Reina Matsuzawa (Sophia University, Japan), Brian Haupt (University of Scranton, Pennsylvania), Terje Jacobsen (University of Bergen, Norway), Minh Mai (Clark University, Massachusetts), John O'Meara (University of Washington, Washington), Andrew Puckett (Roanoke College, Virginia), Karina Sand (University of Bergen, Norway) and Vincent Topping (University of Calgary, Canada).

It is hoped that this study will increase governmental and public understanding of the risks of future foreign-affinity terrorism and provide additional comprehensive short- and long-term responses to the challenge in the coming decades of the twenty-first century. Clearly, a significant historical lesson and practical road map to bear in mind in this effort is the wise guidance offered by President Franklin D. Roosevelt during his first inaugural address on January 20, 1933, facing another national crisis:

> This is preeminently the time to speak the truth, the whole truth, frankly and boldly. Nor need we shrink from honestly facing conditions in our country

today. This great Nation will endure as it has endured, will revive and will prosper. So, first of all, let me assert my firm belief that the only thing we have to fear is fear itself—nameless, unreasoning, unjustified terror which paralyzes needed efforts to convert retreat into advance. In every dark hour of our national life a leadership of frankness and vigor has met with that understanding and support of the people themselves which is essential to victory.[26]

Yonah Alexander
February 18, 2010

Abbreviations

ABC Initiative	Arizona Border Control Initiative
ACLU	American Civil Liberties Union
ALF	Animal Liberation Front
ASALA	Secret Army for the Liberation of Armenia
ATA	Anti-Terrorism Act
ATOC	Anti-Terrorist Operations Center
ATSA	Aviation and Transportation Security Act
BIF	Benevolence International Foundation
BIS	Bureau of Industry and Security
BOP	Bureau of Prisons
CBP	Customs and Border Protection
CIA	Central Intelligence Agency
CISPES	Committee in Solidarity with the People of El Salvador
COT	Committee on Terrorism
CSI	Container Security Initiative
CTFE	counterterrorism financial enforcement
DCI	Director of Central Intelligence
DEA	Drug Enforcement Administration's
DHS	Department of Homeland Security
DIA	Defense Intelligence Agency
DNI	Directorate of National Intelligence
DoD	Department of Defense

EFP	explosively formed penetrator
EMETIC	Even Mecham Eco-Terrorist International Conspiracy
EOTF/FC	Executive Office for Terrorist Financing and Financial Crimes
ERT	emergency response team
FALN	Armed Forces of National Liberation
FARC	Fuerzas Armadas Revolucionarias de Colombia
FATF	Financial Action Task Force
FBI	Federal Bureau of Investigation
FCI	foreign counterintelligence
FI	foreign intelligence
FIGs	Field Intelligence Groups
FinCEN	Financial Crimes Center
FISA	Foreign Intelligence Surveillance Act
FIUs	financial intelligence units
FSRBS	FATF-style regional bodies
FTOs	foreign terrorist organizations
FTTTF	Foreign Terrorist Tracking Task Force
GAO	Government Accountability Office
GIA	Algerian Armed Islamic Group
GRF	Global Relief Foundation
GWOT	Global War on Terror
HCI	Human Concern International
HEU	highly enriched uranium
HLF	Holy Land Foundation
HRT	hostage rescue team
HSPD	homeland security presidential directives
IACP	International Association of Chiefs of Police
IBETs	Integrated Border Enforcement Teams
IC	intelligence community
ICE	Immigration and Customs Enforcement
IEBSA	Immigration Enforcement and Border Security Act
IEDs	improvised explosive devices
IEEPA	International Emergency Economic Powers Act
IG	inspectors general
IIRIRA	Illegal Immigration Reform and Immigrant Responsibility Act

INR	Bureau of Intelligence and Research
INS	Immigration and Naturalization Service
INTERPOL	International Criminal Police Organization
IRT	International Radical Terrorism
ITG	International Terrorism Group
JI	Jema'ah Islamiya
JTTFs	Joint Terrorism Task Forces
KKK	Ku Klux Klan
LTTE	Liberation Tigers of Tamil Eelam
MEK	Mujahedeen-e Khalq
MSA	Muslim Student Association
NAFTA	North American Free Trade Agreement
NATO	North Atlantic Treaty Organization
NCTC	National Counterterrorism Center
NGA	National Geospatial Intelligence Agency
NIEs	national intelligence estimates
NII	nonintrusive inspection
NJTTF	National Joint Terrorism Task Force
NORC	National Opinion Research Council
NRO	National Reconnaissance Office
NSA	National Security Agency
OAE	Operation Active Endeavor
OAS	Organization of American States
OFAC	Office of Foreign Assets Control
OMB	Office of Management and Budget
OSCE	Organization for Security and Cooperation in Europe
PIJ	Palestinian Islamic Jihad
PIRA	Provisional Irish Republican Army
PLO	Palestinian Liberation Organization
POE	ports of entry
REMJA	Reunión Extraordinaria de los Ministros de Justicia de las Américas
RPG	rocket propelled grenade
RPMs	radiation portal monitors
SARs	suspicious activity reports

SBI	Secure Border Initiative
S/CT	State Department Office of the Coordinator for Counterterrorism
SDN	Specially Designated Nationals
SEC	Securities Exchange Commission
SHOW	subject, hostages, objectives, and weapons
SIGI	Special Inspector General of Iraq
SOAR	Special Operations and Research
TEL	Terrorist Exclusion Lists
TFI	Terrorism and Financial Intelligence
TFOS	Terrorist Financing Operations Section
TRAC	Terrorist Research and Analytical Center
TREVI	Terrorism Radicalism Extremism Violence International
TSA	Transportation Security Administration
TSC	Terrorist Screening Center
TTIC	Terrorist Threat Integration Center
UAVs	unmanned aerial vehicles
UNSCR	UN Security Council Resolution
USA PATRIOT Act	Uniting and Strengthening America by Providing Appropriate Tools Required to Intercept and Obstruct Terrorism Act
US-VISIT	U.S. Visitor and Immigrant Status Indicator Technology
WMD	weapons of mass destruction

1

America's Terrorism Challenge: An Overview

Yonah Alexander

Political, social, and economic conflicts within and among nations are as old as history itself. Fear and brutal force as instruments of power have been employed by individuals, communities, substate groups, and sovereign entities in the name of "higher" justifications of "rights," "justice," and even "peace." These tools of psychological and physical violence—constituting random and systematic intimidation, coercion, repression, or destruction of human lives and property—are traditionally regarded as both tactics and strategies in the form of terrorism, insurgency, revolution, asymmetrical conflicts, civil wars, aggression, and full-scale hostilities, to mention a few. Such adversarial conduct is triggered by a wide range of contributing factors including ideological extremism, nationalistic fanaticism, imperial adventurism, religious animosities, ethnic hatred, racial prejudices, and tribal arrogance.

Indeed, from memorial times to the present, humanity's record is characterized by the exploitation of savagery by both weak and strong entities to advance realistic or imaginary goals, notably forcing conversions, maintaining oppression, preserving internal stability, or defeating perceived enemies. Among the numerous precedents frequently highlighted are the attacks mounted by the zealot Jewish group, the Scarii ("dagger" men), targeting the Roman occupiers of Judea and their collaborations during the first century AD; the assassination by the Muslim radical Hashasheen of their co-religionist opponents and Christian "infidels" in the Middle East between the eleventh and thirteenth centuries; the Spanish Inquisition's frequent resort to violence in its effort to "protect" Catholicism during the fifteenth to nineteenth centuries; the "Reign of Terror" of the French Revolution; the illegal underground operations of Narodnaya Volya ("People's Will") in Tsarist Russia in the nineteenth century; and the unprecedented tyranny and brutality of Soviet, Fascist, Nazi, and Maoist regimes during the last century.

It is not surprising, therefore, that a Middle Eastern popular proverb has long observed that "peace is the dream of the wise; war is the history of man." And yet, despite this stark reality, a definitional bankruptcy contributes to a conceptual confusion regarding the meaning and implications of contemporary challenges of terrorism, as one major manifestation of perpetual brutality, within and among nations. Thus, the purpose of this chapter is to provide an analytical context to this study on *Terrorists in Our Midst*,[1] focusing on the experience of the United States in assessing and confronting this particular form of such threat to its security concerns at home and abroad.

The following discussion deals with definitional perspectives, provides a generic overview of terrorism, addresses "diaspora" or "foreign-affinity" dangers, and summarizes various American counterterrorism strategies.

DEFINITIONAL PERSPECTIVES

The seventeenth-century political philosopher John Locke remarked that "a definition being nothing but making another understand by words what the term defined stand[s] for." Locke's observation, however, has evaded the truism that there are no "simple" political or juridical concepts. There exists, therefore, an apparent confusion about the meaning of what constitutes "terrorism" internationally and within the United States itself. The concept "terrorism" presents a more complicated definitional understanding as to its universal meaning. Indeed, the international community and governments speak with a bewildering variety of voices on this subject.[2] Consider, for example, the League of Nations Convention of 1937 that was never enacted by its member states because of contradictory political and moral views. The Convention defined "terrorism" as "all criminal acts directed against a State and intended or calculated to create a state of terror in the minds of particular persons of a group of persons or the general public."[3]

The United Nations (UN), the successor international organization, also failed thus far, at least to provide a global consensus to the meaning of "terrorism." Prior to September 11, 2001, the world body initiated a wide range of definitions and statements on terrorism. For instance, the UN General Assembly, in its resolution titled "Measures to Eliminate International Terrorism," adopted on December 9, 1994, contains a provision describing terrorism: "Criminal acts intended or calculated to provoke a state of terror in the general public, a group of persons or particular persons for political purposes are in any circumstance unjustifiable, whatever the considerations of a political, philosophical, ideological, racial, ethnic, religious, or any other nature that may be invoked to justify them."[4] Similar language was used by subsequent UN resolutions, strongly condemning "all acts, methods and practices of terrorism as criminal and unjustifiable wherever and by whomsoever committed."[5]

Following the 9/11 assault on the United States, Secretary General Kofi Annan described a terrorist attack on one country as "an attack on humanity as a whole." This "zero-tolerance" approach was adopted by the United Nations even without a universally accepted definition.[6] For instance, UN Resolution 1373 (2001) required all member states to criminalize terrorism and to establish as serious criminal offenses any planning, support, and perpetration of terrorist acts.

Clarifications of what constitutes "terrorism" have been incorporated in UN work rather frequently. Thus, UN Resolution 1566 (2004) states that such acts are

> criminal acts, including against civilians, committed with the intent to cause death or serious bodily injury, or taking of hostages, with the purpose to provoke a state of terror in the general public or in a group of persons or particular persons, intimidate a population or compel a government or an international organization to do or to abstain from doing any act, which constitute offences within the scope of and as defined in the international conventions and protocols relating to terrorism, are under no circumstances justifiable by considerations of a political, philosophical, ideological, racial, ethnic, religious or other similar nature, and calls upon all States to prevent such acts and, if not prevented, to ensure that such acts are punished by penalties consistent with their grave nature.[7]

It should be noted that while this resolution asserts that it is "imperative to combat terrorism by all means," member states are obligated to comply with international human rights, refugee, and humanitarian law. Similarly, consistency with international law has been reaffirmed in other UN actions. For example, in its UN Global Counterterrorism Strategy (2006), the world body required the extradition or prosecution of "any person who supports, facilitates, participates, or attempts to participate in the financing, planning, preparation, or perpetration of terrorist acts."

Additional details on the nature of the challenge have been provided in specific UN-sponsored agreements. Thus, in its 2007 International Convention for the Suppression of the Financing of Terrorism, the United Nations asserted that terrorism is an "act intended to cause death or serious bodily injury to a civilian, or to any other person not taking an active part in the hostilities in a situation of armed conflict, when the purpose of such act, by its nature or context, is to intimidate a population, or to compel a government or an international organization to do or to abstain from doing any act."[8]

A similar legal pattern is experienced by other multilateral organizations. For instance, the North Atlantic Treaty Organization (NATO), the regional security body that currently constitutes a global security provider, considers terrorism to present a universal scourge of a multifaceted nature.[9] Nevertheless, the alliance has not as yet agreed upon a precise definition of terrorism. Some of its officials, such as former NATO Secretary General Jaap de Hoop Scheffer, asserted that it is not mandatory for the organization to formulate a definition of terrorism before taking action to combat its threats. The lack of a definitional unanimity, he claimed, does not affect NATO's daily life.[10] After 9/11, for example, NATO invoked Article 5 of its charter and launched "Operation Active Endeavor" (OAE) in supporting the military operation in Afghanistan without having a consensus on a formal definition.[11]

Clearly, the legal confusion regarding what constitutes terrorism stems from the failure of the international community to agree on common practical and moral views on the permissibility and impermissibility of the act. Conceptual differences on who are "terrorists" in contradiction to "resistance" or "freedom fighters" explain partially the dilemma of what is frequently described as an "untenable" definition.

It is not surprising, therefore, that each state reserves to itself the legal authority to define "terrorism" in the context of domestic and international law. For example, Muslim countries, members of the Islamic Conference on Combating International Terrorism, exclude from this act what they regard as "armed struggle for liberation" as an expression of "self-determination."

The United States, like many other Western nations, is, however, more inclusive in its definitional approach. Thus, American perceptions are detailed as follows[12]:

(1) the term "international terrorism" means terrorism involving citizens or the territory of more than 1 country;

(2) the term "terrorism" means premeditated, politically motivated violence perpetrated against noncombatant targets by subnational groups or clandestine agents;

(3) the term "terrorism group" means any group practicing, or which has significant subgroups which practice, international terrorism;

(4) the terms "territory" and "territory of the country" means the land, waters, and airspace of the country; and

(5) the terms "terrorist sanctuary" and "sanctuary" mean an area in the territory of the country—

(A) that is used by a terrorist or terrorist organization—

(i) to carry out terrorist activities, including training, fundraising, financing, and recruitment; or

(ii) as a transit point; and

(B) the government of which expressly consents to, or with knowledge, allows, tolerates, or disregards such use of its territory and is not subject to a determination under—

(i) section 2405(j)(1)(A) of the Appendix to title 50

(ii) section 2371 (a) of this title; or

(iii) section 2780 (d) of this title.

What is particularly noteworthy about this definition is the American meaning of "noncombatant targets." While indiscriminate attacks on civilians appear to always be regarded as illegal in war and peacetime, the United States also includes in "noncombatant targets" military personnel who are at the time of a terrorist incident unarmed and/or not on duty. Additionally, attacks on military bases, installations, and residences are considered illegal such as the bombing of the Marine Headquarters in Beirut in 1983 perpetrated by Hezbollah.

Other clarifications of the meaning of the terms "international terrorism" and "domestic terrorism" are also detailed in American jurisprudence. Thus, the USA PATRIOT (Uniting and Strengthening America by Providing Appropriate Tools Required to Intercept and Obstruct Terrorism) Act (18 U.S.C. Section 2331) states the following[13]:

(1) the term "international terrorism" means activities that—

(A) involve violent acts or acts dangerous to human life that are a violation of the criminal laws of the United States or of any State, or that would be a criminal violation if committed within the jurisdiction of the United States or of any State;

(B) appear to be intended—

(i) to intimidate or coerce a civilian population;

(ii) to influence the policy of a government by intimidation or coercion; or

(iii) to affect the conduct of a government by mass destruction, assassination, or kidnapping; and

(C) occur primarily outside the territorial jurisdiction of the United States, or transcend national boundaries in terms of the means by which they are accomplished, the persons they appear intended to intimidate or coerce, or the locale in which their perpetrators operate or seek asylum;

(5) the term "domestic terrorism" means activities that—

(A) involve acts dangerous to human life that are in violation of the criminal laws of the United States or of any State;

(B) appear to be intended—

(i) to intimidate or coerce a civilian population;

(ii) to influence the policy of a government by intimidation or coercion; or

(iii) to affect the conduct of a government by mass destruction, assassination, or kidnapping; and

(C) occur primarily within the territorial jurisdiction of the United States.

The foregoing definitional sources of American law do not, however, clarify the conclusion that nonetheless exists concerning the United States' policies and activities vis-à-vis terrorism. For instance, during the George W. Bush administration (2001–2009), the official concept "Global War on Terror" (GWOT) was utilized to characterize the juridical and political nature of the asymmetric warfare challenge. Since President Barack Obama assumed power, the conceptual approach has apparently been shifted from the previous "war-like" disposition to a new terminology, labeling "terrorism" as "man-caused disaster" and GWOT as "overseas contingency operations."[14]

Explaining why the Obama administration banned the earlier phrases, John Brennan, head of the White House Homeland Security office, rationalized that "we are at war with al Qaeda. . . . We are at war with its violent extremist allies who seek to carry on al Qaeda's murderous agenda. . . . [Y]ou can never fully defeat a tactic like terrorism any more than you can defeat the tactic of war itself."[15]

Despite this assertion, what is unclear is how long the administration will continue to reject the "war" concept. At least regarding the Afghanistan mission, the president still calls it the "war we need to win."

In sum, the contemporary record amply indicates that the fog over the meaning of the term "terrorism" is not limited to the United States alone. Even the International Court of Justice contributes, partially at least, to the legal definitional confusion. Suffice to mention the following description: "Terrorism is destruction of people or property by people not acting on behalf of an established government for the purpose of redressing a real or imaginary injustice attributed to an established government and aimed directly or indirectly at an established government."[16]

The International Court of Justice's assertion is indeed restrictive simply because it does not provide for considerable acts of terrorism sponsored or supported by state agencies. This limitation weakens efforts to deal with the challenge realistically. And yet, this shortcoming, coupled with the absence of a global common legal definition did not prevent intensive unilateral, bilateral, and multilateral counterterrorism actions. The existing 13 international conventions and the newly developing additional agreements clearly forge a legal basis and road map in this process. Moreover, the international community seems to be moving more speedily than previously in the direction of a worldwide comprehensive juridical instrument in this area of security concerns.

DERIVATIVE "TERRORISM" CONCEPTS: "DIASPORA" AND "FOREIGN-AFFINITY TERRORISM"

The concept of "terrorism," by its very nature, challenges theorists and practitioners alike. The literature on the term described varies as both tactics and strategy are vast and changed. It reflects the proliferation of mainstream and alternative interpretations of definitive terms, ranging from political crime to all-out war.

The previous section focused on the "traditional" and changing articulation of terrorism in light of changing national, regional, and global security circumstances. The following discussion, dealing with the meaning of the terms "diaspora" and "foreign-affinity" terrorism is prerequisite for understanding the dangers facing the United States from terrorists in its midst.

Originally, the concept "diaspora" is a Greek term for "scattering or sowing seeds."[17] It denotes a nation or part of a nation that is separated from its ancestral territory and is dispersed among other countries. Nevertheless, these people are still attached to their national culture, legacy, and aspirations. That term is generally applied to the exile of the Jews from Palestine as a consequence of the occupation of the Kingdom of Judea by the Babylonians in the sixth century and subsequently following the Roman destruction of the Second Temple in Jerusalem in 70 AD.

The characteristics of a "diaspora," a people, vary but generally can be summarized as follows[18]:

- They, or their ancestors, have been dispersed from a specific original "center" to two or more "peripheral," or foreign, regions.
- They retain a collective memory, vision, or myth about their original homeland—its physical location, history, and achievements.
- They believe that they are not—and perhaps cannot be—fully accepted by their host society and therefore feel partly alienated and insulated from it.
- They regard their ancestral homeland as their true, ideal home and as the place to which they or their descendants would (or should) eventually return —when conditions are appropriate.
- They believe that they should, collectively, be committed to the maintenance or restoration of their original homeland and to its safety and prosperity.
- They continue to relate, personally or vicariously, to that homeland in one way or another, and their ethnocommunal consciousness and solidarity are importantly defined by the existence of such a relationship.

These characteristics are attributed not only to the "exiled" Jewish people but also to numerous other ethnic, racial, religious, and national communities throughout the world. From time to time, scholars and policymakers refer to indigenous terrorist groups operating abroad as "diaspora terrorism."

On August 31, 2009, for instance, the Sri Lankan ambassador in the United States, Jaliya Wickramasuriya, claimed that despite the fact that the separatist movement of the Liberation Tigers of Tamil Eelam (LTTE) was defeated recently by government forces in his war-torn country, there are still some ethnic-Tamil expatriates in the diaspora who continue to support the LTTE cause.[19]

Nevertheless, because the concept "diaspora terrorism" invokes sensitive political implications such as charges of "dual loyalty," it appears that a more frequently used term related to "migrant violence" in the broad lexicon of conflict is "foreign-affinity terrorism." Consider, for example, the ordinary dictionary description of the term "foreign":[20] "not native or belonging to a certain country; born in or belonging to another country, nation, sovereignty, or locality." Furthermore, "foreign" is "remote, distant, strange, not belonging, not pertaining or pertinent, not appropriate, not harmonious, not agreeable, not congenial." Similarly, a "foreigner" is "a person belonging to or owing allegiance to a foreign country; one not native to the country or jurisdiction under consideration or not naturalized there; an alien; a stranger."

It is not surprising, therefore, that "foreign" and "foreigner" were "suspect" within their new national environment. The poet John Milton, for instance, defined this label in these words: "whom certain these rough shades did never breed." And William Shakespeare has famously written, "Kept him a foreign man still, which so grieved him that he ran mad and died."[21]

Regardless of countless perceptions of such a concept, for the purpose of this study the following is a working definition of "foreign-affinity terrorist":[22]

International terrorist networks using aliens and U.S. citizens with ties to a foreign country or to ideological or religious groups for several illegal purposes, such as to obtain funds, propagandize anti-American causes, provide military and other training, purchase arms, gather intelligence, and organize operational plans for terrorist targeting in the United States and abroad. The effort to further terrorist interests by foreign nationals with the collaboration of American citizens represents a growing national, regional, and global security concern.

To be sure, some definitive classifications and interpretations of "foreign-affinity terrorism" have been offered and adopted during the past several decades. For instance, in the United States, the Federal Bureau of Investigation (FBI) preferred the phrase "International Radical Terrorism (IRT)" in describing "any extremist movement or group, which is international in nature and conducts acts of crime or terrorism under the banner of personal beliefs in furtherance of political, social, economic, or other objectives." The FBI concluded that IRT, along with state sponsorship of terrorism, poses a "significant threat to U.S. national security."[23]

Before dealing with this political challenge, it is appropriate to present a brief generic overview of the nature and intensity of contemporary terrorism to the international community.

CONTEMPORARY TERRORISM: A GENERIC OVERVIEW[24]

Because terrorism is a cheap, attractive, and effective instrument of fear, it has been repeatedly employed by a variety of groups and even nations in the post–World War II era. Currently, it is becoming a permanent fixture of international life, threatening every nation, large and small. Unlike their historical counterparts, contemporary terrorists have utilized tactics of propaganda and violence on an unprecedented scale, with serious implications for national, regional, and global security.

The following analysis surveys briefly the evolution of terrorism in the West and East. More specifically, terrorism—the unlawful use of physical force and psychological intimidation by substate or clandestine state agents against noncombatant targets, primarily intended to achieve social, economic, political, strategic, or other objectives—is not new in history. In the Middle Ages, several Western states employed pirates to terrorize the seas and further specific foreign policy aims. The "reign of terror" from "above" and "below" became a common practice during the eighteenth century.

Subsequently, a broad spectrum of indigenous groups, ranging from anarchists to national extremists, resorted to violent activities to attain some "higher goals." The assassination of Tsar Alexander II in 1881 is one example of this kind of terrorism. In the twentieth century, the murder of the Austrian Archduke in Sarajevo by a nationalist extremist ignited the First World War. The period between the two World Wars also witnessed terrorist activities in Europe, with the assassination of King Alexander of Yugoslavia as a case in point.

It was not, however, until the 1960s that terrorism became a permanent fixture of life in the West. The Paris students' revolt in 1968, the emergence of indigenous separatist movements, the rise of Middle Eastern violent extremism, and the expansion of state terrorism are some of the contributing factors that encouraged the intensification of terrorism in Europe and elsewhere, such as in Asia and Latin America. The Arab-Israeli conflict, for example, has had for the past six decades many consequences both regionally and globally. Territorial, dynastic, ideological, theological, and personal rivalries within the Arab and Muslim world have also resulted in developing divisive forces, including terrorism mounted by state and nonstate bodies as well as civil wars and all-out military confrontations between and among antagonists.

Indeed, since the end of World War II, the terrorist battlefield extended beyond those traditional geographic areas. The threat engulfed, for instance, Muslim and non-Muslim entities in the East such as decades-long disputes over the control of Kashmir. This and similar regional conflicts will continue to constitute the root cause for further violence in the coming months and years.

Contributing Factors to Terrorism

There are numerous political, social, and economic contributing factors that facilitate modern terrorism. Some of the major types of generic conditions that affect this reality include ethnic, racial, and religious, as well as intolerance and violence; escalation of propaganda and psychological warfare; extreme nationalism and separatism; regional conflicts that defy easy solutions; intensification of criminal activity and narco-trafficking; population explosion, migration expansion, and unemployment; economic gap between West and East; environmental challenges; and arms development and proliferation of conventional and unconventional weapons.

Among the specific reasons for the escalation of contemporary terrorism worldwide, mention should be made of the absence of a universal definition of terrorism; disagreement as to the root causes of terrorism; the religionization of politics; the exploitation of the media; double standards of morality; loss of resolve by governments to take appropriate action; weak punishment of terrorists; violation of international law of states; the complexity of modern societies; and the high cost of security in democracy.

Current and future perpetrators include the following: "free-lance" and substate terrorist groups; individual terrorists; mentally deranged and "crusaders"—"martyrs"; single-issue political extremists; ideological-based groups; ethnic, racial, and religious movements; nationalist and separatist actors; criminal and political mercenaries; and international networks, particularly al Qaeda.[25]

Some of the terrorists' impulses cover a broad range of motivations. These consist of political discontent (a. ideological: anarchism; ambitions; and radicalism; b. nationalistic: resistance; separatism; and irredentism; c. economic discontent: low living standards; lack of opportunity; unfulfilled expectation; loss of squandered resources; and d. cultural discontent: class constraints; ethnic discrimination; religious intolerance; technological irritants; environmental irritants).

Terrorist groups use a variety of means—from the simple to the complex—to secure funds for their activities. The initial sources of terrorist funds include both legal (e.g., personal savings and legitimate business revenue) and illegal (e.g., criminal acts such as drug trafficking and financial fraud). Once the funds are raised, they are distributed to various factions of terrorist groups through a variety of means.

Regardless of the foregoing motivations, the various ways that terrorist organizations fund their deadly activities include the use of traditional and alternative financial services entities (e.g., banks and hawalas—informal money-transfer systems firmly established in Asia and the Middle East); nonprofits' trading in commodities (e.g., "conflict diamonds" and gold); bogus financial instruments; currency smuggling and wire transfers; drug trafficking; extortion; money laundering; smuggling products; securities fraud; and other scams.

To be sure, another contributing factor that encourages terrorism generally and against the United States and its allies specifically is the expansion of international networks of terrorist groups. Osama bin Laden's al Qaeda (the "Base") represents the most dangerous challenge to world security. More specifically, this contemporary Sunni terrorist network and affiliated groups, comprised of supporters, cells, and links in some 100 countries, are now responsible for the spread of a radical *Salafist* ideology of *jihad* (holy war) to all corners of the globe, a development that has already gravely affected many nations.

The ideology and objectives of al Qaeda are crystal clear. It opposes all nations and institutions governed in a manner inconsistent with bin Laden's particular extremist interpretation of Islam, and specifically targets countries such as Saudi Arabia, Egypt, Jordan, Algeria, Morocco, and Tunisia. These militants support the violent overthrow of these countries' governments because, according to their puritanical *Salafist* Islamic beliefs, these governments have been corrupted by Western, particularly American, policies. Al Qaeda's followers believe that all Muslim state boundaries will disappear, and that the broader *umma*, or Islamic community, will be united under the rule of the Caliphs governed by *Shariah*, or Islamic jurisprudence.

The evolution of this brutal and costly ideological and physical conflict between al Qaeda and the United States has been shaped by a series of specific events that have particularly influenced American policymakers, both unilaterally and multilaterally, as they have developed new strategies to confront this continually evolving threat. Four specific benchmarks in this intellectual and physical struggle are worth noting: First, in August 1996, bin Laden issued a Declaration of Jihad against the United States and the Saudi Arabian government; second, in February 1998, al Qaeda's founder along with his senior associate Ayman al-Zawahiri endorsed a fatwah (religious ruling) stating that Muslims should kill Americans, including civilians, anywhere in the world they can be found; third, in May 1998, Mohammed Atef (bin Laden's second in command) sent Khaled al Fawwaz (al Qaeda's spokesman) a letter endorsing a fatwah issued by bin Laden and including a declaration by the "Ulema Union of Afghanistan," calling for a jihad against the United States and its allies; and fourth, in late May 1998, bin Laden issued a statement entitled "The Nuclear Bomb of Islam," in which he asserted that it is the duty of Muslims to prepare as many forces as possible to attack the enemies of God.

Additionally, a series of spectacular attacks by al Qaeda in both the United States and abroad underscored, more than ever before, America's vulnerability and the urgent need to overhaul U.S. counterterrorism policies to confront the threat. The first dramatic attack, which was the largest foreign terrorist operation on American soil at the time, occurred on February 26, 1993, when a large truck bomb exploded in the basement parking garage of the World Trade Center in New York City, killing 8 people, injuring more than 1,000, and causing widespread damage and panic. The attack was perpetrated by a group of foreign terrorists from Egypt, Iraq, Jordan, and the Palestinian Authority. Ramzi Yousef, an al Qaeda operative, and Sheik Omar Abdel-Rahman, the spiritual leader of the Egyptian al-Gama'a al-Islamiya and al-Jihad, with links to bin Laden, were convicted of carrying out this attack and sentenced to life imprisonment.

On October 3–4 of that same year, 18 U.S. servicemen were killed in Mogadishu, Somalia, by local militia men. Al Qaeda claimed credit for helping train them to effectively use rocket propelled grenade (RPG) launchers against U.S. helicopters operating in the area. Other major al Qaeda-affiliated attacks include the November 13, 1995, car bomb explosion outside the American-operated Saudi National Guard training center in Riyadh, Saudi Arabia, killing 5 Americans and 2 Indians; the June 25, 1996, car bombing attack with Iranian support at Khobar Towers, a U.S. Air Force housing complex in Dhahran, Saudi Arabia, killing 19 soldiers and wounding hundreds more; the two virtually simultaneous August 7, 1998, truck bombings of the U.S. embassies in Nairobi, Kenya, and Dar es Salaam, Tanzania, killing 234 people, 13 of them American, and wounding over 5,000 others; and the October 12, 2000, suicide bombing of the USS *Cole* during a refueling stop in Aden, Yemen, which killed 17 and wounded 39 American sailors.

It was not, however, until September 11, 2001, that the most heinous demonstrations of America's unprecedented vulnerability to contemporary terrorism occurred. Bin Laden's "war in the shadows" hit the American homeland in an attack that was described by many as a second "Day of Infamy," causing more casualties than the 1941 Japanese attack on Pearl Harbor. Nineteen al Qaeda suicide terrorists hijacked four U.S. airliners, crashing two into the Twin Towers of the World Trade Center in New York City, and a third into the Pentagon in Arlington, Virginia. A fourth plane, headed towards Washington, DC, and apparently destined for the U.S. Capitol building or the White House, crashed in a field in Shanksville, Pennsylvania, after passengers, alerted by cell phone calls about the earlier New York strikes, attacked the hijackers, who then crashed the plane. The human cost of these attacks was 2,974 dead, with thousands more injured.

Even eight years after this most devastating assault on the American homeland, the United States is still facing daily warnings and threats of terrorism from al Qaeda's leadership.[26]

State Sponsorship of Terrorism[27]

Clearly, there is also a long record of governments providing terror groups with direct and indirect financial and other types of support (e.g., training, intelligence, operations, and weaponry). The roles of Iran, Sudan, and Cuba come to mind. Previously, also Libya and North Korea were considered state sponsors of terrorism by the international community.

More specifically, state sponsorship of terrorism is defined as a government's direct or indirect encouragement of official and unofficial groups to exercise psychological or physical violence against political opponents, adversarial governments, or other entities for the purpose of coercion and widespread intimidation designed to bring about a desired political or strategic objective.

State sponsorship of terrorism is unique in that the groups carrying out the violence are furthering the policy of an established government located outside the territory in which the conflict occurs. Additionally, what distinguishes the use of terrorism from more conventional forms of coercive force at a sovereign state's disposal is the option of plausible deniability, or a complete absence of public accountability. The secretive operational methods employed by state-sponsored terrorists (who range from individual foreign nationals to entire client states) afford sponsoring nations such as Iran the ability to avoid admissions of warlike behavior and evade accountability in the court of international opinion.

The degrees to which a state's involvement with a terrorist group can be reasonably considered "official" vary greatly, ranging from the direct or indirect provision of both moral and material support to direct psychological conditioning, political indoctrination, and propaganda support. Indeed, for the state sponsor, the actual initiation of a terrorist campaign signals the fruition of a long and complex development process. For the terrorists receiving support, external assistance from an organized government in control of sovereign territory and state institutions is an enormous advantage.

Generally, however, if a government is to be held responsible internationally for the actions of a terrorist organization, its assistance to that group has to be measured in concrete terms, e.g., its direction of activities, its supply of funding and armaments, and its use of national assets and territory for training and intelligence activities. Such intimate involvement, however, is usually accompanied by an ideological, religious, or political affinity between a sponsoring government and a group, as well as mutually beneficial propaganda support. However, rather than mere rhetoric, a state's role as "accomplice" or "accessory to the crime" constitutes the most convincing and concrete evidence of terrorism sponsorship.

In international affairs, it is not commonly understood that the domestic criminal law concept of conspiring to commit a crime is itself illegal. This elementary concept, applicable to state sponsorship of terrorism, must be established in international opinion because it justifies self-defense measures and retribution. A terrorist group action in conjunction with, or on behalf of, a foreign government can be used to affect a target country's political stability, commercial ties, and diplomatic relations in a way that direct military confrontation cannot, or will not, achieve; and this effect can be seen regardless of whether or not a state of war exists between the sponsor and target government. Indeed, state sponsorship of terrorism is most detrimental to democratic institutions in cases short of outright warfare.

More specifically, it is amply evident that the major terrorist challenges that have faced the international community and particularly the United States in the post–World War II period consisted of two long "battles" or "wars." The first was the four-decade Cold War, during which the Soviet Union (USSR) employed terrorism via proxy client and cooperative states, including Bulgaria, East Germany, Czechoslovakia, Cuba, and North Korea. In turn, these states directly supported nations such as Libya, Syria, and Iran that openly sponsored specific terrorist organizations with financing weapons, training, and operational assistance. Thus, the USSR was able to reap the geopolitical benefits of terrorist actions from a distance. Indeed, Moscow in pursuing its own global political and strategic objectives, deftly exploited the popular notions of "liberation struggle" and "war of national liberation" to justify its direct and indirect support of both allies and like-minded states as well as numerous left-wing and revolutionary movements throughout the world. That "long war" ended when the Soviet Union finally collapsed in 1991.[28]

The second long "war," which continues today, began on November 4, 1979 when Iranian militants, with the support of Ayatollah Khomeini's government, seized the U.S. Embassy in Tehran, taking some 50 American diplomats hostage. After 444 days in captivity, the hostages were released in January 1981 immediately after Ronald Reagan was sworn in as president, succeeding the Carter Administration.[29] Later, in the early 1980s after Americans were taken hostage in Lebanon, Reagan's top aides initiated the Iran-Contra "arms-for-hostages" deal, in which America sold arms to Tehran in order to persuade Iranian-backed Lebanese Hezbollah (Party of God) terrorists to release the American hostages. These hostages were taken by Hezbollah in an effort to force the United States and other Western countries to pressure Kuwait to release two of the Lebanese who were among the 17 terrorists imprisoned in Kuwait for the December 1983 bombing of the U.S. and French embassies in Kuwait City as well as the failed attacks on a Kuwaiti oil refinery facility and the Kuwait International Airport control tower. The attacks were conducted by the Iranian-backed Islamic Da'wa Party as a result of Kuwait's support of Iraq in the Iran-Iraq War.

Many argue that the U.S. decision to effectively negotiate with Hezbollah via its state-sponsor, Iran, in an effort to secure the release of American hostages, combined with the Reagan administration's withdrawal of the Marine peacekeeping force within months of Lebanese Hezbollah's 1983 suicide truck bomb attack on the Marine barracks, illustrated the United States' weakness in confronting terrorists. This perception led terrorist groups worldwide to conclude that asymmetrical warfare tactics could be effectively employed against American superpower, and therefore encouraged a global escalation of anti-American attacks in the following decades. Even now, three decades after the Tehran embassy takeover, Iran is still engaged in this long "war" against the United States. In the early 1980s, Iran supported Hezbollah which attacked American embassies in Lebanon and Kuwait as well as the U.S. Marine headquarters in Beirut, killing and wounding hundreds of civilian and military personnel.

Iran also was implicated in the 1996 bombing of the Khobar Towers military housing complex in Saudi Arabia. During the summer of 2007, Iran was identified by U.S. officials as having directly and indirectly supported both Islamic and nationalist terrorist and insurgent groups operating in Iraq against American, Iraqi, and allied forces attempting to regain control amid a vicious insurgency. Tehran provides training and weapons, such as improvised explosive devices (IEDs), to include a deadly type of IED called an explosively formed penetrator (EFP) able to disable heavily armored U.S. military vehicles with deadly effect, as well as other assorted light arms. More ominously, according to the U.S. intelligence community's consensus, the expected withdrawal of American troops from Iraq could result in an Iranian intervention in Iraq, either unilaterally or by invitation from Iraqi Shiite factions.

In addition, there are other regional hot spots where Tehran is supporting terrorism. Mention could be made of Afghanistan, where Iranian financial support and weapons have been provided to forces affiliated with the Taliban conducting guerrilla warfare against American and coalition troops present in the country since November 2001 as part of Operation Enduring Freedom and the wider U.S.-led "Global War on Terrorism." Also, Iran, in cooperation with Syria, has long funded and equipped Hezbollah with technologically sophisticated weapons, which enabled the Shiite terrorist movement to launch and sustain a monthlong war against Israel in the summer of 2006. This conflict, which included the launching of thousands of unguided *Katyusha* rockets into Israeli territory, caused civilian casualties and temporarily shut down activity in some northern Israeli towns and villages. Furthermore, Iran continues to provide Palestinian militant groups in the West Bank, as well as Hamas in Gaza, with financial assistance, weapons supplies, and training to further the goal of undermining the Middle East peace process, which the United States and its allies are currently seeking to revive.

However, the most disturbing and challenging current threat to U.S. security interests and, indeed, the security of the Middle Eastern region as a whole is Tehran's decision to actively pursue the development of nuclear materials with weaponized applications. Iran's current activities have focused on the acquisition of fissile materials, such as enriched uranium—a core of any nuclear device. Despite public statements professing its peaceful intentions regarding the production of nuclear materials, the Iranian regime is widely believed to desire a weapons-grade nuclear program.[30] This potentiality, when coupled with its traditional utilization of terrorism as a state instrument, engenders the truly nightmarish possibility (if not probability) that Iran could deploy the ultimate attack via a terrorist proxy against Israel, or a regional Middle Eastern opponent, the United States, or other perceived adversaries elsewhere.

Future Outlook: Super Terrorism

Modern terrorism is characterized by an ideological and theological fanaticism and education in hatred toward one's enemy, which has been coupled with rapid technological advancements in communications (e.g., the Internet), transportation (e.g., modern international air travel), and conventional and unconventional weaponry to create a truly lethal threat.

Indeed, this threat has become much more decentralized, as it now emanates not only from established terrorist organizations, but also from freelance individuals with the motives, means, and opportunities to visit harm upon civil society. As a result of these developments, contemporary terrorism presents a multitude of threats to the safety, welfare, and civil rights of ordinary people; the stability of the state system; the health of national and international economic systems; and the expansion of democracies.

One measurement of evaluating the terrorist threat is to calculate the enormous cost to all societies in terms of the number of incidents, the human toll, and the economic damage. Indeed, since the 1960s, modern society has suffered dearly from the global disease of terrorism, a reality that grows in scope and brutality with every passing year. For example, in the 1970s, a total of some 300 terrorist attacks, both domestic and international, were recorded worldwide. Currently, almost 40 years later, the count has reached over 80,000 incidents.[31]

Clearly, no community, country, or region is immune from the impact of terrorism. In the 9/11 attack in New York City, citizens from 78 countries were killed. That year alone, a total of some 3,537 people died. During the period 2002–2008 approximately over 113,000 persons perished and hundreds of thousands more were wounded in terrorist attacks throughout the world. The economic, political, psychological, and strategic costs must also be considered in this assessment.[32]

What is of particular concern is that unconventional weapons—biological, chemical, radiological, and nuclear—are slowly emerging upon the contemporary terrorist scene.[33] That is, as technological developments offer new capabilities for terrorist groups, the *modus operandi* of terrorist groups may subsequently alter most drastically. Reportedly, at least a dozen terrorist groups, in addition to al Qaeda's network, have shown an interest in acquiring or are actively attempting to obtain mass disruption and destruction weapons (WMD). This worrisome trend presents a clear and present danger to the very existence of civilization itself. Thus, while the probability of nuclear terrorism remains low in comparison to the use of other WMD, the consequences for "super" terrorism could be enormous. If a nuclear bomb is stolen (or built by a terrorist group with reasonable resources and talent), an explosion of about 1 kiloton (one-twentieth the power of the Hiroshima attack) in a major city anywhere will cause more than 100,000 fatalities and result in damages totaling billions of dollars.

The seriousness of this unconventional threat was detailed by former Senator Sam Nunn, who is currently cochairman of the Nuclear Threat Initiative:

> In my view, the threat of terrorism with nuclear weapons and other weapons of mass destruction presents the gravest danger to our nation and the world. We know that al Qaeda is seeking nuclear weapons. We don't know how many other groups may also have similar ambitions. We know that nuclear material al Qaeda desires is housed in many poorly secured sites around the globe. We believe that if they get that material, they can build a nuclear weapon. We believe that if they build a nuclear weapon, they will use it.[34]

Senator Nunn further explained:

> I am not sure we fully grasp the devastating, world-changing impact of a nuclear attack. If a 10-kiloton nuclear device goes off in mid-town Manhattan on a typical work day, it could kill more than half a million people. Ten kilotons, a plausible yield for a crude terrorist bomb, has the power of 10,000 tons of TNT. To haul that volume of explosives, you would need a cargo train one hundred cars long. But if it were a nuclear bomb, it could fit into the back of a truck. Beyond the immediate deaths and the lives that would be shortened by radioactive fallout—the casualty list would also include civil liberties, privacy and the world economy. So American citizens have every reason to ask, "Are we doing all we can to prevent a nuclear attack?" The simple answer is "no, we are not."[35]

And according to an annual report by Harvard University's project on Managing the Atom and the Nuclear Threat Initiative, titled "Securing the Bomb 2007," the worrisome news is that highly enriched uranium (HEU) and plutonium "the essential ingredients of nuclear weapons, exist in hundreds of buildings in more than 40 countries, and terrorists are actively trying to get a nuclear bomb or the materials to make one."[36]

Another dangerous emerging trend of contemporary international life is the growing threat of cyber terrorism. The expanding concern is that not only hackers and criminal crackers but also terrorists will intensify the utilization of this form of electronic "warfare" as "equalizer" weapons.[37]

It is evident that the threat of "nonexplosive" terrorist assaults is growing with every passing day. Three contributing factors account for the reality. First, the "globalization" of Internet users makes government and industry efforts to control cyber attacks much more challenging than ever before.

Second, there are now tens of thousands of hacker-oriented sites on the Internet, thus resulting in "democratization" of the tools to be used for disruption and destruction. With the step-by-step cyber "cookbooks," the exploitation of Trojan horses, logic bombs, and other electronic modus operandi alternatives are becoming a permanent fixture of international life.

And third, terrorist organizations have broken away from their place within the formerly bipolar world and have become multidirectional, causing further complications to our technologically vulnerable societies. These new developments have enhanced the threats and capabilities of terrorist groups to the degree in which they could forever alter our planet's experience.

Counterterrorism Strategies[38]

The vulnerability of modern society and its infrastructure, coupled with the opportunities for the utilization of sophisticated high-leverage conventional and unconventional weaponry, requires states, both unilaterally and in concert, to develop credible responses and capabilities to minimize future threats. Ensuring the safety and interests of its citizens at home and abroad will therefore continue to be every government's paramount responsibility in the coming months and years. Understanding the methods of operation employed by terrorists, identifying the threats and specific targets, both present and future, and realistically assessing consequences that may result from acts of terror violence will assist governments unilaterally and with the cooperation of international and regional bodies, such as the Organization for Security and Cooperation in Europe (OSCE), to confront terrorism for the remainder of the twenty-first century.

The historical record indicates that it is easier to undertake counterterrorism measures at home than it is to promote international action. Thus, governments have given extensive public attention to the terrorist threats; improved intelligence gathering resources against terrorists; enacted appropriate legislation; apprehended, prosecuted, and punished terrorists; and provided greater protection to government facilities and officials. Moreover, certain counterterrorist measures have been taken at places where terrorists have been able to do great damage, most notably airports.

Furthermore, states have engaged in a variety of measures to deal with the international aspects of terrorism. Among the most prominent are the use of diplomacy, implementation of economic sanctions, cooperation in law enforcement, ratification of international conventions, and the employment of military forces in Afghanistan, Iraq, and elsewhere.

AMERICA UNDER ATTACK: HOMEGROWN AND FOREIGN-AFFINITY TERRORISM

Terrorism, at different levels of intensity, has challenged the United States throughout its history. This old-new form of fear and violence will undoubtedly continue to project a sporadic, yet relentless threat, and perhaps even result in some unprecedented grave consequences to national and global security concerns.

The following section provides a general review of the nature and implications of the challenge to America stemming from homegrown and foreign-affinity individuals and groups. Ideological, political, theological, and other social nourishments have motivated these actors. At times they have been encouraged, directed, and supported by state sponsors such as Iran.

More specifically, throughout American history there have been occasional outbreaks of terrorism in the homeland mounted by domestic and foreign groups. Among the early homegrown militants were, for example, the Molly Maguires, a band of militant Irish immigrants, who resorted to vengeance against anti-Catholic, Scotch, Ulster, Welsh, and English Protestants in Pennsylvania during the 1870s.

However, the most notable historical, radical movement employing terrorist tactics is the Ku Klux Klan (KKK). Surviving its early beginnings during the post–Civil War period, the KKK has continued its modus operandi of intolerance, hatred, and violence well into contemporary times. Dramatic attacks by the KKK in the United States during the 1960s Civil Rights Movement included the abduction and murder of two white civil rights workers, Andrew Goodman and Michael Schwerner, along with their African American colleague, Mississippian James Chaney. Only in 2005, some 41 years later, was Klansman Edgar Ray Killen, the mastermind behind the murders, convicted and sentenced to three consecutive 20-year prison terms.

Other historical domestic terrorist groups also failed in achieving their aims. It was not, however, until the turbulent 1960s that a proliferation of radical movements with violent tendencies emerged. The Weather Underground, the New World Liberation Front, the George Jackson Brigade, the Symbionese Liberation Army, the Black Liberation Army, and the Black Panther Party were among the most active left-wing and racist groups in the United States during the late 1960s and 1970s. During the same period, ethnic and nationalist groups (e.g., the Jewish Defense League, Armenian movements, Puerto Rican Armed Forces of National Liberation, Omega

7-Cuban Nationalist Movement, and the Cuban National Liberation Front) operated within the United States and Puerto Rico.

While these domestic U.S. terrorist groups were often less professional and successful than their international counterparts, they succeeded in attacking a variety of targets, including the police, the military, businesses, and others in over 600 attacks during the 1970s. Additionally, foreign terrorist groups were also actively targeting non-American victims in the United States during that decade. Some of these groups included the Croatian Group Otpar (Resistance), the Armenian Secret Army for the Liberation of Armenia (ASALA), and the Palestine Liberation Organization's Black September.

During the 1980s, the number of terrorist activities in the United States, both indigenous and foreign, dropped to around 20, and a further decline was seen during the 1990s, when only 60 domestic attacks were recorded. A significant contributing factor in this three-decade-long downward trend in attacks was the success of proactive operations by the FBI, which included effective cooperation with other law enforcement agencies in the United States and abroad followed by vigorous criminal prosecutions.[39]

The 1990s, however, also registered a variety of new American-born groups committed to ideological and political violence. These included reactionary right-wing movements advancing anti-Semitic and white supremacist causes as well as antigovernment and antitax beliefs (e.g., the Aryan Nations). Additionally, radical environmentalist movements resorted to violent tactics in pursuit of their goals. Groups such as the Even Mecham Eco-Terrorist International Conspiracy (EMETIC) sought to preserve ecological systems by sabotaging perceived despoilers of the environment and the Animal Liberation Front (ALF) damaged laboratories that used animals in medical research and industry.[40]

To be sure, these acts of indigenous violence were occasionally supplemented by individual citizens operating on their own without a specific affiliation to a particular indigenous group. A case in point was the activities of an American former professor Theodore John "Ted" Kaczynski, better known as the "Unabomber." He became infamous in the late 1970s and through the early 1990s for having engaged in a campaign of mail bombings to universities and airlines in an effort to "protect" the environment from destruction by the technologically advanced modern societies.

Mention should also be made of several foreign groups and agents who continued sporadic terrorism support activities within the United States during the 1980s, to obtain fundraising and weapons acquisitions for their colleagues abroad. Examples include activities by the Provisional Irish Republican Army (PIRA), Sikh militants, and Iranian agents. Additionally, other groups supporting Hamas, Hezbollah, and other Middle Eastern terrorist organizations became more active. Thus, in 1990, El Sayyid Nosair, an Egyptian extremist, assassinated Rabbi Meir Kahane, the leader of the

Jewish Defense League in New York City. And in 1999, al Qaeda plotted the opening of a terrorism training camp in Bly, Oregon.[41]

Yet, these activities were not regarded by U.S. authorities as major threats to national security. What was considered more seriously was state-sponsored terrorism. For example, fear of Iraqi-sponsored attacks was widespread during and in the wake of the 1991 Gulf War. Subsequently, various preventive security measures were undertaken by the American government and the private sector. These efforts included a reduction of Iraqi diplomatic staff; scrutiny of Iraqi and other nationals suspected of being linked to radical Arab causes; and upgrading security at government and military installations as well as airports and other commercial industrial sites. As a result of these measures no Iraqi-sponsored incidents occurred.

On the other hand, two dramatic incidents unrelated to the Gulf War have altered American perceptions of the nature of foreign threats within the homeland. First was the surprise February 26, 1993, bombing of the World Trade Center by Islamic terrorists inspired by the Egyptian radical Sheik Omar Abdel Rahman, the spiritual leader of al-Gama'a al-Islamiyya (Islamic Group).

The second major incident unfolded on December 14, 1999, when Ahmed Ressam, a militant linked to the Algerian Armed Islamic Group (GIA), affiliated with al Qaeda, and living in Montreal, Canada, was arrested as he attempted to cross into the United States at Port Angels, Washington, with explosives in the truck of his car. Ressam's thwarted "millennium plot" triggered alarm bells throughout the U.S. government as to the potential foreign-initiated threat to the homeland.

Additionally, domestic dangers have gained momentum from the mid-1990s to the present time. Two major developments ushered in a new era of "American terrorists in our midst." The first was the April 19, 1995, spectacular bombing in Oklahoma City. The second was the unprecedented attack of 9/11 and its lasting political and strategic consequences.

More specifically, two radical right-wing U.S. citizens, Timothy McVeigh and Tony Nichols, perpetrated the Oklahoma City bombing, labeled at the time as the largest act of domestic terrorism in American history. The 7,000-pound truck bomb, constructed of ammonium nitrate fertilizer and nitro-methane racing fuel, destroyed the Alfred P. Murrah Federal Building, claiming 168 lives, including 19 children, and wounding 674 people.[42]

Since that seminal attack, some 75 plots, conspiracies, racist rampages, and violence within the United States were recorded.[43] These illegal acts were planned and perpetrated by a wide range of right-wing groups, including antigovernment "Patriots," tax evaders, survivalists, neo-Nazis, anti-Semites, anti-abortionists, minutemen, and skinheads. These practitioners of reactionary ideologies and extremist theological dogma, aimed to radically alter the "American way of life" by resorting to vicious propaganda, bombings, assassinations, and other tactics of political violence. By 2008, 926 "native" radical entities were identified.

Already in 2009, these far-right actors have operated under a variety of names based in different locations throughout the United States. Suffice to mention the Nevada Lawman Group for Public Awareness; United Aryan Soldiers in Omaha, Nebraska; Aryan Circle in North Richland Hills, Texas; Atlantic City Skins; Nazi Low Riders in Eugene, Oregon; National Vastilian Aryan Party in Georgia; Soldiers of Aryan Culture in Utah; and the American National Socialist Workers Party in Chicago.[44]

These and similar groups were involved in multiple offenses, including robberies, money laundering, tax evasion, illegal weapons possession, arson, assault, and homicide. For example, in May 2009, Scott Rueder, reportedly affiliated with "Sovereign Citizens" who considered themselves subject only to "common law" and therefore opposed the federal government, murdered Dr. George Tiller, an abortion physician. In addition, in the following month, James von Brunn, an 88-year-old neo-Nazi and anti-Semitic militant, killed Stephen Johns, a security guard at the United States Holocaust Memorial Museum in Washington, DC.[45]

This phenomenon is indeed of great concern to domestic stability. After all, the trend based on ethnic, racial, religious, and political intolerance and violence is likely to expand especially at a time of dire economic crisis facing America. Thus, radical U.S. citizens are expected to participate in hate crime and terrorism in the near future.

Concurrently, it is anticipated that foreign terrorist groups such as al Qaeda, Hezbollah, and other militants from the Middle East, Asia, and elsewhere, acting independently, or with the support of states, will reach out and activate American citizens within the country and abroad.

This anticipated development should not be a "new surprise" in light of the long record of Americans involved in terrorism, mostly after 9/11.[46] Some of the better known cases of U.S. nationals (born or naturalized) as well as legal U.S. residents who were arrested, sentenced, or are free-at-large, include the following:

- John Phillip Walker Lindh was an American who fought for the Taliban in Afghanistan.
- Jose Padilla (also known as Abdullah Al-Muhajir) was al Qaeda's "dirty bomb" plotter.
- Adam Yahye Gaddhn (also known as Azzam the American) became the first American to be indicted with treason for his propaganda work for bin Laden.
- Mousa Mohammad Abumarzuq was a former U.S. resident and is currently Hamas' key political leader located in Damascus.
- Al-Arian was a university professor known as the "master manipulator" who provided financial and other services to the Palestinian Islamic Jihad (PIJ).

- And lastly, Ali Al-Timimi, an Islamic lecturer and supporter of al Qaeda and Lashkar e-Taiba ("Army of the Righteous," a Pakistani anti-India and U.S. terrorist group formed in 1989), encouraged Americans to wage war against their country.

Clearly, there are numerous other, less well-known, U.S. citizens and legal residents engaged in terrorist activities within the homeland. Some of these perpetrators have acted individually or as members of sleeper-cells located in places such as Atlanta, Buffalo, Dallas, Houston, Miami, Portland, and Seattle. Their involvement in activities included extortion, racketeering, money laundering, drug smuggling, weapons trafficking, bombing, and assassinations.

Among the aborted plots of American foreign-affinity terrorists were those targeting Jewish synagogues; the Los Angeles International Airport (LAX); a shopping mall in Rockford, Illinois, during Christmas; the New York City subway, bridges, and tunnels; soldiers at the Fort Dix Military Base in New Jersey; the Sears Tower in Chicago; and President George W. Bush.

Reportedly, between 9/11 and August 2006, the United States has arrested 6,500 individuals suspected of being terrorists with foreign ties. In September 2009, the FBI arrested three Americans in Denver and New York in a probe of a possible terrorist plot to detonate improvised explosive devices within the United States and directed against mass transit systems. During the same month, several other plots were revealed: in Springfield, Illinois, an alleged would-be terrorist planned to blow up a federal building by detonating a truck bomb; eight Americans in North Carolina were charged with a conspiracy to attack the U.S. Marine base in Quantico, Virginia; and a Brooklyn resident planned to commit murder and join the al-Shabaab, the terrorist group in Somalia, and to "take up arms against perceived enemies of Islam."[47]

The United States is facing serious homegrown threats from both radicalized right-wing extremists and expanding foreign-affinity American terrorists. The latter are linked with al Qaeda (and its fractured regional networks such as Lashkar e-Taiba). Eight years after September 11, terrorists are still lethal overseas and represent a potential danger of staging attacks within the United States. Other sources of dangers include Hezbollah, Iran, and their American supporters.

AMERICA'S COUNTERTERRORISM STRATEGIES[48]

Because the historical record from America's founding in 1776 until the end of World War II indicates only sporadic terrorist attacks at home and infrequent targeting abroad, U.S. policies and actions combating this form of "warfare-on-the-cheap" were rather limited in scope. In general, terrorism was not considered a major strategic challenge to American national interests, with some exceptions such as the Barbary threats in the nineteenth century.

Domestic radical movements failed to achieve their objectives and adversaries in foreign countries—both state and nonstate actors—were unable to seriously threaten American political, economic, and strategic concerns.

It was not until the 1970s that the United States began to develop a homeland counterterrorism approach. A contributing factor was the major radical riots that erupted in this century during this period, causing casualties, damage, and serious interference with the normal functioning of diverse communities in some American cities. In the aftermath of these events, the U.S. government established a National Advisory Committee on Criminal Justice Standards and Goals. In 1976, this body issued a "Report on the Task Force on Disorders and Terrorism" that recommended a variety of specific steps to assure greater community stability.

Although numerous governmental measures were undertaken by the United States to cope with terrorist threats abroad (e.g., counterterrorism rewards program and legislative action such as the Omnibus Diplomatic Security and Antiterrorism Act of 1986), the focus on domestic challenges was rather limited. During the administration of President Bill Clinton, however, more attention has been given to homeland security concerns. For instance, in 1999, the president established the Advisory Panel to Assess Domestic Capabilities for Terrorism Involving Weapons of Mass Destruction. In its 2000 report, it recommended that an Office for Combating Terrorism be created, along with improved training and response capabilities. Also, a bipartisan panel, the 21st Century Commission, was formed that year. Cochaired by former U.S. Senators Warren B. Rudman and Gary Hart, the commission report in 2000 called, *inter alia*, for the establishment of a Cabinet-level agency to assure responsibility to defend America. However, despite the warnings contained in the various reports, as well as numerous intelligence assessments advising of increased terrorist activity directed against the homeland during the winter and summer of 2001, terrorists were still able to execute the devastating September 11 attacks.

Since that catastrophic day, which resulted in unprecedented human, political, social, economic, and strategic losses from a single terrorist attack, the United States found itself engaged in the most extensive counterterrorism undertaking in its history. On September 20, 2001, President George W. Bush declared war against al Qaeda, accusing it of perpetrating the 9/11 attacks. He then mobilized an international coalition of allied countries to prosecute this new war and on October 6, 2001, the United States initiated Operation Enduring Freedom, a massive military operation against al Qaeda bases and the Taliban regime which had been providing sanctuary to bin Laden's terrorist infrastructure within Afghanistan. This military effort succeeded initially in largely destroying the existing terrorist infrastructure in the country, ultimately resulting in the overthrow of the Taliban regime and the establishment of a freely elected Afghan government in 2005 headed by President Hamid Karzai.

Yet, by winter 2010, more than eight years after the military operation in Afghanistan had begun, America was still fighting a war in that country in order to keep the homeland safe. President Obama worded the battle against the resurgent Taliban as a "war of necessity" that is "fundamental for the defense of our people." On the other hand, apparently the White House, in consultation with Congress, is rethinking future American counterterrorism and counterinsurgency operations in Afghanistan and the problematic border areas with Pakistan.[49]

To be sure, the most significant strategic decision made by the previous Bush administration was to undertake military action against Iraq on the grounds that Saddam Hussein's regime was developing links with al Qaeda and had continued its unilateral efforts to develop weapons of mass destruction. The war against Iraq began in March 2003 and within a month, U.S.-led coalition forces ousted the defeated Saddam Hussein regime. Since the defeat of Saddam and his subsequent capture, trial, and execution, Iraq's designation as a state sponsor of terrorism was formally rescinded in 2004, and the country began to move along the difficult road of political, social, and economic reconstruction under the guidance of American and coalition partners. Yet, despite the ongoing democratization process, as reflected by the December 15, 2005, legislative elections and the presence of 160,000 American troops and some 100,000 contractors in Iraq, the security situation in the country has deteriorated precipitously over the past few years. The situation can be characterized by both an insurgency and classic terrorist acts undertaken by a wide range of actors, including former regime officials, local Islamists, foreign jihadists, tribal groups, and ordinary criminals. The unending violence in the country, marked dramatically by first terrorist and insurgent operations in fall 2003 and subsequently by attacks on coalition forces, the UN Baghdad Office, and Shiite and Sunni religious sites and neighborhoods already resulted in a high cost in terms of human lives, property damage, and negative political consequences.

However, the security situation in the country improved particularly in 2009 as a result of the surge in American forces and the various other efforts to provide a bridge of capability to the Iraqi police and military to undertake stabilization missions. It is expected that a complete withdrawal of the U.S. troops from Iraq will be accomplished by 2011.[50]

The foregoing American policies and actions abroad have been supplemented by intensified counterterrorism strategies at home. These strategies are extensive domestic counterterrorism measures, both traditional and "out-of-the-box"—such as developing emergency medical readiness; upgrading immigration regulations and border control requirements; and increasing the number of domestic law enforcement joint terrorism task forces.

Additionally, there were four critical elements to the evolution of U.S. counterterrorism policies concerning homeland security. The first development was the enactment of the October 26, 2001, USA PATRIOT Act. It intended to better equip the U.S. government to identify, investigate, follow, detain, prosecute, and punish suspected terrorists. As today's terrorists use increasingly sophisticated tools—advanced technology and international money transfers—the government's capabilities must be able to adapt to these methods of operation. In essence, the USA PATRIOT Act sought to significantly improve the surveillance of terrorists and increase the speed with which terrorists are tracked and intercepted.

To be sure, the PATRIOT Act, almost from its inception, has been criticized both within and outside the U.S. government. Among the major criticisms of the act and its implementation are that the legislation allows the government to conduct surveillance of activities protected under the First Amendment; that it radically diminishes personal privacy by removing checks on government power; and that it increases government secrecy while limiting public accountability.

The second major development was the creation of a new Department of Homeland Security (DHS) on July 16, 2003. It involved an extraordinary governmental reorganization on a scale similar to that initiated with the establishment of the Department of Defense. This new 180,000-employee department, which integrated 22 previously separate agencies, consists of four core divisions: Border and Transportation Security; Emergency Preparedness and Response; Chemical, Biological, Radiological, and Nuclear Countermeasures; and Information Analysis and Infrastructure Protection. The reorganization was intended to provide for effective intergovernmental cooperation on national, state, and local levels and, consequently, assure that homeland security is a shared responsibility, although this too has been criticized for an inability to resolve numerous bureaucratic organizational problems inherent in merging so many disparate agencies.

A third significant step undertaken by the George W. Bush administration and Congress was the establishment of the National Commission on Terrorist Attacks upon the United States, better known as the 9/11 Commission (Public Law 107-306, November 27, 2007). In its public report, released on July 22, 2004, the Commission offered some 41 recommendations covering a broad range of topics, such as strategic policies, communications, physical security, intelligence, operational structures, WMD, education, and public offices. While many of these recommendations were implemented, several outstanding recommendations, including airport and seaport security measures, were finally included in a bill passed by both the House and the Senate in late July 2007. This legislation, introduced as HR1, became Public Law 110-53 when President Bush signed it on August 3. The major provisions of the law require that DHS screen all cargo on passenger airlines within three years as well as scan containers for nuclear devices on ships leaving foreign ports within five years. Another aspect of the act provides a formula for awarding homeland security grants to states and cities by placing greater emphasis on terrorist risk assessments of those jurisdictions.

A more controversial law was signed by President Bush on August 5, 2007. The Protect America Act (Public Law 110-055) broadened the executive's authority to eavesdrop without warrant on international telephone calls and e-mail communication of American citizens who are suspected as or known to contact terrorists outside the country. This new legal framework permits surveillance without warrants by the National Security Agency and outside the Foreign Intelligence Surveillance Act (FISA) of 1978.

The final significant step was demonstrated by the legislative action of the development of the Intelligence Reform and Terrorism Prevention Act, constituting the most extensive reform of the intelligence community since 1947. The act brought together some 15 intelligence agencies under a Cabinet-level Office of the Director of National Intelligence. Another important structural change was the establishment of the National Counterterrorism Center. In light of these developments, it seems that the reconstituted intelligence community operated more efficiently than ever before. One recent demonstration of the emerging new "culture of realism" is the August 2007 Department of Defense policy directive for U.S. military intelligence mandating information sharing with domestic agencies and foreign partners. For all practical purposes, this directive replaces the previous "need-to-know" approach with the requirement that the military intelligence has to be coordinated with, and to some extent subordinate to, the directorship of national intelligence. Thus far, both the Bush and Obama positions on related intelligence matters, including interrogations, detentions, renditions, and information classification are increasingly becoming subject to congressional and public scrutiny as well as judicial review.

One example of public concern relates to the claim by some segments of the population, such as the American Civil Liberties Union (ACLU), that the U.S. government is "spying" on private citizens as part of the war on terrorism. The ACLU in its September 2007 report asserted that during the past several years, the USA PATRIOT Act, Real ID, the proliferation of identity checks, health privacy legislation, and the National Security Agency "terrorism surveillance program" have been approved by Congress. It concluded that the "surveillance clock," patterned after the "Doomsday Clock" created by the Bulletin of Atomic Scientists in 1947 to warn against a nuclear holocaust, is now set at six minutes before midnight. This "surveillance clock" is on a digital ticktack display viewable from the ACLU Web site, symbolizing the encroachment of the government spying on private citizens.[51]

While counterterrorism overreaction and expansive tactics could lead to repression and the ultimate weakening of democratic institutions that we seek to protect, the reality is that there are no simplistic or complete solutions to the threat of terrorism. All we can do is to strike a balance between security concerns and civil liberties. Furthermore, we must learn from the historical experience of what works and what does not. Otherwise, as George Santayana rightly concluded, "[t]hose who cannot remember the past are condemned to repeat it."[52]

The subsequent chapters of this book provide in great detail an interdisciplinary analytical survey which focuses on foreign-affinity terrorism affecting the United States and measures undertaken to reduce the threat at home and abroad. Essentially, the research team that was organized initially in 2002 and worked on this study until fall 2009 was guided by three major questions:

First, what are the organizational infrastructures of international networks in the United States and how are they conducting their activities, including propaganda, fundraising, recruitment, arms purchases, training, and other support for terrorist organizations?

Second, which policies and legal protection frameworks are available to reconcile security considerations with those liberal democratic values regarding the suspect aliens (e.g., admission and exclusion, civil rights, and extradition of political offenders) and the suspect citizen (e.g., arrest, detention, and jury trial)?

And third, what are the counter foreign-affinity terrorism lessons learned and which "best practices" responses should be recommended for more effective strategies in reducing future challenges posed by terrorists to the security concerns of the United States?

It is hoped that this volume will encourage further academic work in this evolving field of national and global security concerns in the twenty-first century.

2

The Role of Intelligence in Affinity Terrorism

Raymond Tanter and Stephen Kersting

The attacks of September 11, 2001, unfortunately, were not an aberration. They were part of a continuing worldwide trend that allowed terrorists to undertake an operation that used assets and ideas from multiple continents against the United States. Although the 9/11 attacks prompted this book on foreign-affinity terrorism, those attacks are not examples of such terrorism. In this context, foreign-affinity terrorism occurs when a foreign organization plans or conducts terrorist operations against a target nation's citizens in conjunction with supporters who reside in the host nation by providing or accepting the support of host nation citizens. These supporters may have an ethnic or religious affiliation to the parent group and may or may not have citizenship in their country of residence. To prevent future attacks, an understanding of foreign-affinity terrorism must be applied to the workings of the intelligence community (IC); the new thinking, innovative structuring, and a methodical revamping of intelligence are necessary to prevent future affinity attacks.

For the restructuring to be effective, it must take into account the complexities of foreign-affinity terrorism. Potential foreign-affinity terrorists are difficult to detect because of their ability to hide their affiliations until they are ready to strike. They may be willing to act in isolation for years, keeping their radicalization private, making them difficult for intelligence agents to detect.

Tracking these threats requires using all available resources, from terrorist lists, to threat assessment, to the assets of the U.S. intelligence agencies.

To determine what role intelligence should play in countering affinity terrorism, this chapter addresses three questions:

- What challenges does foreign-affinity terrorism present to the intelligence community?
- How is the intelligence community responding to the threat of foreign-affinity terrorism?
- What further changes must take place for the intelligence community to be most effective against foreign-affinity terrorism?

This paper will argue that agencies must have better interagency communication through the Director of National Intelligence (DNI) if they are to succeed in piecing together the small clues left by those with links to foreign-affinity terrorism. By examining the challenges and solutions facing the IC, the U.S. government will be able to craft a more effective system to defeat the terrorist threat.

THE THREAT

The advent of widespread immigration, ease of international travel, and affordability of long-distance communication have allowed small groups of dedicated terrorists to use connections from across the world to coordinate attacks anywhere. Disheartened youths have taken advantage of these assets to plan and carry out attacks throughout the world. Immigrant groups on one continent can collect assets to build terrorist training grounds in their home regions and send the recruits to a third area. Groups have as much flexibility as they have imagination and ability to dodge intelligence operatives and law enforcement. While no successful foreign attack has occurred on American soil since September 11, 2001, potential affinity terrorism remains a threat; sleepers continue to plan, supporters continue to collect intelligence on targets, and terrorists continue to be trained. In June 2006, authorities arrested 17 Canadian Muslims on charges of planning to use explosives against Canadian targets. American intelligence agencies must remain vigilant to prevent these terrorists before they can strike.

Following Title 22 of the U.S. Code, Section 2656f (d), terrorism is premeditated, politically motivated violence against noncombatant targets by subnational groups or clandestine agents, usually intended to influence an audience. The foreign-affinity variety of terrorism is a subset of "intermestic" terrorism, a combination of international and domestic terrorism: groups targeting Americans and operating in the United States acting under foreign direction, but also functioning with explicit assistance or tacit support of ethnic and/or religious kin and ideological supporters in the United States (unlike satellites that avoid such support).

The most dangerous combination of these characteristics among foreign diaspora populations is a mix that shares foreign terrorists' ethnicity, religion, and especially militant ideology. For U.S. intelligence to counter and stop this threat, it must first understand the adversary.

Islamist Affinity Terrorism

Affinity terrorists can be associated with any region, ethnicity, or religion. The use of terrorist tactics has, in the past, been put toward ethno-nationalist goals, such as the Basques in Spain or the National Liberation Front (FLN) in Algeria. However, a radical religious agenda has replaced anticolonialism as the more common motivating factor of contemporary terrorist movements. In fact, radical Islamists who target Americans are the principal transnational threat to the United States.

Islamism is a political ideology based on revivalist Islam that emphasizes Shariah (Islamic law), rejection of the West, and the belief that integrating state power with religious beliefs is a duty commanded by faith. Although not all Islamists advocate terrorism, most Muslim terrorists are Islamist.

American policymakers need to understand the potential for terrorist organizations to use ethnic and religious affinity groups to infiltrate cells into the United States. While most immigrants do not become terrorists, most terrorists are immigrants.[1] Indeed, "of 212 suspected and convicted terrorists implicated in North America and Western Europe since the first World Trade Center bombing in 1993 through December 2003, ... 86% were Muslim immigrants."[2]

Similarly, all Islamists are Muslims, but all Muslims are not Islamists. Only a very small minority of Muslims are violent Islamists. Intelligence officials need to profile only potentially violent Islamists and not all Muslims; hence, there is a need for an analytic framework to determine whether profiling is a cost-effective means to detect and prevent affinity terrorism.

The concept of affinity terrorism assumes that violent Islamists take advantage of large-scale Muslim immigration to the West to use a "sea of believers" as potential supporters for terrorist activities and/or to gain new recruits.[3] Profiling, though, is further complicated by a new and disturbing trend toward conversion of non-ethnically Arab American and European citizens to a radicalized form of Islam. This movement reflects a deliberate al Qaeda tactic to recruit new members who "don't look Muslim."

Sea of Supporters: Safe Harbor for Sleeper Cells and Satellites

After September 11, Western governments perceived an increased threat of sleeper cells embedded in Muslim communities in their countries awakening to launch terrorist attacks. Sleepers and satellites differ from local affiliates of umbrella organizations. Sleepers are infiltrated foreigners who use domestic Muslim populations for cover while planning terrorist activities in the West.

Satellites are also foreigners who infiltrate non-Muslim countries with the same goal, but without using the domestic Muslim population for cover. They assemble abroad and enter a target country with legal or fraudulent documents for the purpose of conducting a particular terrorist operation.

Sleeper cells consist of individuals of foreign origin who slip into the target country and lie dormant only to rise up to conduct operations. To carry out their assaults, sleepers require safe houses, logistical cover, and financial backup from local communities of sympathetic citizens sharing their ethnic and/or religious identification in the country in which the cells are embedded. September 11 hijackers, however, were satellites and not sleepers. They relied less on local communities and more on central headquarters for support.

Some foreign terrorist organizations use both sleepers and satellites to conduct attacks, and thus the law enforcement community cannot solely focus on either. Only sleeper cells, however, engage in Islamist affinity terrorism, because they make use of the local Muslim communities in the West; satellites can work for the same organization, but they are simply engaging in intermestic terrorism when they conduct attacks in the West.

Sleepers embed in the West to take advantage of Internet access, rapid financial transfers, fundraising of nongovernmental organization front groups, relatively open borders with lax visa requirements, as well as freedom of religion and association. The Islamic principles of "*taqiyyeh*" and "*kitman*"—concealing one's true beliefs from others who would not agree with them until the moment to act is propitious—are important concepts for intelligence and security efforts to understand in this context. Islamist terrorists deliberately may not conform in appearance, association, or behavior with existing concepts of a "typical" Islamist.

A key aspect of sleeper cells is that terrorist operations have a long lead-time, which implies considerable autonomy for cells to make tactical decisions about execution. Assuming that several operations were in progress in addition to the 9/11 attacks, sleeper cells may have been inside the United States for some time.[4] Smoldering cells are like time bombs waiting to be ignited in a benign environment where the cells lay low and receive material support from affinity communities until the time is right to execute a planned operation.[5]

Lyman Faris (Mohammed Rauf), an Ohio truck driver, confessed to his satellite-association with al Qaeda in May 2003. Rauf was also an al Qaeda operative who conspired to provide it with material support and who has since been sentenced to 20 years in prison.[6] By changing his name from Mohammed Rauf, he hid his Muslim identity to become a successful satellite.[7]

The 9/11 hijackers, who were satellites, and not sleepers, used their actual Muslim names while avoiding association with too many Muslims. Moreover, sleepers and satellites may collude: Somali Nuradin Abdi, a sleeper, hid among 30,000 Somalis in Columbus and was involved with satellite Rauf in a plot to blow up shopping malls in Phase Two al Qaeda operations following 9/11 attacks.[8]

Other sleepers include seven al Qaeda operatives, whom the FBI arrested in Buffalo, New York, and who were indicted in September 2002 for "providing material support to terrorism."[9]

In contrast to Rauf, who operated under deep cover as Faris, the so-called "Millennium Bomber," Ahmed Ressam, was a satellite. He lived in Canada for four years before being activated to carry out an attack on the Los Angeles International Airport. U.S. Customs officials apprehended him as he attempted to cross into the United States. He repeatedly surfaced on the radar of the Canadian criminal justice system for petty crimes during 1995–1999 and traveled to Afghanistan to train for a year. Ressam was a satellite because he did not seek to hide in Canada and infiltrate its Algerian Muslim Diaspora.[10]

The cell that executed the 1998 bombing of the U.S. Embassy in Kenya lay dormant for five years before activation. In the East African embassy bombing cases, the benign milieu of Muslim communities gave effective cover for planned operations.

According to one study, "Attacks on the West have been carried out largely through two methods of terrorist attack: the sleeper cell and the hit squad."[11] Sleeper cells embed in the immigrant community and present a threat from the inside; hit squads or satellites also attack from within, but do not seek to hide within Muslim communities. Indeed, another 9/11-type attack in the United States is most likely to come from a satellite of a group like al Qaeda.

Affiliates are a type of domestic terrorist group with links to global terrorist organizations. Most of its operatives are locals, and its origins stem from local grievances. When affiliates obtain support from global terrorist entities or state sponsors, such assistance gives affiliates a foreign element that other domestic terrorist movements lack. Members of El Rukn gang in Chicago agreed to commit treasonable acts against the United States to obtain a huge loan from Colonel Muammar Qadhafi of Libya; hence, the gang falls under the label of affiliate of a state sponsor of international terrorism.[12]

Jema'ah Islamiya (JI) is an al Qaeda affiliate in Southeast Asia, whose leadership came under the sway of radical Wahhabis, which had a global agenda while fighting the Soviets in Afghanistan in the 1980s. By throwing its lot in with al Qaeda, JI is able to increase the threat it poses to Western interests and Southeast Asian governments aligned with the West. From its historical roots in organizations that fought the Dutch colonial power in Indonesia in the 1940s and through many decades of local activities, the JI eventually began to plot covertly through the late 1990s, in pursuit of its goal to create a grand Islamic state comprising Indonesia, Malaysia, Singapore, southern Philippines, and southern Thailand. In this respect, JI is responsible for the Bali, Indonesia, bombings of October 2002, which killed 202 and wounded approximately 300.[13]

While sleepers embed in the West, affiliates operate locally with al Qaeda logistical support in mostly non-Western areas, such as Asia. Affiliates include the Abu Sayyaf Group and Moro Islamic Liberation Front in the Philippines, the Great East Islamic Raiders Front in Turkey, the Front Islamiste du Salut in Algeria, as well as Lashkar e-Taiba and Hizb-ul-Mujahideen on the Indian subcontinent. Most of these groups have had some contact with al Qaeda.[14] In the West, where affiliate groups do not generally exist, the danger comes predominantly from sleeper cells or satellites of al Qaeda and its affiliates.

Some other groups that operate in the West may best be defined as al Qaeda subordinate groups, such as the alleged Abu Hafs al-Masri Brigades. This "group" claimed responsibility for the March 11, 2004, Madrid bombings, but later information indicates that North Africans unrelated to the Brigades were responsible. Other claims by the Brigades include synagogue bombings in Turkey and an August 2003 attack on the UN headquarters in Baghdad.[15]

Another distinction is between infiltrated cells and central headquarters, which provides the foundation for terrorism from abroad: strategic planning, financing, recruiting, and training of personnel. Day-to-day implementation of attacks is then left to individual infiltrated cells, using the sleeper or satellite method.[16] With the fall of the Taliban in Afghanistan and with it al Qaeda's global headquarters, the group's decentralized nature has become even more pronounced. Actual terror cells, whether sleepers or satellites, contrast with "terrorist central," al Qaeda, which is concerned with training, strategy, oversight, and financing.

Consider Mao Tse Tung's dictum: "The guerrilla must move amongst the people as a fish swims in the sea." Guerrillas must blend into their surroundings of local ethnic allies. Modern-day Islamist cells and local affiliates have the potential to exploit ethnic and religious supporters in the American Muslim diaspora that provides a sea in which cells might swim. Ethnic and religious supporters are a potential safe haven for infiltrated terrorist sleeper cells. But infiltration from abroad is only one method of penetration of the West. Another is the process of recruitment and conversion of Western individuals with Islamist affinity.

Conversion and Recruitment to Islam

Within the United States, conversion from Christianity to violent Islamism and recruitment into corresponding organizations are taking place at an increasing rate and may be a harbinger for future affinity terrorism on U.S. soil. Consider the Muslim population base for recruitment. Although there are wide variations in estimates of the size of the Muslim population in the United States, one of the best estimates is that of the National Opinion Research Council (NORC). In a study for the American Jewish Committee, NORC states, "The best, adjusted, survey-based estimates put the adult Muslim population in 2000 at ... 1,401,000. ... The average number being cited by the media at present (6.7 million) is 2.4 to 3.6 times greater than the best available estimates (1.9–2.8 million)."[17]

However, the Council on American Islamic Relations puts the total number of American Muslims at 7 million, with over 2,000 Islamic centers, mosques, and schools throughout the country.[18] Other surveys of Muslims in the United States also exist. One that is rather comprehensive is *The Mosque in America* done by the Council on American Islamic Relations, the product of a larger Mosque Study Project.[19]

The bottom line is that the Muslim population in the United States is huge and growing, and targeting such a group to search for affinity terrorists is both infeasible and unwarranted on civil liberties grounds; the vast majority of Muslims would have nothing to do with violent Islamists.

On one hand, the mosque study is valuable because it surveys Muslims who attend services, reasonably assumed to be the more religious group. These individuals are more likely to be targeted by Islamist or terrorist groups for recruitment because they attend mosque and thus are more easily contacted. This is not to assert that the American mosque is an institutional branch for terrorist organizations, simply that it can become that venue at the hands of those desiring to use it as such.

Regardless of the actual number, Muslims who attend mosque comprise a cohesive group: The average number associated in some way with a mosque is over 1,600, although half of the mosques have fewer than 500 worshipers in attendance at any given service. The average attendance at Friday prayer is almost 300 worshipers.[20] These statistics demonstrate the close-knit nature of the American mosque and ability of Islamist infiltrators to make personal contacts with possible recruits, initiate fundraisers, and meet supporters.

From the perspective of Islamist ideology, consider the growth in individuals associated with mosques in the United States. A 1994 study showed a 300 percent increase in the total number of Muslims associated with mosques, a figure if extrapolated would mean about 3 million Muslims associated with mosques about a decade later.[21]

This trend indicates a higher increase in the number attending mosque than the general growth in Muslim population, which suggests increasing identification with Islam among the American population of Muslims and increased conversion to the faith. In fact, over 30 percent of those attending mosque are converts to Islam.[22] Although the vast majority of Muslim converts are no threat whatsoever, a small percentage may be vulnerable to radical Islamist ideology.

In addition to provision of logistical support, such radical converts are potential foot soldiers in al Qaeda's war against the United States. "Of the 212 individuals implicated in major terrorist attacks around the world since the 1993 World Trade Center bombing, 18 were converts."[23]

During November 2001, U.S. forces captured an American convert to Islam—John Walker Lindh (Suleyman al-Faris)—in Afghanistan, and a grand jury indicted him on ten charges, including conspiracy to murder U.S. citizens and material support for terrorist organizations, during its February 2002 term in Alexandria, Virginia.[24]

In addition to charging Lindh, the FBI charged James Ujaama (Bilal Ahmed) from Seattle with conspiracy to provide material support to terrorists in his effort to establish a terrorist training facility in Oregon during 1999.[25] The FBI charged this American-born Muslim convert with having worked for and provided services to Abu Hamza al-Masri, a radical Muslim cleric based in London.[26]

During 2002, U.S. authorities arrested a native Chicagoan, Jose Padilla (Abdullah Al-Muhajir) for collaborating with al Qaeda to construct a "dirty bomb."[27] During 2004, the FBI sought Adam Pearlman (Adam Yahiye Gadahn) in connection with possible terrorist threats against the United States.[28]

During March 2006, seven Islamist converts in Miami took an oath of allegiance to al Qaeda and plotted to bomb the Sears Tower in Chicago, among other sites. The Miami defendants demonstrate no innate ethnic or religious predilection toward radical Islam. Instead, their attraction to the Seas of David sect has more to do with vulnerability than affinity. As is seen with other radical converts, the members of the Miami Seven are generally disaffected young men who are fodder for radical religious rhetoric.

Simply put, conversion to Islam is not, in and of itself, a threat, but converts are vulnerable to recruitment by violent Islamist groups because they can evade security measures focused on characteristics typically associated with Middle East or Southwest Asian origin.

With respect to leadership, American mosques are not staffed very well. Fifty-five percent have no full-time staff and only 10 percent have more than two paid staff. In most mosques, the leader is a volunteer and has employment elsewhere.[29] Because of the influence of Saudi funding and clerics with a Wahhabi-Salafist ideology, moreover, American mosque leadership tends toward an extreme version of Islam. In 1997, until the International Institute for Islamic Thought created a graduate program to train imams and mosque leadership, all the leadership was imported.[30]

Similarly, there is a lack of domestically trained clerics to lead congregations of European Muslims. As a result, European mosques often rely on imported (or itinerant) imams who sometimes espouse Islamist beliefs. Such clerics gave support to Islamists returning from Afghanistan and Eastern

Europe jihads—among them were some of the 9/11 hijackers. Radical imams also recruit from among Europe's second-generation immigrant youths, some of whom may be rediscovering their religious roots,[31] but others of whom are alienated from their host society, resistant to assimilation, isolated in suburban ghettos (such as the French *banlieues*), and unable to find employment. These factors make them easy prey for a radical ideology that provides a sense of belonging and purpose. In addition, because of the relative prosperity and assimilation of American Muslims, European Muslim immigrant radicalism represents a greater threat.[32]

Muslims in the United States do not come from just the Middle East. In fact, their ethnicities are very diverse:

- 26 percent Middle East (Arab)
- 25 percent South Asia
- 24 percent African American
- 12 percent other
- 10 percent Middle East (non-Arab: Turkish, Persian, etc.)
- 6 percent East Asia[33]

With respect to Arab ancestry in the United States (as opposed to Muslim faith), some 1.2 million people in the United States reported Arab ancestry in Census 2000, which is up from about 860,000 in 1990 and 610,000 in 1980. The Arab ancestry population increased 41 percent in the 1980s and 38 percent in the 1990s.[34]

More telling than ethnicity of the general Muslim population is attendance at mosques by ethnic affiliation. The ethnic breakdown by mosque attendance is as diverse as the general population: 33 percent South Asia, 30 percent African American, and 25 percent Arab. Moreover, only 7 percent of mosques have members of a single ethnicity, and nearly 90 percent have members from all three of these ethnicities.[35]

An increasingly common venue for converting to Islam is the prison system. According to a San Francisco State University study, there are more than 300,000 converted prisoners in the United States, with 30,000 converting each year. Most of these converts are among the African American, Hispanic-American, and Native American prison populations.[36]

Although the U.S. Bureau of Prisons (BOP) is very concerned about prison conversions, at issue is what action is possible in light of freedom of religion and speech; though these freedoms need to be preserved, the FBI and BOP need to coordinate how to deal with Islamist prison preachers whose sermons serve to stimulate inmates to become violent. Freedom of speech does not include speech that incites violence.

Traditionally, any "person of the cloth" could become a prison chaplain and preach a message to inmates. But in the post-9/11 environment, restrictions need to be considered regarding who is qualified to preach in prison. Consistent with religious freedom of association, it might be possible to estimate the extent to which such prisoners are converting to militant Islam, rates of such conversion, as well as which Islamist organizations are driving the process.[37]

In response to political inquiries from Capitol Hill, the Department of Justice Office of the Inspector General reviewed the Federal Bureau of Prisons' policies and procedures for selection of individuals who provide Muslim religious services to federal inmates. The review revealed defects in how the BOP selects and supervises Muslim religious services providers, including the following:

- The BOP typically does not examine the doctrinal beliefs of applicants for religious service positions to determine whether those beliefs are inconsistent with BOP security policies.
- Once contractors and certain volunteers gain access to BOP facilities, ample opportunity exists for them to deliver inappropriate and extremist messages without supervision from BOP staff members.
- BOP inmates often lead Islamic religious services, subject only to intermittent supervision from BOP staff members, which enhances the likelihood that inappropriate content can be delivered to inmates.[38]

The Department of Defense review process to select individuals to provide Muslim religious services in federal prisons provides cracks in the system through which Islamist groups have the opportunity to recruit from the federal prison population.

While conversion to Islam is not worrisome, recruitment into extremist Islamist organizations is a threat, especially if extremist groups are driving the process of conversion. Consequently, there may be a need for infiltration of prisons by intelligence officials to gain insight on potential terrorist cells and operations out of prison. And if government personnel were restricted from engaging in "blanket surveillance" of Islamist groups, private Americans might have to step up to the plate and conduct "citizen surveillance" of suspect organizations.[39]

From the 1990s onward, al Qaeda has made a concerted effort to recruit among the U.S. prison population. Recruits include a high proportion of African Americans but also a high proportion of Hispanics. Prison and American gang populations offer a number of advantages to terrorists: antipathy to U.S. society, values, and law enforcement; a criminal record that makes regular employment difficult; ready-to-go skills, off-the-shelf techniques useful to terrorists (weapons familiarity, document forgery, and knowledge of underground trafficking channels); and in many cases, a predisposition for "belonging" to a group, gang, and potentially a terrorist cell.[40]

Recruitment also occurs in mosques, where in some cases Muslims can be indoctrinated with the more militant beliefs of Islamists. Saudi Islamists have been pouring funds into the United States for the purpose of constructing mosques for many years. Saudi largess also goes for travel expenses for preachers, especially to Islamist clerics who intend to attract additional converts and radicalize those already converted to Islam. Intelligence and law enforcement officials say dozens of Islamists have already been routed through Europe to Muslim communities in the United States, based on secret intelligence information from terrorists and others detained by U.S. authorities.[41]

Consider demographics of Muslims in the United States and Europe to determine how antiterrorism policy might be shaped. In both populations, Muslims constitute roughly 3 percent of the total population. However, there is generally less tension between Muslims and non-Muslims in the United States than in Europe, possibly due to the American immigrant tradition and European colonial history.[42] In the American pattern, and in part due to official U.S. visa policy, immigrants of all backgrounds more often tend to include family units eager to assimilate rather than single young men far adrift from their roots and supportive societies.

Although Muslims are increasing their numbers in both populations, due to the greater fertility rates of the mostly North African immigrants than the indigenous European populations than is the case with Muslim immigrants in the United States, the overall percentage of Muslims among many European national populations is rising faster than it is in the United States. There also is considerably more fragmentation and diversity among the Muslim-American population than its European counterpart, both in terms of beliefs and ethnic origin. Lastly and importantly, most European Muslims come to Europe as working class immigrants and remain largely working class. By contrast, American Muslims often arrive as upper-level students and tend to be well educated and more affluent than their European counterparts.[43] It should be noted that the increasing involvement in extremist activities of second- and third-generation immigrant youth to Europe in particular, but the United States as well, poses a difficult challenge to societies whose own demographic trends will demand a growing supply of immigrant labor for the foreseeable future.

These demographic data suggest conclusions about the potential threat of Islamist organizations radicalizing domestic Muslims to join terrorist groups or simply to shelter foreign terrorists. In Europe, law enforcement efforts can concentrate on relatively cohesive groups of working class Muslims that are distinct from the rest of the population. But in the United States, the task of tracking the Muslim population for violent Islamist tendencies is more complicated than in Europe.

Muslims in America belong to many ethnic and religious groups that are usually well assimilated into the surrounding population. Hence, infiltration by law enforcement becomes less effective, because of the inability to focus attention on a single potentially threatening group. The attraction of American Muslims to higher education also makes college and university campuses a potential source of radicalization, which might need to be monitored with due attention to academic freedom concerns. Europe views the threat of disorder and violence by alienated Muslim youths as a "pressing political reality." Few such fears about Muslim youths per se seem to be on the minds of Americans, who instead concern themselves with "connections between Muslims here and terrorist activities."[44]

This tendency ignores the potential threat that arises if Muslim youths join Islamist groups and if such youths provide cover for foreign sleepers. The general Islamist population need not engage in terrorism for there to be an emerging threat. It will simply be more difficult to provide scarce resources to conduct surveillance on more potentially threatening militant Islamists if they come not only from abroad, but from home as well.

In short, conversion to Islam poses a threat insofar as it increases opportunities for recruitment to violent Islamist organizations and safe haven for sleepers as well as terrorists already in the United States. Europe and America face different potential security threats from Islamized domestic Muslim populations; consequently, the United States must be even more vigilant than Europe, given the diversity of Muslims in the United States.

As a result of such emerging threats, a proportion of the Muslim population in the United States might be considered a potential ally of terrorist organizations. But the threat does not come equally from each ethnic group of Muslims. Arab-American populations may be more vulnerable to penetration by terrorist groups than Muslim Americans from Pakistan, India, and Iran. Why? Muslim Arab-Americans may be more likely to accept radical Islam than non-Arab Muslims who live in the United States. If Islamist preachers prey on those who feel dispossessed by society as a whole, they may find fertile ground between Arab-American Muslims more than Muslims from Asia and Iran.

In contrast to Asian-American Muslims, Arab-American Muslims are likely to be devout and attend radicalized mosques. Such vulnerability, however, need not suggest that these groups are disloyal to the United States; rather, vulnerability only means that sleeper cells from al Qaeda, Hamas, Palestinian Islamic Jihad (PIJ), and Hezbollah may have a better fit within the Arab-American communities than within Asian-American or Iranian-American populations.

Unlike many Arab-American immigrants, and like other Asian-American Muslims, the Iranian Diaspora in the United States immigrated with money, had already studied English, possessed a good education, and had strong backgrounds in business. Iranians, moreover, do not isolate themselves from other cultures and may be the most open of immigrant communities to the views of others.[45]

Policy options should take into account the differing threats presented by each group within Muslim-Americans and respond accordingly to utilize scarce resources for the most gain and also avoid alienating low-risk groups. Thus it is crucial to identify groups, as they may exist, which are more of a threat than others within the United States and monitor conversion and recruitment rates.

Returning to the question that began this section, What is the potential for foreign terrorist organizations to use ethnic and religious affinity groups in a target country to infiltrate cells for later activation and operations? The potential for affinity terrorism depends upon the degree to which Islamist groups seize control of the recruitment and conversion process. And they are more likely to gain control over recruitment and conversion if states like Saudi Arabia and rogue regimes like Iran contribute funds for such tasks. Formal terrorist organizations and Islamist movements also may contribute to the conversion to Islam and recruitment to Islamism within the United States.

An affinity terrorism strategy in the aftermath of September 11, 2001, should take into account a pyramid of terrorism among rogue regimes like Iran, formal terrorist organizations like Hezbollah, and Islamist movements like the Muslim Brotherhood and of late, al Qaeda. Because of their interrelations, it is likely that affinity terrorism by groups like Hezbollah and Hamas will reach the American shores. If the United States targets Iran for regime change in light of Tehran's state sponsorship of international terrorism and development of weapons of mass destruction, Iran may respond by using proxies, such as Hezbollah, against the U.S. homeland and/or Americans abroad. In this respect, a state-centric approach needs to be modified to also focus on groups and transnational movements.

Rogue States, Formal Terrorist Organizations, and Islamist Movements

How do rogue regimes, formal terrorist organizations, and Islamist movements relate to foreign-affinity terrorism? To address this query, consider some distinctions. Rogue regimes are state sponsors of international terrorism (and proliferators, developers, suppliers, or recipients of weapons of mass destruction). These regimes provide support to subnational terrorist groups.[46] In describing links among rogue states, terrorist organizations, and Islamist movements, consider three points in a triangle of necessary conditions to start a fire: fuel, heat, and oxygen. Remove any point and ignition is not possible.[47]

Rogue regimes, terrorist organizations, and Islamist movements create a triad of terror, a threat that is greatest when all the points work in the same direction. Unlike fire, however, any one of the three is a sufficient condition to launch a terror attack; but a combination of three points is more threatening than any one or two points of the terror triad alone. Rogue states not only provide incentives for formal organizations to conduct terrorist operations, but such states also reinforce preexisting motivations by providing financing, political support, and logistics.[48]

First, a terrorist group may rise up, organize, evolve, and then seek state support as well as assistance from a more established terrorist group. According to Human Rights Watch, an Iraqi-Kurdish group—Ansar al Islam—formed as a voluntary amalgamation of Islamist groups in September 2001.[49] Ansar then received aid and support from two rogue states, Iraq and Iran, and perhaps seed money from another formal terrorist organization—al Qaeda. Saddam Hussein's regime provided financial support and military means, mostly mortar rounds, of assistance to the group.[50]

Second, rogue states may spawn a terrorist group, such as Iran's creation of Hezbollah during the Lebanese Civil War: Tehran sent agents to organize the Shiites in the southern part of Lebanon into a cohesive movement.[51] Once established, moreover, relationships between rogue states and terrorist groups may become symbiotic. Third, rogue regimes engage in direct terrorist operations, such as the attack by Libyan intelligence agents against Pan Am flight 103 over Lockerbie, Scotland in 1988.

Iran, of all states, is particularly involved in terrorist activities. According to the Department of State, "Iran remained the most active state sponsor of terrorism [in 2008]."[52] Rather than launch terrorist attacks directly, Iranian security services, such as the Revolutionary Guards, contract with formal organizations like Hezbollah to conduct terrorist operations. Tehran also supplies arms and funds for groups to carry out attacks at a time and place of their choosing. Iran's supply of armaments and money to Hezbollah illustrates a link between a rogue regime and a formal organization. Iran is one of the main sources of Islamist terrorism because the regime helps to sustain its grip on power by demonstrating that it is on the frontline of spreading its radical view of Islam in the region.

Tehran provides Hezbollah with "funding, safe haven, training, and weapons."[53] Such support (estimated by Israeli intelligence at over $100 million per year just on Israel's front with Lebanon) gives Tehran a terrorist proxy of regional and global reach. Recall that Hezbollah suicide bombings against the U.S. Marine barracks and the U.S. Embassy annex in Beirut (in October 1983 and September 1984, respectively) killed some 300 U.S. diplomats and soldiers.

In addition, the 22 individuals on the 2004 FBI list of Most Wanted Terrorists include three Hezbollah operatives accused of the 1985 hijacking of TWA flight 847, during which they were charged with murdering a U.S. Navy diver. The hijacking featured the infamous image of an American pilot peering out of the cockpit with a gun to his head. Moreover, according to a

November 1, 1996, *Washington Post* report, Saudi intelligence concluded that a local group calling itself Hezbollah was responsible for the June 1996 truck bombing of the Khobar Towers—a U.S. military housing complex on the Kingdom's Gulf coast. The Saudis also asserted that this local group was a wing of Lebanese Hezbollah.

In February 2003, an FBI joint terrorism task force took down a Hezbollah financial support cell in the United States operated by a group of Lebanese nationals engaged in racketeering. They purchased contraband cigarettes in Charlotte, North Carolina, a low-sales-tax state, and trucked them to Detroit, Michigan, where they were resold for cash in a high-sales-tax state.

Hezbollah Secretary General Hassan Nasrallah made the following remarks in a speech given in 2003, one week before coalition forces launched Operation Iraqi Freedom (as broadcast on al-Manar, the organization's Beirut-based satellite television station): "In the past, when the Marines were in Beirut, we screamed, 'Death to America!' Today, when the region is being filled with hundreds of thousands of American soldiers, 'Death to America!' was, is, and will stay our slogan."[54]

Iranian dissident sources also contend that Hezbollah has conducted "casing" of coalition assembly centers in Iraq and tracked the timing and order of movements by various coalition vehicles, including tanks, armored personnel carriers, and motorcades. Hezbollah agents reportedly have videotaped various locations in two-person teams, often using public transportation, such as taxis. Footage of targets is sometimes concealed between banal imagery (e.g., wedding festivities) in order to avoid detection by coalition forces. Such reports echo Hezbollah's own public statements, voiced as early as mid-April 2003, regarding its willingness to attack U.S. forces in Iraq and its increasing ability to do so.[55] Nevertheless, despite continuing sectarian violence in Iraq, and intensifying tensions between the United States and Iran, as of mid-2006, Hezbollah had not yet launched any direct attacks against coalition forces in Iraq.

Just because a rogue state is a threat to the United States does not mean that individuals originating from that country are also a threat. The Iranian-American community is a poor recruitment base for state-sponsored terrorist actions by the regime in Tehran. As stated earlier, because many Iranian-Americans emigrated from Iran to escape the extremist nature of that regime, their secular, moderate views contrast sharply with those of the regime in Tehran. Iranian-Americans who emigrated from Iran of the ayatollahs after the 1979 Revolution are similar to Cuban-Americans who escaped Fidel Castro's Cuba: both groups reject the regime from which they fled. But there are Iranian Americans who are apologists for Tehran. Consider the case of Trita Parsi, under investigation for lobbying on behalf of a state sponsor of international terrorism, the Iranian regime, via the cover of the National Iranian American Council (NIAC).[56]

Hezbollah allows Iran to have a link with a formal terrorist organization; it gives Iran an option to hit American targets within both Iraq and, theoretically, also within the United States.

ISLAMIST MOVEMENTS: MUSLIM BROTHERHOOD

The connection of rogue states to terrorist organizations is extremely important. These regimes have the ability to provide funding, supplies, and logistical support that, with the notable exception of al Qaeda, terrorist groups generally cannot obtain elsewhere. However, for the purpose of affinity terrorism, the other two elements of the terrorism pyramid, namely terrorist organizations and Islamist movements, are crucial. For intelligence agencies and local law enforcement to better identify groups that not only espouse an Islamist message, but also may facilitate affinity terrorists, it is worth examining the origins of twentieth century, violent Islamist movements.

The mother of many Islamist movements, including the Egyptian Jihad element of al Qaeda, is the Muslim Brotherhood; indeed, post-9/11 al Qaeda is beginning to act more like a movement than a formal organization. But because the oldest of the modern Islamist movements is the Muslim Brotherhood, it receives the most attention in this discussion of Islamist movements. Launched during 1928 in Egypt, the Brotherhood operates in some 70 countries, according to its Web site.[57]

The Brotherhood began as a social-reform, religious-revival movement in Egypt in the 1920s and morphed into a political movement in the 1930s, finally becoming a political organization in 1939.[58] The Brotherhood opposed the secularism of the Egyptian government and began to engage in terrorist activities in the 1940s. After 1954, the Brotherhood directed attacks against the Arab socialist regime of Gamal Abdel Nasser.[59] Cairo declared the Brotherhood illegal and sought to destroy it. As a result, its members scattered throughout the Middle East during the 1950s, increasing the Brotherhood's global influence.[60] Some of those who immigrated to the United States helped found the Muslim Student Association (MSA) in 1963.[61]

Despite largely operating undercover in the United States, Brotherhood members who arrived in America after the 1950s may have used legitimate businesses and charities to raise and hide money for terrorist operations abroad. Consider how the Brotherhood operates in the United States. It is not unreasonable to assume that this case is a template for how a movement founded abroad can radicalize immigrant students in America.

A *Wall Street Journal* writer reports on the ideological journey of a Muslim immigrant from India, Mustafa Saied. He became a member of the Brotherhood on the campus of a fairly conservative institution—the University of Tennessee. A friend invited Saied to join the Brotherhood, and he found "power" in membership.[62]

The *Journal* article tells how Saied raised what he thought were charitable donations for Muslims in Bosnia and Chechnya and gave them to the Benevolence International Foundation, ostensibly a benign nonprofit group in Chicago, for distribution overseas but actually a primary terror-funding mechanism. Indeed, Saied subsequently learned that the Brotherhood via the foundation distributed funds he helped collect to "holy warriors," fighting on behalf of Islamist causes.

Soon after the September 11, 2001, attacks, the Department of the Treasury froze accounts of the "charity" that sent Saied's donations abroad, designating it as an entity that finances terrorism. Although he received a religious education as a youth in India, his parents taught him equality and tolerance among Muslims and other groups. But Saied's friends in the Brotherhood socialized him into a radical view of Islam. Saied drew upon verses from the Koran, verses that are intolerant of other religions.[63] Saied also began meeting regularly with a few students considered Islamist enough for selection into the Brotherhood and loyal enough to keep the movement's existence on campus a secret.

Saied belonged to an Islamic study group that emphasized the writings of Youssef Al Qaradawi. He is an Egyptian cleric in Qatar, leads a wing of the Brotherhood, and endorses "martyrdom operations" against Israel and Jews.[64] At a conference of the Muslim Arab Youth Association in Toledo, Sheik Qaradawi gave a speech in which he supposedly stated that Islam would overcome all the religions and dominate the world. Saied then contacted the Benevolence International Foundation, and a foundation representative visited Knoxville to pick up contributions.

Saied stated that he had assumed the money was going to civilians but learned in 1995 that the foundation channeled funds to Islamist groups. The *Journal* article states, "In November 2002, the Treasury Department alleged that the foundation had extensive financial ties to al Qaeda. The charity denied the allegations, but its chief executive pleaded guilty in 2003 to illegally buying boots and uniforms for Muslim fighters in Bosnia and Chechnya. As part of the plea deal, prosecutors dropped the charges involving al Qaeda."[65]

Saied subsequently penned op-ed essays advocating moderate views. His sojourn from moderate conservative to radical and supposedly back to moderate is instructive of how Islamic movements relate to formal terrorist organizations.

For the purpose of studying affinity terrorism, the evolution of this Muslim from India reveals how the Muslim Brotherhood embedded itself into the religious life of unsuspecting students to socialize them into the Islamist perspective. The case of Saied sheds light on the operations of the Brotherhood and the ideological journey traveled by Islamist affinity terrorists.

OFFSPRING OF THE BROTHERHOOD: PALESTINIAN ISLAMIC JIHAD AND HAMAS

Not only did the Pyrrhic victory of the Egyptian government over the Brotherhood in the 1950s cause its members to disperse and form branches across the Muslim world, but independent terrorist groups also rose up from the ashes of "defeat." With respect to branches, the Brotherhood appeared in Syria only to be decimated and driven underground when Hafez al-Assad ordered military action against them in the town of Hama during 1982.

The split among factions of the Brotherhood highlights the degree to which, since the 1950s, a multiplicity of Islamist groups, sometimes in competition with each other, has emerged. The proliferation of Islamist groups demonstrates the need for law enforcement and intelligence professionals to identify competing strains of thought among the Islamist community and identify those individuals and ideas most likely to use violent means to achieve their Islamist goals.

Even before the Brotherhood's downfall in Syria, there was a split in which "moderate" members began to cooperate with smaller groups to form the Islamic Front of Syria.[66] The Brotherhood's evolution in Egypt resulted in its remarkable development as a political force, which ostensibly has renounced violence, but retains its long-term objectives to replace Egypt's repressive regime with an Islamic government. Despite intense repression and being banned from overt participation in Egyptian politics, Brotherhood candidates running as individuals still managed to garner more than a quarter of the seats in Egypt's 2005 parliamentary contests. Near destruction in Syria also drove the Brotherhood underground within the area of Greater Syria. In both cases, however, the Brotherhood was able to continue to perpetuate its ideas through evolution into other groups throughout and beyond the Nile Valley, Fertile Crescent, and the region that was once ancient Mesopotamia. And clearly, the Brotherhood and its political philosophy remain potent forces among populations in both Egypt and Syria.

Specific groups split off from the Brotherhood's branches to form terrorist organizations. One product of the Brotherhood is Egyptian Islamic Jihad, which was led by Ayman al-Zawahiri, deputy to al Qaeda's founder, Osama bin Laden. Al-Zawahiri merged his organization with al Qaeda during 1998.[67] Indeed, a close analysis of the evolution of bin Laden's Islamist philosophy can discern the very considerable influence that al-Zawahiri has exerted on his ostensible al Qaeda chief, who did not adopt a universalistic *jihadi* outlook until after the two had merged. Moreover, with al Qaeda's setbacks and subsequent dispersion, al-Zawahiri increasingly is considered the driving strategist behind the movement's transition to the Internet age, with much of its far-flung communications, propaganda, recruitment, and training activities now conducted online.

Violent offspring of the Brotherhood include Hamas and Palestinian Islamic Jihad—militant Palestinian organizations. These "spin-offs" split from the larger parent organization. Spin-offs from the Brotherhood also comprise Turkish Islamic Jihad and Eritrean Islamic Jihad. The general idea is that separate, smaller groups have some kind of ideological similarity that makes their operation appear to fit into an overall strategic plan.[68]

Based in part on the "indestructible" and universal claims of the Muslim Brotherhood, regional groups develop into ones with a global reach. The Muslim Brothers along with schools teaching Islamic jurisprudence and theology—madrasas—socialize and educate youths in an Islamist ideology that makes them more likely to be recruited into organizations like al Qaeda, Hamas, and Hezbollah than those lacking exposure to these groups.[69]

To be sure, formal organizations have their own local recruiting agents, but the Brotherhood helps provide a universal ideology that implicitly permeates doctrines of formal groups, due to the recruitment of Brotherhood members or associates into these groups. Intelligence officials and law enforcement agents should be aware of nuances with which a "global" jihadist message is adapted to the local grievances aired by potential affinity terrorists. While rogue regimes covertly supply fuel for terrorism, the Brotherhood bestows oxygen and hot ideas to formal organizations, one of which is Islamic Jihad.

Palestinian Islamic Jihad

Palestinian Islamic Jihad evolved out of the Muslim Brotherhood's branch in Gaza during 1979–1980 and was officially founded by Palestinian students in Egypt who were influenced by the Iranian Revolution and the militancy of Egyptian Islamist student organizations. Their ideology was pan-Islamist, but they believed the greater unity of the Islamic world would only come as a result of the smaller jihad for the liberation of Palestine. This was a relatively unique position, as was the admiration for Ayatollah Ruhollah Khomeini of Iran, which was somewhat unique for Sunni Muslims. The group's leaders developed links with Iran's Revolutionary Guards and Hezbollah in 1987. PIJ split into several other factions of the same name during the 1980s, but the original remains the dominant group, which has also since developed an operational coordination with Hamas.[70]

These characteristics of PIJ are informative as to the evolution and adaptability of terrorist organizations. Like Hamas, PIJ evolved out of the Brotherhood, demonstrating the groundwork this organization can lay for militant Islam. Moreover, the group grew out of student militancy, which is illustrative of how Islamism among students can create conditions for the rise of terrorism. Although not directly comparable to the situation in the United States, the rise of PIJ does serve as a warning to the effects of youthful Islamism.

Furthermore, the connection with Iran suggests that a Sunni-based Brotherhood can collude with Shia Iran. Such Sunni-Shia cooperation is compatible with reports that Iran shelters al Qaeda leaders regardless of their religious differences. Since 9/11, PIJ has expanded its activities. Islamic Jihad's Web site, which authorities closed down after 9/11, stated that the purpose of contributions is for funding "military Jihad," or holy war.[71] Before the Web site went down, PIJ solicited donations on its site for a violent jihad against Israel. Islamic Jihad provided addresses for donations to be sent to the Charity Association in towns controlled by the Palestinian Authority (PA)—Bethlehem, Gaza, and Jenin. But a high-level PA official testified in a U.S. court that the Charity Association was a front for Islamic Jihad.[72]

Within the United States, Islamic Jihad operated in Florida. During February 2001, federal prosecutors indicted Florida college professor Sami Al-Arian on charges of conspiracy to commit murder via suicide attacks in Israel and the Palestinian territories. For years, Al-Arian had denied that he was an operative of PIJ—which the U.S. government had designated as a terrorist group because of its suicide bombings of Israelis.[73]

Furthermore, although Hamas and PIJ were initially considered rivals in Gaza, their eventual cooperation demonstrates the adaptability of formal terrorist organizations, especially those with similar roots. Thus cooperation should not be de-emphasized in the fight against terrorism, nor should each group be countered individually. Indeed, there should be a strategic approach to understand terrorist groups as a whole, under the assumption that their need for the benefits of collusion might result in strange bedfellows.

Hamas

With the January 2006 victory of Hamas (Islamic Resistance Movement) in the Palestinian legislative elections, an Islamist terrorist organization dedicated to the destruction of the State of Israel has come to power via the ballot box for the first time in the Middle East. Its position at the helm of Palestinian government presented an unprecedented challenge for the foreign policy of the United States and other liberal democracies still seeking a peaceful resolution of the decades-old Arab-Israeli conflict, as well as to the strategies of regional neighbors, including Egypt, Jordan, and, of course, Israel.

Hamas is another group, besides the Palestinian Islamic Jihad, to develop out of the Muslim Brotherhood. Founded formally by Sheik Ahmed Yassin in 1978, the group drew its members from the Palestinian refugee population influenced by the ideas of the Muslim Brotherhood, especially in Gaza. The founding of Hamas reflects the general trend in the Brotherhood movement away from acceptance of Israeli rule to militancy against it. The group built a base on its social and economic programs in the territories, from which it draws political support and recruits for terrorist activities.

Although not widely mentioned, the fact remains that Israel provided some measure of official early support to Hamas in an effort to encourage formation of a counterbalancing force to Yasser Arafat's then-dominant Palestinian Liberation Organization (PLO).

Later, the Hamas leaders built upon the social system constructed by the Muslim Brotherhood to create a widespread and grassroots opposition, evolving away from the original concept of centralized militant activists envisioned by the founding fathers. This strategy helped Hamas play an active role in the first intifada that began in 1987, when the group definitively displayed its role as a terrorist organization.[74] Clearly the Muslim Brotherhood's activities in the territories, particularly Gaza, played a role in both Hamas's emergence and transformation as a terrorist group.

Although Hamas professes to concern itself only with the liberation of Palestine, the group is also active in the United States and commands support from elements of the Muslim Arab-American community.[75] Authorities contend that both groups have sleeper cells in the United States. Much effort by federal law enforcement agencies regarding Hamas is aimed at its financial supporters—including Islamic centers, charities, and criminal rings from Washington to Detroit to Los Angeles.[76]

Unfortunately, Hamas benefits from an assumed and false distinction between its military and political-social sectors. Just as a bird needs two wings to fly, so Hamas has two wings that allow it to carry out terrorist operations. The organization's political side provides welfare for the needy, but the political leadership also directs the military side to conduct operations. But bystanders mistakenly infer that Hamas as a whole is not a terrorist organization. Those who make such a distinction assume that suicide bombings conducted as military operations have nothing to do with "good deeds" carried out by its so-called social wing. Such a distinction "is totally contradicted by the consistent if scattered findings of investigators."[77]

Funds collected for "good deeds" are also used to finance terrorism operations. In 2002, a U.S. federal judge in Washington, DC, ruled that the Holy Land Foundation, a Hamas charity, has had financial connections to violent elements of Hamas since its creation in 1987, such as supporting the families of Hamas suicide bombers and paying for trips by Hamas authorities to the United States.

According to the federal judge in the 2002 case, "Islamic social welfare groups must not be given a free pass simply because they provide humanitarian support alongside their support role for terrorism."[78]

Though Palestine Islamic Jihad and Hamas are well-established terrorist organizations on the radar screens of intelligence communities in countries around the world, their experience sheds light on the manner in which local grievances can become an occasion for the spawning of a local, affinity terrorist group.

ROLE OF INTELLIGENCE

Of the many U.S. intelligence agencies, the FBI has held the lead role in detecting terrorist activities among domestic affinity groups, but it is the new Directorate of National Intelligence, including the reorganized National Counterterrorism Center (NCTC), that has assumed most of the interagency action on terrorism. Consequently, the DNI and NCTC should have greater input to the terrorist-designation process.

Consider the operation of the FBI in the period before the outbreak of Operation Iraqi Freedom in March 2003 as a template for how the Bureau has acted previously within the interagency process against affinity terrorist organizations. The FBI created a list of individuals who may have had knowledge of Iraqi leadership, military facilities, or potential Iraqi actions in support of terrorism against the United States. Some of them had fled Iraq for a safe haven in America.

The Bureau then conducted some 10,000 interviews. To prepare for these encounters, agents obtained training and received guidelines to conduct the interviews. And before interviewing, FBI executives personally met with Muslim- and Arab-American civic leaders to explain the interview process, a dialogue that has been ongoing since September 11, 2001. Agents informed selected individuals of the Bureau's jurisdiction and responsibility to investigate hate crimes, which were of great concern especially to this leadership.

The process produced 250 reports on possible weapons production, storage, and underground facilities. Director Robert Mueller stated that the FBI furnished these reports to the Pentagon, which informed the Bureau that the reports were timely, relevant, and helped bridge gaps in intelligence.[79] Once the war began, the Bureau activated command posts in its 56 field offices throughout the United States. Agents, support personnel, as well as state and local law enforcement staffed such posts on a 24/7 basis. The posts investigated intelligence about threats of possible terrorism.

These procedures the FBI developed to guard against potential terrorist attacks by Saddam's Iraq also might be used as a model for the Bureau's investigation of certain groups on the U.S. terrorism lists, under the guidance and leadership of the DNI. Preparations for the Iraq War demonstrate that, provided the proper supervision of an IC element with responsibility for the full scope of transnational terrorism, the FBI has experience in both creating and managing lists of individuals, and then setting priorities based on perceived importance.

Within the reorganized context of the overall IC, the DNI should direct the consolidation of watch lists and implement a public government-wide multitiered system for categorizing terrorist groups. Specifically, the DNI should take the lead in the interagency process to revise the various terrorist lists, including determining which individuals and organizations should appear on which lists based on their activities and capabilities.

Meanwhile, law enforcement personnel should approach populations vulnerable to terrorist cells and local affiliates of terrorist organizations in order to alert these populations to the risks of providing material support to terrorist groups. Finally, U.S. officials should seek to win the hearts and minds of vulnerable American ethnic populations before terrorist groups are able to seek material support from such communities.

For diplomatic and bureaucratic reasons, the Department of State must still have a say in the foreign terrorist organization (FTO) designation process, but the DNI and NCTC roles must be enhanced. The state department also should set threat priorities on its public list of state sponsors of terrorism, because Iran is far more dangerous to the United States than other members on that list. This priority-setting process should be repeated for all designated terrorist organizations outside of classified channels.

In order to use the resources of the domestic antiterrorism community effectively, the U.S. government needs to streamline its public terrorist list system to reflect threats posed by different types of groups with different intentions. The separate lists should contain categories that mirror threat levels posed by each group, including whether the organization has mainly a domestic or foreign theater of operations

Because the distinction between foreign and domestic antiterrorism efforts of U.S. agencies is not black and white, one list should be created for foreign terrorist groups (major global terrorists and state sponsors are a different category). The post-9/11 FBI operates abroad with increasing frequency, such as investigating the suicide attacks against Western housing compounds in Saudi Arabia during 2003; its contributions to the full spectrum of intelligence reporting (including that obtained through national technical means, the CIA, and the Defense Intelligence Agency) must be merged more effectively to combat domestic terrorism. In this respect, the NCTC fuses intelligence from multiple sources, including the FBI and CIA, and employs modern methods of data sharing.

With a new list system, it is important to distinguish between the different types of "intermestic" terrorism. Sleepers and satellites employ differing tactics and thus must be addressed differently by government agencies. Sleepers pose the greatest threat in the future, and their ability to operate is enhanced by Islamization of certain segments of American society.

Critics might ask, "What is the value of making such distinctions between different terrorist organizations, because they all conduct terrorism?" By making such distinctions based on the nature, intentions, and theater of operations of each group, the United States can have a much more valid perception of the threat it faces. And from a resource allocation point of view, these distinctions might be a valuable guide in determining which groups to monitor and to what extent.

There is a high potential for FTOs to use ethnic and religious affinity groups to infiltrate cells for later activation and operations in Western countries in general and the United States in particular. A foreign-affinity terrorism strategy in the aftermath of September 11, 2001, should take into account a pyramid of terrorism among rogue regimes, formal terrorist organizations, and Islamist movements.

Based on these relationships, there should be a restructuring of the various terrorism lists maintained by the U.S. government, an enhanced role for the DNI and NCTC in designating FTOs, and a more limited role for the Department of State in FTO designation. In addition, the DNI and NCTC should continue as the lead interagency organizations for fusing and interpreting intelligence on domestic and international terrorism.

It is most likely that affinity terrorism will reach the American shores in great magnitude and with high frequency in the near future. A reconstituted FTO list would be a useful vehicle for highlighting groups that have committed acts of terrorism in the past and have the capability and intent to conduct affinity terrorism in the future.

Threat Assessment

Abroad, the United States takes precautions to disrupt terrorist activities targeted against Americans or allied countries and peoples. Domestically, the strategy of counterterrorism by law enforcement and intelligence communities employs a system of lists to highlight organizations and individuals that might conduct terrorist activities. These lists, however, fail to reflect the level of threat to American civilians posed by designated organizations. Moreover, the distinctive law enforcement culture of the FBI is poorly suited to the kinds of extended intelligence gathering that are so critical to penetration of transnational terrorist networks.

Attempts to change the FBI's criminal investigation focus, from the current system where wrongdoers are brought to justice after commission of a crime to an emphasis on defense of national security through preemption and prevention before terrorists can perpetrate an attack of mass destruction, are not likely to succeed. The United States is unlikely to establish a domestic intelligence agency, analogous to Britain's MI-5, for Constitutional reasons.

To provide American law enforcement and intelligence agencies with effective tools to monitor and prevent terrorist activities, the lists should take into account varying levels of threat posed by different groups. Agencies of the U.S. government then would be able to devote the proper amount of resources to each level according to such threat assessment.

The four principal lists related to the threat of terrorism are (a) State Sponsors of [International] Terrorism, (b) Foreign Terrorist Organizations, (c) Executive Order 13224, and (d) Terrorist Exclusion Lists (TEL).[80]

The Secretary of State designates a government as a state sponsor of terrorism if that entity "has repeatedly provided support for acts of international terrorism." This designation requires imposition of sanctions, such as

- ban on arms exports and sales,
- restrictions of dual-use items,
- prohibitions on economic assistance (except humanitarian), and
- miscellaneous trade restrictions and liability for officials in U.S. courts.

Cuba, Iran, Sudan, and Syria are on the state sponsors list.[81] The primary concern is that these states aid terrorist activities within the United States or against Americans abroad.

The legal basis for FTO classification stems from section 219 of the Immigration and Nationality Act as amended by the Antiterrorism and Effective Death Penalty Act of 1996. The Secretary of State, as before, has the authority to designate or redesignate FTOs if they "conduct international terrorism and threaten the interests of the United States," and the FBI has responsibility for monitoring their activities.

The FTO designation allows authorities to block assets and visas and criminalizes material support for the group.[82] Labeling an entity as an FTO thereby curtails support for terrorist activities and pressures groups to get out of the terrorism enterprise. The state department's Office of the Coordinator for Counterterrorism (S/CT) monitors activities of terrorist groups around the world to identify potential targets for designation.[83] S/CT has the responsibility to review the FTO list every two years. This process involves examining terrorist attacks that a group has carried out, in addition to preparations, capabilities, and intentions for possible future acts.[84] In October 30, 2003, two independent analysts classified 18 out of 37 groups on the FTO list as "Islamist."[85]

Executive Order 13224 of September 23, 2001, established a third watch list that primarily targets terrorist finances. With the Departments of State and Treasury in the lead, the U.S. government is able to block assets of individuals or groups that provide financial or other support to designated terrorists.[86]

The U.S. PATRIOT Act of 2001 authorizes the Terrorist Exclusion List (8 U.S.C. § 1182). Organizations are placed on the list if they

- commit or intend to commit a terrorist activity with an intention to cause death or serious bodily injury;
- prepare or plan a terrorist activity;
- gather information on potential targets for terrorist activity; or
- provide material support to further terrorist activity.[87]

The Secretary of State is given the power to exclude individual members of TEL groups from entering the country.

This list classification system tries to combat terrorism by delineating terrorists and their support network to make them easier to target. However, the system of lists places too much designation authority with the Department of State given that many groups operate both in foreign countries and domestically. Intelligence agencies with overseas collection and tracking responsibility should have a greater input into which groups belong on lists. In particular, the NCTC and DNI, which combine both domestic and international intelligence, should have greater authority in deciding which groups deserve to be designated.

The Department of State should retain primary responsibility for the State Sponsors of Terrorism list and share the TEL with the Department of Treasury because both have an international focus.

Treasury should have primary responsibility to designate under Executive Order 13224 because this list tracks terrorist financing. The DNI, working with State, CIA, and NCTC, should take the lead in designating and monitoring compliance for the FTO list because the activities are intermestic: both international and domestic.

Public versions of the four lists also do not take into account the level of threat that different terrorist groups pose to the United States. For example, Cuba and Iran are both on the State Sponsors of Terrorism list, yet Iran is the more dangerous state to the safety of Americans abroad as well as in the U.S. homeland. The FTO list includes al Qaeda, which has conducted terrorist attacks against American targets for well over a decade, but it also includes the Real Irish Republican Army, which has never targeted the United States.

The unclassified lists are therefore useful for monitoring different facets of terrorism—funding, support, conduct—but fail to designate terrorist organizations by how dangerous they are to the United States. While there may be classified lists that give priority to threat level, keeping such information secret is a disservice to the American public. Furthermore, some groups might modify their behavior if they better understood their offense.

Determining Threat Levels

Department of Defense threat assessment criteria, which are widely used in the government, evaluate terrorist group's capability, motivation and intentions, prior history, and current targeting activity. These criteria are ranked: the nature of the organization is a primary indicator and group intention is a secondary criterion.

A group's nature can either be that of true believers or secularists. True believers follow a faith-based ideology and have a supranational mission. Although they may be willing to make temporary concessions for a

short-term benefit, in the long term they will not compromise their absolutist goals. Nothing will end their violent struggle except all-out victory or
utter destruction.[88] In contrast to true believers, secular terrorists downplay
faith as a motivation for terrorism. For example, secular motivations for terrorism include anticolonialism. These are generally nationalists who may
accept a resolution short of all-out victory.

The intentions of a group reveal both its choice of targets and its motivation. A group's objectives can be evaluated regardless of whether they have
attacked before or not. While the nature of a group tends to be fixed over
time, its intentions and targets do vary. In this chapter, two intentions are
explored: the intention to target Americans or not to do so.

When we combine the group's nature and intentions, we can determine
that the most dangerous groups to national security are those that are "true
believers" who target Americans. Next in order of most dangerous are secularists who target Americans, followed by true believers who do not target
Americans, and ending with secularists who do not target Americans. Inherently, true believers are more dangerous because of their absolutist purposes
and unwillingness to compromise. It is also important to examine motivations (and thus perceived targets) because any group that targets Americans
is more dangerous than a group that does not.

Al Qaeda is the quintessential example of true believers targeting Americans.
Osama bin Laden outlined his grievances against the United States, including the presence of American troops in the Gulf and support for Israel, and
is unwilling to negotiate his goals. Even if the United States were to withdraw from the Middle East and Islamic world, Al Qaeda would continue
targeting American targets; the United States is the one power in the world
that can pose a credible threat to the unlimited ambitions of the international *jihad* movement. A combination of true believer nature and hostile
motivations against the United States makes a group like al Qaeda an
implacable foe.

Less of a threat than true believers are secular groups that target Americans.
Foreign secularists generally only target American citizens when U.S. action
interferes with their goals. For example, if the U.S. government supports a
government battling such a group, or if Americans are caught in the areas of
operations, the terrorist groups may seek American targets. Secular terrorists
have targeted Americans abroad. The Greek group November 17, for
instance, assassinated Americans in Greece to protest U.S. support for the Greek
government. Colombia's Fuerzas Armadas Revolucionarias de Colombia
(FARC) and the Palestinian Liberation Organization have also targeted
Americans abroad. Because secularists' goals, unlike true believers, are limited,
they do not feel the need to make their battle global.

Also, because these secularist groups have grievances which are localized
abroad, they pose much less of an affinity threat. "True believers," whose
grievances are global and against the very existence of the United States,

are much more likely to emerge from within the homeland as affinity terrorists.

Other groups find themselves on terrorism lists more for political reasons than terrorist activity.

The Clinton administration designated the Mujahedeen-e Khalq (MEK) as an FTO on October 8, 1997, primarily because the White House and Secretary of State Madeline Albright desired to create a climate conducive to improving relations with Mohammad Khatami's inauguration as president. Indeed, she may have designated the MEK as an FTO to send a signal to Iran that the United States was interested in making a diplomatic deal.

A senior Clinton administration official said inclusion of the People's Mujahedeen [MEK] was intended as a goodwill gesture to Tehran and its newly elected moderate president, Mohammad Khatami.[89] The unnamed official agrees with then Assistant Secretary of State Martin Indyk. In an interview five years after the MEK designation, Indyk states that, "[There] was White House interest in opening up a dialogue with the Iranian government. At the time, President Khatami had recently been elected and was seen as a moderate. Top Administration officials saw cracking down on the [MEK], which the Iranians had made clear they saw as a menace, as one way to do so."[90]

While there is no question that al Qaeda, Hamas, and Hezbollah have engaged in terrorist activities during 2001–2009, and encouraged affinity attacks, it is clear that the MEK has not done so. In fact, after the war to topple Saddam Hussein began in March 2003, U.S. forces negotiated a cease-fire with the MEK in Iraq, placed the group's weapons in storage, and granted protected persons status under the Fourth Geneva Convention to individual MEK members in Iraq.

The MEK may not meet criteria for membership on the FTO list. Consequently, its status should be reviewed. At the very least, sparse intelligence and law enforcement resources should not be spent defending against organizations, like the MEK, which never posed an affinity threat.

While groups that directly threaten the United States are the largest danger to Americans at home and abroad, the U.S. government has defined its goal in the War on Terrorism to be rooting out "terrorism with a global reach."[91] So the United States has an interest in stopping terrorist activities, even if such activities do not support operations against Americans. To do so, it is important to consider a group's general theater of operations. If a terrorist group, even one not targeting Americans, operates in the United States in any way, it must be designated as such in order to alert domestic law enforcement officials as to the nature of the threat and the span of operations of the group.

Both threat nature and motivation criteria are important in highlighting dangerous groups. The U.S. government ought to use this matrix to determine threat levels and determine funding and personnel allocation within and among agencies combating terrorism.

CHANGES IN INTELLIGENCE SINCE SEPTEMBER 11, 2001, AND RECOMMENDATIONS FOR THE FUTURE

The intelligence lapses preceding 9/11 highlighted the lack of coordination and inadequate sharing of information among government agencies. To correct the problems, Congress mandated and the intelligence community instituted a number of far-reaching structural changes. The Intelligence Reform and Terrorism Prevention Act of 2004 decreed an ambitious program to reorganize the national intelligence system. In February 2005, President George W. Bush appointed Ambassador John Negroponte to be the first Director of National Intelligence, with authority to manage the entire IC and serve as principal advisor to the president on intelligence matters. Vice Admiral John Michael McConnell succeeded Negroponte on February 13, 2007, and on January 29, 2009, Admiral Dennis C. Blair took over as Director of National Intelligence.

Key among the DNI's assigned tasks are management of the overall budget for all national intelligence agencies, ensuring the sharing of information among IC agencies and the establishment of common standards for all IC personnel.[92] One of the most important implications of the DNI title is the inclusion of domestic intelligence authority, which the Director of Central Intelligence (DCI) previously held nominally, but in fact, never effectively exercised because of FBI dominance in the domestic arena.[93]

In May 2006, Air Force General Michael Hayden, a career intelligence official, took over as head of the CIA, following the stormy 18-month tenure of political appointee, Porter Goss. After the inauguration of President Obama in January 2009, Leon Panetta was nominated and confirmed as Director of Central Intelligence. In his capacity as CIA director, Panetta reports directly to the DNI and is tasked with returning stability to the CIA as well as improving that agency's record of performance in the wake of widely acknowledged failures prior to the attacks of 9/11.[94]

Additionally, several other new entities were created to help unify interagency processes and enhance an integrated IC performance in the Global War on Terrorism. Among these were the Terrorist Threat Integration Center (TTIC), the Foreign Terrorist Tracking Task Force (FTTTF), and the Terrorist Screening Center (TSC). Elements from across the IC seconded personnel to serve in the TTIC, while FTTTF and the TSC were placed under the authority of the Attorney General and the FBI, respectively, and essentially staffed by the FBI and its government contractors.

Although administratively contained within the CIA at its inception, TTIC was an interagency body intended "to provide a comprehensive, all-source-based picture of potential terrorist threats to U.S. interests."[95] Elements of the Department of Homeland Security (DHS), the Counterterrorism Division of the FBI, the Counterterrorism Center of the Director of Central Intelligence, and the Department of Defense combined to form

TTIC. Agents and analysts were moved into a secure building where it was expected (somewhat idealistically) that close proximity would enable them all to work more closely together than ever before. TTIC later evolved into the NCTC and was removed from the CIA to be placed under the authority of the newly created Directorate of National Intelligence, which was building a staff that neared 1,500 members by mid-2007.

A continuing problem with this reorganization is the potential for NCTC friction with the CIA's CTC, which retains a closer link to frontline operations officers but lacks the NCTC's analytical strengths and domestic intelligence role.[96]

NCTC now holds primary responsibility for collection, analysis, fusion, and dissemination of intelligence on terrorist groups that cut across foreign and domestic boundaries (i.e., transnational terrorists). The FBI continues to contribute to the overall goal of "connecting the dots" through its Counterterrorism Division (now a part of the NCTC), the FTTTF, and the TSC. The FBI remains the lead IC organization for strictly domestic terrorism and acts in a supporting role to the NCTC when transnational terrorism (including that which crosses into U.S. domestic security purview) is at issue.

The FTTTF was another specialized interagency organization; it was placed within the Office of the Deputy Attorney General and included participants from the Department of Defense, DHS's Bureaus of Immigration and Customs Enforcement (ICE) and Customs and Border Protection, the Department of State, the Social Security Administration, the Office of Personnel Management, the Department of Energy, and CIA. FTTTF's mission is to provide information that helps keep foreign terrorists and their supporters out of the United States or leads to their removal, detention, prosecution, or other legal action. The FTTTF's principal feature was creation of a unified, cohesive lookout list with which to identify foreign terrorists and their supporters who have entered or seek to enter the United States or its territories. In keeping with its criminal law perspective, FTTTF also was charged with detecting such factors as violations of criminal or immigration law which would permit exclusion, detention, or deportation of such individuals.[97]

Finally, the TSC was yet another interagency organization, set up at the end of 2003 and administered by the FBI, that included elements from DHS, the Department of Justice, the FBI, the Department of State, and other IC representatives. Not an information or intelligence collector, the TSC rather was created to consolidate terrorist watchlists and provide 24/7 operational center support for federal screeners across the United States and around the world. The TSC was to receive the majority of its information from the TTIC, after TTIC had assembled and analyzed the raw information. The FBI was to provide the TSC with information about purely domestic terrorism, with no connection to international terrorist activities. With this input, the TSC was tasked to consolidate the information into an unclassified terrorist screening database, and then to make the database available to queries from federal, state, and local agencies.[98]

The good news is that the U.S. government is organizing to combat the threat of terrorism via increased synchronization and enhanced sharing of information. The bad news is that such organizing still falls short of what it takes to detect and prevent future terrorist threats against the United States. For optimal detection and prevention, clear lines of authority and genuine coordination and cooperation across the IC must become far more of an established reality than has been the case to date.

If the new Directorate of National Intelligence becomes simply a new level of bureaucracy, interposed between the 15 or so constituent agencies of the IC and the Executive Branch, but with the same limitations attendant to the former DCI, the IC reorganization will not have accomplished what it was designed to do. Many problems remain, some minor and some major; many are the same problems that plagued the IC with the infighting and inefficiencies cited by the 9/11 Commission. Some time will be required before it is clear whether the appointments of Blair and Panetta can impose order on America's sprawling and unruly intelligence system.

Among the problems the new team must address are the key challenges of intelligence sharing and interagency cooperation. For instance, not until June 2006 did NCTC elements from the CIA and FBI cease to be merely seconded from their parent organizations instead of being completely reassigned as dedicated employees of the new entity; because their loyalties (and career tracks) remained with their organization of origin, the sought-for cohesiveness across IC elements also remained an elusive objective.

Previously, because CIA retained overall control over the TTIC (which was physically located within the CIA's CTC at Langley before its redesignation as NCTC within the Directorate for National Intelligence), while the FBI retained administrative control over its Counterterrorism Division, the intended fusion of capabilities, functions, and intelligence never happened. IC elements within the TTIC did not trust one another or share intelligence, especially with those elements from DHS, which often found itself frozen out of classified conversations and excluded from sharing in reporting collected by other IC players. The DHS Directorate of Information Analysis and Infrastructure Protection has since been split into its two component elements, but in any case, never grew into its assigned role of coordinating and analyzing terrorist threat intelligence for the IC.

As if this were not bad enough, the TTIC operated as though it were in competition with the FTTTF, the FBI's terrorist tracking and database system, and with the FBI's TSC. In addition, TTIC participants could not access each other's databases and could not even communicate via e-mail because they were all on different and nonconnected systems. Clearly, all-source intelligence collection, analysis, fusion, and dissemination were not achieving the results intended with the establishment of these specialized post-9/11 intelligence organizations.

Two other major organizational flaws impeded the effective functioning of the IC prior to this reorganization and have not yet been addressed adequately by it. Namely, the continued ownership by the Department of Defense of the national technical intelligence agencies—the National Security Agency (NSA), the National Reconnaissance Office (NRO), and the National Geospatial Intelligence Agency (NGA)—allows an intelligence-sharing barrier to remain between the powerful U.S. military structure and the primarily civilian organizations of the rest of the IC. As well, the FBI's dominance of domestic intelligence becomes increasingly problematic in an age of transnational terrorism, in which the preponderance of overseas collection remains the responsibility of the CIA, but intelligence about the domestic crossover of foreign-origin terrorism often falls into the hands of a system primarily geared to track down and prosecute criminal lawbreakers.[99]

Another continuing problem not yet satisfactorily resolved by this most recent IC reorganization is the issue of which agency should have primary action to designate terrorist groups to the official FTO list. The state department, whose only element that participates formally in the IC is the Bureau of Intelligence and Research (INR), has the primary designation authority in this regard, exercised however, not through INR, but through its Office of the Coordinator for Counterterrorism. But because neither the S/CT nor INR has either collection authority or responsibility, these offices rely on the input with which to make the department's terrorist group designation decisions on other members of the IC—which, as noted above, continue to function in a disorganized and competitive, rather than cooperative, spirit. In the absence of strong, centralized IC authority over the FTO list, political considerations have crept into the designation process, eroding and weakening the overall credibility of the list.

The Directorate of National Intelligence, relying on both the CIA and the NCTC, should have increased authority to designate organizations that have engaged in transnational terrorism that threatens U.S. persons, facilities, or interests. Although the Department of State is likely to resist yielding primary designation authority to the DNI, this change is necessary if political considerations are ever to be removed from the process of compiling the FTO list.

The structure of the intelligence community must incorporate an understanding of foreign-affinity terrorism, especially its "intermestic" characteristics, to prevent future attacks. A new outlook and reformed structure of intelligence are necessary to prevent future affinity attacks.

3

Intelligence: An Endangered Species

William H. Lewis

Intelligence is a never-ending, constantly evolving work in progress. From time immemorial, tribes and nations have sought strategic advantage over adversaries through the accumulation of information regarding the intentions and capabilities of their opponents. Intelligence, properly informed, has served as the bedrock for planning preventive actions, in the process shaping diplomatic initiatives and appropriate military tactics.

In the view of many informed observers, no other intelligence agency approximates the overall capabilities of the American intelligence community. During the Cold War period, encompassing four plus decades of competition with the Soviet Union, U.S. intelligence agencies proved effective in dealing with Soviet efforts to expand communist global influence. Advantages in signal intelligence, high-resolution satellite imagery, espionage, and disinformation campaigns proved decisive in safeguarding U.S. security forces. The final chapter was written during the period 1989–1991, hallmarked by the collapse of the Warsaw Treaty Organization and the dissolution of the Soviet Union. Then President George H. W. Bush posited at the onset of the 1990s that a new international order was emerging where the United States hoped to witness the peaceful resolution of disputes under the auspices of the United Nations and other multilateral organizations.

Only dimly perceived were future emergent threats to U.S. national security interests. By the end of the decade, however, President Bill Clinton acknowledged that the international landscape had altered and had become more threatening. In a Presidential Decision Directive (PDD) on homeland defense, issued in 1998, he observed that threats to our national security could no longer be fully anticipated. The PDD suggested that the government might best focus less on specific threats than on "identifying and remedying the country's vulnerabilities." Not to be outdone, Congress had produced a number of comprehensive studies detailing intelligence community deficiencies in its efforts to provide information on the goals and activities of terrorist organizations, including al Qaeda.[1]

Members of the Senate Intelligence Committee, in particular, had devoted special attention to the need for structural changes in the CIA and the NSA for the express purpose of enhancing their collection and analytical capabilities. After a lengthy debate, and at White House urging, Congress authorized a presidential commission to examine the advisability of intelligence community reorganization. In due course, it became evident that the sponsors had modest goals in mind—i.e., to maintain the existing agencies' place while pacifying outspoken critics seeking far-reaching reforms.[2] Part of the failure to conduct a meaningful, comprehensive review is partially attributable to the partisan politics of the period, including impeachment proceedings initiated against the president.

An additional factor in weakening the review conducted was a misapprehension on the part of the legislative and executive branches of the nature and global reach of militant Islamic entities, a number of which had penetrated deeply into American society for financial and other forms of material assistance.[3] Their recruiting within America's melting pot communities and political activism, while troubling, was not viewed as a major strategic threat. As a result, no organizing guideline was fashioned to deal with them for purposes of developing a domestic counterterrorist surveillance program. Primary responsibility continued to be lodged in the law enforcement community (e.g., the FBI), which was inhibited by severe legal constraints. Even in those instances where local religious activists were found to be supportive of al Qaeda and comparable organizations, their activities were viewed as of marginal importance. A further consideration, most FBI staff resisted counterterrorism assignment as career endangering and therefore to be avoided wherever possible. There appeared to be only limited awareness within the intelligence community of the new brand of terrorism that was about to descend on the United States and its ties with the diaspora communities emanating from the Middle East and South Asia.

THE "NEW" WORLD OF TERRORISM

Until the shocks registered on September 11, 2001, the majority of U.S. domestic intelligence specialists tended to view terrorism in divergent terms. Among the lead agencies, no common definition of the term "terrorism" existed, as a result, hindering efforts to hammer out a government wide strategy.

- According to the defense department, "Terrorism was the calculated use of violence or the threat of violence to inculcate fear, intended to coerce or intimidate governments or societies as to the pursuit of goals that are generally political, religious, or ideological."
- The state department defined terrorism as being "premeditated politically motivated violence perpetrated against the noncombatant targets by subnational groups or clandestine agents, usually intended to influence an audience."
- The FBI defined terrorism as "the unlawful use of force or violence against persons or property to intimidate or coerce a government, the civilian population, or any segment thereof, in the furtherance of political or social objectives."

None of these efforts at delineation capture the width and depth of emerging Islamic jihadist extremism. The defense department effort appeared to ignore the all-encompassing nature of jihadism; the state department preferred to bypass any religious connotations; the justice department appeared focused primarily on homegrown militia group terrorism.[4] Of more than passing interest, none of these delineations were compatible with definitions adopted by West European intelligence agencies, many of which had long-standing experience with foreign-sponsored domestic terrorism.

Misguided American perceptions were grounded in the belief that the principal threat to be confronted would arise abroad. The expectation appeared confirmed during much of the 1990s: two bombings in Saudi Arabia, one in Riyadh in November 1995 and the other on the Khobar Towers in Dhahran in June 1996. They were followed by bombings of U.S. embassies in Tanzania and Kenya in 1998; two years later, the audacious attack on the USS *Cole* took place in Aden, a key port of Yemen. The latter event was received with a mixture of astonishment and pleasure by large sections of Arab communities throughout the Middle East. The U.S. military had been humiliated by two young "martyrs " in a "motorized skiff."

The United States was far from passive as these challenges to American interests began to emerge. Between 1996 and 2000, the U.S. budget for counterterrorism rose to $11.3 billion: the number of agents assigned to counterterrorism almost doubled. Assistance to foreign intelligence agencies in the Middle East and Western Europe rose significantly during this period.

The number of FBI agents assigned to U.S. embassies as legal attachés also rose, as did the cadre of CIA analysts dedicated to analysis and early warning of impending terrorist attacks.

These initiatives proved less than successful for several reasons: (1) Throughout much of this period, none of the multiple agencies theoretically concerned with protecting U.S. interests, at home and abroad, shared a single action agenda. (2) As a result, no common priorities or agreed strategies obtained. (3) With skewered priorities, bureaucratic rivalries tended to proliferate with only intermittent sharing of information, thus impeding agreement on intelligence collection targets. Post-September 11 initial studies have shown that parochial agency interests led to constriction of intelligence collection on a community-wide basis—e.g., the Defense Intelligence Agency (DIA) and the assorted service agencies concentrated on "force protection" needs, the CIA on rogue regime ties to sundry terror organizations, and the FBI on foreign espionage. Little attention was devoted to the free-floating anti-Americanism encountered in the Islamic arc extending from North Africa through the Middle East, South Asia, and into the broad reaches of Southeast Asia.

Nor was appreciable attention devoted to the spread of Islamic radicalism within diaspora communities in western Europe. The configuration of these communities was changing as political groups, frustrated with their inability to topple autocratic regimes at home, transformed their operational cells in Germany, the United Kingdom, France, Spain, and Italy where local intelligence agencies had limited surveillance capabilities. Most disturbing, diaspora terrorists had developed evasive techniques, developed secure communications, had access to financial resources, and enjoyed freedom of international travel.

In due course, the U.S. government concentrated its intelligence collection efforts on Osama bin Laden. The scion of a wealthy Saudi family, he had volunteered his services in the "mujahedeen" campaign against the Soviet occupation of Afghanistan during the 1980s. Restless and resourceful, bin Laden remained in South Asia after the Soviet occupation ended. Representative of a generation of Islamic activists who had become disillusioned with repressive governments in their home countries and increasingly critical of Western secularist values and institutions, bin Laden attracted a generation of rejectionists who found in the theology of holy war opportunity to express their dissatisfactions.[5]

The Washington intelligence community soon came to perceive that war against terrorism had no geographic borders. On the other hand, some analysts came to believe that religion could be a useful weapon, as demonstrated in Afghanistan. Eric Rouleau has observed: "The United States, in fact, joined forces with Saudi Arabia and Pakistan to recruit, arm, finance, and train tens of thousands of mujahedeen for the 'Islamist International' that was assembled to help drive the Soviets out of Afghanistan."[6] Ultimately, bin Laden would build on Islamic fervor to fashion an anti-U.S. jihad-driven crusade.

With the arrival of the second Bush administration, there was growing awareness in some quarters that religion had become a poisoned fruit profoundly shaping terrorist doctrine in Middle and South Asia. Geography mattered less, however, than the strength of Islamist rage and jihadist messianic visions. (As Daniel Stevenson and Steven Simon have recently observed, the al Qaeda belief system is consonant with traditional Islamic teachings— e.g., Taq al Din ibn Taymiyya and Muhammed ibn Abd al-Wahab.) However pernicious, bin Laden's religious beliefs cannot be separated neatly from the mainstream of Islamic principles and beliefs.[7] His issuance of religious decrees or fatwas against the U.S. and the Saudi government is taken seriously by many Muslims.

CHALLENGE AND RESPONSE

The carnage unleashed against the United States on September 11, 2001, shook the nation. It also revealed the face of an adversary dedicated to the destruction of America's institutions and values. The victims included 3,000 killed and twice that number in what an observer called "the bloodiest day on American soil since the battle of Antietam in 1862." The country awakened to a cosmic reality—the United States was at war with an enemy that accepted no civilized norms or constraints.

The immediate effect was an upsurge in outrage and national unity, reflected in a closing of congressional ranks. The percentage of Americans who rallied in support of President George W. Bush rose from the 50s prior to 9/11 to an astounding 90s after the tragedy, the highest score ever for a sitting president.

Declaring the country at war against a global threat, President Bush assumed the mantle of "commander in chief" claiming powers beyond public scrutiny or congressional reach. He promised an unrestrained campaign against predatory Islamic enemies, one in which traditional rules of engagement would be set aside.

Intelligence would serve as the core of the antiterror campaign, with multiple roles and responsibilities. At the same time, the administration's list of terrorist organizations was greatly expanded, embracing more than 40 entities, many with a cadre of supporters in the United States. This required a remolding of counterterror and counterintelligence, as well as a blurring of past distinctions between domestic and internationally driven covert action. No longer would there be a "Chinese wall" separating law enforcement and pure counterterrorism.

These changes were pursued with a sense of wartime urgency. Emblematic was the speed with which the PATRIOT Act received congressional approval. The act freed the FBI and other agencies to conduct investigations of foreign nationals resident in the United States, as well as U.S. citizens suspected to be supporters of Islamic extremist organizations. Agents armed with a court order could now eavesdrop on private telephone conversations, read e-mail, and seek library records, bank statements, and medical records without having to show "reasonable cause." At the same time, the president in an apparent breach of existing law, secretly authorized the NSA—the nation's premier code breaking organization—to conduct warrantless surveillance of communications between suspected international terrorists and Americans. Comparable authorization was given to the treasury department to survey and monitor financial transactions between American entities and terrorist organizations abroad.[8]

The administration, contending that the threat of global terrorism had altered the rules by which to conduct war, reshaped conventional American understanding governing the use of covert action. The Geneva Conventions relating to the treatment of prisoners and their right to fair trial under military justice was set aside. *Habeas corpus* rights and protections were surrendered when exigent circumstances warranted. Overriding was the White House contention that customary international conventions and norms should be set aside to protect our national security. Even more disconcerting to law makers and members of the American legal community, the president contended that covert action secrecy trumps the public's "need to know."[9] In short, a national security firewall must be maintained between congress and the executive branch, presumably to preclude congressional involvement and oversight in sensitive security matters.

Consonant with White House guidance, the CIA was authorized to establish covert centers of incarceration in eastern Europe and Asia where "high value detainees" could be subject to coercive interrogation measures outside the purview of the International Committee of the Red Cross. Access to real-time intelligence was to be elicited through coercive measures which international conventions might characterize as torture. (In 2006, 14 "high value detainees" were transferred to Guantanamo Bay to await trial by military tribunals.) In addition, under presidential edict, CIA officers were authorized to apprehend suspected terrorists for imprisonment in "black sites" abroad or for transfer to other governments for final disposition. All of these activities, when revealed in published reports, generated widespread demands for reform in covert action programs.

As public revelations widened, the most deleterious consequence was the weakening of collaboration between the CIA and friendly foreign government intelligence services. The latter have experienced public opprobrium for their reported participation in secret detentions and renditions. The depth of criticism was recently captured by a respected journalist, Eugene Robinson:

> If the president needed a "hot pursuit" to allow some specific forms of coercive interrogation, he should have asked Congress to give it to him—rather than

rely on a vague blanket authorization to pursue the War on Terrorism. If the judgment was that coercion had to be applied . . . absent a law allowing it, then the officials who ordered the coercion should have had to defend their actions in a court of law.[10]

The administration's position is that Islamic terrorism is a transnational phenomenon which the old international order is unprepared to address and eliminate. Confronted by an elusive enemy that regards jihadism as a legitimate form of warfare wherein Western-imposed conventions and norms should be ignored, the United States must deal with extremists by adopting extralegal measures. In the treatment of detainees, the administration requires unfettered freedom of action—a maximalist reading of executive power not readily sustainable in the existing American political system.

The White House notes that the intelligence community must cover a wide spectrum of imperatives—*protection* of the American homeland (involving detection, surveillance, interdiction, and trial and prosecution of terrorists and their supporters); *preemption* of groups abroad planning to attack U.S. interests and those of our allies; and *prevention* which requires intelligence gathering to forestall the acquisition of weapons of mass destruction by rogue regimes or terrorist organizations. Sixteen departments and agencies staffed by 100,000 intelligence personnel are in theory mobilized to meet these mission requirements. There is reason to doubt that they are fully prepared to do so.

INTELLIGENCE FAILURES

As historians often declaim, "the past is not always decipherable." However, the abject failure of the CIA and the FBI "to connect the dots" of 9/11 and the warping of intelligence leading up to the U.S. invasion of Iraq (March 2003) demanded explanation. The initial inclination of the White House was to avoid official finger-pointing assessments. It remained for Richard Clarke, erstwhile senior White House counterterrorism official, to acknowledge before the Senate Intelligence Committee that the country's counterterrorism agencies and the White House had failed to protect the American people.[11]

The president initially opposed creation of an independent commission with a mandate "to understand an event that was unprecedented with the destruction it had wrought on the American homeland, and appalling even within the catalogue of human brutality" (words by Thomas A. Kean and Lee H. Hamilton, co-chairs of the 9/11 Commission). Only in the face of unrelenting pressure by congress and families that had lost relatives in the carnage of 9/11 did the White House set aside its reservations. The commission did, however, continue to face obstacles by the executive branch as it pursued the painful question: "What went wrong?"

Not to be outdone or outflanked, the administration set about organizing its own investigations within the CIA, FBI, and state department. In addition, in the wake of the intelligence community's inept performance in evaluating Iraq's WMD programs, the president approved the creation of a "Commission on Intelligence Capabilities of the United States Regarding Weapons of Mass Destruction," cochaired by former Senator Chuck Robb and Laurence Silberman, a senior appellate court judge. In its report issued on April 1, 2005, the commission offered a scathing evaluation of the intelligence community. In addition to being "dead wrong" in its assessments of Iraq's WMD capabilities before the U.S. invasion, it found that the community knows "disturbingly little" about the weapons programs and intentions of many of our "most dangerous adversaries."

With respect to the dysfunctional organization, poor management, and lack of coordination among various intelligence agencies, the cochairs offered no recommendations for improvement in the commission's nearly 600-page report to the president. The main thrust of the report found the following:

The "community" demonstrates serious errors in analyzing in what information it could gather and a failure to make clear just how much of its analysis was based on assumptions rather than good evidence.

The need is for "stronger" and more centralized management of the intelligence community, and in general, the creation of a more integrated community, "rather than a loose confederation of independent agencies."

It won't be easy to provide ... leadership to the intelligence components of the Defense Department or to the CIA. Sooner of later they will try to "run around" the newly established Director of National Intelligence (DNI).

With regard to organizations, the report (1) called for far-reaching changes within the FBI, including creation of a new National Security Service that could merge the agency's counterterrorism and counterintelligence divisions; and (2) recommended establishing a National Counter Proliferation Center to oversee intelligence on nuclear, biological, and chemical weapons; a new human intelligence center in the CIA and (3) mission managers to coordinate analysis on specific topics across the entire intelligence community.

The Kean-Hamilton 9/11 Commission was even less kindly disposed than Robb-Silberman in outlining the failures and incompetence of the American "system" of intelligence. They pointed, *inter alia*, to the structural barriers to performing joint intelligence work, the lack of common standards across the foreign-domestic divide, weak capacity to set priorities, and divided management of national capabilities. Changes in organization and direction of U.S. intelligence recommended by the commission will be addressed in the following sections. Critics of the 9/11 report applaud many of the proposed changes, but contend that more reforms must be addressed.

To the surprise of many informed observers, neither the CIA nor the FBI suffered severe penalties for their failure to provide early warnings of the September 11 attacks. Both received substantial increases in funding and personnel hirings to strengthen their covert action and counterterrorism capabilities. The administration has also sought legislation permitting the CIA to conduct operations in the United States. Such an effort in the decades of the 1970s and the 1980s would have been rejected out of hand.[12] The White House effort was set aside in 2007.

At the onset of the twenty-first century, traditional boundaries between domestic law enforcement and domestic spying have been breached, however. The administration recognizes that intelligence, when properly organized, enables participating agencies to operate in a more coherent and coordinated fashion. However, the president has yet to provide the country with a convincing strategic vision on how the administration proposes to conduct its global war on terrorism or offer comprehensive guidelines to intelligence agencies on measures to enhance collection and analysis of intelligence gleaned.

Some proponents of reform within the intelligence and law enforcement communities recommend far reaching institutional changes. These include proposals to create a separate agency to cope with domestic terrorist groups—as in the United Kingdom's MI5—while continuing to relegate traditional anticrime responsibilities to the FBI. Others propose that the FBI be detached from the justice department and become an autonomous entity. The Department of Defense has not established major reforms but a position of deputy secretary of defense intelligence had been created. His responsibility is to oversee intelligence collection efforts and to initiate covert action programs. Others have recommended that the military service agencies dealing with counterterrorism be incorporated into the DIA. The CIA has also received public scrutiny. Institutional changes proposed include separation of the National Intelligence Center from the remainder of the agency to become the central analytical entity under the personal direction of the Director of Central Intelligence (DCI).

Prior to considering ongoing reorganization of the intelligence community, several difficulties should be addressed. The new administration beginning in 2009 should step back from a crisis perspective to assess the weaknesses of the current approach to counterterrorism. The review should include a senior level policy study to identify problems in information gathering and analysis by intelligence agencies. In addition, there is a need to address deficiencies in the preparation of intelligence estimates, recently characterized by one senior defense department official as "an art form rather than pure science." The intelligence estimate process should guide program managers in setting information target goals and provide a more effective basis for exchanges of data and analyses. The White House should make clear that it is no longer willing to tolerate traditional stovepipe approaches and poor coordination at the interagency level. The military departments appear to have taken the initiative in developing an analytical framework that reaches beyond the military to include diplomatic, law enforcement, and treasury department's resources. Reportedly, emphasis is being placed on organizational innovation to promote "synchronicity of effort." This has led to the insertion of liaison teams into selected "agencies" that operate under the command of defense attachés or, as circumstances warrant, military group commanders. Yet, to be fully resolved, however, is the span of control to be exercised by U.S. ambassadors, their need to know highly sensitive information, and their degree of involvement in ongoing, covert operations.

A source of growing contention has been the expanding involvement of military units in pacification and nation-building activities absent effective state department involvement and concurrence. Several such efforts have been directed towards intelligence collection and elimination of suspected al Qaeda sanctuaries in Africa and the Maghreb (e.g., North Africa) region. The defense department by late 2007 was seeking to create a new regional unified command based in North Africa. Lack of receptivity to this imitative by governments in that region led the command to be lodged in Stuttgart, Germany, early in 2008.

With respect to oversight, three critical areas require strengthening— congressional review, White House priority setting, and the areas of responsibility exercised by agency inspectors-general. In theory, passage of the Intelligence Oversight Act of 1980 set in motion requirements that the intelligence community keep select intelligence committees fully apprised of all covert activities—past, present, and anticipated. Over the past two decades, congressional oversight has had little impact in shaping decisions on the advisability of launching sensitive operations abroad and overseeing the allocation of resources for counterterrorism operations. The committees are frequently handicapped by partisan political considerations, an inability to conduct public hearings, the lack of professional competence of their staffs, and failure to agree on joint hearings.

The recently established White House Office of the National Counterintelligence Executive is understaffed and overwhelmed with far-reaching alert responsibilities. The president, as a result, has a limited capacity to insure effective oversight of interagency coordination. Many of these responsibilities might be delegated to a specially formed counterterrorism group within the Office of Management and Budget. *Inter alia*, the latter could provide annual assessments of intelligence agency performance with clear indication that such assessment will impact on annual budget allocations for each agency.

INSPECTORS GENERAL

During 2007, serious deficiencies in the existing inspectors general "system" began to emerge, including reports of malfeasance within the state department office which led its inspector general (IG) to resign in late

December. The CIA office faced its own challenge in the wake of disclosures that the agency's clandestine branch had destroyed, in 2005, classified tapes of "extreme measures" (including frequent water submergences, called "water boarding") undertaken several years previous in CIA interrogations of "high profile" al Qaeda terrorists. The public admission generated widespread Congressional expressions of outrage and multiple investigations, including a joint Department of Justice-CIA Inspector General initiative. The CIA representative is placed in the unenviable position of participating in a process that requires agency accountability and possible public opprobrium for actions that could be deemed illicit.

Equally significant have been steps initiated by some members of Congress to terminate a special IG created to eliminate corruption and ineffective management of reconstruction programs, whose reports have produced acute embarrassment with respect to the Bush administration's "post-conflict reconstruction efforts in Iraq." Efforts by some members of Congress to have this IG's operations terminated in 2008 have failed to secure the support of fellow legislators.[13]

Inspector general performance clearly requires marked improvement. The existing reality is that the inspector general function is debilitated by compartmentalization of classified information, which involves walling off access to intelligence. To overcome these barriers, the White House Counterintelligence Executive should serve as an ombudsman when interagency disputes arise over access to sensitive information. Considerable advantage might be found in the formation of a special body bringing together agency inspectors for review of extant issues, under the auspices of the White House Counterintelligence Executive.

ORGANIZATION AND REFORM

After extensive legislative-executive branch negotiation, as already alluded, the White House accepted the need for an independent commission to examine failures in policy supervision and intelligence early warning leading up to 9/11. The various agencies initially sought to avoid providing written data on the grounds that "sources and methods" might be revealed. Moreover, the commission proposed to examine the credibility and reliability of intelligence sources, the "track record" of analytical staff, and the failure of agencies to share early warning data.[14]

The commission included all of the above in examining failures in the national intelligence estimates (NIEs) system. The record of estimates intended to predict challenges and threats has been parlous at best. The CIA, which has the primary responsibility for the preparation of NIEs, failed abysmally to predict the 1973 Yom Kippur War, the Soviet invasion of Afghanistan, and most tellingly, the degradation of the Soviet economy and its armed forces in competition with the United States. To ignore the lack of warning of the al Qaeda attack in September 2001, the commission felt, would be self-defeating.

In its preparatory work, the commission received special assessments and critical input that focused on four areas.

Organizational Compartmentation

The intelligence community is a community in name only. The then DCI, George Tenet, had little effective oversight responsibility for the programs of the DIA, NSA, military service organizations, and the state department's Bureau of Intelligence and Analysis. Each reports to separate "masters"; each establishes separate collection requirements; each protects its assets (so-called "family jewels"); and each maintains separate and distinct bureaucratic cultures. This stovepipe system frustrated efforts to organize a coordinated community-wide collection and analytical effort.

System Overload

The absence of a coordinated community-wide collection effort presented difficult challenges when sorting "wheat from chaff." Competing agency priorities based on demands by the White House, other senior executive branch officials, and the armed services produces high "paper volume" and marginal "actionable material." For national security council staff, the perpetual overhang of crisis generates combat fatigue and frustration.[15]

Given the vague boundaries between domestic and foreign security concerns, information system demands have escalated. Evaluation of input has been dependent on systems that have been in place over five decades, which are obsolescent and unreliable.

Alternative Inputs

Competing information sources distort threat assessments presented by various intelligence agencies. While NIEs are expected to provide consensus on issues of concern to the president, they are frequently shaded in subtle ways to reduce differences and to accommodate the competing views of participating agencies. When disagreements go unresolved, on occasion, dissenting estimates are "leaked" to the media and congressional staff in expectation that contentious issues would be revisited.[16] Policy makers, themselves, seek information inputs from nonofficial sources, goaded in part by intelligence reports that raise doubts about the likely efficaciousness of existing policy courses. *In extremis*, senior officials will seek to create special intelligence assessments. These competing inputs tended to slow efforts to deal with the al Qaeda threat prior to 9/11.

Robert Woodard reports that the CIA director and several associates had briefed the president-elect in 2001 on bin Laden and his network, observing that they constituted an "immediate threat." There was no doubt in the director's mind that bin Laden "was coming after the United States ... but it was not clear when, where or how." Director Tenet had urged that the anti-Taliban Northern Alliance warlords be "armed" but the state department opposed the proposal until Richard Armitage, Secretary Powell's deputy, interceded in April 2000. Additional approaches were under consideration but they were overtaken by the tragic events of September 11. Why had the Clinton and Bush administrations failed to deal with bin Laden's challenge in a timely fashion? As Woodard notes:

> The question that would always linger was whether they had moved fast enough on the threat that had been identified by the CIA on one of the top three facing the country, whether September 11 was as much a failure of policy as it was of intelligence.[17]

Cultural Rigidities

In the immediate aftermath of September 11, Vice President Dick Cheney urged that the administration "go after anyone in the U.S. who might be a terrorist." He also asked, "Are we aggressive enough?" and urged that the question of homeland security be addressed with a heightened degree of urgency.[18] On September 22, FBI Director Robert Mueller reported to the president that his agency had placed 331 individuals located in the United States on a "terrorist watch." The president expressed shock since the FBI had been responsible for domestic intelligence surveillance. He felt that the FBI had "dropped the ball." He also felt that the FBI mind-set devoted to capturing criminals and espionage agents had to change with greater emphasis placed on counterterrorism.[19] His complaint has since been echoed in other quarters accompanied with recommendations for drastic FBI organizational surgery (see following section.)

The sheer inability of FBI leaders to meet the need for an integrated information management system in the wake of 9/11 was revealed in mid-2006. Mueller acknowledged four years after 9/11 that the bureau had expended more than $400 million in failed efforts to upgrade its 1980s system, which impeded expeditious transmittal of information within the bureau and to other intelligence agencies. The failed attempt was attributed to poor conception and execution, inadequate attention by the director, and an inadequate number of information technology specialists to oversee project implementation at every state of evolution. As a result, the FBI does not, in the words of the 9/11 Commission staff report, have an adequate ability to "know what it did not know."[20]

The commission ultimately agreed with much of this criticism. Its final report noted that the post-Cold War world had changed drastically, becoming one in which the United States faces challenges that surpass the boundaries of traditional nation-states. To deal with them, the United States has "good people," but they should not have to operate in systems and structures accustomed to "doing business" rooted in a different era. The commission, therefore, felt obligated to recommend significant changes in the organization of the intelligence agencies to strengthen unity of effort. Five recommendations were put forth to meet this goal:

1. Unify strategic intelligence and operational planning against Islamist terrorists across the foreign-domestic divide with a National Terrorism Center.
2. Unify the intelligence community with a new National Intelligence director.
3. Unify the many participants in the counterterrorism effort and their knowledge in a network-based information sharing system that transcends traditional governmental boundaries.
4. Unify and strengthen congressional oversight to improve quality and accountability.
5. Strengthen the FBI and homeland defenders.

The imperative to restructuring the intelligence community, according to the commission, arises out of six problems that had become apparent before and after 9/11: (1) structural barriers to performing joint intelligence work; (2) lack of common standards and practices across the foreign-domestic divide; (3) divided management of national oversight capabilities; (4) weak capacity to set priorities; (5) too many jobs by the DCI; and (6) operations that were so "complex and secret," to the point of defying public comprehension.

Proposed remedial actions to be taken are encapsulated in Chapter 13 of the commission report. At its core is the proposal that the existing position of DCI be replaced by a Director of National Intelligence (DNI). The quintessential mission of the DNI should be to oversee the National Intelligence Centers of the CIA, FBI, and the DoD (Department of Defense), to provide all source analysis, and plan intelligence operations for the whole government on major national security problems. In the process, he should serve as the principal intelligence adviser to the president. In addition, the director should have far-reaching budget authority, including submission of a unitary community budget to the National Security Council and, upon receipt of an appropriation, apportionment of funds to the several agencies. He would also submit to the president for approval and nomination of leaders of the country's intelligence agencies, as well as the newly established Department of Homeland Security.

The commission recommended that the DNI manage the intelligence community effort with the support of three deputies: (1) foreign intelligence (the director of the CIA); (2) defense intelligence (the undersecretary of defense for intelligence); and (3) homeland security (either a senior FBI official or an undersecretary of Homeland Security). The DoD's military intelligence programs would remain part of the department's responsibility.[21]

The reaction in Congress to the commission's recommendations was tepid at best. The jurisdiction of various oversight committees was at risk, and few chairmen were prepared to surrender roles where partisan issues were fully engaged (witness the Senate Select Committee on Intelligence divided by Roberts-Rockefeller's political maneuverings). The White House was equally noncommittal, pressured by various intelligence agency mandarins, led by the CIA. Intelligence professionals, retired and otherwise, claimed the proposed reorganization was a wiring diagram simply involving super-imposition of another bureaucratic layer of supernumeraries lacking in field experience. For many critics, the need was to protect covert action programs from congressional oversight and the intervention of an unsophisticated DNI superstructure. For many others, the NSA warrantless communications surveillance program and the equally valued treasury efforts might well be jeopardized.

A PROGRAM IN PROGRESS

Only after the 9/11 Commission managed to conduct hearings and secure widespread public support did the entrenched opposition relent and half-heartedly enacted legislation creating a DNI with attendant support staff. However, the authority accorded the director was diluted and the autonomy of the intelligence agencies largely retained, including their ability to circum-vent the DNI through congressional supporters and the public media. A notable example of the latter was the inclination of former congressman Porter Goss, newly appointed CIA director, to constantly oppose DNI deci-sions until Goss's ouster by the president in mid-2006. Being contentious, the FBI and DoD have managed to avoid usurpation of their missions, roles, and authority thereby retaining much of their autonomy.

Inspired by 9/11 Commission urgings, the DNI has managed to use the cudgel of his limited authority to fashion new networks of coordination. In addition to formation of a headquarters staff numbering in the several hun-dreds, his accomplishments include (1) increases in the ranks of "all source" analysts who focus on human intelligence collection involving priority targets; (2) the strengthening of the National Counterterrorism Center (NCTC) which integrates 28 agency networks; (3) creation of the National Security Branch of the FBI whose purpose is to expand and connect the bureau's intelligence, counterterrorism, and counterintelligence capabilities; (4) integration of state and regional "fusion centers" with more than 100 FBI joint terrorism task forces assigned to ensure actionable threat information is disseminated in a timely fashion; and (5) establishment of an FBI WMD division to enhance domestic counterterrorism expertise on weapons of mass destruction.[22] These initiatives are intended to end the tradition of compartmentation and "stove piping" that have impeded integrated intelligence collection and analysis. In the DNI estimate of progress made, "we are 'connecting the dots' both nationally and internationally, integrating counter-terrorism analysis across the intelligence community, and removing bureaucratic barriers to information sharing."[23]

The 9/11 Commission believes that the claims of progress in wire diagramming realignment of bureaucracies and analysis are Panglossian. The commission, which in December 2005 assessed the administration's reform record as mediocre at best, has remained unimpressed. Six months later, its chairman Thomas H. Kean, informed congress "our perspective now . . . is just about the same. There is still a great deal we have to do and still haven't done to protect the American people." One commission member, John Lehman, decried FBI failure to form a national security system that focuses on preventative intelligence rather than on law enforcement. His frustration led him to propose the creation of a separate domestic intelligence service, without police powers, comparable to Britain's MI-5. The Lehman proposal was counterintuitive to the 9/11 report but was suggestive of mounting impatience within the commission.[24]

There has been ample reason for concern. While recommended reforms and reorganization are a work in progress—however, halting and incomplete—intelligence and covert action programs have been multiplying. While the official personnel rolls are pegged at 100,000 and the annual budget estimated at $40–$50 billion, the actual figures are much greater. When the number of special operations troops dedicated to counterterrorism and covert action is added, together with out-sourced research analysis, use of advanced technology, and private protective services, the real intelligence "community" probably aggregates 200,000 personnel with a budget in excess of $65 billion. Since these activities are "stove piped," they escape close DNI review and budgetary control. Much of the DNI remit essentially involves loose coordination rather than direct supervision. Agencies continue to resist making operational time-sensitive information available to the newly formed NCTC, a joint interagency staff created to support oversight responsibilities of the DNI.

At the onset of 2008, major gaps in the DNI approach to "fusion" remained uncovered. The FBI automated data system remained incomplete and beyond possible levels of interface with DNI systems, as well as with those operational within the CIA, DIA, and NSA. Equally troubling, the Department of Homeland Security, embracing multiple agencies, lacks a coherent integrated information and data management system capable of timely early warning and data sharing with intelligence agencies.

To achieve a measure of mission coherence, the administration introduced, after lengthy interagency review, its vaunted National Implementation Plan. Intended to establish priorities in the "long war" against terrorism, the plan, issued in 2006, contends the fight is "all encompassing" and must draw back from purely military initiatives and be balanced with diplomacy and "hearts and minds" campaigns. It designates lead and subordinate agencies to carry out more than 500 discrete counterterrorism tasks, among them defeating al Qaeda, protecting the homeland and wooing allies, training experts in foreign languages and cultures, and understanding and influencing the Islamic "world view." To gain agreement on the plan required intense negotiations among more than 200 departments and agencies. To achieve the desired goals will require a reconfiguration of the intelligence budget, clearly a Herculean task.

The plan has not produced the solidarity envisioned in the 2004 Intelligence Reform and Terrorism Prevention Act. The DNI-NCTC pyramid remains outclassed in power and number of personnel—an estimated 400 analysts by 2008 compared to the FBI's 3,000 existing analytical staff. The DIA has 8,000 employees collecting and analyzing intelligence. The CIA reportedly had twice that number in 2007. Particularly worrisome, morale within CIA ranks has slumped, because the agency's erstwhile responsibility for integrating and analyzing all-source intelligence has been transferred to the DNI and the NCTC. For the agency, its primary remaining responsibility is to strengthen its clandestine human intelligence collection network that congress had found wanting in coverage of the Middle East.

The CIA is now directed to build clandestine network and analytic resources focused on penetrating and eliminating known terrorist organizations, leaving to the DNI-NCTC responsibility for comprehensive analysis for the executive branch as a whole. Overlaying the diminished CIA access to the oval office in the form of daily briefings (written and oral) was the insertion of Porter Goss and his congressional staff to control leaks of information, test the loyalties of agency executives, and to appoint ill-trained personnel in senior ranks. The Goss period of stewardship (2004–2006) proved a disaster from which the agency is only now recovering.

The Goss experience revealed the extent to which partisan politics had infected intelligence agencies over the past several years. Political influence by external sources has long been a factor in shaping U.S. foreign policy. However, the shock of 9/11 produced an inverted pyramid in policy-intelligence dynamics. Policy became the engine guiding intelligence, wherein personalities and rogue intelligence offices could shape perspectives and policy outcomes.

The Department of Defense's senior civilian leaders, in collaboration with White House operatives, adopted a multifaceted approach to ensure the input of "information" to support policy objectives: (1) creation of an "office of special plans" to cull information from Iraqi exiles—for the White House without vetting by other agencies—in short a special "stove pipe" within the DoD to compete with the CIA, DIA, and FBI; (2) establish a "B team" to test and challenge national intelligence estimates prepared by the collegial NIEs system; and (3) rely on external collateral sources to reinforce opinions and prejudices within the senior reaches of the national security policy bureaucracy. Operating deductively rather than inductively, officials within DoD's "special plans office" stoked the fires regarding the WMD threat and the need to seek regime change in Iraq, despite the absence of supporting data:

> [much] of the data was doubted or even dismissed by the CIA, the Defense Intelligence Agency, the State Department's Bureau of Intelligence and Research and the Energy Department. In the eyes of the Pentagon civilians, the methods of these intelligence agencies were deeply suspect, and mainstream analysts had a long record of failure in the Middle East.[25]

A final cautionary note is required. Failures in intelligence are most likely to occur in the final stages of the evaluation process after information has been collected, interpreted, and communicated to senior policymakers. Failure may occur in the analysis stage where the actions of terrorist forces cannot always be predicted with confidence. But, policymaker perceptions and abuse of intelligence is a crucial element in most intelligence failures. Any system that encourages the polarization of intelligence invites distortion of the process. If intelligence becomes a weapon for policy debate, it will lose credibility with the American public and invite further intelligence failure.

Particularly disturbing has been the failure of congressional oversight committees to objectively review intelligence agency activities, provide criticism, and to assess overall performances. Created in 1975 after revelations of wrongdoing, the Senate and House committees were intended to be bipartisan, setting well-defined limits on intelligence activities at home and abroad. Since 9/11, the oversight promised in the original legislation was set aside to permit the CIA to initiate Draconian measures against al Qaeda captives and others. The minority party members often turned a blind eye to excesses. However, after the 2006 midterm elections, with the minority assuming the rule of majority leadership, the committees have become increasingly embroiled in controversy over access to information regarding "harsh interrogation techniques, renditions, *habeas corpus* questions, judicial oversight." By early 2008, bipartisanship had ended. The administration, including the justice department, was engaged with efforts to limit access to what it deemed "sensitive information."

INTELLIGENCE AND CONSTITUTIONAL ISSUES

Establishing an equilibrium between national security imperatives on the one hand and the ongoing rights and freedoms of American citizens on the other is a daunting challenge. Intelligence operations, even those undertaken by law enforcement agencies, require a substantial measure of secrecy if they are to be successfully conducted. The Constitution, when applied to protections and civil rights, requires disclosure of measures taken and accountability. In periods of national crisis (e.g., in the aftermath of the 9/11 attacks),

Congress and much of the American public were prepared to accept an abridgement of some constitutional safeguards. Similarly, as the administration declared open-ended war on terror (a nebulous theoretical construct), there was acceptance of stern intelligence collection and interrogation approaches adopted by intelligence agencies operating abroad.

With the passage of time, disclosures of excesses in intelligence collection interrogations aroused growing public concern. The initial outcry was prompted by exposés at Abu Gharib which revealed questionable approaches adopted in 2004 by U.S. military intelligence officers in their efforts to elicit information from prisoners. Allegations of torture of Afghan prisoners and other captives transferred to an American center at Guantanamo Bay, Cuba, soon followed. In 2005, the *Washington Post* reported that the CIA had been maintaining clandestine interrogation centers where "high value" al Qaeda and Taliban captives were subjected to torture techniques such as water boarding. The centers were situated in Eastern Europe and Asia.[26]

In 2006–2007, various newspapers were also reporting that the government was concomitantly engaged in so-called extraordinary renditions—the abduction of Arab, Afghani, and other nationals suspected of terrorist activities and their transfer, without judicial review, to third countries for harsh interrogation. Reportedly, 100 suspects were seized in various countries and transformed to detention centers in Jordan, Egypt, Saudi Arabia, and other Arab countries. In the case of Italy, press reports of illegal seizure and sequestration of suspected Arab terrorists by U.S. agents produced a public outcry and led an Italian magistrate to initiate proceedings against more than a dozen CIA agents who were involved. One dozen have been officially charged and are to be tried in absentia.[27]

The revolution of "harsh interrogations" by the U.S. military and CIA generated widespread calls for judicial review and congressional investigation. In due course, the FBI announced that its agents would terminate participation in CIA interrogations of terrorists. The Army Field Manual was amended in 2006 to ensure adherence to the International Conventions (Geneva) on the treatment of prisoners, which precludes water boarding, beating, shocking, or burning of detainees, etc.[28] In December 2007, the lower house of congress approved comparable guidelines including strict adherence to the Geneva Conventions. The measure was approved by a largely party-line vote 222 to 199; it was passed by the senate a short time later.

The White House had threatened to veto the aforementioned legislation, contending that limiting the CIA to U.S. Army interrogation techniques "would prevent the United States from conducting lawful interrogations of al Qaeda terrorists to obtain intelligence needed to protect Americans from attacks." Moreover, the president had claimed that Geneva Convention protections did not apply in the case of "unlawful enemy combatants," a designation formulated by the administration in 2002–2003. It contended Convention protections and safeguards did not apply to foes who are not a member of official armed forces or organized resistance movements, do not carry arms openly, wear no uniform or other distinctive sign, and refuse to heed the laws of war. Contrary to initial administration claims, many detainees captured in Afghanistan and Pakistan (2001–2003) were not battlefield combatants but were surrendered to American agents by Afghan bounty hunters; others were seized in Bosnia and Zambia. Moreover, despite administration contention, "unlawful enemy combatants" are now presumed by several U.S. courts to be entitled protections, including humane treatment and chance to a fair trial by a "regularly constituted court."

Increasingly, the Bush administration clashed with congress and the Supreme Court in its expansive view of executive power when addressing policies and practices adopted in the unprecedented war on terror. Military legal issues have been commingled with civilian constitutional questions. Surveillance and counterintelligence are procedures legislated by congress to protect against invasion of privacy. Should terrorism be prosecuted under the laws of armed conflict or the criminal justice system? Is a terrorist action a criminal violation or a political act? Which international conventions govern the confinement of prisoners and any legal processes attending evidentiary hearings? To what extreme should habeas corpus apply? Are renditions an acceptable policy, unguided by rules of war and judicial review?[29]

By February 2008, virtually all of these questions remained to be answered. The recently appointed DNI admiral, Mike McConnell, contended in January that CIA detention and interrogation programs had saved lives and provided information that could otherwise not have been obtained. At the same time, he declared that the U.S. government does not use torture techniques. It was also noted that then CIA Director Michael Hayden had directed that torture would be prohibited.[30]

As the 2008 presidential campaign unfolded, the courts assumed a significant role in shaping decisions on Constitutional issues. Throughout, the Bush administration persisted in its view that questions relating to wartime decision-making should not be handcuffed with Constitutional principles and precepts—i.e., that practical intelligence needed to protect national security should be accorded higher priority than a legally recognized "hierarchy" of rights found in the Constitution.

By mid-2007, revelations that the administration had authorized clandestine wire tap surveillance of communications (international and domestic) between U.S. nationals and sources abroad suspected of involvement in terrorist activities generated expressions of public concern. Particularly disturbing revelations were: (1) the oversight court mandated by legislation in 1974 to approve such activities had been side-lined; (2) senior congressional leaders had not been fully briefed about the enterprise launched in 2002 by the NSA; and (3) then Attorney General Ashcroft, the director of the FBI, and the Deputy Attorney General had threatened to resign if comprehensive new legal guidelines governing the surveillance were not established. In due course, issues associated with treatment of prisoners and habeus corpus were left with Congress, the Supreme Court, and the lower courts to disentangle—with mounting pressure directed toward Congress to provide legislative guidance and more effective oversight than had been the case since 2001–2002.[31]

4

The Role of Law Enforcement Agencies in Combating Terrorism: The Threat and Challenge

Oliver (Buck) Revell

In June 1993, the FBI issued its annual report on Terrorism in the United States; however, this report documented the incidents of terrorism for the 10-year period from 1982 through 1992.[1] The report reflected a continuing decline of terrorist incidents during the 10 years prior to 1993. In 1982, 51 terrorist incidents were reported, but by 1992 the total number of reported incidents had declined to 4. The report also cited the fact that 74 intended acts of terrorism had been prevented during this 10-year period. The vice president's Task Force on Combating Terrorism report published in February of 1986 had documented an increased threat to Americans and American interests internationally.[2] Domestically it appeared that the terrorism threat was being dealt with effectively. However, in the preface to the FBI's report an ominous warning was set forth. The FBI director stated:

> When this publication was being prepared, the United States had been relatively free of terrorism. Since the end of 1983, there had been only one act of international terrorism inside the United States, and the level of domestic terrorism had been reduced significantly. The record of the past decade gave reason for optimism. However, on February 26, 1993, the bombing of the World Trade Center in New York issued a cruel reminder that the United States is not immune from terrorism within our Borders.

The warning of America's vulnerability and the intent of international extremist groups to directly attack the United States was again starkly stated and well documented in a widely read and quoted book, "Final Warning: Averting Disaster in the New Age of Terrorism," written by Dr. Robert Kupperman and Jeff Kamen and published in 1989.[3] Kuppermann and Kamen predicted that terrorist groups would attempt to inflict mass causalities on American citizens both within the United States and abroad, and that these extremist groups would attempt to obtain and utilize weapons of mass destruction against America. They stated that

> the United States, its allies, and the Soviet Union face more violent, more disruptive terrorists attacks than have ever been seen. Ordinary citizens are more likely to become victims, even if they do not place themselves in high risk areas such as international airports. Americans and their interests have come under increasingly innovative terrorist assaults at home and abroad. . . . Government often behaved as though it were powerless just as a new age of domestic and international terrorism appeared to be on the horizon.

I was a participant in and observer of the attempts by the U.S. government and many of its allies to meet and defeat the daunting challenges posed by the various forms of terrorist organizations from 1964 to 1994. During 10 of these years, 1982 to mid-1991 the counterterrorism program was part of my responsibility as the FBI's assistant director in charge of criminal investigations and then as the associate deputy director of investigations which included all criminal investigative, counterintelligence, counterterrorism, and international programs. Where my actions and/or opinions are cited in this chapter, they will be clearly delineated. I will cite reasons for mistakes that were made, but I will not try to excuse those of us who made them.

The terrible events of September 11, 2001, shall ever remain in our collective memories. Many Americans lost relatives and friends in the attacks. Could the attacks have been anticipated and are we likely to face such devastation again? Unfortunately, the answer to both questions is yes. For it is very clear we have been the target of a sustained campaign of terrorism since 1979. The fall of the Shah of Iran and establishment of a fundamentalist Islamic State in Iran under the Ayatollah Khomeini, and the invasion of Afghanistan by the Soviet Union in 1979 were the predicates of the tragedy that we suffered on September 11. In Iran, Islamic extremists found that they could take and hold Americans hostage without serious repercussions.

Out of that experience the Iranian-backed Hezbollah bombed our embassies in Beirut twice, and Kuwait once, and killed over 200 Marines in a suicide truck bombing. The Hezbollah took Americans hostage and hijacked our airliners, and we seemed impotent to respond. Before we even knew of Osama bin Laden, Imad Mugniyah of the Hezbollah was the leading terrorist against the United States. He was directly responsible for the attacks against our personnel and facilities in Lebanon, and yet he and his organization have never been punished for their crimes against our nation. This example was not lost on the founders of al Qaeda, members of the Afghan Mujahidin primarily from Arab countries. Osama bin Laden and his associates learned firsthand that guerilla warfare and terrorist tactics could defeat a world "super power" such as the Soviet Union, and he learned from Mugniyah experience that the United States was not likely to fight back.

Beginning with the first attack on New York's World Trade Center in February 1993, and the ambush of American military personnel carrying out a humanitarian mission in Somalia in October 1993, Osama bin Laden and his associates have implemented a steady and increasingly deadly campaign against the United States and its citizens. The following are but the publicly known events:

1. World Trade Center, New York, February 1993
2. Somalia, October 1993
3. Planned attacks against multiple targets (bridges, tunnels, and buildings) in New York during the Fourth of July 1993 holiday
4. Planned assassination of Pope John Paul in the Philippines, 1994 (Americans were in the Pope's entourage)
5. Planned assassination of President Bill Clinton in the Philippines, 1995
6. Planned bombings of 11–13 U.S. airliners over the Pacific Ocean, 1995
7. Car bombing of U.S. military mission in Riyadh, Saudi Arabia, 1995
8. Truck bombing of U.S. Air Force housing area Khobar Towers, Dhahran, Saudi Arabia, 1996
9. Truck bombing of U.S. Embassy, Kenya, 1998
10. Truck bombing of U.S. Embassy, Tanzania, 1998
11. Plot to bomb Los Angeles International Airport, New Years Day, 2000
12. Plot to bomb the U.S. East Coast,, New Years Day, 2000
13. Plot to attack U.S. naval ship in Yemen, January 2000
14. Suicide boat attack on USS *Cole*, Yemen, October 2000

By September 11, 2001, we certainly should have known that we were the principal target of an international terrorist campaign unlike any we had ever faced. And yet we as a society totally failed to recognize the impending disaster that stalked our nation. Some of us in the counterterrorist arena tried to warn of the danger; however, we were generally considered to be alarmists.[4] Congress in general and the national press, for the most part, ignored the warnings. The following statement published in 1998 is one example specifying the warnings and the reasons for concern among knowledgeable terrorist experts:

The rather abrupt end to the Cold War was expected to bring about a substantial improvement in international cooperation, and a concordant change in the manner in which governments dealt with transnational issues such as terrorism and organized crime. However, the expected improvements in overall safety and security of U.S. citizens and interests have not materialized except at the strategic level.

Terrorism remains a constant and viable threat to American interests on a global basis even though the sources of the threat may be evolving into unknown or undetected elements/organizations. The threat is increasing because the philosophy, motivation, objectives, and modus operandi of terrorists groups, both domestic and international, have changed. New terrorist groups are not concerned with the consequences of inflicting mass causalities, and in many instances that is precisely their goal.

Terrorist groups today have ready access to massive databases concerning the entire U.S. infrastructure, including key personnel, facilities, and networks. Aided by state sponsors or international organized crime groups, terrorist can also obtain weapons of mass destruction. The Internet now allows even small or regional terrorist groups to have a worldwide C3I (Command, Control, Communication, and Intelligence) system, and highly effective propaganda dissemination capabilities. Domestic antigovernment extremists have proliferated, and pose a significant threat to the federal government and law enforcement at all levels. Militia organizations have targeted the federal government for hostile actions, and could target any element of our society deemed to be their adversary. Islamic extremism has spread to the point where it now has a global infrastructure, including a substantial network within the United States.[5]

The attacks of September 11, 2001, demonstrated these warnings were not alarmist, but in fact understated. In a major speech and follow-up article in a national journal in 1995, I tried to warn of the dangers of complacency and ignorance in facing the growing threat of international terrorism.[6]

THE THREAT

The United States has a long history of domestic terrorism, which includes, on the right, the Ku Klux Klan, the Minutemen, the American Nazi Party, the Christian Identity Movement, and the Jewish Defense League; and on the left, the Weather Underground Organization, the Armed Forces of National Liberation (FALN), and the Black Panther Party. But by far, the greatest threat to the United States at this time comes from elements associated with radical fundamentalist Islam. Groups associated with this movement include Hezbollah (Party of God), Hamas (Islamic Resistance Movement), Islamic Jihad, Palestine Islamic Jihad, and the Muslim Brethren (also known as the Muslim Brotherhood).[7]

Hezbollah and Hamas are very active and extremely dangerous; however, it is the Iranian government, aided by its Sudanese counterpart, which drives fundamentalist Islam. Without the intensive support of these two regimes, the fundamentalist groups would not pose nearly the threat they do.

These governments continue to work toward Ayatollah Khomeini's oft-stated goal: the spread of his vision of the true nature of Islam and the creation of Islamic states throughout the Muslim world. Fundamentalist terrorism against Americans is all the more lethal due to Iran's sponsorship of such well-organized groups as Hezbollah and Hamas. State sponsorship allows the groups to be far reaching in carrying out their attacks. Israeli intelligence has traced to Hezbollah the July 1994 bombings of the Jewish center in Buenos Aires and contemporaneous bombings in London. It seems highly unlikely that Hezbollah would have undertaken such serious actions without Tehran's direct approval and support. Pro-Iranian terrorist groups receive critical support and, possibly, direction through Iranian embassies and intelligence services. Iran's support makes the militant groups far more dangerous than other religious-based extremist groups. Only a state can provide the broad range of services needed to carry out terrorism on a global basis.[8] Nevertheless, the emergence of al Qaeda, a virulent form of Sunni Muslim extremism, demonstrated a multinational network of terrorists can exist and carry out a campaign of attacks against Western democracies. However, even al Qaeda required sanctuary in Afghanistan and support from "friendly" governments to function effectively.

HOSTILITY TO THE UNITED STATES

Muslim militants are hostile to the West, the United States in particular, for three main reasons. First, they view the United States as the primary supporter of the State of Israel, a Jewish and European creation in the midst of the Muslim world. Fundamentalists sometimes go further and see the U.S. support of Israel as part of a covert crusade by the Christian West against Islam, where Israel serves as a proxy. Second, the U.S. government backs moderate Muslim governments that fundamentalist militants regard as apostate regimes opposed to the implementation of true Islam and the creation of a unitary Islamic state. This category includes the governments of Algeria, Egypt, Jordan, Kuwait, Saudi Arabia, and Turkey. And third, the United States offers an attractive culture with materialistic and individualistic qualities fundamentalist Muslims view as dangerously seductive and incompatible with the ethos of an Islamic moral order.

The cultural aspect is a subtle but important one. Fundamentalist Muslims tend to look at American culture through the prism of their own societies, and see in it a reflection of religious motives. For example, they view the American University in Beirut, the product of American Protestant missionaries in the nineteenth century, as part of a U.S. government conspiracy to subvert Islamic culture. Just as Middle East governments closely control the content of books and the media, so Muslim militants assume news reports coming from the United States, or even works of fiction coming from the United Kingdom (such as Salman Rushdie's *The Satanic Verses*), reflect calculated attempts by the West to undermine Islam. The extreme reaction by many in the Islamic world to the publication of cartoons in Danish newspapers depicting the Prophet Mohammed and Islam in a manner deemed to be blasphemous caught the Western world by surprise. But, knowledgeable observers knew that this sense of outrage was simmering just below the surface and that violent reaction in the Islamic world would likely follow any apparent offense against Islam.

For Americans doing business in the Middle East, this notion of America as a "cultural enemy" has significant importance. As countries such as Egypt and Algeria move away from the old, centralized, state-managed enterprises, they become increasingly more dependent on investment, technology, and expertise from abroad. When American business people and technological consultants set up offices abroad, they do more than provide work for a specific project; they represent their civilization and culture. To those who see the United States as the cultural enemy, American business people are targets. This feature points to the fact that it is who Americans are—and not their actions—that make the fundamentalist extremists hostile to them. It does not matter if you inadvertently offend them or use the utmost diplomacy dealing with them; they are hostile in either case.

These perceptions of Western affronts to Islam are likely to continue and provoke violent reactions, including terrorist threats and attacks against American citizens. U.S. diplomatic and military facilities overseas have been prepared for such attacks. Therefore, terrorists in countries like Egypt and Algeria have turned their attention to more accessible targets, including foreign businesses, tourists, and hotels or restaurants catering to expatriates.

Although the stereotype of Muslim militancy portrays their methodology as irrational or fanatical, the leaders of these groups have displayed a very calculating and cold rationality. They are not inclined to sacrifice their assets or their own security recklessly. Terrorist acts are usually planned to invoke a specific response that in their minds will advance the cause. This warning, first made in a speech in 1994 and published in 1995, along with many others, was ignored by most in Congress and the American news media.[9]

ISLAMIC EXTREMIST TERROR IN THE UNITED STATES

Radical and militant organizations have learned that the United States provides an almost perfect sanctuary for their activities. In a remarkable piece of investigative journalism, Steven Emerson has shown in his film documentary *Jihad in America* (featuring Ambassador L. Paul Bremer and me [Buck Revell] as the principal commentators) that Muslim extremism has important strongholds in the United States. The documentary, first aired on vis the Public Broadcasting Service in November 1994, revealed that Muslim radicals have infiltrated so deeply that they are now using the United States as a base of operations and support for their organizations worldwide. Emerson also showed that the extremist who masterminded the 1993 World Trade Center bombing had ties to other radical groups still operating in the United States, and he establishes that these groups exploit the freedoms guaranteed by the U.S. Constitution to spread a message of hate and violence. Emerson wrote a book *American Jihad: The Terrorist Living among Us*, which elaborated on the information provided in the PBS documentary and gave further documentation to the degree which radical Islamists infiltrate the United States and the threats they pose.[10]

The attacks of September 11 and the massive investigations mounted in both the United States and internationally afterwards have further demonstrated the substantial infiltration of our society by Islamic extremists. Al Qaeda, Hamas, Hezbollah, the Palestinian Islamic Jihad, and many other similar groups have established a substantial stronghold in America. The open borders we share with Mexico and Canada and the unwillingness or inability of these nations to control or limit the use of their territories as staging areas for infiltration into the United States give rise to an even greater threat to the citizens and vital infrastructure of the United States.

The train bombings in Madrid in March 2004 that killed 191 and wounded 2,050 and the subway and bus bombings in London in July 2005 dramatically demonstrated the ability of Jihadists to operate covertly in the Western world and to strike with deadly consequences when they choose.

ENHANCED TERRORIST CAPABILITIES

One of the outcomes of the globalization of economies and technologies, the phenomenon that President George H. W. Bush in 1991 termed "A New World Order," is the relatively new linking and intermingling of disparate crime and narcotics organizations with terrorists. Analysts have been dismayed to find that even the most notorious crime groups with global reach, such as the Italian mafia, Russian mafias, Nigerian criminal enterprises, Chinese triads, Colombian and Mexican cartels, and the Japanese Yakuza, are developing new working relationships. They are making cooperative arrangements and networking with one another and with insurgent and terrorist organizations to take advantage of each oother's strengths and to make inroads into previously denied regions.

This feature has allowed terrorists a new means to raise money, as well as to provide them with a marketplace to purchase sophisticated weaponry and other high-tech equipment. This cooperation, for example, has long been seen among Colombian drug lords and Italian crime groups in exploiting the West European drug market; and now it is seen in New York City and in eastern Europe with drug and financial crime networks linking Russian and Italian groups. As organized crime groups become increasingly international in the scope of their activities, they are also less constrained by national boundaries.

The new lowering of political and economic barriers permits them to establish new operational bases in commercial and banking centers around the globe. The willingness and capability of these groups to move into new areas and cooperate with local groups are unprecedented, magnifying the threats to stability and even governance.

This undermining of civil authority is now very evident in Afghanistan where tribal warlords have quickly taken advantage of the weak central government of Kabul after the temporary defeat of the Taliban and have reinstituted heroin smuggling operations. These smuggling operations are providing great wealth to not only the warlords, but also to the many international organized crime organizations with which they deal.

All of these transnational groups are becoming more professional in their criminal endeavors, especially in their business and financial practices, as well as in the application of technology. Many of them use state-of-the-art communication security, better than some nations' security forces can crack. The business nexus between international organized crime and terrorist organizations compounds the threat terrorism poses and raises the danger of more sophisticated and deadly attacks in the future. If terrorists obtain weapons of mass destruction, it is likely that international organized crime will have aided and abetted their acquisitions.[11]

LAW ENFORCEMENT ORGANIZATION AND TACTICS TO ADDRESS TERRORISM PRIOR TO SEPTEMBER 11, 2001

In 1985, the United States and the Western world were subjected to an unprecedented level of terrorist attacks. In the United States, the hijacking of TWA flight 847 and the cruise liner *Achille Lauro*, and the brutal attacks on the Rome and Vienna airports finally led to an awakening of the American public and political leaders to the real threat of international terrorism. President Ronald Reagan appointed Vice President Bush to head a task force to study the phenomenon of international terrorism and to make recommendations to him, the Congress, and the American public on how best to combat this growing threat. In February 1986, the Public Report of the Vice President's Task Force on Combating Terrorism was issued. This report summarized the current problems facing the U.S. government and made recommendations for more adequately addressing the continuing problem of terrorism. Outlined in this report was the federal government's plan to combine its resources to respond to and combat terrorist acts.

Within the federal government, various agencies are given "lead" responsibilities in responding to terrorist incidents. The U.S. Department of State is responsible for coordinating the U.S. government's response to terrorist incidents outside the United States and its territories; the Department of

Justice, through the FBI, is responsible for responding to terrorist incidents that take place within the United States and its territories; and the Federal Aviation Administration is responsible for responding to terrorist incidents aboard aircraft which take place within U.S. jurisdiction. In addition to the various lead agencies, there are also a number of interagency groups, such as the Interdepartmental Group on Terrorism, that coordinate the activities of different components of the U.S. government.[12]

The U.S. Congress also took action against terrorism by enacting legislation that enabled the United States to bring terrorists to trial for crimes committed against U.S. citizens' interests abroad. In the aftermath of the April 1983 bombing at the U.S. Embassy in Beirut, Lebanon, and the October 1983 bombing at the Marine Corps barracks in Beirut, Lebanon, Congress enacted legislation that made the United States a party to the International Convention against the Taking of Hostages. This legislation, which was contained in the Comprehensive Crime Control Act of 1984 (Title 18 USC, Section 1203), gives the FBI investigative jurisdiction both inside and outside the United States in hostage events when U.S. interests or citizens are involved. In effect, it gives the U.S. government, via the FBI, the ability to respond to terrorist events anywhere in the world. However, the caveat is that any extraterritorial investigative activity on the part of the FBI needs the permission of host governments and coordination with U.S. foreign policy agencies.

A second statute that has extraterritorial application for the FBI was enacted as part of the Omnibus Diplomatic Security and Anti-Terrorism Act of 1986 (Title 18, USC, Section 2331). This statute enabled the U.S. government to prosecute, in U.S. courts, persons who assault or murder U.S. citizens abroad. Furthermore, prosecution can be considered when it is proven that there exists a conspiracy to commit these acts against U.S. citizens. Before a person can be prosecuted under the statute, the Attorney General must certify that the act was perpetrated with the intent to coerce, intimidate, or retaliate against the government or the civilian population. Until the passage of the PATRIOT Act in the aftermath of the 9/11 attack, these were the only major legislative acts regarding terrorism passed by the Congress.

The desire of all terrorists to focus media attention on their cause by staging attacks at locations or events of international interest has made it necessary for government and law enforcement authorities to closely coordinate preparations for special events. The killing of Israeli athletes by Palestinian terrorists at the 1972 Summer Olympic Games in Munich, West Germany, tragically illustrated the necessity for law enforcement authorities to be prepared to respond to any situation during such an event. Elaborate security measures for special events, such as the Olympic Games, World Fairs, Bicentennial celebrations, and the rededication of the Statute of Liberty, have become mandatory. All elements of the federal government must work closely with numerous state and local agencies to ensure everything that can be done is accomplished regarding the security of participants in the events.

The preparation that U.S. law enforcement and intelligence collection authorities undertook for the 1984 Summer Olympics in Los Angeles, California, has served as a model for how divergent agencies should cooperate in order to successfully manage these events. A primary concern during the Los Angeles Games was the application of intelligence information in a law enforcement context. In order to ensure that this was properly managed, an Interagency Intelligence Subcommittee, cochaired by the FBI, the Los Angeles Sheriff's Department, and the Los Angeles Police Department, was established. This subcommittee, designated as the Anti-Terrorist Operations Center (ATOC) was the intelligence center for all Olympic participants and functioned as the mechanism for receiving and evaluating threats. Raw intelligence information received by the center was processed, analyzed, and disseminated to appropriate Olympic security components. The center's staff, composed of command-level representatives from the ATOC agencies, had authority to order further investigation if it was deemed appropriate. On a daily basis, the center assessed potential threats to the Games and identified the event that had the greatest potential of being disrupted.

In preparing for an event with a magnitude of the 1984 Summer Olympics, contingency plans were also formalized for responding to a terrorist incident. The emergency response team (ERT) under the control of the Los Angeles FBI field office was available to establish an initial federal presence and to handle incidents falling under FBI jurisdiction. The ERT is a self-contained unit designed to control serious or escalating problems until additional resources report to the scene and integrate into the operation. Had an incident occurred, the law enforcement response was to be determined by evaluating four factors: subject, hostages, objectives, and weapons, or SHOW. The on-scene commander would have then assigned a threat or risk level, and appropriate forces would have been mobilized. Both the Los Angeles Police Department and Sheriff's Office had similar highly trained and well-equipped units dedicated to Olympic security.

Major events with potential for being terrorist targets rely heavily on cooperation and management coordination among the various law enforcement agencies. Because of the large number of law enforcement officers needed in the event a terrorist incident occurred, local law enforcement agencies play a vital role; particularly since these agencies may have investigative interests because the criminal activity committed may be a violation of the state or local laws. The 1984 Olympic Games illustrated the cooperation and coordination among the multiple federal, state, and local law enforcement agencies having varying roles of responsibility. These agencies combined their efforts to provide a synchronized response had a terrorist incident occurred during the 1984 Olympic Games. Subsequently, this model was used in the United States at both the Atlanta and Salt Lake City Olympics and the

World Cup Soccer Championship matches held in 1994. This same Special Events Management model continues to be extensively applied by law enforcement and security services in other Olympics.

Preparing to respond to terrorist incidents at special events is just one area in which U.S. law enforcement authorities may have to deal with terrorism. Because of the very real possibility that a terrorist could attack anywhere, at any time, specialized law enforcement techniques have been developed to prevent, respond to, and/or control terrorist incidents. These include hostage negotiation and crisis management teams trained to defuse hostage situations and prevent violence; psychological and behavioral profiling techniques to assist in identifying terrorists; and specialized surveillance techniques to monitor the activities of suspected terrorists. Law enforcement techniques modified to deal with the threat of terrorism include the use of undercover operations and intelligence analyses. Undercover operations have been used effectively against various terrorist groups operating weapons acquisition networks in the United States or attempting to purchase weapons for use in assassinations. In recent years, the FBI and ATF (Bureau of Alcohol, Tobacco, Firearms and Explosives) have introduced undercover agents as weapons brokers, successfully foiling the efforts of terrorists to acquire such weapons. Law enforcement intelligence-gathering capabilities have also enabled authorities to closely monitor the activities of international terrorist groups and assess the likelihood of a terrorist attack through the collection and analysis of intelligence data. Through documentation, the modus operandi of terrorist groups can be recorded and analyzed, enabling law enforcement to be alert for certain types of behavior by suspected individuals.

Specialized counterterrorism response squads and analytical capabilities have also been developed to assist law enforcement authorities in response to terrorist attacks in the United States. The FBI's hostage rescue team (HRT), consisting of 50 special agents trained in counterterrorism tactics, was established in 1982 to provide nonmilitary response capability to a terrorist incident. Each member of the team receives extensive training in emergency medical treatment, the use of breaching and diversionary devices, and specialized entry techniques. Team members are also trained in a variety of other skills, including the use of special weapons and tactics in siege or hostage situations in which usual law enforcement apprehension techniques would not be effective.

The HRT has been in place at events such as the Olympics, presidential conventions, and other similar events in order to provide response should a situation arise. In September 1987, during the FBI's first exercise in extraterritorial jurisdiction authority, involving elements of the CIA, the U.S. Navy, and FBI, components of the HRT were used in the arrest of Fawaz Younis, an international terrorist wanted in connection with the hijacking of a Royal Jordanian airliner in June 1985.

The HRT was again deployed in the November 1987 prison uprisings in Oakdale, Louisiana, and Atlanta, Georgia, after Cuban refugees seized prison personnel as hostages. These incidents were eventually settled without the use of the HRT through negotiations; however, the team was prepared to take the necessary action to resolve the hostage standoff had it been necessary. The HRT was also later used to assist in the protection of first responders during the Los Angeles riots of 1993.

To merit the increasing threat of both domestic and international terrorism, the FBI created additional resources, such as the Special Operations and Research (SOAR) Unit, the Bomb Data Center, and the Terrorist Research and Analytical Center (TRAC) during the 1980s. The SOAR Unit studied terrorists and serial criminals for tactical and psychological insights. In addition to preparing psychological profiles, SOAR assisted in the training of Special Weapons and Tactics teams in the United States and conducted training liaison with various international counterterrorism groups.

The Bomb Data Center was responsible for training FBI, state, and local bomb investigators; establishing the technical collection and distribution of information concerning details of bombings by terrorist groups; and becoming active in research and development supporting hostage rescue activities. TRAC conducted research on terrorism by analyzing available data and assessing the likelihood of a terrorist attack. It also produced an annual incident summary identifying all terrorist acts that had taken place in the United States in the preceding year.

In combating terrorism in the United States, the cooperation of all levels of the law enforcement community has been the key, and remains so, for the successful prevention and investigation of terrorist activities. Terrorism cases often involve the jurisdiction of state, local, national, and foreign agencies. To avoid duplication of investigative efforts and to increase effectiveness and efficiency, cooperation has replaced competition among law enforcement personnel. One of the best methods for accomplishing cooperation was the development of joint task forces, which combine the investigative talents and manpower of several law enforcement agencies within a specified area. Task forces are staffed and supervised by police detectives, state troopers, and FBI agents, all participating equally in the formulation and implementation of investigative strategies.

This concept was developed in 1981 after the Brink's armored car robbery of $1.6 million in Nanuet-Nyack, New York. Cooperation among the New York City Police Department, the New York State Police, the New Jersey State Police, the Rockland County District Attorney's office, the Nyack Police Department, and the New York FBI field office resulted in the identification of the terrorist network that committed the crime. The investigation produced valuable information about the way domestic terrorist groups operated at the time and provided the impetus for expanding the task force concept to other metropolitan areas of the United States.

In fact, joint terrorism task forces (JTTFs) have been vital in the investigation of several domestic terrorist groups. The first task forces were located in Boston, Chicago, Houston, Los Angeles, Philadelphia, and Washington, DC. All police officers on the task forces were deputized as U.S. marshals and given the same security clearances as FBI agents. A memorandum of understanding between the local police and the FBI was required in the creation and operation of JTTFs. At the time of the 9/11 attacks there were 34 JTTFs in place[13] (by July 1, 2008, the FBI and cooperating law enforcement agencies had established 106 JTTFs).

The strength of the task force concept lies in the ability of the various agencies to share information, and in fact one of the strongest tools in the fight against terrorism is the ability to share information. International law enforcement organizations such as the International Criminal Police Organization (INTERPOL) provide for the rapid transmission of information needed by law enforcement throughout the world.[14] INTERPOL originally stood back from the issue of terrorism because Article III of its constitution prohibited members from intervening in or investigating matters considered to be racially, politically, militarily, or religiously motivated.

However, at the General Assembly meeting held in 1984, member countries adopted a resolution which determined that though the acts of terrorism may have a political motivation, this motivation should not be considered, and the acts are determined on the basis of the nature of the crime. This interpretation of the INTERPOL constitution opened the door for the world's law enforcement community to exchange information on terrorists and use the INTERPOL network to trace and apprehend terrorists charged with criminal offenses. The FBI's executive management, with the support of the chief of the U.S. National Central Bureau of INTERPOL, and the newly elected president of INTERPOL John Simpson, the director of the U.S. Secret Service, successfully lobbied for this important change in the role of INTERPOL to combat international terrorism.

Further developments in INTERPOL's effort to combat terrorism resulted in the approval by member countries of a special unit within INTERPOL that would deal with information concerning terrorist activity and compile and analyze the available data on terrorist groups. This group, established at INTERPOL headquarters in France, became operational in 1986 and is known as the International Terrorism Group (ITG). An experienced FBI counterterrorism agent, Don Lavey, was appointed as the first chief of ITG. It was the intention of this group to conduct organized symposia on terrorism to better foster cooperation among law enforcement organizations in the international fight against terrorism and to be a repository of information on terrorist organizations.[15] The current head of the group is an experienced FBI counterterrorist expert. We are also fortunate to have the former Undersecretary of Treasury for enforcement, Ronald K. Noble, as the current secretary general of INTERPOL. Noble, the first American to serve in this position, is a highly skilled professional, dedicated to improving international law enforcement.

U.S. government participation in various bilateral and multilateral forums has also made it possible to share information on terrorists. Additionally, proclamations, such as those issued by the industrialized nations that comprise today's G-8 (United States, Canada, France, the United Kingdom, Germany, Italy, Japan, and Russia) serve to identify and bring to light areas of common concern.

In 1986, the United States through the Attorney General established an informal, but productive, relationship with the ministers of justice and interior of the European Economic Community in an organization known as the TREVI (Terrorism Radicalism Extremism Violence International) Group. TREVI met semiannually to consider specific measures to combat terrorism through joint international initiatives and cooperation. The FBI director and executive assistant director (EAD) for investigations participated with the Attorney General in the conferences and worked with their counterparts from European police and security agencies to establish supportive programs and cooperative relationships.[16]

After the attacks on the United States in 2001 and the Madrid railroad bombings on March 11, 2004, the European Union elected to more closely coordinate and facilitate counterterrorism activities by appointing a counterterrorism coordinator with Union-wide responsibilities.[17] The United States had urged the creation of such a position within the EU for a considerable time.

In 1986, the president and board of directors of the International Association of Chiefs of Police (IACP) determined that international terrorism was of such continuing concern to the international police community that the IACP should establish a committee on terrorism in order to focus continuing attention and scrutiny to this problem. The IACP asked the FBI's EAD for investigations to form and chair this committee to address the issue of cooperative police activities in combating international terrorism. Then FBI Director William H. Webster supported this responsibility and concurred with me, then FBI EAD–Investigations , accepting this responsibility. In structuring the committee, IACP President Bob Landon, Executive Director Jerry Vaughn, and EAD Revell agreed that the committee should be international in scope; composed of individuals heading agency operations; and involved with specific responsibilities or demonstrated competence in the counterterrorism arena.[18]

The first meeting of the Committee on Terrorism (COT) took place on March 3, 1987, at FBI Headquarters in Washington, DC. At the request of the chairman, a vice chairman was elected by the committee members. Commissioner Norman D. Inkster of the Royal Canadian Mounted Police was unanimously elected to this position. Thereafter, the committee decided by consensus that the COT would break down into four subcommittees along functional lines and that the subcommittees would, in turn, report back to the committee on various projects and activities that should be taken up by the committee on behalf of the IACP. The subcommittees were established as follows:

- Information Sharing/Intelligence Systems
- Law Enforcement Operational Capabilities
- Threat Assessment-Risk Analysis and Contingency Planning
- Training/Public Information

The members agreed that the committee would meet four times a year with one of the meetings being held during the annual IACP conference. It was also agreed that the committee would sponsor workshops on combating terrorism and provide leadership and oversight for the IACP on all matters relating to the fight against terrorism. The second meeting of the committee was held in July 1987. Colonel Lester Forst, Connecticut State Police, was selected to be chairman of the Information Sharing/Intelligence Systems subcommittee; Colonel Jeremy Margolis, director, Illinois Division of State Police, was selected to be the chairman of the Law Enforcement Operational Capabilities subcommittee; Colonel Dave Luitweiler, New York State Police, was selected as chairman of the Threat Assessment-Risk Analysis and Contingency Planning subcommittee; and Colonel Frank Mazzone, Maryland State Police, was selected as chairman of the Training/Public Information subcommittee. Each of the subcommittees assumed specific tasking with regard to its area of responsibility, and the subcommittee membership was expanded to include, as ex officio members, other IACP members who could bring specific expertise to the subcommittee responsibilities.

At the end of 1987, the IACP COT had held three meetings; established the four subcommittees; and sponsored workshops in Hamburg, Germany, during the International Policing Conference and the 1987 Annual IACP conference held in Toronto, Canada. The membership represented eight countries: Vice Chairman Norman Inkster, Royal Canadian Mounted Police; John Dellow, deputy commissioner of the Metropolitan Police, New Scotland Yard, London, England; Sir John Hermon, chief constabulary, Royal Ulster Constabulary, Northern Ireland; and senior law enforcement officials from Australia, India, Israel, Japan, and Korea. The chief of the Anti-Terrorism Group of INTERPOL from the secretariat general in St. Cloud, France, was appointed as a member as well. Furthermore, senior officials from 10 U.S. federal agencies, the heads of 10 state police agencies, and the chiefs of 10 major U.S. city police departments, such as Chief Daryl Gates of the Los Angeles Police Department; Superintendent Leroy Martin of the Chicago Police Department; Commissioner Kevin Tucker of the Philadelphia Police Department; and Director Fred Taylor of the

Metropolitan Dade County, Miami, Florida Police Department, were included. Enhanced cooperation, better sharing of information, improved educational opportunities, and enhanced investigative techniques among law enforcement agencies, both international and domestic, were the objectives of the IACP COT.[19] The COT continues to this day; its chairman is the FBI's EAD–National Security Branch, Arthur Cummings, a highly respected career agent and former U.S. Navy SEAL who has specialized in counterterrorism during the majority of his career. The committee has 30 members from U.S. law enforcement agencies and 10 members from foreign agencies. The COT held its most recent meeting in October 2009 in Denver, and received briefings on the November 2008 swarm terrorist attack against Mumbai by the Pakistani terrorist group (Lashkar e-Taiba), the status of security planning for the 2010 Vancouver Winter Games, and the rise of al Qaeda in the Arabian Peninsula (AQAP).

Despite the exceptional efforts of U.S. law enforcement agencies, there was not wide support for intelligence collection and analysis against terrorism, even after the first World Trade Center bombing in 1993 and the 1995 bombing of the Murrah Federal Building in Oklahoma City.

The prevention and investigation of a terrorism activity in the United States has always been a joint responsibility of the three levels of government within our country. While local, state, and federal responsibilities are often shared, they are not always clearly defined. Many local law enforcement agencies have been constrained from collecting intelligence on potential terrorist organizations by restraining orders or consent decrees issued by courts in response to civil suits alleging violation of Constitutional rights and privacy laws by police agencies. The so-called "Red Squads" of most police departments were abolished in the 1960s and 1970s, and there was an expectation that the federal agencies, particularly the FBI, U.S. Secret Service, and ATF, would fill the void. However, substantial limitations on the principal U.S. counterterrorism agencies substantially thwarted effective intelligence collection and preemptive action by federal agencies. Furthermore, police departments of New York City, Chicago, Los Angeles, and San Francisco were prohibited from collecting intelligence on groups in their territories, if their activities could not be directly connected to a current and specific criminal act.[20]

THE BREAKDOWN OF INTELLIGENCE GATHERING

During the 1960s and 1970s there had been no consensus in this country on how to deal with the antiwar movement and with the more radical elements of the civil rights movement. The Executive Branch of the government had taken certain actions that had not been by consensus. They had been essentially presidential decisions. Some of the tactics used would today be considered illegal; at the time they were not illegal, but perhaps were unwise. In seeking to determine who was behind certain movements and groups that carried out violent acts, the FBI and military intelligence, as well as the CIA, engaged in such improper activities as wiretaps and surreptitious entries, without court authorization. In most of the world today, including Great Britain, France, and Germany, these types of intelligence-seeking activities can still be authorized by executive order of the government. In the United States they cannot, and in my view they should not. But at the time they were.

In the mid-1970s, Watergate and the turmoil it brought to our political system led to a series of hearings by the Church (Senate) and Pike (House) investigative committees. The intelligence components of the U.S. government were highly criticized for some of the things they had done during this period, particularly for spying upon individuals and groups that, though radical, were not a direct threat to the nation's existence. There was no consensus in the body politic on the extent to which the domestic law enforcement and intelligence services could be used to investigate the causes, structure, and membership of groups that, in fact, made use of systemic violence.

While the criticism that arose out of the Church and Pike hearings was primarily directed at the CIA, the FBI got its share, especially for a very ill-considered program called COINTELPRO. This program had adopted counterintelligence methods meant to be used against a foreign power for use against domestic groups. In COINTELPRO, the FBI used extralegal tactics to determine who was behind certain movements and their involvement in subversive activities.[21] After this became known, the Bureau was quite traumatized about its proper role and about the legal use of executive authority to combat domestic terrorism. In the late 1970s, the FBI practically shut down its entire domestic security operation. It was dealing with specific criminal acts after the fact only; it did virtually no collection or analysis of intelligence prior to the commission of a violent act by some politically motivated organization.[22]

THE REBUILDING OF INTELLIGENCE GATHERING

By 1980, the level of terrorist incidents in the United States had risen to the point where the leadership of the FBI believed it had to become proactive again, but very carefully and under a set of guidelines that it participated in designing. These guidelines, called the Attorney General's Guidelines, were intended not only to tell the Bureau the limitations of its authority but also to sanction those actions that it did take, and to make sure people understood that this was a legitimate exercise of the legal authority of the president, the Attorney General, and those charged with carrying out their directives. In 1982 I, then assistant director of the FBI's Criminal Investigative Division, recommended to then FBI Director William Webster that terrorism be designated as a national priority of the FBI, as were the counterintelligence, organized crime, and white-collar crime programs.

In the late 1970s and early 1980s, in addition to domestic groups with domestic political concerns, numerous groups with foreign-interest concerns had been committing violent acts in the United States. There was Sikh terrorism, Armenian terrorism, Croatian terrorism, terrorism from virtually every continent. There were groups carrying out attacks against the Soviet Union, Turkey, and India, all operating in the United States. It was a precursor to what exists today.

In 1982, there were 51 terrorist incidents in the United States, in which at least 7 people were killed and 26 were injured. Between 1982 and 1988, because of the renewed vigor of the counterterrorism program, the FBI and cooperating American law enforcement agencies were able to reduce that level to only 5–10 incidents a year. The FBI was able to prevent 56 terrorist incidents that would have resulted in massive loss of life in the United States and the assassination of some visiting foreign leaders. Some incidents, similar to the blowing up of Pan Am flight 103 in 1988, were prevented because of the Bureau's ability, although limited, to collect and utilize information under the Attorney General's Guidelines, and because of the cooperative relationships that had been built with domestic and foreign law enforcement agencies.

THE CISPES AFFAIR

By 1988, only three or four terrorist groups continued to function within the United States. Through the use of existing legal procedures, the FBI had been able to preempt, prosecute, or neutralize most of the domestic and foreign organizations committing acts of terrorism in the United States. However, this was the time when President Reagan's policy in Central America became very controversial, and another situation developed that once again set back the FBI's counterterrorism program.

This was a series of cases concerning CISPES, the Committee in Solidarity with the People of El Salvador. In 1982, the FBI learned from the CIA that this group in the United States was affiliated with the front organization for communist guerrillas in El Salvador and was largely funded by Cuba and by the Sandinista regime in Nicaragua. The FBI developed a Salvadoran informant who reported that CISPES had been formed to assist revolutionary elements in El Salvador, which directly supported terrorist organizations there, particularly the Farabundo Marti National Liberation Front. Information gathered also indicated that CISPES was operating illegally in the United States to raise money, procure arms, and even recruit supporters to go to El Salvador.

An investigation began within the FBI's terrorism section, using field offices in several locations. The case was one of several hundred pending in the terrorism section and was never sent up the FBI's chain of command because no extraordinary investigative techniques were used. There were no wiretaps, no undercover operations; the information was gathered from public meetings, physical surveillance, and the use of informants, all of which were authorized under the Attorney General's Guidelines. Due to heightened political sensitivity and the disagreement between the Republican president and the Democratic-controlled Congress, the case was drawn into the national spotlight.

Unfortunately, at about this time the FBI agent who happened to be the case agent for the CISPES investigation in Dallas came under scrutiny. The FBI determined he had abused his authority in dealing with the informant, fabricated information, and had not done a proper job in controlling and directing the informant. Subsequently, the agent was fired. Although the FBI recommended prosecuting the former agent, the Department of Justice chose not to do so. The Salvadoran informant became disenchanted and went to political opponents of the administration to allege that this had been a politically motivated investigation. Because the Bureau had closed the case, CISPES was able to obtain access to information contained in the case files using the Freedom of Information Act. It became a *cause célèbre*, resulting in Congressional hearings and news media frenzy.

As it happened, the FBI had a new director, William Sessions, a federal judge from Texas. In October 1987, when Sessions came in, he knew almost nothing about the FBI's responsibilities with regard to counterintelligence and terrorism. In fact, he stated he had not known the FBI even had counterintelligence responsibilities before he became director. Obviously, the Bureau was at a considerable disadvantage in the representation of its position. The charges against the FBI were (1) it was involved in a political investigation, (2) it had used illegal tactics, and (3) it had violated the Constitutional rights of those involved in this movement.

Investigation by the FBI's Office of Professional Responsibility, the Department of Justice, and the Senate Intelligence Committee found none of these allegations to be true. There had been no political involvement whatsoever on the part of the Reagan administration. The investigation had been reviewed by the Department of Justice's Office of Intelligence Policy and Oversight early on and had been sanctioned as a legitimate investigation. No one's constitutional rights had been violated. No one had been obstructed or intimidated with regard to attending meetings, expressing his or her views, or engaging in any other protected activities. Nor had any FBI agent other than the Dallas case agent, who was involved in a financial fraud in dealing with informant payments, committed any violation of law. What was determined was that mistakes had been made in the investigation and some Bureau regulations had been violated. But the media's appetite for sensationalism had not been satiated and the *New York Times* and *Washington Post* construed this finding by stating "the FBI admits that it engaged in illegal activities just as it did during COINTELPRO," which was nonsense.

In looking back at the case, I (then the FBI's EAD–Investigations) believed that there was substantial justification for at least part of the investigation and was extremely worried that the Bureau would again suffer and that the Congressional inquiry and media misrepresentation would jeopardize careers of people who were honestly trying to prevent acts of terrorism in the United States—people who had no motive except to defend their nation against terrorism. I testified to committees of both the House and the Senate about the findings in the CISPIS inquiry and about my concerns.[23]

Unfortunately, as feared, the minimal findings of error were exploited and adversely affected the FBI's ability to combat terrorism. In 1988, the FBI found itself at almost ground zero in carrying its counterterrorism responsibilities, just as it had a decade earlier. While the FBI and JTTFs responded to terrorist-related crimes, they could not conduct intelligence collection or analysis activities.

THE KAHANE ASSASSINATION

All this set the stage for what happened at the World Trade Center in February 1993. A few years earlier in November 1990 there was a murder in New York of Rabbi Meir Kahane, an extremist who had created an organization—the Jewish Defense League—that engaged in acts of terrorism in the United States. Kahane also created a group in Israel that committed, or at least facilitated, terrorist acts. Some of his more active followers fled from the United States while under investigation for assassinating a Palestinian American in Los Angeles and were given sanctuary in Israel. The investigation of the assassination of Kahane was conducted for the most part by the New York City police, with the FBI and the New York JTTF looking over their shoulders to see if there was anything indicating a terrorist conspiracy.

As it turned out, information was available that, had it been properly translated, processed and analyzed, could have provided a direct association between the assassin of Kahane and the group that later bombed the World Trade Center, a group conspiring to carry out a number of other heinous acts of terrorism. Due to the political climate, FBI agents and New York City police were loath to undertake anything that had any appearance of being involved in the political process, and the Kahane assassination was not properly analyzed. The "political process" included anything that could be construed to be protected by the Constitution, such as religious activity, freedom of assembly, and free speech. Therefore, the safest avenue was to consider only the direct crime committed and not the potential, and much more threatening, conspiracy that was the root cause of the crime. The message was clear—stay away from political and religious organizations, even if they might be at the heart of a terrorist movement.

WARNINGS

There were ample warnings of the dire threat we faced as a nation prior to the 9/11 attacks. They included the vice president's Task Force on

Combating Terrorism in 1986; the president's Commission on Aviation Security and Terrorism convened in 1989 following the Pan Am 103 tragedy; a prescient book *Final Warning: Averting Disaster in the New Age of Terrorism*, written in 1989 by the late Dr. Robert Kupperman, a CSIS Senior Fellow, and Jeff Kamen a respected Washington journalist; the Center for Strategic and International Studies (CSIS) ongoing study of global organized crime and transnational threats (a TNT project chaired by Judge Webster and coordinated by Arnaud de Borchgrave) begun in 1994; the president's Commission on Critical Infrastructure Protection in 1996; the Advisory Panel to Assess Domestic Response Capabilities for Terrorism involving Weapons of Mass Destruction (Gilmore Commission), established by Congress in 1998 (final report issued December 2003); the U.S. Commission on National Security (Hart, Rudman Commission), 1998 to present, convened by the secretary of defense, supported by the president and Congress; the National Commission on Terrorism (Bremer Commission), authorized by Congress in 1999 (final report issued June 2000); and numerous books and articles by Dr. Yonah Alexander.

In each of these detailed studies, the significant threat to the United States by international terrorist organizations was carefully documented and highlighted. Congress held hearings and there were numerous debates in the media concerning the specifics and extent of the threat. The limitations on our intelligence and law enforcement agencies were cited with rising concern. Documentation of the escalating attacks against U.S. targets abroad was presented, and yet no comprehensive restructuring of U.S. counterterrorism capabilities was undertaken. The CIA was not given the authority to return to a heavy emphasis on human intelligence resources, nor was it allowed to utilize assets with unsavory backgrounds. It was not tasked with or given the resources to make substantial inroads with foreign services in problematic areas. The CIA was not authorized to receive intelligence or evidence on U.S. citizens even if that information had been collected under the authority of a Foreign Intelligence Surveillance Act (FISA) court order. The FBI had not received authority to deviate from the Attorney General's Guidelines in the face of a perceived increasing threat level. The FBI could not share FISA information with other agencies, or even with FBI agents working criminal cases.

The Federal Rules of Criminal Procedure (rule 6e) restricted grand jury information, even documents obtained by grand jury subpoenas; and unlike the Drug Enforcement Administration's (DEA) administrative subpoena authority in drug cases, the FBI had no similar authority in terrorism cases. The FBI's information technology infrastructure was antiquated; even after the difficulties of the Timothy McVeigh trial; it had not been adequately addressed. The FBI's operating budget was also severely strained by the necessity to respond to numerous overseas investigations, such as Kohbar Towers, the bombing of our East African embassies, and the attack on the USS *Cole*; and yet no supplemental funds were provided by Congress.

Congress has refused to create contingency funds for the Bureau similar to funds established for the CIA's contingency operations. FBI legal attaché offices were opened and strategically located, using funds that had originally been designated for operations and equipment. This development caused severe shortfalls in areas such as the FBI's motor vehicle fleet, or Bucars as they are called, which were virtually parked because there were no funds for gasoline and maintenance.

Congress failed to provide legislation authorizing roaming wire taps in terrorism cases, even though similar authority had been established for drug and organized crime cases. The Department of State's visa process was a virtual sham and, consequently, was of little value from an intelligence or law enforcement perspective. The Immigration and Naturalization Service was understaffed and overwhelmed by its responsibilities and was largely dormant in efforts to prevent terrorism. State and local authorities for the most part ignored large populations of illegal immigrants, even when they suspected that significant elements of these groups were involved in criminal conduct. Advocacy groups in essence ground to a halt any effective enforcement of immigration laws; and the sheer number of violators overwhelmed border control agencies.

In the face of these well-established and fully documented limitations and shortcomings, it is highly hypocritical for members of Congress and the national media to harp on so-called failures in intelligence and "dot connecting." The system that Congress strove to create was not capable of meeting its expectations in hindsight, nor was it capable of defending America from well-planned acts of international terrorism. Informed members of the news media certainly knew the limitations as well.[24]

The root causes of the so-called intelligence failures before the attacks of September 11, 2001, have been and are being debated in commissions and before congressional committees, but few are looking for the underlying weakness in our system of governance that allowed and, in fact, ensured that we would fail. In remarkably candid and succinct testimony on December 8, 2003, before the National Commission on Terrorist Attacks against the United States (9/11 Commission), Stewart A. Baker, former general counsel of the National Security Agency, set forth the issue of privacy versus intelligence and spelled out in vivid detail why the system failed and why it is still failing. His testimony in part follows:

> I said that it is dangerous to write rules restricting access to data based on theoretical fears of abuse. Let me be more plain. The reason we could not find al-Mihdhar and al-Hazmi in August of 2001 was not just that we didn't have enough tools. It was that we had imposed far too many rules on antiterrorism investigators—rules designed to protect against privacy abuses were mainly theoretical. In fact, we missed our best chance to save the lives of three thousand Americans in August because we were spending more effort and imagination guarding against those theoretical privacy abuses than we spent guarding

against terrorism. I feel some responsibility for sending the government down that road. Having gone down it once, though, we know where it leads—to death on our shores in numbers we can hardly fathom. And yet I fear that we are already starting down that road again.

How the rules failed us. Let me go back to the two and a half weeks that began in August 2001. It is true that the agents looking for al-Mihdhar and al-Hazmi didn't have the computer access they needed to do the job alone. But if this was a job for shoe leather and contacts, why not ask for help from the Bureau's criminal investigators—who had plenty of shoe leather and contacts and who outnumbered the counterintelligence agents three to one? Or from state and local police officers, who number more than a million? If those resources had been tapped, it's likely that al-Mihdhar and al-Hazmi would have been located quickly even without sophisticated new tools, and we would have had a fighting chance to roll up the rest of the plot as well. Why didn't the New York agent use those resources? It was not for lack of trying. He fought for the help, and he was turned down flat. Acting on legal advice, FBI headquarters refused to involve any criminal agents: "If al-Midhar is located, the interview must be conducted by an intelligence agent. A criminal agent CAN NOT be present at the interview. This case, in its entirety, is based on intelligence. If at such time as information is developed indicating the existence of a substantial federal crime, that information will be passed over the wall according to the proper procedures and turned over for follow-up criminal investigation."

It breaks my heart to read this exchange. The agent in New York protested the ban on using law enforcement resources in eerily prescient terms. "[S]ome day someone will die—and wall or not—the public will not understand why we were not more effective and throwing every resource we had at certain 'problems.' Let's hope the [lawyers who gave the advice] will stand behind their decisions then, especially since the biggest threat to us now, UBL [Usama Bin Laden], is getting the most 'protection.'"

The "wall" between intelligence and law enforcement was put in place to protect against a theoretical risk to civil liberties that could arise if domestic law enforcement and foreign intelligence missions were allowed to mix. In fact, in 1994, after I left my job as General Counsel to the National Security Agency, I regret to say that I defended the wall for just that reason, arguing that it should be left in place because foreign "Intelligence-gathering tolerates a degree of intrusiveness, harshness, and deceit that Americans do not want applied against themselves." I recognized then that the privacy risks were still just theoretical, but proclaimed the conventional wisdom of the time: "However theoretical the risks to civil liberties may be, they cannot be ignored." I foresaw many practical problems as well if the wall came down, and I argued for an approach that "preserves, perhaps even raises, the wall between the two communities." I was wrong, but I was not alone in assigning a high importance to theoretical privacy risks. In fact, over the 1990s, the wall grew higher and higher, well beyond anything I could have imagined. Indeed, in 2000 and 2001, as Al-Qa'ida was slowly bringing its September 11 plans to fruition, the FBI office that handled Al-Qa'ida wiretaps in the U.S. was thrown into turmoil because of the new heights to which the wall had been raised. The special court that oversees national security wiretaps, known as the Foreign Intelligence Surveillance Act, or FISA Court, had ordered strict procedures to ensure that its intelligence wiretaps were not contaminated by a law enforcement purpose. When those procedures were not followed strictly enough, the court barred an FBI agent from the court because his affidavits did not fully list all contacts with law enforcement.

In the spring and summer of 2001, with Al-Qa'ida's preparations growing even more intense, the turmoil apparently grew so bad that numerous national security wiretaps were allowed to lapse. Let me say that again. It is a shocking statement. In the months before the worst foreign attack on our nation in history, one of our best sources of information was allowed to lapse—something that had never happened before in the history of the program. It isn't clear what intelligence we missed as a result of that lapse. But it does seem clear that the loss of those wiretaps was treated as less troubling than the privacy scandal that now hung over the antiterrorism effort. Knowing how such matters are usually handled, I'll wager that the agent who provoked the FISA Court's wrath was being measured for disciplinary action and perhaps even a perjury indictment. And the Joint Intelligence Committee Inquiry has concluded that the lesson was not lost on the rest of the office: "FBI personnel involved in FISA matters feared the fate of the agent who had been barred and began to avoid even the most pedestrian contact with personnel in criminal components of the Bureau or DOJ because it could result in intensive scrutiny by OIPR [the Justice Department office that reviewed national security wiretaps] and the FISA Court."

Against this background, it's easy to understand why FBI headquarters and its lawyers refused so vehemently to use law enforcement resources in the effort to find al-Mihdhar and al-Hazmi. To do so would be to risk a further privacy scandal and put their careers in jeopardy. Viewed in this light, the New York agent's fight to get law enforcement involved looks like an act of courage that borders on foolishness. We can all be thankful for his zeal. But in the end, one agent's zeal was not enough to overcome the complex web of privacy rules and the machinery of scandal that we built to enforce those rules. He lost. And on the 11th, so did we all.

What lessons can we learn from this tragic unfolding of events? I would offer two. First, we must admit that the source of this tragedy was not wicked or uncaring officials. The wall was built by smart, even wise, professionals who thought they were acting in the country's and their agency's best interest. They were focused on the theoretical privacy risks that would come if foreign intelligence and domestic law enforcement were allowed to mix, and by a fear that in the end the courts and Congress would not understand if we put aside those theoretical concerns to combat a threat that was both foreign and domestic. They feared, and with good reason, that years of successful collaboration would end in disaster if the results of a single collaboration could be painted in the press and public as a privacy scandal. To protect against that possibility, they drafted ever more demanding rules—created an ever higher wall—to govern operations at the border between domestic law enforcement and foreign intelligence. As drafted, the rules still allowed antiterrorism investigators to do their jobs—at least in theory. The drafters counted on the fierce determination of law enforcement and intelligence agents to accomplish their mission. They weren't wrong. The New York agent's determination is palpable.

But even if he could in theory have found a route through the maze of rules, it was the FISA court scandal that finally choked off any practical hope of getting that job done. No one at headquarters wanted to thread that needle. No one wanted to find a way to say "yes" to the New York request, because they knew that that kind of creativity was likely to end in disgrace.

And so the first lesson is that, with the best will in the world, we cannot write rules that will both protect us from every theoretical risk to privacy and still allow the government to protect us from terrorists. We cannot fine-tune the system to perfection, because systems that ought to work can fail, as this one did so catastrophically in August of 2001. That is why I am so profoundly skeptical of efforts to write new privacy rules to go on top of all the rules we had in August 2001, and why I would rely instead on auditing for actual abuses. Now we know that the cost of protecting against theoretical risks to privacy can be thousands of American dead. That cost was too high. We should not again put American lives at risk for the sake of some theoretical risk to our civil liberties.

And now to the second lesson. Perhaps it isn't fair to blame all the people who helped to create the wall for the failures that occurred in August of 2001. No one knew then what the cost of building that wall would be. But now we do know. Or at least we should. We should know that we can't prevent every imaginable privacy abuse without hampering the fight against terror. We should know that an appetite for privacy scandals hampers the fight against terror. And we should know that, sooner or later, the consequence of these actions will be more attacks and more dead Americans, perhaps in numbers we can hardly fathom. We should know that. But somehow we don't. The country and its political leaders have had more than two years to consider the failures that occurred in August 2001 and what should be done to correct them. These were failures bad enough for people to lose their jobs over. But only one man has been forced out in those two years. Adm. John Poindexter. He tried to build information technology tools (including privacy tools) to address the failings of August 2001. But he was enmeshed in a "scandal" over privacy abuses that were entirely theoretical—when they weren't simply false. And so he and his program went the way of the TIPS program, also killed because of theoretical privacy worries. Next up for the same treatment are Section 215 of the USA PATRIOT Act, attacked for allowing library searches that, it turns out, have never occurred, and CAPPS II, designed to use information that will improve airline security while reducing the humiliating searches that now occur at airports around the nation but attacked because it poses a theoretical risk of abuse by airport security officials. Libertarian Republicans have joined with civil-liberties Democrats to teach the law enforcement and intelligence communities the same lesson that FBI headquarters taught its New York agent in August 2001. You won't lose your job for failing to protect Americans, but if you run afoul of the privacy lobby, you're gone.

And so, the effort to build information technology tools to find terrorists has stalled. No one wants to be the next John Poindexter. Worse, the wall is back.

Intelligence experts in the Terrorist Threat Integration Center (TTIC) have been barred from examining law enforcement reports due to an overly cautious (and scandal-haunted) reading of the executive order that creates a charter for the intelligence community. In short, bit by bit, we are again creating the political and legal climate of August 2001. And sooner or later, I fear, August will again lead to September 11.

Baker's concerns about the "Privacy Lobby" once again unilaterally disarming our counterterrorist agencies are not without merit.

Former Attorney General John Ashcroft had been in office nine months when the 9/11 attacks occurred. During this period he had shown virtually no interest in the terrorist threat to the United States and had turned down the Bureau's request for budget enhancements for the program. In his book, *Never Again: Securing America and Restoring Justice*, published in late 2006, Ashcroft acknowledges that the laws and regulations in existence at the time of the 9/11 attacks made it virtually impossible to have prevented the attacks.

In the decades prior to 9/11, the U.S. Congress and Department of Justice officials had designed a system that actually made it more difficult for our nation to protect itself against terrorism. Indeed, it was a tragedy waiting to happen, a system destined to fail.

As recently as 1995, the Justice Department had arduously augmented the separation of law enforcement and intelligence agents, strengthening and reinforcing the "wall" between the two groups charged with the responsibility for keeping our nation secure. For example, prosecutors—who had the power to take potential terrorists off the streets were generally restricted in their ability to communicate with or receive information from intelligence officials who were keeping terrorists under surveillance. It wasn't simply that the CIA could not share information with the FBI or the military; the FBI intelligence division could not even freely share information with the criminal arm of the Bureau. Ostensibly this dividing wall was put in place in an effort to make sure that the various agencies didn't taint evidence that could later be used in court to prosecute effectively cases involving foreign intelligence gathering. But Justice officials kept raising the invisible wall higher and higher. More about that later, but for now let me say that by 2001, and especially after September 11, we knew we had to do something to change this situation and we needed to do it fast.

One of the first matters we had to address following 9/11 was the aforementioned "wall" between intelligence and law enforcement agencies. We had to find some way the two groups could legally and freely share the information they were gathering about terrorists and suspected terrorists. Indeed, it surprised most Americans to know that prior to 9/11 our nation's intelligence agents, military intelligence officers, and criminal law enforcement officers were not permitted to help one another by freely sharing information about their investigations. Average citizens were astounded to discover the invisible barrier existing between them. And agents and prosecutors knew that ignoring or crossing over the wall was a surefire way to damage your career in law enforcement or intelligence gathering.

In truth, I hadn't paid much attention to the wall's existence when I took office as attorney general. It was described to me simply as part of the law. Moreover, the courts had issued opinions that seemed to condone the wall, so I accepted that fact.

This was obviously not the type of proactive Attorney General that the United States needed to face an enemy that had repeatedly stated its determination to attack the United States and its vital interests both at home and abroad. But he was no different than the Attorney General he replaced, Janet Reno, who was not at all interested in or knowledgeable concerning the FISA Statute and Court; or her Deputy Jamie Gorelick, who actually further complicated the use of the court and the exchange of intelligence and then had the audacity to criticize the law enforcement and intelligence agencies for not collecting and sharing intelligence when she served as a member of the 9/11 Commission; and unfortunately the FBI director, Louis Freeh, who took no effective actions to get relief for his beleaguered agency.

President Bush became so concerned about efforts to repeal the PATRIOT Act that he started a campaign to retain the act and clearly stated that he would veto any Congressional efforts to repeal it. Once again we are seeing the ill-conceived concerns of the few undermining legitimate and Constitutional measures to protect our society. The almost immediate passage of the PATRIOT Act after the 9/11 attacks was intended by Congress and the president to provide the U.S. intelligence and law enforcement communities with the legal tools to prevent and preempt terrorism that had long been sought by the agencies, but denied by Congress.

Almost immediately the PATRIOT Act came under criticism from the privacy lobby and without any showing of abuse or adverse consequences. The critics began a constant campaign to repeal many of the act's most important provisions. On May 10, 2004, one of America's most experienced and respected federal judges put the criticism of the act in proper prospective. Chief Judge Michael B. Mukasey of the Southern District of New York in an oped article in the *Wall Street Journal* stated in part:

> We are now in a struggle with an extremism that expresses itself in the form of terror attacks, and in that we face what is probably the gravest threat to this country's institutions, if not to its physical welfare, since the Civil War. When one tries to assess people who can find it in themselves to fly airplanes into buildings and murder 3,000 of us in a single morning, whatever else you can say about such people, they are very sure that they are right; and wouldn't it be music to their ears to hear that our spirit says we're not too sure that we are right?
>
> ...Recently, a statute called the USA Patriot Act has become the focus of a good deal of hysteria, some of it reflexive, much of it recreational. My favorite example is the well-publicized resolution of the American Library Association condemning what the librarians claim to believe is a section of the statute that

authorizes the FBI to obtain library records and to investigate people based on the books they take out. Some of the membership have announced a policy of destroying records so that they do not fall into the hands of the FBI. First a word on the organization that gives us this news. The motto of this organization is "Free people read freely." When it was called to their attention that there are 10 librarians languishing in Cuban prisons for encouraging their fellow countrymen to read freely, an imprisonment that has been condemned by Lech Walesa and Vaclav Havel, among others, this association declined to vote any resolution of condemnation, although they did find time at their convention to condemn their own government.

In addition to the library association, many towns and villages across the country, notably Berkeley and Amherst, have announced that they will not cooperate with any effort to gather evidence under the statute. A former vice president has called for the statute's repeal, and a former presidential candidate has called the act "morally wrong," "shameful" and "unconstitutional."

I think one would have to concede that the USA Patriot Act has an awkward, even an Orwellian name, which is one of those Washington acronyms derived by calling the law "Uniting and Strengthening America by Providing Appropriate Tools Required to Interrupt and Obstruct Terrorism." You get the impression they started with the acronym first, and then offered a $50 savings bond to whoever could come up with a name to fit. Without offering my view on any case or controversy, current or future, I think that that awkward name may very well be the worst thing about the statute.

Most of the provisions have nothing to do with the current debate, including provisions authorizing purchase of equipment for police departments and the like, and provisions tightening restrictions on money laundering, including restrictions on the export of currency, which is the life-blood of terrorists. Recall that when Saddam Hussein was captured, he had with him $750,000 in $100 bills.

The statute also breaks down the wall that has separated intelligence gathering from criminal investigation. It allows intelligence information to be shared with criminal investigators, and information that criminal investigators unearth to be shared with those conducting intelligence investigations. I think many people would believe this makes sense, although a series of bureaucratic decisions and a stark misreading of the Foreign Intelligence Surveillance Act for years made this impossible, and thus prevented the government from fulfilling its most basic responsibility under the Constitution: "to provide for the common defense [and] promote the general Welfare."

What difference would this make? Well, there is one documented incident involving an FBI intelligence agent on the West Coast who was trying to find two men on a watch list who he realized had entered the country. He tried to get help from the criminal investigative side of the FBI, but headquarters intervened and said that was not allowed. That happened in August 2001. The two men he was looking for were named Khalid al-Midhar and Nawaf al-Hazmi. A few weeks later, on Sept. 11, they were at the controls of the airplane that struck the Pentagon. This provision of the statute, permitting information sharing, could not pass Congress without an agreement that it would sunset on

Dec. 31, 2005, and so unless that provision is changed, come Jan. 1, 2006, we will be back to the rules that prevailed in August 2001.

The provisions in the law that have generated the most opposition have to do with investigative techniques, including electronic surveillance and the gathering of business records. The electronic surveillance provisions give investigators access to cable-based communications, such as e-mail, on the same basis as they have long had access to telephone communications, and give them access to telephone communications in national security cases on the same basis on which they already have such access in drug cases.

I think most people would have been surprised and somewhat dismayed to learn that before the Patriot Act was passed, an FBI agent could apply to a court for a roving wiretap if a drug dealer switched cell phones, as they often do, but not if an identified agent of a foreign terrorist organization did; and could apply for a wiretap to investigate illegal sports betting, but not to investigate a potentially catastrophic computer hacking attack, the killing of U.S. nationals abroad, or the giving of material support to a terrorist organization. Violations like those simply were not on the list of offenses for which wiretaps could be authorized.

The statute also codifies the procedure for issuing and executing what are called "sneak and peek" warrants that allow agents, with court authorization, to enter premises, examine what is there and then leave. These warrants had been issued by courts before the Patriot Act was passed, including my own court—although I have never issued one myself—on the fairly simple logic that if it is reasonable under the Fourth Amendment to enter premises and seize things, it should also be reasonable to enter premises and not seize things. The statute permits agents to delay disclosure of their presence to the person who controls the premises, again with court authorization. Here too, the logic seems obvious: If you leave behind a note saying "Good afternoon, Mr. bin Laden, we were here," that might betray the existence of an investigation and cause the subjects to flee or destroy evidence. There are analogous provisions that were in existence long before the Patriot Act permitting a delay in notifying people who are overheard on wiretaps, and for the same reason.

What about the section the librarians were so concerned about, Section 215? Well, it bears some mention that the word library appears nowhere in that section. What the section does authorize is the issuance of subpoenas for tangible things, including business records, but only upon approval by the Foreign Intelligence Surveillance Court. Such a subpoena can direct everyone, including the record keeper, not to disclose the subpoena to anyone, including to the person whose records were obtained. That section also specifically forbids investigation of a citizen or a lawful alien solely on the basis of activity protected by the First Amendment. It requires that the Justice Department report to Congress every six months on subpoenas issued under it. At last report, there have been no such subpoenas issued to libraries. Indeed, there have been no such subpoenas, period.

Let me hasten to add that it is not impossible to imagine how library records might prove highly relevant, as they did in one case, very much pre-9/11—the case of the "Unabomber," Ted Kaczynski. Some of you may recall that Kaczynski was apprehended soon after a newspaper agreed to publish his manifesto, and was caught based principally on a tip from his brother, who read the manifesto, and recognized the rhetoric. But one of the ways that tip was proved accurate was through examination of library records, which disclosed that the three arcane books cited in the manifesto had been checked out to Ted Kaczynski from a local library—a devastating bit of corroborative circumstantial evidence.

Like any other act of Congress, the Patriot Act should be scrutinized, criticized and, if necessary, amended. But in order to scrutinize and criticize it, it helps to read what is actually in it. It helps not to conduct the debate in terms that suggest it gives the government the power to investigate us based on what we read, or that people who work for the government actually have the inclination to do such a thing, not to mention the spare time ...

The hidden message in the structure of the Constitution—is that the government it establishes is entitled, at least in the first instance, to receive from its citizens the benefit of the doubt. If we keep that in mind, then the spirit of liberty will be the spirit which, if it is not too sure that it is right, is at least sure enough to keep itself—and us—alive.

Judge Mukasey was nominated to be Attorney General by President George W. Bush on September 17, 2007, and confirmed by the U.S. Senate on November 8. He entered duty on November 9, 2007.

On March 9, 2006, President Bush signed two pieces of legislation that reauthorized the key provisions of the PATRIOT Act. This was done after protracted debate and deliberation in both Houses of the Congress. However, two, of the act's most important sections were once again placed under a "Sunset" provision of the Law, namely, the roving wiretap authority and the access to business records provisions. Even though there had been no showing of abuse of these authorities and senior officials of the government, including the president, Attorney General, and FBI director who had directly supported reauthorization of these provisions, the Senate found it necessary to limit the time that these provisions would be allowed without Congressional reauthorization. A perplexing aspect of this debate for law enforcement has been the fact that these authorities have been available to the FBI and DEA in drug and organized crime investigations for many years and there is no record of significant abuse. Are illegal drugs and organized crime more important to Americans than the threat of terrorism? The American law enforcement community does not think so.

There have certainly been mistakes and miscalculations by the government in responding to the 9/11 attacks including holding American citizens without charge and denying citizens and permanent resident aliens the right of the *writ of habeas corpus* and application of the Speedy Trial Act, in addition to the arrest and detention of illegal aliens without publicly identifying these detained persons, and ensuring due process procedures smacks of police state tactics and is totally unnecessary in efforts to combat terrorism. The most

dramatic departure from acceptable actions on the part of American authorities, but not law enforcement agencies, came in the area of permissible methods of interrogation. American values were violated and our standing in the
world community suffered because of dubious abuses which violate our laws
and moral standards. Fortunately, both candidates for president in the 2008
election have taken strong positions against torture or excessively coercive
interrogation techniques. These excesses have come from the White House
General Counsel, certain Department of Defense officials, and the Attorney
General and senior officials of the justice department, all of whom have
departed. But long after their departure, the agencies that were mandated to
execute these policies will be called upon to justify their actions in carrying
out the war on terrorism. And in the past, such exercises in self-flagellation
have put our nation at risk.

LAW ENFORCEMENT SUBSEQUENT TO 9/11

Virtually, the first consequence of the 9/11 attacks was the realization that
the first responders to acts of terrorism in the United States were going to be
state and local police, fire, and emergency service personnel. The second
realization was that these brave and valiant men and women were poorly
equipped and inadequately trained to deal with such catastrophic events.
We also learned, or at least finally acknowledged, that our border and air
transportation systems were highly vulnerable. And lastly, it became gravely
apparent that impediments to the collection, analysis, and sharing of information among intelligence, security, and law enforcement agencies had, in
fact, compromised our nation's ability to proactively defend itself from
terrorism.

After the initial round of finger-pointing and rhetorical excuses, law
enforcement agencies focused immediately on improving our national security. The protection of airports and public buildings was deemed a high priority, and enforcement measures were implemented swiftly. All major and
most medium-sized, local law enforcement agencies joined and supported
the JTTFs in covering their territories, or assisted the FBI's regional efforts
in creating task forces appropriate to the needs. The process of obtaining
security clearances for task force members and police chiefs who desired
them was expedited. The FBI saw its JTTFs increase from 34 before the
9/11 attacks to 106 as of July 1, 2008, according to Kirsten Sheldon, special
assistant to EAD Art Cummings who is in charge of the FBI's National
Security Branch.

The FBI also created at FBIHQ an ad hoc group of representatives from
federal agencies. In July 2002, they formally created the National Joint Terrorism Task Force (NJTTF) to act as a liaison and conduit for information
on threats and leads from FBIHQ to the local JTTFs and 38 participating
agencies. The NJTTF now includes representatives from members of the

intelligence community; components of the Departments of Homeland Security, Defense, Justice, Treasury, Transportation, Commerce, Energy, State, and the Interior; the City of New York Police Department; the Nuclear Regulatory Commission; Railroad Police; U.S. Capital Police; and others.[25]

All members are provided with access to the FBI intranet, including the internal e-mail system, and to the FBI's investigative databases for purposes of counterterrorism investigations. In turn, members provide access to their organizations' respective databases. In addition, daily secure video conferences, coordinated by the National Security Council, are held within FBIHQ and attended by NJTTF members, ensuring that all member agencies of the NJTTF receive the latest threat briefings.[26]

President Bush proposed and supported the creation of a new federal Department of Homeland Security (DHS) and gave the new department and its secretary broad powers after it was created by an act of Congress. The president (March 2004) set forth the following mission for DHS:

> The Department of Homeland Security was created with one single overriding responsibility: to make America more secure. Along with the sweeping transformation within the FBI, the establishment of the Department of Defense's U.S. Northern Command, and the creation of the multi-agency Terrorist Threat Integration Center and Terrorist Screening Center, America is better prepared to prevent, disrupt, and respond to terrorist attacks than ever before.

DHS set forth the following response to the president's tasking:

- Border and Transportation Security: DHS has unified the agencies responsible for securing our borders—many now wearing the same uniform—to keep out terrorists, criminals, and dangerous material. To do so, DHS is implementing a layered security strategy—including an increased DHS presence at key foreign ports, improved visa and inspection processes, strengthened seaport security, and improved security technology at airports and border crossings. DHS is implementing background checks on 100% of applications for U.S. citizenship and has registered over 1.5 million travelers into the U.S. VISIT program. The Coast Guard also seized over 136,000 pounds of cocaine and arrested more than 280 drug smugglers in 2003 with this layered approach.

- Critical Infrastructure: DHS has worked to better protect our communications systems, power grids, and transportation networks. During the holiday terror alert, DHS coordinated with private and civic partners to upgrade security at key facilities around the country. DHS also established a National Cyber Security Division to examine cyber-security incidents, track attacks, and coordinate response.

- Chemical and Biological Threats: DHS has established the BioWatch program, which protects many large U.S. cities by monitoring the air for biological agents that could be released by terrorists. Additionally, with the funding of the president's Project BioShield, America is able to develop and acquire more advanced vaccines and treatments for biological agents.

- Helping our First Responders: The federal government has provided more than $13 billion to equip and train local officials such as firefighters, police officers, and EMS workers to respond to terrorism and other emergencies and created a national incident management system. Over 500,000 responders have been trained in weapons of mass destruction awareness and response since September 11, 2001.

- The USA PATRIOT Act: The PATRIOT Act has played a vital role in protecting the homeland, enabling the federal government to better track terrorists, disrupt their cells, and seize their assets. By breaking down unnecessary barriers between intelligence and law enforcement officers, the PATRIOT Act is helping to ensure that the best available information about terrorist threats is provided to the people who need it most.

While DHS does add additional resources and capabilities to our nation's ability to protect itself from terrorism and weapons of mass destruction, it still remains the principal responsibility of the FBI and CIA working with their domestic and international partners to carry the largest burden in this effort.

In addition to the DHS, a new apparatus has been established for coordination, evaluation, and dissemination of intelligence. The 9/11 Commission recommended the creation of a national intelligence director. After much debate and consternation about the wisdom of such a restructuring of the intelligence community, the president signed the Intelligence Reform and Terrorism Prevention Act of 2004. Ambassador John Negroponte, then serving as ambassador to Iraq, was nominated to be the first director of national intelligence and took office on April 21, 2005, along with his designated deputy director, General Michael Hayden, USAF, the immediate past director of the National Security Agency. On February 13, 2007, Admiral John M. (Mike) McConnell, USN (ret.) was sworn in as the second DNI after Ambassador Negroponte became the Deputy Secretary of State. Hayden left the Office of the Director of National Intelligence (ODNI) to become the director of the CIA on May 30, 2006; he was replaced as the deputy director of National Intelligence by Dr. Donald M. Kerr on October 4, 2007.

Four offices were created in the ODNI. They are

1. The Office of the Program Manager, Information Sharing Environment, headed by Ambassador Thomas E. "Ted" McNamara.
2. The National Counter-Terrorism Center, headed by Admiral John S. Redd with FBI Executive Kevin R. Broch as deputy director.
3. The National Intelligence Council, directed by Dr. Thomas Fingar, formerly the Assistant Secretary of State for intelligence and research.
4. The Office of National Counter-Intelligence Executive, headed by Dr. Joel F. Brenner, former inspector general of the National Security Agency.

In April of 2008 Colonel Bart Johnson, New York State Police (ret.), an active member of the IACP COT, became the first director of Homeland Security and Law Enforcement in the ODNI.

The DNI was assigned three important duties that directly relate to law enforcement agencies at all levels in the United States: (1) devise and implement an intelligence and information sharing process that will serve the needs of the law enforcement, homeland security, and defense communities; (2) establish and ensure that a National Counter-Terrorism Center was established to serve the all-source intelligence requirements of these communities; and (3) provide oversight of the intelligence community including the newly created National Security Branch of the FBI. The DNI was assigned co-appointing authority with the FBI director for the official picked to lead the National Security Branch as an EAD of the FBI. That position is now held by EAD Art Cummings.

FBI Director Robert Mueller took office the week of 9/11/01. He was immediately confronted with the necessity of overcoming many shortcomings in personnel, budget, and authority for the FBI to actively and effectively deal with the terrorism threat. There was much criticism of the Bureau for "failing to connect the dots" in identifying and preempting the 9/11 terrorists, but little attention was given to the legal limitations imposed on the Bureau by the FISA law and the Attorney General's Guidelines and the failure of the previous director to address these issues and the FBI's antiquated information technology infrastructure.

Director Mueller made no excuses and simply proceeded to remake the Bureau to face the now obvious threat of international terrorism. He quickly expanded the number of JTTFs until there were 106 functional task forces covering all areas of the United States. Field Intelligence Groups were set up in each field office to independently collect intelligence and report to the newly established intelligence directorate at FBIHQ. In order to oversee, coordinate, and facilitate the counterterrorism, counterintelligence, and weapons of mass destruction programs of the Bureau, the National Security Branch was established.

On January 22, 2007, the FBI cited the following initiatives in restructuring to support collaborative law enforcement efforts:

Task Forces and Joint Centers

- Increased number of JTTFs from 35 to 101
- Established national JTTF with 40 member agencies
- Established interagency National Counterterroism Center
- Established interagency Terrorist Screening Center
- Established interagency Foreign Terrorist Tracking Task Force
- Established interagency Terrorist Explosive Device Analysis Center

- Participating in state and regional intelligence fusion centers and other regional multiagency intelligence centers
- Established six regional computer forensics laboratories
- Established National Gang Intelligence Center

In testimony before the Senate Select Committee on Intelligence on January 17, 2007, Mueller provided a threat assessment that clearly demonstrated the challenge facing the Law Enforcement and Homeland Securities agencies in the United States and much of the world. His testimony included the following judgments:

From the FBI's perspective, it's a sobering assessment:

- **International terrorism in general.** The "United States homeland faces two very different threats from international terrorism: the attack planning that continues to emanate from core al Qaeda overseas and the threat posed by homegrown, self-radicalizing groups and individuals—inspired, but not led by al Qaeda—who are already living in the U.S. While they share a similar ideology, these two groups pose vastly different threats due to their differences in intent and attack capability."
- **Al Qaeda.** We believe "al Qaeda is still seeking to infiltrate operatives into the U.S. from overseas who have no known nexus to terrorism using both legal and possibly illegal methods of entry. . . . It is also possible, however, that al Qaeda's strategy for attacking the U.S. homeland includes using the U.K. as a stepping stone for al Qaeda operatives to enter the United States."
- **The homegrown international terrorism threat.** The director cited cases involving three separate groups—two with the intent to attack within the United States and one operating "independently of any known terrorist organization"—that reflect the diverse threat posed by homegrown terrorists.
- **The threat from other international terrorist groups,** such as Iranian-supported Lebanese Hezbollah, Shia extremists, and Palestinian terrorist groups.
- **Domestic terrorism.** White supremacist groups, the militia/sovereign citizen movement, some U.S.-based black separatist groups, and animal rights extremism and ecoterrorism pose a threat.
- **Weapons of mass destruction.** Both the pursuit of and proliferation of chemical, biological, radiological, and nuclear weapons continue to be a concern. "Few if any terrorist groups are likely to have the capability to produce complex biological or chemical agents needed for a mass casualty attack, but their capability will improve as they pursue enhancing their scientific knowledge base by recruiting scientists as some groups are doing."
- **Foreign intelligence and espionage.** "Through partnerships with other government agencies and the private and academic sectors, the FBI has not only corroborated long-standing assumptions concerning high-level foreign

intelligence activities in the United States, but [also] has detected far greater levels of activity than originally projected; stealing and compromising of classified and nonclassified technologies are occurring at levels previously unknown."

- **Cyber Security Threats,** "which may come from a vast array of groups and individuals with different skills, motives, and targets," including terrorists, foreign governments, criminal hackers, and con artists.

Mueller also cited several steps that the FBI is taking to address these threats and cases and success stories from the past year.

On May 29, 2008, Dr. Donald M. Kerr, the principal deputy director of National Intelligence made a presentation at a symposium hosted by the Washington Institute for Near East Policy. Dr. Kerr is a highly respected professional who has served in many agencies of government and important positions in the private sector including as the assistant director in charge of the FBI laboratory, the deputy director for research and development of the CIA, and as the director of National Reconnaissance. He was confirmed as the principal deputy director of National Intelligence on October 4, 2007. He worked with me in the early 1980s when he was director of the Los Alamos National Laboratory to establish our nation's first responders to the nuclear threat by participating with the FBI, the Department of Defense, and the Department of Energy to create the Nuclear Emergency Search Teams. These teams still exist and exercise together on a regular basis. In his remarks, Dr. Kerr set forth the current consensus of the intelligence community on the threat of terrorism. He stated in part the following:

Let me begin simply: There has been no attack against our homeland since 9/11. This was no accident. In concert with federal, state and local law enforcement, the intelligence community helped disrupt cells plotting violent attacks. For example, last summer, we and our allies unraveled terrorist plots linked to al-Qa'ida and its associates in Denmark and Germany, and earlier this year our allies disrupted a network plotting attacks in Turkey. We were successful because we were able to identify key personalities in the planning. We worked with our European partners to monitor the plotters and disrupt their activities. One of the intended targets was a US facility.

Our partners throughout the Middle East and elsewhere continued to attack aggressively terrorist networks involved in recruiting, training and planning to strike American interests. Pakistani authorities—who have helped us more than any other nation in counterterrorism operations—increasingly are determined to strengthen their performance, even during a period of heightened domestic political tension exacerbated by the assassination of Benazir Bhutto and formation of a new government after the February elections. Al-Qa'ida remains the preeminent terror threat to the US at home and abroad. Despite our successes, the group has retained or regenerated key elements of its capability, including its top leadership, operational lieutenants, and a de facto safe haven in Pakistan's border area with Afghanistan known as the Federally

Administered Tribal Areas (FATA) to train and deploy operatives for attacks in the [W]est. Al-Qa'ida's Homeland plotting is likely to continue to focus on prominent political, economic, and infrastructure targets designed to produce mass casualties, visually dramatic destruction, significant economic aftershocks, and foment fear among the population.

In spite of all that is being done to prevent and deal with the terrorist threat, it is extremely important for our Congress and the national news media to mature and realize that even though it is the paramount goal of the intelligence and law enforcement agencies to prevent and preempt terrorist attacks, that will not always be possible, particularly in a democracy. The blame game now being played out in our nation's Capitol is an unwise attempt to affix blame instead of correcting systemic problems; problems that both the Congress and news media were well aware of and failed to properly address. Bombastic and partisan finger-pointing by political partisans during an election campaign will not help in creating a safe and secure America.[27]

If the Israeli Knesset (Parliament) and media conducted themselves as many of our legislators and media commentators have done, they would have undermined the morale and effectiveness of the very agencies that they depend upon to protect their society. And even though Israel is attacked much more frequently than the United States, they realize that as good as their agencies are they cannot possibly always preempt terrorists, particularly those who are willing to sacrifice themselves for their cause. We need the same balance and perspective within our society if we are to prevail in this long, difficult, and bloody struggle. And prevail we must, for the fight against terrorism and the extremist ideologies they represent is a fight for our very civilization.

5

Combating the Financing of the International Terrorism Network in the United States

Bruce Zagaris

In the aftermath of the September 11 terrorist attacks, the U.S. government and the international community reviewed typologies for the financing of transnational terrorism and examined ways to combat such financing. Unfortunately, evidence indicates that al Qaeda and other terrorist groups apparently affiliated with or inspired by al Qaeda have worked quite economically, using low-budget methods to operate. After reviewing two typologies, this chapter discusses applicable legal mechanisms for preventing and prosecuting the financing of transnational terrorist networks and considers proposals for improving the effectiveness of efforts to combat foreign-affinity terrorist financing.

TYPOLOGIES

The evolving effects of globalization and the transnational nature of terrorism have combined to create almost limitless possibilities for terrorists looking to finance operations.[1] One problem with combating terrorist financing is that many forms of terrorism—such as suicide bombings—require minimal financial resources. Terrorists often self-finance such attacks by working and/or borrowing from their immediate families. In addition, the bulk of the money may come from legitimate or quasi-legitimate sources. Anti-money-laundering laws have a negligible chance of detecting terrorist financing activities under a regulatory framework built for different purposes.[2] Hence, the first typology describes a legal income source, a relief organization in the Middle East. In the second typology, foreign-affinity terrorist groups perpetrate crimes in order to generate money.[3]

Enforcement authorities working to deny potential terrorists access to financial resources must contend with the problem of "fresh faces," especially ones without criminal records or with legitimate academic credentials. Intelligence agencies often have no information linking these "fresh faces" to terrorist organizations or other criminal connections. Considering the dynamic efforts surrounding terrorist groups, the number of new and unknown faces may be very large.[4] The absence of knowledge about potential new terrorists, the extremely small amount of resources they use, and the self-generation of funds, including legitimate funds to conduct their activities, impose severe limitations on potential legal means to deny such groups or individuals financing.

Legal Income Typology—Relief Organization in the Middle East

According to a state department report, the Financial Crimes Center (FinCEN) of the U.S. Department of Treasury identified 649 suspicious activity reports (SARs) that seven U.S. depository institutions filed during a three-and-a-half-year period. These reports involved transactions worth $9 million involving structured cash deposits and deposits of business, payroll, and Social Security benefit checks. Within one or two days of deposits, the funds were transmitted to a company in the Middle East. Thirty-seven individuals were involved in the deposit and wire transfer activity, conducting transactions through 44 accounts on behalf of four businesses. Two of the businesses were wire remittance companies. One was described as a relief organization at the same location as one of the wire remittance businesses. The fourth undescribed business, located in the Middle East, was the beneficiary of the wire transfer activity. The majority of the wire transfers went to two accounts in the Middle East. Other wire transfers were made to accounts at three different banks in foreign locations. The majority of the transactions (83 percent) were structured; that is, they were arranged to fall below the $10,000 threshold that triggers reporting requirements. The deposit amounts ranged from $350 to $636,790. Most deposits were between $2,000 and $8,000.[5]

Illegal Income Typology—Cigarette Smuggling

Individuals or groups often engage in common criminal activities, using the proceeds to fund terrorist groups. In May 2002, two men were convicted in

Charlotte, North Carolina, of providing, and conspiring to provide, material support to the Palestinian group Hezbollah, a designated foreign terrorist organization. The criminal group engineered an interstate cigarette tax evasion scheme whereby inexpensive cigarettes from North Carolina were transported to and then sold in Michigan to avoid the latter state's higher taxes. Profits from the operation were sent to Hezbollah. International law enforcement authorities have discovered that cigarette smuggling networks can produce enormous profits. Additionally, cigarette trafficking is often the precursor to other types of contraband smuggling, including weapons and narcotics smuggling.

The investigation started when a deputy sheriff working part-time at a large tobacco wholesaler in North Carolina noticed the same individuals buying large quantities of cigarettes. These individuals drove vehicles with out-of-state license plates. Federal, state, and local authorities began a joint investigation. Surveillance of the suspects revealed a large-scale cigarette smuggling ring involving the use of tobacco storefront operations in North Carolina to justify the large purchases and bulk sale of cigarettes. Based on the surveillance, authorities obtained search warrants for the subjects' businesses and residences. Utilizing the warrants, law enforcement officials seized photos of the subjects counting large amounts of cash, a Hezbollah banner, a Hezbollah propaganda video of suicide bombers, and materials showing the involvement of some of the suspects with military training and/or operations. During the searches, law enforcement found a receipt from a Hezbollah leader for money received from the smuggling ring. The search turned up a number of false identification documents for the subjects. Additional evidence showed that the criminal group intended to buy a variety of items for Hezbollah, including night vision devices, radios and receivers, and metal detection devices. In the end, 25 individuals were charged with various offenses, including material support to a terrorist organization, money laundering, conspiracy, bank fraud, credit card fraud, and visa entry fraud. The Bureau of Alcohol, Tobacco, and Firearms played a large role during the initial stages of the investigation. The FBI contributed during the later stages by helping to develop the link to a terrorist organization.[6]

U.S. POLICIES

Much of U.S. counterterrorism financial enforcement (CTFE) is based on U.S. financial or economic sanctions. Under the Trading with the Enemy Act,[7] the International Emergency Economic Powers Act (IEEPA),[8] and certain other statutes, the Treasury's Office of Foreign Assets Control (OFAC) administers sanctions programs that target specific countries, including Cuba, Iran, and Sudan. In addition, the Treasury administers programs targeting designated persons including international terrorists, as well as persons acting on behalf of the governments of sanctioned countries. Such persons are identified on the ever-expanding list of Specially Designated Nationals (SDN list) maintained by the Treasury.[9]

The increased resort to sanctions, both unilaterally and multilaterally through the United Nations, has prompted extensive debate about their efficacy and operation. Such sanctions have long been used to fight terrorism.[10] U.S. economic sanctions and export controls are blunt instruments with a long history that the U.S. private sector carefully follows due to the harsh sanctions for violating them.[11] Compliance with export controls and economic sanctions requires that the private sectors have a comprehensive awareness and due diligence in place. While this subject is beyond the scope of this chapter, the complexity and cost of these programs should be considered.[12] Lawyers and bar associations have played a leading role in helping educate and counsel the private sector on compliance. The U.S. executive branch imposes sanctions against countries and individuals associated with terrorism.[13]

United States Initiates Sanctions against Osama bin Laden and Associates [14]

On September 23, 2001, President George W. Bush issued Executive Order 13224, immediately freezing U.S. financial assets of, and prohibiting U.S. transactions with, 27 different entities.[15] The entities include terrorist organizations, individual terrorist leaders, a corporation that serves as a front for terrorism, and several nonprofit organizations.[16] This section discusses the legal framework and aspects of the order and the responses and implications for foreign governments and financial institutions.

Executive Order 13224

Bush issued Executive Order 13224 under the IEEPA,[17] section 5 of the UN Participation Act of 1945, as amended,[18] and section 301 of title 3, U.S. Code. Bush also cited as legal bases UN Security Council Resolution (UNSCR) 1214 of December 8, 1998, UNSCR 1267 of October 15, 1999, UNSCR 1333 of December 19, 2000, and multilateral sanctions contained therein, and UNSCR 1363 of July 30, 2001, establishing a mechanism to monitor the implementation of UNSCR 1333.

Because many of the groups and individuals operate primarily overseas and have little money in the United States, the United States has been notifying foreign governments that do not freeze or block terrorists' ability to access funds in foreign accounts and share information that the U.S. government has the authority to freeze their bank's assets and transactions in the United States. Legally the executive order authorizes this action by empowering "persons determined by the Secretary of the Treasury, in consultation with the Secretary of State and the Attorney General," and "after such consultation, if any, with foreign authorities as the Secretary of State, in consultation with the Secretary of the Treasury and the Attorney General, deems appropriate, in the exercise of his discretion."[19]

The following persons are subject to the blocking order:

1. foreign persons determined by the Secretary of State to have committed, or to pose a significant risk of committing, acts of terrorism that threaten the security of U.S. nationals or the national security, foreign policy, or economy of the United States;

2. persons determined by the Secretary of Treasury to be owned or controlled by, or to act for or on behalf of any persons listed under the Order or any other persons determined to be subject to it;

3. persons determined by the Secretary of Treasury to assist in, sponsor, or provide financial, material, or technological support for, or financial or other services to or in support of, such acts of terrorism or those persons listed under the Order or determined to be subject to it;

4. persons determined by the Secretary of Treasury to be otherwise associated with those persons listed under the Order or determined to be subject to it.[20]

The executive order's other principal prohibitions include

1. no transaction or dealing by U.S. persons (including their overseas branches, but not their foreign subsidiaries) or within the United States in blocked property;

2. prohibition against U.S. persons or persons in the United States from evading or avoiding, or attempting to evade or avoid any of the Order's prohibitions;

3. prohibition against any conspiracy to violate any of the Order's prohibitions;

4. prohibition against donations intended to relieve human suffering to persons listed under the Order or determined to be subject to it.[21]

Practically speaking, the new terrorist sanctions largely overlap existing U.S. terrorist sanctions administered by OFAC, i.e., the Terrorism Sanctions Regulations (31 CFR Part 595) and the Foreign Terrorist Organizations Regulations (31 CFR Part 597). Under the Terrorism Sanctions Regulations, OFAC has blocked the property of persons posing a significant risk of disrupting the Middle East peace process. Under the Foreign Terrorist Organizations Regulations, U.S. financial institutions must block all funds in which foreign terrorist organizations have an interest. Most of the persons listed in President Bush's September 23, 2001, executive order are already listed as specially designated terrorists under Part 595 or as Foreign Terrorist Organizations under Part 597.

The new sanctions significantly enlarge existing sanctions. First, they are broader than the Terrorism Sanctions Regulations, extending beyond terrorists who pose a significant risk of disrupting the Middle East peace process.

Second and most importantly, they are broader than the Foreign Terrorism Organization Regulations in that they require blocking actions by all U.S. persons, not just U.S. financial institutions. Third, the new sanctions make it easier to designate terrorists because anyone "associated" with terrorists can be listed. As mentioned above, the Bush administration intends to block the U.S. assets of and bar U.S. market access to foreign banks that can be linked to terrorists in any way and which refuse to freeze terrorists' assets. Previously, the United States has had difficulty convincing allies and foreign banks to impose sanctions on terrorists.[22]

Foreign subsidiaries of U.S. companies now deal with terrorists at their peril. While the subsidiaries appear to be beyond the scope of the executive order, any link between a foreign subsidiary and a terrorist could be treated as an "association" warranting sanctions.[23] Bush explained that the foreign terrorist asset tracking center announced by the United States the preceding week is operational and is coordinating information from among government agencies with the express purpose of identifying and obliterating the financial network that funds terrorism.

Second U.S. Counterterrorism List [24]

On October 11, 2001, the United States named 39 additional persons linked to the al Qaeda network, including a series of charitable organizations, businesses, and individuals with close contacts with governments in the Middle East and Central Asia.[25] The new list of persons adds to the 27 identified in Executive Order 13224 and exerts pressure on a number of key governments. On November 2, 2001, the Bush administration added 22 additional groups to the list.

The new list adds Yasin al-Qadi, also known as Mr. Kadi, a Saudi businessman who has directed the Muwafaq Foundation, a foundation with trustees who have included some of Saudi's most prominent families. The treasury alleges the foundation has sent millions of dollars from Saudi businesses to bin Laden.

The Bush administration consulted with European allies, but not Saudi Arabia before releasing the new list. (Before the release of the second list, Saudi Arabia faced—and continues to face—stringent criticism from some American political figures for the country's perceived failure to fight terrorist financing. However, state department figures have recently praised the government for stepped up anti-money-laundering efforts and a crack down on many charities believed to be fronts for terrorist financing.)[26] Although U.S. officials contemplated listing the Saudi-based Muwafaq Foundation, or Blessed Relief, they compromised at listing its head, Yasin al Qadi, partly because the foundation has been defunct since 1996.[27]

Rabita Trust, a Pakistani charity over which Pakistan's President General Pervez Musharraf was a board member, is another politically sensitive entity on the list. The United States had warned Musharraf of the impending order and encouraged him to disassociate himself from the organization.[28] Top Pakistani officials helped establish Rabita, which has aided resettled refugees from Bangladesh. According to Pakistani news accounts, the Rabita Trust is affiliated with a much larger and better-known charity, usually called Rabita Alam-e-Islami, or the Muslim World League. It is headquartered in the holy city of Mecca and operates a multibillion-dollar budget contributed by many wealthy Saudis.

According to the Treasury, the secretary-general of the Rabita Trust is Wa'el Hamza Jalaidan, who it characterized as "logistics chief" and cofounder of bin Laden's organization. According to information attributed to terrorism expert Steve Emerson, Jalaidan resided in Arizona in the early 1980s and directed an Islamic center there before joining bin Laden in the fight against the Soviets in Afghanistan.[29]

Three entities on the new lists are said to be al Qaeda fronts in Yemen: Al-Hamati Sweets Bakeries, Al-Nur Honey Press Shops, and Al-Shifa Honey Press. While bin Laden has been identified as owning and deriving income from construction companies, currency trading firms, and export-import businesses, the honey businesses were only recently identified.[30] The owner of the last of the three businesses is Mahmud Abu al-Fatuh Muhammad, who is linked to the Islamic Cultural Institute in Milan, which U.S. officials characterize as "the main al-Qaeda station house in Europe" and is supposedly used to "facilitate the movement of weapons, men and money across the world," according to a U.S. Treasury statement.

Treasury officials also alleged that a relief group based in Canada— Human Concern International (HCI)—was connected to al Qaeda operations and froze the assets of Ahmad Sa'id Al-Kadr, who directed HCI's Afghan operations until his arrest by Pakistani police for the bombing of the Egyptian embassy in Islamabad.[31]

The Bush administration also named Jaish-e-Mohammed, a militant Pakistani group that has attacked Indian targets in Kashmir and claimed responsibility for the suicide bomb that killed 38 in Kashmir's capital during the first week of October. Kandahar-based Society of Islamic Co-operation is listed due to its alleged connections to bin Laden and his closest associates. Another person named in the new list is Haji Abdul Manan Agha, described as "a large scale hawala dealer" (hawala are the informal undocumented asset transfers used with frequency in the Middle East and Asia) whose Al-Qadir Traders business is based in Pakistan.[32]

Third U.S. Counterterrorism List

On November 22, 2001, the Bush administration added 22 organizations to the list of groups against whom financial sanctions apply. Included are a number of Arab organizations, such as Hamas, Hezbollah, Islamic Jihad, and the Popular Front for the Liberation of Palestine, three Colombian groups, the Real Irish Republican Army, and the Basque group ETA (Basque Homeland and Freedom).[33]

The addition of Hamas and Hezbollah will exert enormous pressure on Egypt, Saudi Arabia, Jordan, Kuwait, Syria, and other Arab nations to take steps against the fundraising and other activities of Hamas and Hezbollah. Support for these organizations is quite open and widespread. Hamas operates numerous schools and hospitals aimed at poor Palestinians and solicits money openly in mosques across the Arab world. The group receives large donations from mainstream companies and executives.[34]

All of the groups mentioned on the third list were already on the Department of State's list of foreign terrorist organizations, which requires U.S. financial institutions to freeze their assets and makes it illegal to offer them support. Their addition to the counterterrorist financial sanctions list will enable the United States to take action against them and deny access to U.S. financial markets to foreign banks that do not cooperate.[35] With the Financial Action Task Force (FATF) decision to add counterterrorist financing to its recommendations along with countermeasures, the United States can exert pressure on the rest of the world to follow suit.

The Use of Terrorist Lists

U.S. diplomatic efforts to convince other countries to maintain some groups on domestic terrorism blacklists—particularly Hamas—have met with mixed success. In March 2005, international press outlets reported that France and Spain were trying to remove Hamas from the European Union blacklist, a decision the countries characterized as a step toward engaging Hamas with an eye toward progress in the Middle East.[36] A major problem for banks outside the United States is the multiplicity of terrorism blacklists—these include the United States,[37] the European Union,[38] the United Nations,[39] and ones maintained by other countries. Some persons and even professionals who do not specialize in CTFE confuse terrorist lists with lists of the FATF for countries who do not meet international standards for anti-money-laundering due diligence and the lists of the Organization for Economic Cooperation and Development of uncooperative countries in its harmful tax practices initiative.

Effective monitoring of the lists requires a substantial investment in human resources and software, a requirement which many medium-sized and small financial institutions may have difficulty making. An additional problem is that, even multinational firms spending significant resources to check the lists, almost on a daily basis trigger "false positives" or gray areas. In other words, because the buyer (company or person with whom the company has a proposed transaction) has a name very similar to the name of the list and because the names are translated into English and/or the determination of whether the buyer's appearance on the list depends on the jurisdiction in which the buying entity is registered, the seller or often the seller's counsel needs to actually communicate with the regulatory agency (in the United States it is OFAC) or organization administering the list to ascertain if the proposed transaction can be consummated. Hence, the process of just determining whether the proposed buyer is not on the list can seem prohibitively expensive for some sellers.

Executive Order 13382

On June 28, 2005, pursuant to one of the recommendations of the report of the Commission on Intelligence Capabilities of the United States Regarding Weapons of Mass Destruction, President Bush issued Executive Order 13382.[40] The executive order is an authority aimed at freezing the assets of proliferators of weapons of mass destruction (WMD) and their supporters, and isolating them financially. Designations under Executive Order 13382 prohibit all transactions between the designees and any U.S. person and freeze any assets the designees may have under U.S. jurisdiction. The action effectively denies those parties access to the U.S. financial and commercial systems. U.S. persons, meaning any U.S. citizen, permanent resident alien, U.S. company (including their foreign branches), and any person or company in the United States, are prohibited from engaging in any transaction or dealing with any party designated under Executive Order 13382. In addition, all property within the possession or control of any U.S. person in which a target has an interest is blocked and must be reported to OFAC within 10 days.[41]

This order creates a powerful new mechanism for the United States to broadly assert extraterritorial jurisdiction and impose sanctions on entities engaged in the proliferation of WMD or persons providing support, financial or otherwise, to such activities. OFAC administers this blocking program, which initially applied to eight organizations in North Korea, Iran, and Syria. The Treasury, together with the Department of State, is authorized to designate additional WMD proliferators and their supporters under the new authorities provided by this executive order.[42] As of April 7, 2007, 36 entities were identified as proliferators or supporters whose assets must be frozen.[43]

Changes to U.S. Infrastructure on Investigating Financial Aspects of Terrorism[44]

One issue that arises in developing counterterrorism financing enforcement is the establishment of a proper infrastructure to undertake this work successfully. The U.S. government has established, as mentioned above, a Foreign Terrorist Tracking Center to prioritize the identification and blocking of financial activities of terrorists.

On October 25, 2001, the Treasury announced a new investigative team to target charities, nongovernmental organizations, and underground remittance systems used by al Qaeda.[45] Named "Operation Green Quest," the new team includes prosecutors from the justice department and investigators from several financial agencies, including the Internal Revenue Service, the Customs Service, and the FBI.

According to Robert Bonner, the customs commissioner, the new task force would be more proactive, trying to identify future sources of financing and either disrupt or dismantle their activities. The new team will rely substantially on the New York-based El Dorado Task Force, a 200-person money laundering task force that has seized $425 million and arrested 1,500 people since its start in 1992.[46]

Kenneth Dam, then the Assistant Secretary of Treasury, said the Treasury would rely significantly on "friends and allies" to pursue the charities and nongovernmental organizations used by terrorists overseas. Dam noted that 153 countries have agreed to combat counterterrorism financing.

In addition to targeting hawala, illicit charities, and corrupt financial institutions, the task force has closely examined other activities connected with terrorist financing, including counterfeiting, credit card fraud, drug trafficking, and cash smuggling.[47]

The establishment of the task force shows the expansion of one law enforcement mechanism, established for counternarcotics enforcement, to counterterrorism. Increasingly, the United States is applying counternarcotics procedures to counterterrorism enforcement. The extent to which other governments will emulate the U.S. approach will depend on the diplomatic skill of the United States. Clearly, the announcement of the new task force illustrates that a shift in law enforcement resources is occurring, reallocating resources from counternarcotics to counterterrorism enforcement.

The FBI formed the Terrorist Financing Operations Section (TFOS), formerly called the Terrorist Financial Review Group, in response to the urgent need for a more comprehensive, centralized approach to investigate the financing of terrorists and terrorism. Its goal is to provide a coordinated financial investigative component to terrorism investigations and to develop predictive terrorist identification mechanisms to identify terrorists and their networks, in addition to disrupting and dismantling those networks and their funding mechanisms. TFOS initially focused on conducting and coordinating a comprehensive financial analysis of the 19 September 11 hijackers in order to connect them and identify their financial support structure within the United States and internationally.[48]

TFOS assists with the financial aspects of terrorism investigations to FBI field offices. It assists the Joint Terrorism Task Forces operating in the FBI field offices and the 44 FBI legal attaché offices located in foreign countries. Depending on resource needs and expertise, it helps with investigative, analytical, and document handling support, or the conduct of all aspects of financial investigation. TFOS employs a relational database to organize, capture, and analyze all TFOS financial documents. When information is put into the database, link analysis and queries can be conducted to identify associations and further expand the scope of an investigation. The process aims to help investigators and analysts identify and clarify the activities of individuals, illicit charities, and corrupt financial institutions engaged as facilitators of terrorist funding.[49]

On March 31, 2003, the U.S. Treasury created a new Executive Office for Terrorist Financing and Financial Crimes (EOTF/FC). In December 2004, after a series of bureaucratic reorganizations, the EOTF/FC was renamed and folded into the Treasury's Office of Terrorism and Financial Intelligence (TFI). TFI is chartered with a number of goals, including "freezing the assets of terrorists, drug kingpins, and their support networks" and "developing and enforcing regulations to address U.S. vulnerabilities to terrorist financing."[50]

TFI is responsible for coordinating and leading theTreasury's efforts to combat terrorist financing and other financial crimes, both within the United States as well as abroad.[51] The new office has the following responsibilities:

1. developing and implementing U.S. government strategies to combat terrorist financing domestically and internationally together with the Treasury's International Affairs Task Force on Terrorist Financing;
2. developing and implementing the National Money Laundering Strategy, as well as other policies and programs to combat financial crimes;
3. participating in the Treasury's development and implementation of U.S. government policies and regulations in support of the USA PATRIOT Act, including outreach to the private sector;
4. participating in the representation of the United States at focused international bodies dedicated to fighting terrorist financing and financial crimes; and
5. developing U.S. government policies relating to financial crimes.

In January 2006, William Fox left his position as head of FinCEN to become senior compliance executive at Bank of America. U.S. Treasury Secretary John Snow named Robert Werner to replace Fox. FinCEN's most recent strategic plan emphasizes fighting terrorist financing, noting that the group wants to increase the scope of data collection "to enhance the value of [its] efforts to combat terrorism and money laundering."[52] FinCEN also intends to hire more analysts to work on combating terrorist financing.

USA PATRIOT Act and Implementation[53]

On October 26, 2001, President Bush signed into law the USA PATRIOT Act of 2001, H.R. 3162. Title III concerns international money laundering abatement and anti-terrorism financing.

The USA PATRIOT Act expanded the anti-money-laundering obligations of U.S. domestic financial institutions and as a result they have had to substantially revise existing compliance policies and procedures. The law requires foreign financial institutions with assets in the United States that have not been directly subject to U.S. financial regulation to meet new anti-money-laundering requirements as a condition for doing business in the United States. The provisions in the USA PATRIOT Act to make intrusive searches, freeze property, expand jurisdiction over foreign bank accounts (e.g., the correspondent bank account provisions), designate foreign jurisdictions, financial institutions, and transactions as of "special money laundering concern" all have transformed significantly the U.S. Constitutional and criminal law and procedural protections for a vast part of the country. A discussion of some selected relevant provisions follows.

Section 311 (31 U.S.C. § 5318A) gives the Secretary of the Treasury, in consultation with other government officials, authority (in the secretary's discretion), to impose one or more of five new special measures against foreign jurisdictions, foreign financial institutions, transactions involving such jurisdiction's institutions, or one or more types of accounts, that the secretary, after consultation with the Secretary of State and the Attorney General, determines to pose a "primary money laundering concern" to the United States. The measures include the following:

1. requiring additional record keeping or reporting for particular transactions;
2. requiring identification of the foreign beneficial owners of certain accounts at a U.S. financial institution;
3. requiring identification of customers of a foreign bank who use an interbank payable-through account opened by a foreign bank at a U.S. bank;
4. requiring the identification of customers of a foreign bank who use certain correspondent accounts opened by that foreign bank at a U.S. bank; and
5. after consultation with the Secretary of State, the Attorney General, and the chairman of the Federal Reserve Board, restricting or prohibiting the establishment or maintaining of certain interbank correspondent or payable-through accounts.

Measures 1 through 4 cannot be imposed for more than 120 days except by regulation, and measure 5 may only be imposed by regulation.

Section 311 addresses the concern that certain jurisdictions outside the United States that offer offshore banking and related facilities designed to provide anonymity, coupled with weak financial supervisory and enforcement regimes, enable transnational criminals to disguise ownership and movement of criminal funds, derived from, or used to commit, diverse transnational crimes. Transactions involving such offshore financial centers make it difficult for law enforcement officials and regulators to trace the proceeds of crimes. See Section 302(a)(4) and (5). Section 311 also responds to the objective of the Bush administration to take coordinated action against money laundering threats, including giving guidance to U.S. financial institutions regarding international money laundering risks and initiating appropriate countermeasures against noncooperative countries and territories. The power to designate countries and banks has been used sparingly. The United States designated Ukraine and Nauru in 2002 and Banco Delta Asia for allowing North Korea to engage in corrupt activities in Macao.[54]

Section 313 added a new subsection (j) to 31 U.S.C. §5318, prohibiting depository institutions and brokers and dealers in securities operating in the United States from establishing, maintaining, administering, or managing correspondent accounts for foreign shell banks, other than shell bank vehicles affiliated with recognized and regulated depository institutions. This section addresses the concern that U.S. banks and securities brokers and dealers should not have bank accounts with unregulated banks with no physical presence in any jurisdiction. Under Section 312, financial institutions must undertake steps to identify the owners of any non-U.S. bank that is not publicly listed who have a correspondent account with them, along with the interests of each of the owners in the bank. It is expected that additional scrutiny will be applied by the U.S. institution to such banks to make sure they are not engaging in money laundering. They must also identify the nominal and beneficial owners of any private bank account opened and maintained in the United States by non-U.S. citizens and must undertake enhanced scrutiny of the account if it is owned by, or is being maintained on behalf of, any senior political figure where there is reasonable suspicion of corruption. As a result of Secs. 312 and 313, the U.S. financial system has been more secure from terrorist financing through shell banks. However, a number of small and medium-sized indigenous banks and their customers have lost their access to the U.S. financial system because they have not been able to meet the due diligence requirements they needed to show their U.S. banks. When in doubt, U.S. banks have closed correspondent banking relationships rather than endure the risk of an adverse regulatory impact.

Under Section 314, the Secretary of the Treasury issued regulations encouraging cooperation among financial institutions, financial regulators, and law enforcement officials and permitting information sharing by law enforcement and regulatory authorities with such institutions regarding persons reasonably suspected, based on credible evidence, of engaging in terrorist acts or money-laundering activities. FinCEN also developed a 314 electronic exchange system, allowing financial institutions and governments to share financial information about suspected terrorist operations. The section also allows (with notice to the Secretary of the Treasury) the sharing of information among banks of possible terrorist or money laundering activity, and requires the Secretary of the Treasury to publish semiannually a report containing a detailed analysis of patterns of suspicious activity and other appropriate investigative insights derived from SARs and law enforcement investigations.

Section 315 amends 18 U.S.C. §1956 to include foreign criminal offenses, certain U.S. export control violations, certain customs and firearm offenses, certain computer offenses, and felony violations of the Foreign Agents Registration Act of 1938, to the list of crimes that are "specified unlawful activities" for purposes of the criminal money laundering provisions.

Under Section 316 of the USA PATRIOT Act, if the case goes to trial under civil forfeiture proceedings, Section 981(a)(1)(G), and the property involves the assets of "suspected international terrorists," the normal burden of proof is reversed: once the government makes its initial showing of probable cause, the claimant has the burden of proving, by a preponderance of the evidence, that his property is not subject to confiscation. The amendments in Section 316 impose an additional burden on the owner or interested parties in assets confiscated due to terrorist prosecutions to show that the property should not be subject to confiscation or that the interested parties are innocent owners and the amendments enable the court to have a broader discretion in admitting evidence, especially where it may want to protect national security interests of the United States, unless the owner of the property can make an argument under the U.S. Constitution or the Administrative Procedure Act. Nevertheless, Section 316 responds in part to one of the purposes of the act: to ensure that the forfeiture of any assets in connection with the antiterrorist efforts of the United States allows for adequate challenge consistent with providing due process rights. See Section 302(b)(8). The use of IEEPA for the counterterrorism forfeiture strengthens the legislative framework.

Despite the provisions of Section 316, U.S. law enforcement has only sought to seize or forfeit terrorist assets under the new statute in a few cases. The treasury department already had separate authority to freeze and confiscate terrorist assets under the IEEPA, which is specifically exempted from the Civil Asset Forfeiture Reform Act of 2000 and from virtually all of the other evidentiary and due process requirements of federal forfeiture law.[55] Therefore, since September 11, 2001, virtually all of the press reports concerning the freezing of terrorist-related bank accounts have been IEEPA cases, not cases brought by the justice department under Section 981(a)(1)(G).

Section 317 gives U.S. courts "long-arm" (e.g., extraterritorial) jurisdiction over foreign persons committing money laundering offenses in the United States, over foreign banks opening bank accounts, and over foreign persons who convert assets ordered forfeited by a U.S. court. It also permits a U.S. court dealing with such foreign persons to issue a pretrial restraining order or take other action necessary to preserve property in the United States to satisfy an ultimate judgment.

Section 318 expands the definition of financial institution for purposes of 18 U.S.C. §§1956 and 1957 to include those operating outside of the

United States. Section 319 amends U.S. asset forfeiture law 18 U.S.C. §981 to treat funds deposited by foreign banks in interbank accounts with U.S. banks as having been deposited in the United States for purposes of the forfeiture rules. It grants the Attorney General authority, in the interest of jurisdiction consistent with U.S. national interest, to suspend a forfeiture proceeding, based on that presence. U.S. financial institutions must request information from a U.S. regulator relating to anti-money compliance within 120 days of receipt of such a request.

Section 319(b) also requires foreign banks that maintain correspondent accounts in the United States to appoint agents for service of process within the United States. The Attorney General and Secretary of the Treasury are authorized to issue a summons or subpoena to any such foreign bank, seeking records, wherever located, relating to such a correspondent account, and it requires U.S. banks with correspondent arrangements with foreign banks that do not either comply with or contest any subpoenas to provide to appropriate federal banking agencies information and account documentation for any account opened, maintained, administered, or managed in the United States by the financial institution. U.S. courts are given authority to order a convicted criminal to return property located abroad and to order a civil forfeiture defendant to return property located abroad pending trial on the merits.

Section 319(b) provides that the covered financial institution must provide the information requested to the requesting federal law enforcement officer within seven days of receipt of the request.[56] The covered financial institution "shall terminate any correspondent relationship with a foreign bank not later than 10 business days after receipt of written notice from the Secretary or the Attorney General . . . that the foreign bank has failed—(I) to comply with a summons or subpoena issued under [this provision]; or (II) to initiate proceedings in a United States court contesting such summons or subpoena."[57] The failure to terminate the correspondent relationship in accordance with this provision "shall render" the covered financial institution liable for a civil penalty of up to $10,000 per day until the correspondent relationship is terminated.[58]

The summons/subpoena provision in Section 319 is significant. The authority of the Secretary of the Treasury and the Attorney General to issue and enforce subpoenas is almost without limits and apparently such subpoenas can be issued for any arguable law enforcement or regulatory purpose, not just money laundering or antiterrorism enforcement. Although the provision suggests that an interested party (e.g., non-U.S. bank) can challenge the summons or subpoena in U.S. courts, the challenger would have difficulty doing so successfully. The USA PATRIOT Act is likely to be construed as a piece of "national security" legislation and, as such, U.S. courts are likely to give greater than normal deference to the government agencies that seek to enforce it. Presumably, if the facts support them, foreign banks could assert burden or relevance arguments in challenging summonses, but it is not clear what other arguments would be available. For instance, the relevant provision authorizes the Secretary or the Attorney General to seek all records relating to correspondent accounts, "including records maintained outside the United States relating to the deposit of funds into the foreign bank."[59] This authorization of extraterritorial jurisdiction is unprecedented.

Under preexisting law, if a U.S. government agency served a summons or subpoena on a U.S. bank seeking the production of not only records kept in the United States, but also records outside the United States, the recipient of the subpoena could resist producing offshore records on a number of grounds. The challenger could argue lack of possession, custody, and control and the fact, if true, that production of those records from an offshore jurisdiction would violate the domestic confidentiality laws of the offshore jurisdiction and constitute a criminal violation in that jurisdiction there. The U.S. courts would then typically engage in a balancing test of the interests of the U.S. government and those of the foreign government, as well as looking at other legal issues, and determine whether the offshore aspect of the subpoena should be enforced.[60] Given the language of Section 319, it is not clear whether a U.S. court would entertain these types of arguments in the context of a challenge of a Section 319 subpoena by a U.S. or a non-U.S. bank.

The Treasury has issued regulations on record keeping and termination requirements for correspondent accounts of foreign banks. Under 31 U.S.C. §5318(k), as added by Section 319(b) of the PATRIOT Act, any covered financial institution that maintains a correspondent account in the United States for a foreign bank must maintain records in the United States identifying: (1) the owner(s) of such foreign bank; and (2) the name and address of a person (as defined in 31 C.F.R. §103.11(z)) who resides in the United States and is authorized to accept service of legal process for records concerning the correspondent account.

With the new authority of the USA PATRIOT Act (Section 319, which has become 18 U.S.C. §918(k)), if the government can show that forfeitable property was deposited into an account at a foreign bank, the government can now recover the property by filing a civil forfeiture action against the equivalent amount of money that is found in any correspondent account of the foreign bank that is in the United States. Hence, the United States need not trace the money in the correspondent account to the foreign deposit. Additionally, the foreign bank does not have standing to object to the forfeiture action. Only the customer who deposited the forfeitable funds into the foreign bank has standing to contest the forfeiture.

For instance, if the United States obtains information that the assets of an international terrorist are on deposit in a bank in a Caribbean jurisdiction, and that bank has a correspondent account at a bank in Miami, the government may effectively seize the terrorist's assets by bringing a civil forfeiture action under Section 981(k) against the equivalent sum in the correspondent account of the foreign bank in Miami.

The rationale of U.S. prosecutors proposing these provisions was that when the U.S. forfeiture action results in the forfeiture of a given sum of money from the correspondent account of the foreign bank, the bank will then debit the customer's account abroad, leaving the bank in a wash situation and depriving the foreign customer of the funds that have been forfeited to the United States. Prior to the enactment of Section 981(k), U.S. law enforcement would have not taken this tact because the foreign bank would have had the right to object to the forfeiture of funds in its correspondent account, claiming that the money belongs to it, not its customer, and raising the innocent owner defense. Because of the controversial nature of this action, however, forfeitures under Sec. 981(k) require approval from justice department headquarters.[61] The U.S. government has rarely used these new authorities.

Section 320 amends 18 U.S.C. §981 to allow the United States to institute forfeiture proceedings against the proceeds of foreign predicate offenses found in the United States. Section 323 allows the government to seek a restraining order to preserve the availability of property subject to a foreign forfeiture confiscation judgment. The provisions of Section 320 broaden the ability of the United States to institute forfeiture proceedings where proceeds of foreign crimes are involved. Because the United States is the most important capital market in the world and an investor can make significant yields on such proceeds, many proceeds of foreign crimes find their way to the United States. A recent example is that a number of the Central Asian governments that have helped the United States in the counterterrorism war have requested help from the United States in forfeiting and returning to them proceeds of crimes that occurred in their country.

Section 325 authorizes the Secretary of the Treasury to issue regulations concerning the maintenance of concentration accounts by U.S. depository institutions, to ensure such accounts are not used to prevent association of the identity of an individual customer with the movement of funds of which the customer is the direct or beneficial owner. A concentration account is a single account used for the internal purposes of a financial institution to facilitate the processing and settlement of multiple or individual customer transactions within the bank, usually on the same day.[62] Such accounts can lead to the concealment by financial institutions of transactions made by customers. Section 325 bans their use for such purposes by forbidding financial institutions to allow clients to direct transactions that move their funds into, out of, or through the concentration accounts of the financial institution.

Section 326(a) requires the Secretary of the Treasury to prescribe by regulation, jointly with each functional regulator, minimum standards for financial institutions and their customers regarding the identity of the customer that must apply in connection with the opening of an account at a financial institution; the minimum standards that must require financial institutions to implement, and customers (after being given adequate notice) comply with, reasonable procedures concerning verification of customer identity, maintenance of records for identity verification, and consultation at account opening of lists of known or suspected terrorists provided to a financial institution by a government agency.

Section 326(b) requires the Secretary of the Treasury, in consultation with the federal functional regulators and other appropriate agencies, to submit a report to Congress within six months of the date of enactment containing recommendations about the most effective way to require foreign nationals to provide financial institutions in the United States with accurate identity information comparable to that required to be provided by U.S. nationals, and to obtain an identification number that would function similarly to a U.S. national's Social Security or tax identification number.

Section 328 requires the Secretary of the Treasury, in consultation with the Attorney General and the Secretary of State, to take all reasonable steps to encourage foreign governments to require the inclusion of the names of the originator in wire transfer instructions sent to the United States, and to report annually to the House Committee on Financial Services and the Senate Committee on Banking, Housing, and Urban Affairs concerning meeting that goal. Section 351 creates a safe harbor from civil liability for banks that provide information in employment references sought by other banks.

An aspect of the U.S. anti-money regime is that tainted funds follow the path of least resistance to enter the legitimate financial system. Hence, a comprehensive approach to minimizing money laundering and terrorist financing risks within the United States necessarily involves extending controls to the full range of financial services industries that may be susceptible to abuse. Sec. 352 of the USA PATRIOT Act takes this approach by ordering the Treasury to expand the basic anti-money-laundering program requirement to all financial institutions that present risks of money laundering by virtue of the products or services offered. The challenge for Treasury is to take the broad statutory mandate and implement that to rules that apply to each of the diverse industries defined as financial institutions under the Bank Secrecy Act. An anti-money program must include

1. the development of internal policies and procedures;
2. the designation of a compliance officer;
3. an employee training program; and
4. an independent testing function to verify that the program is operating as required.

In April 2002, the Treasury, with the assistance of the Securities Exchange Commission (SEC), the Commodities Futures Trading Commission (CFTC), their respective self-regulatory organizations, and the banking regulators, issued regulations requiring firms in the major financial sectors to establish an anti-money-laundering program. In addition to the banks, which already had an anti-money-laundering program requirement, Treasury covered securities brokers and dealers, futures commission merchants and introducing brokers, mutual funds, money services businesses, casinos, insurance companies (e.g., life insurance and annuities), dealers in precious metals, stones, or jewels, travel agencies, operators of credit card systems, and a business engaged in vehicle sales, including automobiles, airplanes, and boats. Treasury prepared and issued separate rules for each financial industry to ensure that the programs would be appropriately customized to the risks posed by their operations.

Section 356 directs the Secretary of the Treasury, in consultation with the SEC and Federal Reserve Board, to publish regulations, on or before July 1, 2002, requiring broker-dealers to file SARs. The provision sets a schedule for regulating future commission merchants, commodity trading advisors, and commodity pool operators and sets the basis for future money laundering regulations of investment companies.[63] On December 31, 2002, the Department of Treasury issued a §365(c) report, proposing a number of changes to certain types of investment companies.

Section 359 clarifies that the Bank Secrecy Act treats certain underground banking systems—money transmitting businesses—as financial institutions for purposes of the funds transfer record keeping and other anti-money-laundering rules. The Secretary of the Treasury must report to Congress within one year of the date of enactment on the need for additional legislation or regulatory controls relating to underground banking systems.

Section 360 authorizes the Secretary of the Treasury to instruct the U.S. Executive Director of each international financial institution to use such directors' "voice and vote" to support loans and other use of resources to benefit nations that the president determines are contributing to U.S. efforts to combat international terrorism, and to require the auditing disbursements at such international financial institutions to ensure that funds are not paid to persons engaged in or supporting terrorism. In November 2002, the Department of Treasury issued a §359 report, calling for licensing and regulation of money-transmitting business and hawalas but noting that an outright ban would simply drive them underground.[64]

Section 377 provides extraterritorial jurisdiction for the financial crimes committed abroad where the tools or proceeds of the offense pass through or are in the United States (e.g., account issuer, credit card system).

A plethora of proposed and final regulations implementing Title III of the USA PATRIOT Act have been issued. They total in excess of 1,000 pages. There is still an intensive dialogue between the private sector and the U.S. government over the regulations. This dialogue will continue for some years due to the breadth of the regulations and their relative newness for certain subsectors.

On March 2, 2006, the U.S. Senate passed legislation renewing the USA PATRIOT Act by a vote of 89 to 10. On March 9, 2006, President Bush signed into law "The USA PATRIOT Improvement and Reauthorization Act of 2005" (the "PATRIOT Reauthorization Act"). Section 402 of the PATRIOT Reauthorization Act amended the IEEPA to increase the maximum civil penalties from $10,000 to $50,000. Section 402 also increases the maximum term of imprisonment for individuals from 10 to 20 years. This increase took most of the exporting community by surprise. The new language raises civil penalties to half the levels that had been imposed under the Export Administration Act (EAA) before it lapsed for national security controlled items (which were subject to $100,000 in civil fines). Because the EAA only imposed $10,000 fines on exports other than those controlled for national security reasons, it is not clear whether the Bureau of Industry and Security (BIS) of the U.S. Department of Commerce will assert that penalties for those fines should also be increased to $50,000 (and whether it would be lawful if they were to do so).

According to BIS's Office of Chief Counsel, the new penalties will apply to BIS administrative penalties for violations occurring after March 9, 2006. BIS is currently assessing the potential impact of the new penalty amount on its administrative penalties practices. In particular, Commerce's Office of Export Enforcement and BIS management are determining whether and to what extent they will still charge multiple violations for the same substantive offenses as penalties increase under this recent change and perhaps under legislation under consideration in Congress. OFAC officials have said that they will also apply the new maximum penalty to civil violations under IEEPA-based embargo/sanctions programs. By law, the increases can only apply to violations occurring after March 9, 2006.[65]

While the USA PATRIOT Act has enhanced the authority of U.S. law enforcement and regulators and increased the due diligence requirements for U.S. financial institutions, including a wide range of sectors now deemed financial institutions for purposes of the CTFE legislation, the utility of the new authorities has yet to show its cost-effectiveness. Terrorist attacks around the world have increased. Many of the attacks occur in the Middle East and continue to use low-budget mechanisms, such as improvised explosive devices, suicide bombers using automobiles, and explosives attached to individuals' clothing. The number of terrorist financing convictions is indeed small. The burden on U.S. and non-U.S. financial institutions is great: they have increased their investment in hardware and software, training, and overall due diligence as a result of the addition of terrorist financing to their anti-money-laundering programs.

In April 2006, OFAC issued new Syria/Lebanon sanctions, extending the president's designation authority under prior Executive Order 13338, which implements the Syria Accountability and Lebanon Sovereignty Act of 2004. The April 25, 2006, executive order authorizes blocking of assets of persons implicated in the assassination of former Lebanese prime minister Rafiq Hariri and 22 others, as well as other bombings in Lebanon since October 1, 2004.[66] A UN commission investigating the assassination has preliminarily implicated members of the Syrian intelligence apparatus and other parties in Lebanon sympathetic to Syria. So far, no individuals have been named. These sanctions follow on the designation of a senior Syrian intelligence official as a blocked party under Executive Order 13338 on January 18, 2006. These actions build upon the nearly complete export ban applicable to U.S.-origin goods bound for Syria and reflect a moderate increase in pressure on the Syrian government.[67]

U.S. Initiatives and Enforcement Action with Respect to U.S. Islamic Charities

The U.S. government has taken enforcement action against a number of Islamic charities in the United States. In December 2001, the FBI raided the Holy Land Foundation's (HLF) Texas office, seizing more than $5 million in assets, along with all documents and property. OFAC designated HLF a supporter of terrorism under IEEPA and Executive Orders 13224 and 12947. The United States alleges that HLF sent millions of dollars to Hamas, a designated terrorist organization since 1995, and provided funds to families of suicide bombers. Although HLF vigorously contested the charges and challenged the asset seizure, the U.S. District Court for the District of Columbia and the U.S. Court of Appeals for the D.C. Circuit upheld the Treasury's action.[68] Litigation over HLF's frozen assets continues. Meanwhile, on December 8, 2004, a jury awarded the parents of David Boim, a U.S. citizen killed in a terrorist shooting in Israel in 1996, $52 million against HLF and other defendants because of their ties to Hamas. The award was partially based on the Treasury's allegations in the 2001 designation and the criminal indictment.[69]

On October 22, 2007, a federal judge declared a mistrial in the HLF case after prosecutors failed to convince a jury to convict five leaders of the Muslim charity on any of the charges, or even reach a verdict on many of the 197 counts, including providing material support to a foreign terrorist organization.[70] The jurors acquitted Mohammad el-Mezain, the former chairman of HLF, on virtually all the charges brought against him and deadlocked on the other charges that had been brought against four other former leaders of the charity.[71]

Jimmy Gurulé, the Undersecretary of the Treasury when the Bush administration froze the HLF's assets, described the HLF's verdict as "the continuation of what I now see as a trend of disappointing legal defeats" in terror-financing cases.[72] As David Cole, a professor at Georgetown

University Law School observed, the inability to secure convictions even for providing material support to terrorists calls into question the fairness of blocking and freezing assets of charities using secret evidence that the charities cannot see, much less rebut.[73]

On December 14, 2001, the Treasury seized and froze the assets of the Global Relief Foundation (GRF), an Islamic charity based in Illinois, pending an investigation into ties to terrorist organizations. GRF contested the action in U.S. District Court, seeking an order unblocking assets and returning seized property. The court upheld the Treasury action. GRF appealed to the U.S. Court of Appeals for the 7th Circuit. On December 31, 2002, the appeals court upheld Treasury's action as authorized under IEEPA and under the limited standard of review on appeal. GRF's assets remain frozen, although no criminal charges have been filed against the group.

On December 14, 2001, the FBI searched the Benevolence International Foundation's (BIF) offices in Illinois and New Jersey, seizing financial records and other documents and property. The FBI searched the home of Enaam Arnaout, BIF's chief executive officer, and seized personal effects belonging to him and his family. Treasury eventually put BIF on the Specially Designated Global Terrorist list. BIF filed suit and moved for a preliminary injunction, asking that the order blocking its assets be lifted and its property returned.[74] The U.S. government filed criminal charges against BIF and Arbaout, alleging that their sworn statements in support of the March 2002 motion used false material. In May 2002, the U.S. District Court for the Northern District of Illinois stayed the civil case pending the outcome of the criminal case and dismissed the civil case on its own.[75] The charges against BIF were dismissed. Arnaout plead guilty to a lesser charge of fraud, admitting he misled BIF donors to believe funds were being used for humanitarian purposes when in fact some funds were diverted to Chechen and Bosnian soldiers. He was sentenced to 11 years in prison. In 2002, OFAC denied BIF's application for a license to dispense funds earmarked for charitable causes abroad. BIF's resources have been exhausted on legal actions and the organization is permanently closed.[76] U.S. law enforcement has also acted against the Islamic American Relief Agency, Al-Haramain Islamic Foundation, and KindHearts USA.[77]

As seen by the enforcement actions described above, the U.S. government started and has maintained a comprehensive campaign against terrorists and their support networks, including the sources and conduits of terrorist financing. Investigations carried out during this campaign have revealed consistent terrorist abuse of the charitable sector through the diversion of charitable funds and services to terrorist organizations such as al Qaeda and Hamas. In response to this threat and to assist charities in adopting protective measures against terrorist abuse,[78] the Treasury released the Anti-Terrorist Financing Guidelines: Voluntary Best Practices for U.S. Based Charities ("Guidelines") in November 2002. On December 5, 2005, based on an ongoing terrorist financing dialogue with other government author-ities and the charitable sector, the Treasury revised the Guidelines to improve their usefulness and effectiveness and asked for comments.[79]

The Guidelines are intended to increase awareness in the donor and chari-table communities of the kinds of practices that charities may adopt to reduce the risk of terrorist financing or abuse, and to comply with various sanctions programs administered by OFAC. The Guidelines are voluntary and do not create, supersede, or modify current or future legal requirements applicable to U.S. persons. The Guidelines are for helping charities to develop, re-evaluate, or strengthen a risk-based approach to guard against the threat of diversion of charitable funds or exploitation of charitable activ-ity by terrorist organizations and their support networks.[80]

The Guidelines also instruct charities to maintain a risk-based approach that includes all prudent and reasonable measures that are feasible under the circumstances. They encourage charities and donors to consult the Guidelines when considering protective measures to prevent infiltration, exploitation, or abuse by terrorists. Effective internal controls that incorporate the principles and practices contained in the Guidelines can prevent the diversion of chari-table resources from their proper uses, as well as identify situations involving terrorist financing or abuse.[81]

The guidelines call for, *inter alia*, charitable organizations to comply with fundamental principles of good charitable practice and adopt practices in additional to those required by law that provide additional assurances that all assets are used exclusively for charitable or other legitimate purposes; good governance standards; financial practice and accountability standards; disclosure/transparency in governance and finances; and antiterrorist financ-ing best practices.[82] The section of the Guidelines on "Governance Account-ability and Transparency" requires charitable organizations to have independent oversight.[83] While this requirement has potential to be imple-mented, many charitable organizations in the United States and throughout the world are startups without any full-time employees. They are operated by volunteers. Requiring independent oversight of their charitable opera-tions is a non-starter for these organizations because of the inordinate expense that would be involved.

Critics say that the Treasury's broad powers to freeze and seize assets make the Guidelines mandatory in practice. The "best practices" section, they say, has suggestions and procedures that are impractical, unrealistic, and unlikely to offer charities additional protection against diversion of funds. Some critics have urged Treasury to reexamine its assumptions about the nature and role of the nonprofit sector.[84] One group criticizes the Guidelines for failing to incorporate the Principles of International Charity,[85] a proposed alternative to the earlier guidelines developed by a working group of nonprofit organiza-tions and released in late 2004 but moves in the wrong direction by adding new and onerous requirements on nonprofits.

INTERNATIONALIZATION OF CTFE EFFORTS

The bulk of the CTFE efforts has been internationalized, especially through the work of international organizations, governments, and private sector groups.

Work of International Organizations

The United Nations has taken major steps to combat the financing of international terrorism, facilitating the development of a major convention and promulgating of resolutions by the Security Council.

The 1999 Convention for the Suppression of the Financing of Terrorism, now in effect, applies to the offense of direct involvement or complicity in the international and unlawful provision or collection of funds, whether attempted or actual, with the intention or knowledge that any part of the funds may be used to carry out any of the offenses described in the Conventions listed in the Convention's Annex, or an act intended to cause death or serious bodily injury to any person not actively involved in armed conflict in order to intimidate a population, or to compel a government or an international organization to do or abstain from doing any act. The provision or collection of funds in this manner is an offense whether or not the funds are actually used to carry out the proscribed acts.

The Convention requires each signatory to take appropriate measures, in accordance with its domestic legal principles, for the detection and freezing, seizure, or forfeiture of any funds used or allocated for the purposes of committing the offenses described. (Art. 8). The offenses referred to in the Convention are deemed to be extraditable offenses (Art. 11) and signatories must establish their jurisdiction over the offenses described, make the offenses punishable by appropriate penalties, take alleged offenders into custody, prosecute or extradite alleged offenders, cooperate in preventive measures and countermeasures, and exchange information and evidence needed in related criminal proceedings. The offenses referred to in the Convention are deemed to be extraditable offenses between signatories under existing extradition treaties, and under the Convention itself.

Article 18(1) of the Convention requires signatories to subject financial institutions and other professionals to requirements of Know Your Customer and identification and filing of suspicious transaction reports. In addition, Article 18(2) requires that signatories cooperate in preventing financing of terrorism insofar as the licensing of money service businesses and measures to detect or monitor cross-border transactions. Article 18(3) requires signatories to cooperate through exchanging information with respect to terrorist financing.

On September 28, 2001, the UN Security Council adopted U.S.-sponsored Resolution 1373, requiring all member states to take action to stop the financing, training, and movement of terrorists and to cooperate in any campaign against them, including ones that involve the use of force.[86] The Resolution calls on all states to do the following: "prevent and suppress the financing of terrorists"; "freeze without delay" the resources of terrorists and terror organizations, though none were specifically cited; prohibit anyone from making funds available to terrorist organizations; suppress the recruitment of new members by terrorism organizations and eliminate their weapon supplies; "deny safe haven to those who finance, plan, support or commit terrorist acts, or provide safe havens"; "afford one another the greatest measure of assistance" in criminal investigations involving terrorism; and "prevent the movement of terrorists or terrorist groups by effective border controls" and control over travel documentation. UNSCR 1373 established a counterterrorism control committee to implement that resolution. It monitors and facilitates the provision of technical assistance in implementing the resolution.

On October 31, 2001, the FATF issued new international standards to combat terrorist financing and called on all countries of the world to adopt and implement the standards.[87] The FATF Special Recommendations on Terrorist Financing commit members to the following:

1. take immediate steps to ratify and implement the relevant UN instruments;
2. criminalize the financing of terrorism, terrorist acts, and terrorist organizations;
3. freeze and confiscate terrorist assets;
4. report suspicious transactions linked to terrorism;
5. provide the widest possible range of assistance to other countries' law enforcement and regulatory authorities for terrorist financing investigations;
6. impose anti-money-laundering requirements on alternative remittance systems;
7. strengthen customer identification measures in international and domestic wire transfers; and
8. ensure that entities, especially nonprofit organizations, cannot be misused to finance terrorism.

To achieve the swift and effective implementation of these new standards, FATF agreed to a comprehensive plan of action. On October 22, 2004, FATF added a ninth special recommendation concerning cash couriers. The ninth recommendation calls for countries to more carefully track, scrutinize, and interdict cross-border cash couriers.[88] FATF has also published international best practices on the use of cash couriers.[89]

On October 12, 2007, FATF, responding to entreaties by the United States,[90] issued guidance[91] regarding the implementation of activity-based financial prohibitions of UN Security Council 1737 concerning countering the proliferation of WMDs.[92]

The guidance, which is not binding, has the purpose of assisting jurisdictions in implementing the activity-based financial prohibitions in paragraph 6 of S/RES/1736(2006) by providing background information, definitions, and general principles that jurisdictions should consider when applying this guidance; describing information that jurisdictions should encourage their financial institutions to consider for purposes of identifying high-risk customers and transactions that may be related to activities prohibited under paragraph 6 of S/RES/1737(2006); describing enhanced scrutiny that jurisdictions should encourage their financial institutions to apply to such high-risk customers and transactions to promote compliance with paragraph 6 of S/RES/1737(2006); and describing follow-up actions that jurisdictions should encourage their financial institutions to take to address concerns about high-risk customers or transactions that may be related to activities prohibited under paragraph 6 of S/RES/1737(2006).

The guidance will be useful to industrialized countries and FATF members. However, for other countries, many of which do not even have export control authorities, the guidance will be more difficult to implement. It is likely to have the effect of making it more difficult for Iran to obtain WMD materials and require increased indirect purchases, e.g., through third countries. The guidance illustrates how the United States, in particular, has succeeded in persuading international organizations and informal groups, such as FATF, to assist in its effort to deny WMD to Iran. Simultaneously with the announcement of FATF's guidance, the U.S. government announced its own nonproliferation enforcement initiative.[93]

Regionally, a number of organizations, such as the European Union and the Organization of American States, have adopted proactive programs to help combat terrorist financing, mostly interacting with and trying to implement regionally the UN and FATF measures. FATF has continued to expand, approving two new FATF-style regional bodies (FSRBS) in 2004: the Eurasian Group (October 6, 2004) and the Middle East and North African FATF (November 9, 2004).[94] There are now eight FSRBS, all of which are working to implement FATF's recommendations to combat the financing of terrorism.

Internationalization of Laws and Institutions

Through the use of international organizations, hard law in the way of international treaties, such as the UN Suppression of Terrorist Financing Convention, and soft law in the way of UNSCR and FATF special recommendations, and institutions to implement the new legal obligations, FIUs, the Egmont Group (an informal organization to which FIUs obtain legitimacy and source of support), and the UN Counter-Terrorism Committee, CTFE is becoming increasingly internationalized.

WORK OF THE PRIVATE SECTOR

The adjustments by the banking and financial sectors in their due diligence for anti-money-laundering policies to accommodate the demands to prevent financing of terrorism are illustrated by the Wolfsberg Statement on the Suppression of the Financing of Terrorism. In October 2000, in the wake of revelations of abuse of private banking operations for money laundering purposes, 12 multinational banks issued Global Guidelines for Private Banking Principles. Subsequent to the September 11, 2001, incidents, the Wolfsberg Group issued a Statement on the Suppression of the Financing of Terrorism.

The statement includes the Know Your Customer policy. It provides that the proper identification of customers can improve the efficacy of searches against lists of known or suspected terrorists issued by competent authorities having jurisdictions over relevant financial institutions ("applicable lists"). In addition to the continued application of existing customer identification, acceptance, and due diligence procedure, the Wolfsberg Group is committed to (1) implementing procedures for consulting applicable lists and taking reasonable and practicable steps to determine whether a person involved in a prospective or existing business relationship appears on such a list; (2) reporting to the relevant authorities matches from lists of known or suspected terrorists or terrorist organizations consistent with applicable laws or regulations regarding the disclosure of customer information; (3) exploring with governmental agencies ways of improving information exchange within and between jurisdictions; and (4) exploring ways of improving maintenance of customer information.

The Wolfsberg Group is committed to applying enhanced and appropriate due diligence in relation to those of their customers engaged in sectors and activities that the competent authorities have identified as being widely used for the financing of terrorism, such as the underground banking business and alternative remittance systems. This will include the adoption, to the extent not already in place, of specific policies and procedures on acceptance of business from customers engaged in such sectors or activities, and increased monitoring of activity of customers who meet the relevant acceptance criteria. In particular, the Wolfsberg Group is committed to restricting their business relationships with certain problematic businesses, including those used as a conduit to launder the proceeds of terrorism.

The Wolfsberg Group is also committed to the continued application of existing monitoring procedures for identifying unusual or suspicious transactions. In particular, the Wolfsberg Group is committed to (1) exercising heightened scrutiny with respect to customers engaged in sectors identified by competent authorities as being widely used for the financing of terrorism; (2) monitoring account and transactional activity against lists generated by competent authorities of known or suspected terrorists or terrorist organizations; and (3) working with governments and agencies to recognize patterns and trends in terrorism financing.

The Wolfsberg Group also proposes revised policies for enhanced global cooperation. The following areas have been identified for discussion with government agencies. The idea is to enhance the contributions financial institutions can make, and particularly:

- the provision of official lists of suspected terrorists and terrorist organizations on a globally coordinated basis by the relevant competent authority in each jurisdiction;

- the inclusion of appropriate details and information in official lists to assist financial institutions in efficient and timely searches of their customer bases (for individuals, this requires the date and place of birth, passport or identity card number; for corporations, this involves the place of incorporation or establishment, details of principals, to the extent possible, reason(s) for inclusion on the list, and geographical information, such as the date and time of transactions);

- the provision by governments of prompt feedback to financial institutions on reports made following circulation of official lists;

- the provision of meaningful information in relation to patterns, techniques, and mechanisms used in the financing of terrorism to assist with monitoring procedures; and

- the development of guidelines on appropriate levels of heightened scrutiny in relation to sectors or activities by competent authorities as being widely used for terrorist financing.

ANALYSIS AND RECOMMENDATIONS

The creation of the Department of Homeland Security has required large-scale reorganization of many of the agencies and subagencies (e.g., Treasury, Justice, Alcohol Firearms and Tobacco, Customs Service, Border Patrol, Immigration and Naturalization Service) that are on the frontline of terrorist financing. The initial impact is to create some uncertainty and delay for terrorist financing, especially in the context of uncertainty and delays about U.S. budgetary allocations for these agencies. Indeed, U.S. budgetary and fiscal deficits put a continuing cloud over future resources.

Despite all the creation of new groups to undertake terrorist financing, the ability of the different agencies and subagencies to effectively communicate and efficiently divide tasks is unknown and will remain so for the short term.

The creation of the EOTF/FC responds to criticisms and suggestions of outside groups that the U.S. government's efforts towards terrorist financial enforcement need to be more centralized and at a higher level.[95] The new office also responds to fill the void created by the transfer of institutions to the Department of Homeland Security. In that regard, it remains to be seen whether the U.S. government is creating surplus agencies that will be able to effectively cooperate with each other. In particular, in the actual operation of anti-money-laundering, financial crime, and terrorist financing, the U.S. government sometimes has multiple agencies investigating the same people. The overlapping sometimes shows itself when undercover agents track and lure each other, not knowing that each are undercover agents until sometimes they tragically have a violent encounter. Sometimes foreign governments complain that they receive multiple requests for mutual assistance about the same matter from multiple U.S. agencies. A major issue will be the extent to which the allocation of resources and prioritization of combating terrorist financing will diminish other financial crimes, including anti-money-laundering. In this regard, the impact of the new efforts on the private sector will be important to monitor. The USA PATRIOT Act has expanded significantly the enlisting of the private sector in the efforts to combat terrorist financial and simultaneously anti-money-laundering at a time when the U.S. economy and foreign direct investment have declined.

Another trend to monitor will be whether the U.S. government's reorganization efforts will have any impact internationally. Already in the last five years, the international community has tried to digest the formation on a national level of FIUs and their networking through the Egmont Group. With the technical and financial assistance of international financial institutions, many countries are still trying to adopt legislation and establish, train, and practically empower FIUs to investigate financial crimes, especially with respect to political corruption, transnational organized crime, and other offenses, including terrorist financing.

Indeed the national governments and the international community are challenged to be able to design, establish, and equip new institutions and mechanisms as fast as criminals who operate in a borderless world and use modern technology to act.

Developing proper infrastructure to undertake counterterrorism financing enforcement requires law enforcement officials equipped with experience in financial enforcement and knowledgeable about terrorism. Excellent links with counterpart foreign law enforcement officials are also useful. Successful counterterrorist financial action requires excellent relationships and cooperation with the private sector. Most countries have an FIU for conducting anti-money-laundering investigations and prosecutions. In most countries, CTFE will be linked to FIUs.

The designation lists of persons and entities suspected to be associated with terrorism, which the U.S. government and various international organizations maintain, are very burdensome and costly for both governments and the private sector to implement, especially because they change daily.[96] Among the problems are that the information is often vague, sometimes inaccurate or out of date, and includes so many names that are common or sound like names of additional persons that the lists' enforcement and effectiveness are weakened. This process often slows everything down and does not seem to have produced any noteworthy counterterrorism assistance.[97]

Countries are overwhelmed and overburdened by such a regulatory over-load, which covers not only these and related terrorism standards, but also regional and UN conventions, such as those against transnational organized crime and corruption. Indeed, in the United States alone financial institutions must add to their lists "Narcotic Kingpins"[98] and soon Internet gaming entities,[99] even though the World Trade Organization has declared the U.S. laws illegal. As the U.S. government persuaded FATF to add to terrorism financing WMD financing, this illustrates the continual onslaught of counterterrorism financial regulatory requirements. The implementation of all such rules and, in many instances, the fundamental legal and institutional reforms they may entail, necessitates technical and other assistance from developed countries. Yet, the capacity for quality technical assistance does not exist in actuality, either in developing or developed countries.[100]

Some have suggested the need for the United States to lead international efforts and establish a specialized international organization dedicated solely to combat terrorist financing. The organization would undertake responsibility for various counterterrorist financing initiatives undertaken by the FATF since September 11, 2001, and support and reinforce the activities of the UN Counter-Terrorism Committee that it has undertaken.[101]

The bulk of efforts to counterterrorist financing depend on the ability of the United States to lead international coalitions in international organizations. The United States will need to strengthen substantially its relationships with key allies if it is to achieve proactive implementation of multilateral CTFE. Given the number of new recruits and the low-scale financing of the latest terrorist attacks, and the expenditure of U.S. resources already on counterterrorism efforts, true multilateralization of CTFE will be required to stop potential safe harbors for certain groups.

If private sector groups can establish best practices internationally for dealing with terrorist financing, like the Wolfsberg Group has done, then the private sector will find it easier to implement new rules and will have a level playing field. The U.S. government may want to encourage such groups through the Bank Secrecy Act Task Force and other government-private sector fora.

To the extent the U.S. government imposes and/or enforces terrorist financing laws much stricter than do other countries, the United States will undermine its economic security. Indeed, current statistics on foreign direct investment and tourism to the United States reflect a sharp downturn in both of these sectors, in part due to counterterrorism controls.

The global CTFE regime needs to be strengthened through development of a systematic research program using economic tools, starting with a more sophisticated assessment of the costs of the CTFE regime. Another important research-related activity is the creation of a database of existing cases that provides a detailed description of the prices, methods, and predicate crimes involved. This would represent a first step in analyzing the existence and mechanisms of the market for CFTE services. An elaborate system of laws and regulations that affects the lives of millions of people and imposes several billion dollars in costs annually on the U.S. public has been based to a substantial degree on untested assumptions that do not look particularly plausible. Both the U.S. Congress and FATF operate normally by postulating problems based on anecdotal information and then legislating based on such information and whether it is likely to fly with political constituents. The constituent base of the FATF is narrow: the law enforcement and regulatory agencies of about 30 countries. While the failure to systematically evaluate the CFTE regime has not as yet impeded its expansion either in the United States or elsewhere, at some stage it should and most likely will. The system needs careful examination before any further expansion is actively contemplated.[102]

To the extent prospective acts of terror are planned by new recruits without international criminal records and creative, small-scale financing is used to conduct unorthodox acts in which terrorists are willing to sacrifice their own lives, the United States and any other country will have difficulty identifying and stopping the financing of terrorist acts. In this regard, it must be acknowledged that counterterrorism financial enforcement has strict limits.

Another challenge is that to the extent U.S. post-9/11 legislation and initiatives are over-inclusive in efforts to end terrorist financing, they also block benign use of funds. For instance, to the extent the laws and initiatives target hawalas and hawaladars, they tend to have a negative impact on benign use while not deterring the malign.[103] The U.S. counterterrorism financial initiatives are so strict that they sometimes affect true humanitarian aid at a time when vulnerable areas dealing with civil strife are suffering from poverty, unemployment, and the massive destruction of infrastructure. The result is counterproductive: the initiatives exacerbate the hopelessness, contributing to an environment that breeds new terrorists.

6

Border Security

Bruce Zagaris

In the aftermath of the terrorist attacks of September 11, 2001, the United States has made significant changes in its border security. This chapter outlines the salient changes and discusses the various potential initiatives that are pending and may occur.[1]

The topic of border security potentially embraces many diverse topics. The border is where domestic law enforcement activities, such as apprehending fugitive criminals and ordinary policing—becomes internationalized. It constitutes the dividing line between sovereign jurisdictions with distinct regulations, law enforcement systems and political interests, constituencies and upheavals. For criminals, borders often provide an advantage. On the one hand, there is a business advantage: they may be able to bring into the United States illegal migrants and contraband in the way of drugs. They can return with guns, money, and precursor chemicals. On the other hand, they have an advantage because it is often difficult for law enforcement on each side to cooperate effectively, enabling them to successfully engage in criminal business.[2]

Terrorists are one type of modern group who want to take advantage of borders to commit spectacular crimes and bring terror to the lives of persons in a country, such as the United States. This chapter discusses border security from the perspective of U.S. counterterrorism policy.

The first section discusses threats to the U.S. border due to transportation-related vulnerabilities, especially those due to aviation issues. The second section deals with threats from immigrants and gaps in the nonimmigrant visa process. The third section addresses threats from terrorists attacks from containerized cargo. The fourth section discusses fortifying the infrastructure to U.S. land and other borders. The fifth and final section provides some analysis.

TRANSPORTATION-RELATED VULNERABILITIES

Because the attacks of September 11, 2001, originated from hijacking regularly scheduled airliners and flying them into the World Trade Center and the Pentagon, many of the border security initiatives have focused on preventing terrorist attacks from airlines and airplanes. The challenge is great because the U.S. transportation system is huge. In an open society the United States cannot possibly secure fully against terrorist attacks, especially since there are hundreds of commercial airports, thousands of planes, and tens of thousands of daily flights carrying more than half a billion passengers yearly. The 9/11 Commission recommended that the U.S. government identify and evaluate the transportation assets that require protection, establish risk-based priorities to defend them, select the most practical and cost-effective means of doing so, and then develop a plan, budget, and funding to implement the effort. In measuring effectiveness, the commission recognized that perfection is not attainable. However, terrorists should perceive that potential targets are defended, so that they may be deterred by a significant potential of failure.[3]

Progress in Minimizing Aviation-Related Vulnerabilities and Enhancing Layers of Defense Directly Exploited by Terrorist Hijackers

Since 9/11 the United States has made significant progress to eliminate risks of terrorist attacks upon commercial aviation. U.S. agencies have reduced aviation-related vulnerabilities and improved the layers of defense that terrorist hijackers previously exploited. The United States has developed better airline passenger screening procedures to identify and prevent known or suspected terrorists, weapons, and explosives from being brought onto aircraft. Nevertheless, threats remain (i.e., from bringing liquid explosives aboard aircraft).[4]

Creation of TSA

To strengthen transportation security, on November 19, 2001, Congress enacted the Aviation and Transportation Security Act (ATSA).[5] The law's primary goal was to strengthen the security of the country's aviation system. The ATSA established the Transportation Security Administration (TSA) as an agency within the Department of Transportation with responsibility for securing all modes of transportation, including aviation.[6] As part of this responsibility, TSA oversees security operations at the more than 400 commercial airports in the United States, including passenger and checked baggage screening operations. The ATSA had various requirements with deadlines for TSA to implement in order to strengthen the various aviation layers of defense. For instance, ATSA required TSA to create a federal workforce to assume the job of conducting passenger and checked baggage screening from air carriers at commercial airports. Before this work was done by private companies under contract to the airlines. The law also gave TSA regulatory authority over all transportation modes.

Homeland Security Act of 2002 Consolidated Most Federal Agencies Dealing with Border Security

The Homeland Security Act of 2002 consolidated most federal agencies charged with providing homeland security, including securing the borders of the United States into the newly formed Department of Homeland Security (DHS), which was established to improve, among other things, coordination, communication, and information sharing among the multiple federal agencies responsible for protecting the homeland.[7]

Congress enacted legislation to strengthen various aspects of border security. For instance, the Homeland Security Act confers on DHS exclusive authority to issue regulations on, administer, and enforce the Immigration and Nationality Act and all other immigration and nationality laws relating to the functions of U.S. consular officers with respect to the granting or denial of visas. The Homeland Security Act authorized DHS, among other things, to assign employees to U.S. embassies and consulates to provide expert advice and training to consular officers regarding specific threats concerning the visa process.[8]

Better Airline Passenger Screening

After 9/11, President Bush issued 16 homeland security presidential directives (HSPD), providing additional guidance related to the mission areas outlined in the National Strategy. For instance, HSPD-6 concerns policy related to the consolidation of the government's approach to terrorism screening and provides for the appropriate and lawful use of terrorist information in the screening process. HSPD-11 sets forth the U.S. policy with respect to comprehensive terrorist-related screening procedures through detecting, identifying, tracking, and indicting people and cargo that pose a threat to homeland security, among other things.[9]

As mentioned above, by November 2002 TSA assumed responsibility for passenger checkpoint and baggage screening.

Better Prescreening Procedures

In December 2004, Congress enacted the Intelligence Reform and Terrorism Prevention Act of 2004,[10] containing provisions designed to address many of the transportation and border security vulnerabilities identified and recommendations made by the 9/11 Commission. For instance, it required that TSA develop a passenger prescreening system that would compare passenger information for domestic flights to government watch list information, a function that air carriers performed at the time and still perform.[11]

Prescreening Identity-Matching Process and Problems of Customs and Border Patrol

At the direction of the president and Congress, DHS and other federal agencies have acted to develop better airline passenger screening procedures which help to identify and prevent known or suspected terrorists, weapons, and explosives from being allowed onto aircraft. For instance, since 9/11, domestic airline passenger prescreening procedures, whereby passengers who may pose a security risk are identified before boarding aircraft, have been strengthened through an identity-matching process that compares prospective passengers' names against an expanded list of terrorist suspects taken from a consolidated terrorist watch list. The prescreening process has been buttressed by requiring certain passengers to undergo greater scrutiny prior to boarding.[12]

TSA has not yet carried out a congressional requirement that it assume responsibility for the passenger identity-matching process from domestic air carriers, in part to improve accuracy in the matching process and to end disclosure of sensitive information on possible terrorists to air carriers. Passengers on international flights departing from or traveling to the United States undergo prescreening by DHS's U.S. Customs and Border Protection (CBP). This process has challenges because the flights take off before the CBP completes the passenger identity-matching process. Hence, the flights are vulnerable to a terrorist takeover and other risks. CBP is working to address the problem. The Government Accountability Office (GAO) has recommended that DHS make key policy and technical decisions required to more fully coordinate CBP's international prescreening program with TSA's prospective domestic prescreening program.[13]

Efforts to Improve Security of Other Transportation Modes

In addition to improving the security of commercial airlines, priority federal attention was directed towards improving the security of other transportation modes, including aviation, passenger rail, maritime, and surface transportation in order to better identify critical assets and to prioritize and allocate finite security resources for protecting these assets. DHS and other federal agencies are still working on coordinating security-related priorities and activities with domestic and international stakeholders and acting to enhance such cooperation. For instance, DHS and other federal agencies are evaluating foreign passenger rail security practices not currently in use in the United States. TSA is working with foreign counterparts to share and ascertain best practices.[14]

The U.S. government has devoted significant efforts to improve the security of transportation modes other than aviation. In doing so, DHS has adopted a risk management approach to identify and prioritize transportation security needs and investments. The following section discusses efforts to strengthen the security of seaports, the rail system, and the highways.

Congress and Federal Agencies Are Addressing Security Needs of Transportation Modes in the Post-9/11 Era Through Legislation, Risk Management, and Enhanced Cooperation with Domestic and International Partners

Congress, the 9/11 Commission, federal agencies, and others have recognized the need to develop strategies and take actions to protect against and prepare for terrorist attacks on critical parts of the U.S. transportation system other than aviation, which are also considered vulnerable to attack. These areas include passenger rail and the maritime industry—both considered vital components of the U.S. economy—as well as the country's highway system.[15]

Multiple Federal Agencies Have Taken Actions to Enhance Passenger Rail Security

A number of federal agencies have started acting to enhance security for the passenger rail sector. The U.S. passenger rail sector is an important component of the country's transportation infrastructure, with railways, subway, commuter rail systems, among others, carrying more than 11 million passengers each weekday. The characteristics of some rail systems—such as high ridership, expensive infrastructure, economic importance, and location in large metropolitan areas or tourist destinations—make them attractive targets for terrorists because of the potential for mass casualties and economic damage and disruption.[16]

In response to the commuter rail attacks in Madrid, and federal intelligence on potential threats against U.S. passenger rail systems, TSA issued security directives for rail operators in May 2004. The directives required rail operators to implement a number of general security measures, such as conducting frequent inspections of stations, terminals, and other assets, or utilizing canine explosive detection teams, if available. Since these directives were issued with limited input and review by rail industry and federal stakeholders, they may not provide the industry with baseline security standards based on industry best practices. No permanent rail security standards have been issued. Rail operators lack clear guidance. The GAO has recommended that, to ensure future rail security directives are enforceable, transparent, and feasible, TSA should collaborate with the Department of Transportation and the passenger rail industry to develop rail security standards that reflect industry best practices and that can be measured, monitored, and enforced.[17]

Federal Agencies and Stakeholders Have Taken Steps to Identify and Reduce Vulnerabilities and Enhance Security at Seaports

The maritime sector is a vital area of transportation. Since 9/11 the 361 seaports of the United States have been increasingly viewed as potential targets for future terrorist attacks because they are sprawling, interwoven with complex transportation networks, close to crowded metropolitan areas, and are easily accessible. Ports have a number of specific facilities that terrorists could target. For instance, military vessels and bases, cruise ships, passenger ferries, terminals, locks, and dams, factories, office buildings, power plants, refineries, sports complexes, and other critical infrastructure. The large cargo volumes transiting seaports, such as containers destined for further shipment by other modes of transportation such as rail or truck, also represent a potential conduit for terrorists to smuggle weapons of mass destruction or other dangerous materials into the United States. The potential consequences of the risks created by these vulnerabilities are significant as the U.S. economy relies on an expeditious flow of goods through seaports.[18]

After 9/11, federal agencies such as the Coast Guard, CBP, and TSA have been responsible for making seaports more secure, such as monitoring vessel traffic or inspecting cargo and containers, and procuring new assets such as aircraft and cutters to conduct patrols and respond to threats. In addition to these federal agencies, seaport stakeholders in the private sector and at the state and local levels of government have acted to improve the security of seaports, such as conducting security assessments of infrastructure and vessels operated within the seaports and developing security plans to protect against a terrorist attack. The actions are directed at three types of protections: (1) identifying and reducing vulnerabilities of the facilities, infrastructure, and vessels operating in seaports; (2) security of the cargo and commerce flowing through seaports; and (3) developing greater maritime domain awareness through enhanced intelligence, information-sharing capabilities, and assets and technologies.[19]

New information-sharing networks and command structures have been established to permit more coordinated responses and increased awareness of activities in the maritime domain.

TSA Has Identified the Nation's Highway Infrastructure and Commercial Vehicles as Vulnerable for Terrorist Attacks

Concerns exist about the U.S. highway infrastructure, which facilitates transportation for a vast network of interstate and intrastate trucking companies and others. Vehicles and highway infrastructure play an essential role in the movement of goods, services, and people, yet more work is required to assess or address vulnerabilities to acts of terrorism that may exist in these systems. Among targets, attackers can target bridges, tunnels, and trucks, including using hazardous material trucks as weapons. The diversity of the trucking industry poses challenges in effectively integrating security in both large, complex trucking operations and smaller owner/operator businesses.[20]

Agencies Have Begun Using a Risk Management Approach to Identify and Prioritize Transportation Security Needs and Investments

The predominant approach to ensure that resources are assigned and appropriate strategies are selected to address the greatest risk is through risk management. This approach requires defining and reducing risk. The risk management approach is a systematic process for analyzing threats and vulnerabilities, together with the criticality or the relative importance of the assets involved. The process involves a series of analytical and managerial steps, basically sequential, that can be used to assess vulnerabilities, determine their criticality, determine the relative importance of the assets being considered, determine the threats to the assets, and assess alternatives for reducing the risks.[21]

Analysis

The TSA has improved passenger and baggage screening significantly since 9/11. Air cargo in the underbody of the plane is still vulnerable, since the system used to target what is inspected is problematic. The tools and the resources to determine what is inspected do not exist.[22]

STRENGTHENING THE NONIMMIGRANT VISA PROCESS

The U.S. visa process allowed terrorists to exploit its system and gain extended stays within the United States. Recognizing this defect, terrorists concentrated on ways to exploit legal entry into the United States, whether by lying on entry forms or using manipulated or fraudulent documents.

All but two of the nonpilots involved in the 9/11 attacks were admitted as tourists and were granted automatic six-month stays. This allowed them to maintain a legal immigration status through the end of the 9/11 attacks. Policymakers have advocated that the United States examine the process by which length of stay is determined to ensure that inspectors grant an appropriate time period to those seeking to enter the country.

All of the 9/11 attackers entered the United States through a legitimate port of entry, passing through border security 68 times prior to carrying out their deadly attacks. These border encounters are the time to detect and arrest those who use document fraud and manipulation to enter. Immigration inspectors must receive periodic updated training about document manipulation, fraud, and other illicit methods used to enter out country because these inspectors are in the best position to stop those who come to the United States to perpetrate terror.[23]

All 15 of the visa applications filed by the 9/11 hijackers contained significant inaccuracies or omissions that should have prevented them from obtaining visas, and only two of the hijackers were personally interviewed by the Department of State. The remainder were simply approved sight unseen.[24]

The 9/11 Commission staff report added that Immigration and Naturalization Service (INS) inspectors were inadequately trained in the essentials of identifying terrorists, that they had received no counterterrorism training, were remarkably undertrained in conducting primary inspection and in recognizing fraudulent documents, and that they were not taught the content and value of the numerous databases at their disposal, which might have helped them identify members of the 9/11 terrorist group.[25]

Visa Waiver Program

Before 9/11, U.S. visa operations concentrated primarily on illegal immigration concerns, such as whether applicants sought to reside and work illegally in the United States. After 9/11, Congress, the Department of State, and DHS implemented several measures to improve the entire visa process as a mechanism to combat terrorism. These agencies, especially State, implemented new policies and programs to improve visa security, improve applicant screening, provide counterterrorism training to consular officials who administer the visa process overseas, and help prevent the fraudulent use of visas for those seeking to gain entry to the country. For instance, U.S. agencies have expanded fivefold since 2001 the number of records available to check the identities of visa applicants against the consolidated terrorist watch list and criminal records. The state department also has taken steps to mitigate the potential for visa fraud at consular posts by undertaking visa fraud investigators to U.S. embassies and consulates and conducting more in-depth analysis of the visa information collected by consulates to identify patterns that may indicate fraud, among other things. State department and DHS officials have also started reviewing potential security risks in immigrant visas.[26]

Intensification by DHS of Oversight of Visa Waiver Countries to Ensure Compliance with Programs Statutory Requirements

The Visa Waiver Program, which enables citizens from 27 countries to travel to the United States without a visa for business or tourism for 90 days, has a number of security risks. The program has inherent security, law enforcement, and illegal immigration risks. For instance, visa waiver travelers are not subject to the same degree of screening as travelers who must first obtain visas. Convicted 9/11 terrorist Zacarias Moussaoui is among those who carried a passport issued by a visa waiver country (France).[27]

Lost and Stolen Passports

Terrorists, criminals, and others seeking to hide their identity have utilized lost and stolen passports from visa waiver countries to gain entry into the U.S. Congress, DHS's Office of Inspector General, and the GAO have helped DHS to address these challenges in the context of strengthening border security. Sine 2003, DHS has intensified its oversight of visa waiver countries to ensure they comply with the program's statutory requirements.[28]

More Human Resources and Training for CBP Officers in Fraudulent Document Detention

A critical element to proper visa implementation to prevent the entry of potential terrorists requires more and better trained human resources. DHS and State have focused their available resources and high priority initiatives in high threat areas of the world. DHS visa security officers in Saudi Arabia reviewed over 20,000 visa applications last fiscal year. In 2004, DHS deployed a permanent delegation to two locations in that country, half of whom are trained in the local language. In 2005, DHS deployed visa security officers to five additional locations, consistent with its threat-based approach.

Boots on the ground also applies to U.S. border patrol and various border initiatives that the United States is employing such as expedited removal at parts of the Southern border, deployment of additional border patrol agents, and the implementation of the Arizona Border Control Initiative or the ABC Initiative.[29]

A survey by the American Federation of Government Employees in the summer of 2004 found that a majority of the 500 custom and border protection officers say they do not have the tools, training, or support to stop potential terrorists from entering the country. According to a 9/11 Commission staff report, al Qaeda altered passports in four ways: by substituting photos, by adding false entry/exist stamps, by removing visas and bleaching stamps, and by counterfeiting passports and substituting pages.[30]

To mitigate the misuse of lost or stolen passports, DHS provides additional training for CBP officers in fraudulent document detection. On October 26, 2005, passports of visa waiver travelers issued on or after that date, and until October 25, 2006, had to have a digital photograph as an antifraud measure. Passports issued to visa waiver travelers after October 25, 2006 must be electronic (e-passports). GAO has recommended that DHS take additional steps to mitigate the risks from lost or stolen passports, including requiring all visa waiver countries to provide the United States and Interpol with data on lost or stolen issued passports as well as blank passports. Some visa waiver countries have been reluctant to provide this information. The United States must find ways to address these and other challenges since many countries are actively seeking admission into the program.[31]

CBP now recruits, hires, and trains its enforcement officers at the ports of entry (POE) as CBP officers. New officers begin their careers with a 20-day training and orientation program at a new duty post, followed by 73 days of training at the CBP Academy. After graduation, the new officers return to their duty posts and begin a formal program that includes 37 distinct modules of specific training and supervised application in the workplace of the training and skills that have been acquired. CBP is very active in preparing its frontline officers to do their jobs properly.[32]

US-VISIT

A border security initiative known as US-VISIT (U.S. Visitor and Immigrant Status Indicator Technology) is designed to serve as a comprehensive system for integrating data on the entry and exits and verifying the identity of most foreign travelers coming through the U.S. air, land, and sea ports, to mitigate the likelihood that terrorists or criminals can enter or exit, at will, or that persons stay longer than authorized.

The US-VISIT faces operational and strategic challenges. DHS has achieved progress installing the entry portion of this system, which permits CBP border officers to verify travelers' identities by, among other things, scanning and comparing digital fingerprints and photographs and checking biographic information against various federal databases, including the consolidated terrorist watch list.

The goal for the US-VISIT program is to record the entry, reentry, and exit of travelers, including those who surpass their authorized stay—has not been met. The DHS has found that an exit capability using comparable biometric scanning tools is not yet technologically feasible. It would be very costly and is not likely to be developed or deployed for up to 10 years.

The GAO has recommended that DHS should report to Congress describing how a comprehensive biometrically based entry and exit system would work in order to achieve US-VISIT's intended goals.

Agencies need to address other border-related vulnerabilities as well. In this connection, CBP and the Departments of Energy, Defense, and State have acted to combat the smuggling of hazardous materials and cargo at POE through use of better radiation detection equipment and interagency coordination, among other things.[33]

Information Sharing among Agencies

One of the most import strategic challenges involves improving the sharing of information related to terrorism. The 9/11 Commission observed that information collected about terrorist suspects by the CIA and FBI at the time of the attacks was not shared with the Federal Aviation Administration. The GAO designated information sharing for homeland security as a government wide high-risk area in 2005. Hence, the GAO and 9/11 Commission recommended information sharing as an area that needs urgent attention and transformation to ensure that appropriate government agencies function in the most economical, efficient, and effective manner possible.

Congress and federal agencies have acted to improve information sharing across the federal government and in conjunction with state and local governments and law enforcement agencies. They have created a consolidated terrorism watch list, as aforementioned. It has been more broadly shared among key federal agencies to provide information that can be used to identify terrorists traveling to and within the United States. Furthermore, the FBI has increased its field-based joint terrorism task forces that bring together personnel from all levels of government to combat terrorism by sharing information and resources. DHS has implemented homeland security information networks to share relevant information with states and localities. Congress has required establishing an information sharing environment that would combine policies, procedures, and technologies that link people, systems, and information among all appropriate federal, state, local and tribal entities and the private sector.[34]

The Intelligence Reform Act Congress passed in December 2004 calls for a strategy to combine travel intelligence, operations, and law enforcement in a joint effort to intercept terrorists and identify those who facilitate their travel. It also requires improvements in technology and training to assist border, consular, and immigration in this mission.[35]

New Legislation on Enhanced Technology at Borders

New legislation was enacted that has provisions affecting a major border security that had started prior to 9/11—a system for integrating data on the entry and exit of certain foreign nationals into and out of the United States, now known as US-VISIT.

Utilization of Biometric Technology and Development of Tamper-Resistant Documents Readable at Ports of Entry

The USA PATRIOT Act provides that, in developing the integrated entry and exist data system (US-VISIT), the Attorney General (now Secretary of Homeland Security) and Secretary of State must focus especially on the utilization of biometric technology (such as digital fingerprints) and the development of tamper-resistant documents readable at POE (either a land, air, or sea border crossing associated with inspection and admission of certain foreign nationals).[36]

Establishment of a Database of the Arrival and Departure Data from Machine-Readable Visas, Passport, and Other Travel and Entry Documents Possessed by Aliens and the Interoperabilty of All Security Databases

The Enhanced Border Security and Visa Entry Reform Act of 2002[37] required that, in developing the integrated entry and exit data system for POE, the Attorney General (now Secretary of Homeland Security) and Secretary of State implement, fund, and use the technology standard that was required to be developed under the USA PATRIOT Act at U.S. POE and at consular posts abroad. The law also required the establishment of a database containing the arrival and departure data from machine-readable visas, passports, and other travel and entry documents possessed by aliens and the interoperability of all security databases relevant to making determinations of admissibility under section 212 of the Immigration and Nationality Act.[38]

Development of a Passenger Prescreening System That Would Compare Passenger Information for Domestic Flights to Government Watch List Information

In December 2004, the U.S. Congress enacted the Intelligence Reform and Terrorism Prevention Act, containing provisions designed to address many of the transportation and border security vulnerabilities identified and recommendations made by the 9/11 Commission. It included provisions designed to improve aviation security, information sharing, visa issuance, border security, and other areas. The law required that TSA develop a passenger prescreening system that would compare passenger information for domestic flights to government watch list information. The act also required the development of risk-based priorities across all transportation modes and a strategic plan describing roles and missions concerning transportation security for encouraging private sector cooperation and participation in the implementation of such a plan. The law required DHS to develop and submit to congress a plan for full implementation of the US-VISIT as an automated biometric entry and exit data system and required the collection of biometric exit data for all individuals required to provide biometric entry data.[39]

Analysis

The border security staff identified several deficiencies in the training of border personnel and several defects with regard to U.S. visa policy. The report noted that U.S. immigration inspectors, now called CBP officers, received little counterterrorism and behavioral science training, no cultural training, and rarely received follow-up training.[40]

The United States has made a number of significant improvements since 9/11 but no one would argue that the United States has adequately repaired the broken system of intelligence, border security, and immigration. Better information sharing and training are essential to enable the U.S. frontline officers and inspectors to detect and intercept potential terrorists before they cause harm. Critical intelligence on terrorist travel indicators is still not being declassified and distributed to frontline officers on a timely basis.

The Attempt of a Comprehensive Immigration Reform

Comprehensive Immigration Reform

Various attempts have been made in the past few years to restructure immigration laws. Naturally, some of the proposed legislation touched on the issue of border security and counterterrorism. The Comprehensive Immigration Reform Act 2006[41] contained several provisions on the enforcement of border security, providing, *inter alia*, the increase of personnel such as border patrol agents. However, it also introduced controversial immigration changes, allowing for longtime illegal aliens to gain citizenship and also establishing a new type of visa program (so-called "blue card"), giving employers the opportunity to bring guest workers to the United States. On May 25, 2006, the bill was passed in the Senate, but it was not passed in the House.

The Comprehensive Immigration Reform Act 2007[42] would have also increased enforcement on the southern border of the United States, providing for funding of 300 miles of fencing along the border with Mexico. Moreover, this act would have allowed for an additional 20,000 border patrol agents and for extra technologic equipment such as unmanned vehicles. This bill, however, was not passed by the Senate; the last vote on cloture failing by 46–53 on June 28, 2007. Mexican President Felipe Calderón criticized the United States for rejecting the immigration reform.[43]

While these bills did not provide for specific counterterrorism measures, they would have strengthened the enforcement component of border security, especially on the border with Mexico.

Pending Legislation

The Immigration Enforcement and Border Security Act of 2007[44] (IEBSA) is currently on the Senate's calendar. It provides, *inter alia*, for 300 miles of vehicle barriers and 700 miles of fencing to be installed on the border with Mexico. Furthermore, the IEBSA prescribes that 105 radar and ground-based camera towers be installed as well as four unmanned aerial vehicles (UAVs); 500 more duty officers would be employed by U.S. CBP; and 2,400 border patrol agents would be working at the border.

Border Security and Access of Foreign Scientists and Engineers to the United States

Need for Foreign Scientists in the United States

In the past, the United States has greatly benefitted from the many foreign scientists and engineers who came to the country in order to study and work. For instance, of the Nobel Prizes awarded to U.S. citizens between 1990 and 2004, over one-third was awarded to foreign-born U.S. nationals.[45] The industry and the economy depend on the technological progress owed to, among others, the foreign scientists in the United States.

Problems Owing to Counterterrorism Measures

Foreigners who decide to study, research, or work in the United States are exposed to the measures implemented after 9/11, as mentioned above. After the attacks of 9/11, changes in U.S. immigration laws made it mandatory for all visa applicants to personally appear at a U.S. embassy or consulate for an interview before obtaining a visa to enter the United States. Also, biometric data is collected from each applicant in order to verify the individual's identity upon entry to the United States. In addition to the new measures adopted, already existing measures were applied to a greater number of applicants.[46] For example, the process known as "Visas Mantis" was applied to a greater number of cases[47] and substantially delayed entry for foreign scientists and engineers to the United States.[48] According to this process, visa applications for persons to study or work in certain sensitive scientific and technical fields are subject to an interagency clearance in Washington, D.C. This clearance process is used in order to protect against illegal technology transfers.

As a result of these and other changes, a backlog was created, which again resulted in increased delays in issuing the visas.[49] In addition to the increase in time, there was also increased uncertainty as to whether the visa would be issued at all. These post 9/11 changes in the processing of visa applications have had repercussions on the number of students seeking to enter the United States. The year 2004 marked the third consecutive year of decline in full-time enrollments of foreign graduate students in U.S. science and engineering programs.[50] Between the years 2001 and 2004, enrollment in these programs by foreign students dropped by 20 percent.[51] While other changes, such as the fingerprinting and photographing of visitors at the POE to the United States, have not brought about delays, they have contributed to a negative perception of U.S. immigration policy.[52]

Study and research programs for foreign students entail a potential risk to U.S. security. Therefore, the United States must scrutinize foreigners entering the country. However, it is in the interest of the U.S. scientific community and the U.S. economy to put in place screening mechanisms that do not discourage foreigners from entering the United States. It has been suggested that it is even in the interest of U.S. security to facilitate the entry of foreign scientists and engineers, as this largely contributes to the United States's military ascendancy.[53]

Recommendations and Measures to Solve Issue

In order to balance the interests of national security on the one hand and openness to international scientists and engineers on the other, a study by the Center for Strategic and International Studies proposes various measures.[54] One recommendation includes the nonapplication of the Visa Mantis to foreigners accepted into programs based on catalog courses at accredited institutions.[55] This recommendation has been supported by the fact that instruction in such programs is excluded from export controls. Moreover, it has been suggested to exclude visitors from the Visa Mantis procedure who will be conducting fundamental research, as the results of such research is made publicly available through scientific publications.[56] Fundamental research is also excluded from export controls.

The Department of State acted upon the concerns raised with respect to foreign scientists. In February 2005, the Visas Mantis procedure was amended insofar as the clearance is now valid for a period of up to four years, i.e., no additional screening is required within that period. Therefore, students are no longer subject to another review after the course of one year if they exit and reenter the United States.

CONTAINERIZED SECURITY INITIATIVE

Containerized shipping is a critical component of international trade. According to the CBP: about 90 percent of the world's trade is transported in cargo containers. In addition, almost half of incoming U.S. trade (by value) arrives by containers onboard ships. Nearly seven million cargo containers arrive on ships and are off-loaded at U.S. seaports each year.[57]

As terrorist organizations have increasingly turned to destroying economic infrastructure to make an impact on nations, the vulnerability of international shipping has come under scrutiny. Under the CSI program, the screening of containers that pose a risk for terrorism is accomplished by teams of CBP officials deployed to work in concert with their host nation counterparts.

In the aftermath of the terrorist attacks on September 11, 2001, the U.S. Customs Service started developing counterterrorism programs to help with border security. Within months of the attacks, U.S. Customs Service had established the Container Security Initiative (CSI). Announced in January 2002, CSI proposes a security regime to guarantee all containers that pose a potential risk for terrorism are identified and inspected at foreign ports before they are placed on vessels destined for the United States. CBP has developed multidisciplinary teams of U.S. officers from both CBP and Immigration and Customs Enforcement (ICE) to work together with U.S. foreign government counterparts. Their mission is to target and prescreen containers and to develop additional investigative leads related to the terrorist threat destined for the United States.[58]

CSI's Core Elements

CSI has three core elements:

1. Identify high-risk containers. CBP uses automated targeting tools to identify containers that pose a potential risk for terrorism, based on advance information and strategic intelligence.
2. Prescreen and evaluate containers before they are shipped. Containers are screened as early in the supply chain as possible, generally at the port of departure.
3. Use technology to prescreen high-risk containers to ensure that screening can be done rapidly without halting international commerce. The technology includes large-scale x-ray and gamma ray machines and radiation detection devices.[59]

CSI Interaction with Other Countries

Through CSI, CBP officers work with host customs administrations to establish security criteria for identifying high-risk containers. Those administrations use nonintrusive inspection (NII) and radiation detection technology to screen high-risk containers before they are shipped to U.S. ports.

CSI, a reciprocal program, offers its participant countries the opportunity to send their customs officers to major U.S. ports to target oceangoing, containerized cargo to be exported to their countries. Similarly, CBP shares information on a bilateral basis with its CSI partners. Japan and Canada currently station their customs personnel in some U.S. ports as part of the CSI program.

Some Results

In the first four years, 26 customs administrations committed to joining CSI and are at various stages of implementation. CSI is now operational at ports in North America, Europe, Asia, Africa, the Middle East, and Latin and Central America. CBP's 58 operational CSI ports now make approximately 90 percent of all transatlantic and transpacific cargo imported into the United States subject to prescreening prior to importation.

CSI continues to expand to strategic locations around the world. The World Customs Organization, the European Union, and the G8 support CSI expansion and have adopted resolutions implementing CSI security measures introduced at ports throughout the world.[60]

The CSI has not been able to target all U.S.-bound shipments from CSI ports because of staffing imbalances. CBP has developed a staffing model to determine staffing requirements. However, it has not been able to fully staff some ports due to diplomatic considerations, such as the need for host government permission, and practical considerations, such as workspace constraints. Hence, a GAO report in April 2005 found that 35 percent of the shipments were not targeted and hence not subject to inspection overseas.[61]

A limitation has been that CBP has not established minimum technical requirements for the detection capability of NII and radiation detection equipment that CSI deploys. Ports participating in CSI use various types of NII equipment (e.g., x-ray or gamma ray scanning equipment) to inspect containers, and the detection and identification capabilities of such equipment differ.[62] Technologies to detect other weapons of mass destruction have limitations. Hence, CBP has limited assurance that inspections conducted under CSI are effective at detecting and identifying terrorist weapons of mass destruction.

In July 2003, the GAO recommended that CBP develop a strategic plan and performance measures, including outcome-oriented measures, for CBI. In February 2004, CBP developed a strategic plan that contains three of the six key elements required for agency strategic plans. CBP officials are continuing to develop the other three elements. CBP has also made progress in the development of outcome-oriented performance measures, especially for the program goal of increasing information sharing and collaboration among CSI and host country personnel.[63]

The GAO has recommended that CBP further refine its staffing model to help improve the program's ability to target shipments at foreign ports, develop minimum technical requirements for the detection capabilities of equipment used in the program, and complete development of performance measures for all program goals.[64] Other commentators cite as a main problem this lack of sufficient funding and resources to carry out the program.[65]

FORTIFYING THE BORDER INFRASTRUCTURE

Since the terrorist attacks of September 11, 2001, the U.S. Congress, law enforcement, 9/11 Commission, and other bodies have focused on trying to fortify the border infrastructure of the United States. The border infrastructure embraces POE and unprotected border points. It involves the controversial issue of immigration.

According to the 9/11 Commission, U.S. borders and immigration system, including law enforcement, should "send a message of welcome, tolerance, and justice to members of immigrant communities in the United States and in their countries of origin. We should reach out to immigrant communities. Good immigration services are one way of doing so that its valuable in every way—including intelligence."[66]

The 9/11 Commission states that the United States must be able to monitor and respond to entrances between its POE, working with Canada and Mexico as much as possible. The commission report says that an increasing role exists for state and local law enforcement agencies. They need more training and work with federal agencies so they can cooperate more effectively with the federal authorities in identifying terrorist suspects.[67] This section will discuss overall border security programs, especially since the start of the Bush administration, and then the northern and then southern borders of the United States.

Securing U.S. Borders and Counterterrorism Generally

The DHS through its Secure Border Initiative (SBI) and other efforts has strengthened security only in its northern and southern borders through the integrated use of increased manpower and infrastructure, technology, enhanced immigration enforcement, and cooperation with state, local, and international partners.[68]

Expanding Infrastructure and Building a Virtual Fence

The Bush administration built new fencing and barriers and improved and expanded existing infrastructure. DHS deployed new technology to enhance the effectiveness of operations. Through the use of radiation detectors, sensors, cameras, and biometric information, DHS significantly increased the likelihood of apprehending criminal or terrorist elements trying to enter the United States.

DHS built fencing and barriers where it was effective to improve security along the border. Former President Bush's $1.9 billion supplemental request in 2006 included $500 million for additional infrastructure including more barriers, lighting, roads, fencing, communications equipment, and new stations and bases along the border. In many areas, infrastructure enhancement is already underway.[69]

DHS used SBInet and other efforts to obtain and deploy a virtual fence along the borders comprised of detection equipment, sensors, cameras, and other high-tech mechanisms. DHS is integrating its improved technology with new investments in infrastructure and will greatly increase the apprehension capabilities of the Border Patrol.

Since 9/11, the DHS has used more than $122 million in technology for the northern border, including $8.7 million in tactical communications, $60 million in radiation portal monitors (RPMs), and $40 million in other large-scale nonintrusive equipment. Future deployments include $150 million for RPMs and large-scale nonintrusive equipment. Additionally, DHS used $200 million to strengthen the truck arrival and cargo entry processes along the northern border.[70]

Increasing Human Resources and Assets along the Borders

The Bush administration significantly increased the size and budget of the Border Patrol and trained and assigned additional agents to the northern and southern borders. Border security funding increased 66 percent. As of November 29, 2006, there were approximately 11,600 agents compared to 9,096 when Bush took office, an increase of 27 percent. By the end of 2008, there were 18,000 agents.

The Bush administration tripled the number of CBP agents along the northern border from 340 agents in 2001 to 980 agents as of November 29, 2006. The increase in human resources improved CBP's ability to detect, apprehend, and deter illegal aliens, criminal elements, and terrorist threats along the border with Canada. The CBP has moved agents from administrative positions to the field. With National Guard support, approximately 600 Border Patrol agents along the southern border will be moved from nonlaw enforcement jobs and be made available for border operations, apprehensions, and interdictions.

The DHS used supplemental appropriations to buy more than a dozen new helicopters, over 650 new vehicles, and two new UAVs for use along the border. In one year, a single DHS UAV alone was responsible for the apprehension of 2,300 illegal migrants and four tons of marijuana.

The Bush administration increased the number of air and marine branches along the northern border. Before September 11, 2001, no CBP Air and Marine branches were deployed along the northern border. After 9/11, the first two were opened, in Bellingham, Washington, and Plattsburgh, New York. A third air wing in Great Falls, Montana, became operational by the end of 2006. And, subsequently, two additional air branches were opened, located in Michigan and North Dakota.

The Bush administration deployed thousands of Coast Guardsmen to protect the northern border. Coast Guard districts in the Pacific Northwest and Great Lakes have 3,500 active duty military personnel, 19 cutters, and 38 small boat stations serving along northern border waterways. As mentioned above, US-VISIT biometric verification technology was deployed at 154 land POE and screened roughly four million visitors entering the country.[71]

Enhancing Immigration Enforcement

The Bush administration emphasized enhancing immigration enforcement, apprehending and returning millions of illegal aliens, increasing funding for interior enforcement substantially, and replacing the policy of "catch and release" with "catch and return." During the Bush administration, as of November 29, 2006, more than six million people had been apprehended for entering the country illegally, including more than 400,000 with criminal records.

Since the start of the Bush administration, the number of immigration investigators had grown 25 percent and increased funding for interior enforcement by 42 percent. Former President Bush's fiscal year 2007 budget requested funds to increase the number of ICE fugitive operational teams from the current number of 32 to 70.

Expedited removal substantially diminishes the amount of time an illegal migrant spends in processing before being returned to his home country. Before the SBI, the average length of stay in ICE detention was approximately 90 days for all removals, and could be as high as 32 days for those in expedited removal. Today, the average length of stay for persons in expedited removal along the southern border is 26 days. Secretary of Homeland Security Michael Chertoff expanded the practice of expedited removal to all U.S. borders—northern, southern, and coastal.[72]

Northern Border

The terrorist attacks of 2001 in the United States imposed pressure on the United States and Canada to develop closer cooperation on border security. Among the controversies have been Canada's decision to not participate in the 2003 war in Iraq, leading the U.S. government to doubt Canada's reliability in defense matters. The U.S. detention and sending a Canadian citizen named Maher Arar to Syria, where he suffered inhumane treatment or even torture, has led to a loss of confidence by Canadians in U.S. border procedures and adherence to the rule of law.[73] Despite the problems, the two governments have significantly strengthened their border security and infrastructure. For instance, on December 12, 2001, Canada and the United States signed the Smart Border Declaration, which gave rise to the 30-point Smart Border Action Plan.[74]

History of U.S.-Canada Border Security Cooperation—Ogdensburg Declaration of August 1940

To understand the current climate and border security issues between the United States and Canada requires some understanding of the history of U.S.-Canada border security cooperation. When Canada and the United States encountered defense and national security issues in the early years of World War II, they negotiated an arrangement whereby the United States permitted Canada to keep all military authority over its own territory in return for a commitment to deny Canadian territory to a foreign power seeking to threaten the United States.

The arrangement was set forth in the Ogdensburg Declaration of August 1940 and created a Permanent Joint Board of Defense. It contained a shared commitment to North America's security and contained the security basis for the close integration of the two countries. It enabled Canada to promote international security in a way that complemented but did not mimic the foreign policy of the United States.[75]

Renewal in 1947 and Thereafter

When the Ogdensburg Declaration was renewed in 1947, Canada and the United States committed to exchange military officers; conduct joint exercises and test new weapon systems; standardize equipment and military procedures; make their army, naval, and air facilities available to each other on request and expedite requests for passage through territorial lands and waters; and respect each country's control over all activities in its territory.[76]

The Ogdensburg arrangement adapted to circumstances that ensued. Additional formalization of the arrangement came with the signing of the North Atlantic treaty, which required each member to consider an attack against any one of them an attack against all of them.

During the Cold War, North America came under threat of long-range ballistic missiles fired across the Arctic. The threat led in 1958 to the United States and Canada forming the North American Air Defense Command. The two armed rorces patrolled the air with radar installations. Warning of an attack would produce a response by a single air command reporting to the heads of state in both countries.[77]

More Recent Security Cooperation: Drugs, Organized Crime, and Terrorism

In the last two or three decades, new threats to North American security arose from the flow of drugs, organized crime, and terrorist organizations. The mutual commitment of both countries to North American security resulted in the spread of cooperation from the military to law enforcement, immigration, and customs agencies. New informal institutions were established, such as the Cross Border Crime Forum, the Shared Border Accord, and Border Vision, to coordinate security policies.[78]

Immigration reforms adopted by the Canadian Parliament after the 2001 attacks in the United States constituted a positive step toward addressing the problem and showed that the government was taking the problem seriously.[79] In this regard Canada enacted the Anti-Terrorism Act (ATA), which allowed Canada to meet its many international obligations to implement counterterrorism measures and to show leadership with respect to UN requirements. The ATA enabled Canada to ratify and implement the International Convention for the Suppression of Terrorism Bombings (1997) and the International Convention for the Suppression of the Financing of Terrorism (1999) to implement the UN Security Council Resolution 1373 (2001) and the commitments by leaders of the G8, APEC, the OSCE, and the Organization of American States (OAS).[80]

As of November 14, 2007, the Canadian government had listed 40 entities under section 83.05(1) of the Criminal Code and had arrested and prosecuted various persons for terrorism-related offenses under the Criminal Code. Since the enactment of the ATA in 2001, the minister of public safety has published four annual reports (2002–2005) on the use of arrests without warrant pursuant to the ATA. Canadian law enforcement also has taken action against suspected financing of terrorism.[81]

New Threats Post 9/11 and Options

The challenge in the post-9/11 era is for Canada and the United States to cooperate in security matters even though there are no supranational political institutions to manage the issues that inevitably arise from such close cooperation. Aside from bodies that manage narrowly defined issues, such as the International Joint Commission or the Secretariat of the North American Agreement on Environmental Cooperation, Canada and the United States utilize traditional bilateral channels to resolve political disputes.[82] The difficulty is that while Canada and the United States have divergent policies on important security issues, they still need to cooperate closely. For instance, Canada has tight control over the personal ownership of handguns while the United States has one of the most liberal polices over ownership of guns. In contrast, while the United States continues its war on drugs, Canadian provinces have decriminalized the possession of marijuana, which has led to the growth of marijuana in provinces such as British Columbia for export to the United States.[83]

Since 1997 the Cross Border Crime Forum has offered an annual venue to discuss threat perceptions and opportunities for coordination and cooperation among law enforcement organizations, the U.S. Department of Justice, and the Canadian Ministry of Justice. This forum has given birth to the idea for Integrated Border Enforcement Teams (IBETs) that operate as binational and joint interagency task forces to tackle shared problems and complex, multijurisdictional investigations. As of mid-2006, there were 23 IBETs operating along the border.[84]

When Congress enacted legislation in 2004 requiring U.S. citizens to show passports (where a birth certificate and photo identification had before been adequate) when reentering the United States from several foreign countries (including Canada), the legislation renewed a long-standing struggle over border management between the United States and Canada. Canadians have been able to enter the United States at land border crossings without a passport for years. They only occasionally were asked to present photo identification and a birth certification. However, with unilateral U.S. legislative initiatives in the aftermath of 9/11 Canadians have lost the courtesy. The current Harper administration has acknowledged the U.S. sovereign right to secure its borders, while focusing its diplomacy on the implementation of the new requirement and pressing U.S. officials to make passports and secure travel documents less onerous for U.S. citizens to obtain.[85]

Canada and the United States should redefine the commitment to the security of North America in terms of the new threat to the continent, namely, another major terrorist attack on the United States. Three potential options are the variable approach, the integrated approach, and the coordinated approach.

Variable or Ad Hoc Approach.—One approach would be to extend security cooperation in isolated policy areas, rather than take a high-profile political commitment to an overarching security goal in favor of a pragmatic, case-by-case ad hoc approach to security cooperation. The two governments have followed this approach since 2001. High-level political attention has focused on U.S. and Canadian customs, and immigration agencies had met regularly since 1995 under the Shared Border Accord.[86]

The ad hoc approach has disadvantages. The Smart Border process showed that high-level political attention and commitment is required to achieve progress in security issues. The attention is difficult to sustain over a long period of time, especially in the United States with its broader national security agenda. By approaching these various issues separately, both countries will have difficulty making progress beyond one or two pressing areas at a time. Another disadvantage of the variable approach is that it makes it difficult to develop significant momentum on a broad range of security issues, especially given the divergence in national security policy issues, such as guns and drugs.[87]

Integrated Approach.—The two governments could decide to take an integrated approach, whereby they implement a common commitment to preventing terrorist attacks by adopting the same rules governing immigration policy, customs enforcement, and transportation security.

The approach would have Canada and the United States adopt the same laws criminalizing terrorism-related activities and governing immigration policy, customs enforcement, and transportation security. Such an approach would also require the renegotiation of agreements that govern the collection and sharing of intelligence data, and necessitate common approaches to public health emergencies and to the protection of critical infrastructure.

The integrated approach would eliminate inconsistencies between the security policies of the two countries that terrorists could exploit. The advocates of this approach believe it would also serve to improve the economic and social linkages between the two countries by removing the need for immigration and customs checks at the common land border.

Neither country is likely to be interested in full integration of domestic security policy due to the aforementioned policy divergences. The process of harmonizing security policy would also threaten critical national security policies.[88]

Coordinated Approach.—A third approach would draw inspiration from the Ogdensburg arrangement. To apply the Ogdensburg arrangement, Canada and the United States would have to recognize that the two governments represent one common space for the purposes of keeping terrorists out of North America. They would also have to agree to cooperate as equal partners. The United States would profit from this approach because it would benefit from a farther-reaching alignment of domestic security policy than it has been able to achieve until now. Canada would profit from preserving its ability to set policy in relevant areas while regaining a degree of U.S. confidence required to forestall any threat to the model of economic and social links.

The disadvantages would be that for Canada it may raise concerns about its capacity to maintain its important differences in social policy. However, the security policies of both need not be identical so long as they meet goals that derive from the commitment the two governments make. They can choose to exclude the areas in which policies diverge. Hence, there need be no contradiction between security and social policy goals.[89]

Mutual recognition would need to be more than a one-off event. Instead, it would have to be a process of constant review and negotiation between the two countries as they pursue their commitment to shared security. For this reason, it may be worth considering a formal treaty to implement the commitment to shared security.[90] The arrangements to align North American domestic security measures could be expanded to include Mexico when it is ready to make a similar commitment to the security of the other two, and when Canada and U.S. authorities have confidence in the capacity of their Mexican counterparts to fulfill such a commitment.

The two governments would establish a mechanism to review the implementation of the shared commitments. It could be a board of military, law enforcement, immigration, and homeland security officials. They could have periodic meetings and have the staff of each functioning as a dedicated secretariat. There could be an annual meeting of the heads of state and ministers.[91]

Southern Border with Mexico

Congress has continually expanded the barriers currently deployed along the U.S. international land borders. Within the DHS, Customs and Border Protection (CBP) has the responsibility to secure the U.S. land and maritime borders between official POE to deter and interdict terrorists, weapons of mass destruction, and aliens trying to enter the country unlawfully. To discharge its duties, the CBP deploys personnel, technology, and tactical infrastructure such as vehicle barriers and fencing.

Fencing

The U.S. Attorney General used its broad powers to control and guard the U.S. border.[92] The construction of fences along the U.S. southern border with Mexico has for years been a major border security initiative. Fencing is erected on the border to impede the illegal entry of unauthorized aliens, while vehicle barriers are designed to impede the entry of vehicles but do not impede the entry of individuals.[93]

During 2007, the government built 270 miles of pedestrian and vehicle fencing. By the end of 2008, DHS had added 225 miles of pedestrian fencing, for a total of 370 miles, in addition to 300 miles of vehicle fencing along the southwest border section. This established a natural and a manufactured barrier over the heaviest illegal traffic areas from the Pacific Ocean to the Texas-New Mexico border.[94]

The Primary Fence in San Diego.—In 1990, the CBP started erecting a barrier known as the "primary fence" directly on the border to deter illegal entries and drug smuggling in its San Diego sector.[95] The San Diego fence was part of the CBP's "prevention through deterrence" strategy,[96] which called for reducing unauthorized migration by placing agents and resources directly on the border along population centers in order to deter would-be migrants from entering the country. In 1993 the San Diego fence was finished, covering the first 14 miles of the border from the Pacific Ocean. The fence was constructed of 10-foot-high welded steel army surplus landing mats[97] with the assistance of the Corps of Engineers and the California Nation Guard. The CBP also maintains stretches of primary fencing in several other sectors along the southwest border, including Yuma, Tucson, El Centro, and El Paso.[98]

In 1996, Congress enacted the Illegal Immigration Reform and Immigrant Responsibility Act (IIRIRA), which, among other things, expressly gave the Attorney General wide authority to build barriers along the border. It authorized the Immigration and Naturalization Service to construct a secondary layer of fencing to complement the completed 14-mile primary fence.[99] Construction of the secondary fence stalled after 9.5 miles had been completed as a result of the California Coastal Commission's environmental concerns. In 2005, Congress passed the REAL ID Act, which, among other things, authorized the secretary of the DHS to waive all legal requirements to speed the construction of the border fences.[100] In 2006, Congress enacted the Secure Fence Act, which, among other things, directs DHS to construct five separate stretches of fencing along the southern border totaling 850 miles.

In addition to border fencing, the CBP uses both permanent and temporary vehicle barriers at the border. The CBP typically chains together temporary vehicle barriers and can move them to different locations at the CBP's discretion. The CBP embeds permanent vehicle barriers in the ground and are meant to remain in one location. The CBP is currently erecting a 150-mile stretch of vehicle barriers in conjunction with the National Park Service near Yuma, Arizona.[101]

The CBP's San Diego sector extends along the first 66 miles from the Pacific Ocean of the international border with Mexico. It covers approximately 7,000 square miles of territory. The sector is located north of Tijuana and Tecate and has no natural barriers to entry by unauthorized migrants and smugglers.[102] Due to the large numbers of unauthorized aliens crossing the border in the area, in 1990, the CBP started erecting a physical barrier to deter illegal entries and drug smuggling. The ensuing "primary" fence covered the first 14 miles of the border, starting from the Pacific Ocean, and was constructed of 10-foot-high wielded steel.[103]

Operation Gatekeeper.—Because the primary fence did not have a significant impact on the influx of unauthorized aliens crossing the border in San Diego, the CBP announced Operation Gatekeeper in the San Diego sector on October 1, 1994. Its principal components were large increases in the overall human resources of the sector, and the deployment of CBP personnel directly along the border to deter illegal entry.

The strategic plan provided for three tiers of agent deployment. The first tier of agents was deployed to fixed positions on the border. The agents in the first tier were charged with preventing illegal entry, apprehending those who tried to enter, and generally observing the border. A second tier of agents was positioned north of the border in the corridors that were heavily used by illegal aliens. The second tier of agents had more freedom of movement than the first tier and were charged with containing and apprehending those aliens who made it past the first tier. The third tier of agents was typically placed to man vehicle checkpoints further inland to apprehend the traffic that eluded the first two tiers.[104]

Operation Gatekeeper resulted in significant increases in the manpower and other resources used in the San Diego sector. Agents received additional night vision goggles, portable radios, and four-wheel drive vehicles, and light towers and seismic sensors were deployed. Between October 1994 and June 1998, the San Diego sector experienced the following increases in resources: CBP agent manpower increased by 150 percent; seismic sensors deployed increased by 171 percent; vehicle fleet increased by 152 percent; infrared night-vision goggles increased from 12 to 49; permanent lighting increased from 1 mile to 6 miles, and 100 portable lighting platforms were used; helicopter fleet increased from 6 to 10.[105]

Due to the increase in resources and the new strategy resulting from Operation Gatekeeper, in 1998 the CBP estimated that the entire 66 miles of border patrolled by the San Diego sector's agents could be brought under control in five years.[106]

Sandia National Laboratory Study.—A 1993 Sandia Laboratory study commissioned by the former INS recommended a three-tiered fence system. The study said the use of multiple barriers in urban areas would increase the CBP's ability to discourage a significant number of illegal border crossers, to detect intruders early and delay them as long as possible, and to funnel a reduced amount of illegal border crossers to geographic locations where the CBP was better able to deal with them.[107] The Sandia study stated that segments of the border could not be controlled at the immediate border due to the ruggedness of the terrain. It recommended the use of highway checkpoints in those areas to contain aliens after they had entered the country illegally.[108] The study said that aliens trying to enter the United States from Mexico were able to bypass or destroy obstacles in their path, including the existing primary fence. Hence, it concluded that "[a] three-fence barrier system with vehicle patrol roads between the fences and lights will provide the necessary discouragement."[109]

2005 REAL ID Act

In 2005, Congress enacted H.R. 418, the REAL ID Act of 2005. It required the secretary of DHS to waive all laws necessary to ensure expeditious construction of the security barriers. Federal district courts have exclusive jurisdiction to review claims alleging that the actions or decisions of the secretary violate the U.S. Constitution. The law provides that only the U.S. Supreme Court can review district court rulings.[110]

The waiver authority contained in § 102 of the REAL ID Act appears to be a wide grant of authority since it authorizes the waiver of all legal requirements determined necessary by the secretary for the expeditious construction of authorized barriers and only permits judicial review for constitutional claims. The new waiver authority appears to apply to all the barriers that may be constructed under IIRIRA. In other words, it applies both to barriers constructed in the vicinity of the border in areas of high illegal entry and to the barrier that is to be constructed near the San Diego area.[111]

Many persons have been concerned with the apparent breadth of the waiver provision and the limited judicial review. DHS Secretary Chertoff construed the provision to allow him to waive laws in their entirety. While some take the position that the waiver authority can extend to any law, including those apparently unrelated to building a fence (e.g., civil rights or child labor laws), the provision is conditioned by the requirement that the DHS secretary must determine the law (subject to the waiver) is necessary "to ensure expeditious construction" of the barriers. Hence, the secretary may be limited to laws that, in effect, will delay the construction of the fence and not those that only tangentially relate to or do not necessarily interfere with construction. In this regard, the legislative history shows that several members called for the waiver provision because of laws that were complicating and ultimately preventing the completion of the fence.[112]

Status of San Diego Triple Fence

The 2006 Appropriations Bill included $50 million for construction of the border fence in San Diego, and $50 million for border infrastructure, including fences and vehicle barriers, in Arizona. On September 14, 2005, DHS said it was applying its new waiver authority to complete the San Diego fence.[113] DHS had been in the land acquisition phase of the project, and construction was to start sometime thereafter.[114]

In terms of the success of the San Diego fence, the CBP has used apprehension statistics as a performance measure. However, the number of apprehensions may be a misleading statistic for several reasons, including the data's focus on events rather than people and the fact that no reliable estimates exist for how many aliens successfully evade capture. As a result, it is difficult to establish a firm correlation between the number of apprehensions in a given sector and the number of people trying to enter through that section. Nevertheless, apprehension statistics remain the most reliable way to codify trends in illegal migration along the border.[115] Statistics indicate that the installation of border fencing, in combination with an increase in agent manpower and technological assets, has had a significant effect on the apprehensions made in the San Diego sector. The lower number of apprehensions suggests that fewer unauthorized aliens are trying to cross the border in the San Diego sector as a result of the increase in enforcement measures, including fencing, manpower, and other resources that were deployed to that sector.[116]

Permanent and Temporary Border Barriers

Since 1991, the CBP has constructed and maintained barriers along the international land border. These barriers have historically been limited to selected urban areas as part of the CBP's overall strategy of rerouting illegal migration away from urban areas towards geographically isolated areas where their agents have a tactical advantage over border crossers. Two principal types of border fencing have been built: primary fencing located directly on the border along several urban areas; and Sandia fencing, also known as secondary or triple fencing in San Diego. In addition, the CBP has installed permanent vehicle barriers in various segments of the border. The latter are intended to impede the entry of vehicles while allowing individuals and animals to cross the border freely.[117]

Permanent vehicle barriers are not designed to be moved but instead are permanent installations. The barriers are typically steel posts, or bollards, that are excavated five feet deep and inserted into a poured concrete base. The posts alternate in aboveground height in order to dissuade individuals from forming a ramp over the barrier. They are spaced so as to permit foot and animal traffic but not vehicular traffic. The CBP recently started building permanent vehicle barriers in the Yuma sector, with a substantial stretch ready to be built along the Organ Pipe Cactus National Monument. When connected with the 30 miles of vehicle barriers built by the National Park Service, the total 123-mile length of the project will make the largest continuous physical barrier along the U.S. border.[118]

Temporary vehicle barriers are typically built from welded metal, such as railroad track, but can also be constructed from telephone poles or pipe. These barriers are built so that they cannot be rolled or moved manually. They can only be moved with a forklift or a front-end loader. Normally the CBP builds them at its stations and transports them to areas of high vehicle entry, where they are placed and chained together. The main advantage of the temporary vehicle barriers is their ability to be redeployed to different areas to address changes in smuggling patterns. The principal disadvantage of these barriers is that they are easier to compromise than permanent vehicle barriers.[119]

Policies of Mexican Government

The U.S. government has not tried to engage the Mexican government as much as it has engaged and cooperated with the Canadian government on its border infrastructure program. To the extent the United States does engage the Mexican government on border issues, it does so on an ad hoc basis, such as the regular meetings among the attorney generals of the two governments and the border states.

The policy of the Mexican government has been to guarantee its national security and preserve the physical integrity and property of Mexicans over all other interests. In this regard its National Development Plan calls for strengthening the capacities of the armed forces through training and modernization of its equipment in order to guarantee the effective protection of its national territory and seaports, land and maritime borders, natural resources, air space, and strategic installations. Mexico is especially concerned with the economy of organized crime that permits them to engage in the black market of arms and buy information.[120]

The Mexican government's policy is to make the border area an example of fulfilling the rule of law, at the same time respecting completely human rights of everyone. Goal 14 is to safeguard the security of the frontiers, as well as the integrity and respect of human rights of the residents of these areas, as well as migrants. To achieve this goal, the Mexican policy calls for integrating mixed police units composed of the federal police and border and state police, so that, with the support of the armed forces, they guarantee the security of Mexicans and all residents of the border regions. The border security strategy focuses on the protection of migrants and the population of these regions, which is exposed to groups of persons trafficking contraband, illegal aliens, and drugs.[121]

The Mexican policy is to work with its neighboring countries to work together to develop mechanisms of exchange of information to permit sufficient control of the transit of persons between one country and the other, to protect the rights of migrants, and simultaneously, close the path to crime and international terrorism.[122]

Strategy 1.10 of the Mexican National Development Plan calls for combating terrorism and organized crime. In this regard, Mexico will maintain its provisions to cooperate with other countries to bring security, respect for international law, and the free determination of people and the sovereignty of states.[123]

Indeed, Mexico has enormous illegal migration problems of its own. Chinese and Asian aliens often first enter Mexico with the aim of later entering the United States. Its southern border is regularly crossed by Central American illegal aliens, including many gang members. Its Caribbean or eastern border is regularly besieged by boats carrying Cubans who hope to eventually enter the United States. Many of these illegal aliens spend their lives or much of their lives in Mexico, which offers them a better livelihood than their prior residences. These illegal aliens produce all kinds of challenges and crime in Mexico.

Mexican governments, including heads of state, have continually objected to and protested the construction of fencing as counterproductive, harmful to human rights, and adverse to environmental policies. They have regularly also objected to and protested the harsh treatment in the United States to illegal migrants, especially children and women.

Prospects: More Border Barriers

In recent years, Congress has continued to enact laws to build and fund border barriers. The 109th Congress enacted three pieces of legislation concerning border fencing. The REAL ID Act, as discussed above, expanded DHS's waiver authority to expedite the construction for border fending. The Secure Fence Act of 2006 (P.L. 109-367) directed DHS to construct approximately 850 miles of border fencing. The FY2007 DHS Appropriations Act (P.L. 109-225) provided $1.2 billion for the installation of fencing, infrastructure, and technology along the border. Congress considered a number of other bills with fencing related provisions.[124]

Policy Issues

The construction of barriers along the border raise a number of policy issues, including their effectiveness, overall costs compared with benefits, possible diplomatic ramifications, unintended consequences, and the locations in which they are to be constructed. While these issues apply to all potential barriers at the border, the current policy focus is on building new fencing at the border.

Effectiveness

Proponents of border fences argue that construction of fencing has substantially reduced in apprehensions along the San Diego sector and hence fences succeed in reducing cross-border smuggling and migration where they are constructed. Opponents attribute some of the decrease in apprehensions to the increase in manpower and resources in the sector. They note the increase in apprehensions in less-populated sectors. Opponents state that the fence only succeeds in rerouting unauthorized migration (around and under the fences) and not in stopping it. A possible issue for Congress and U.S. policymakers is whether border fencing is effective unless it is constructed across the entire border in question.[125]

Costs

Border fencing is a relatively new and limited phenomenon along the U.S.-Mexico border. As a result, a dearth of information exists concerning its overall costs and benefits. The Congressional Budget Office has estimated that border fencing would cost $3 million a mile to construct. That does not include the cost of maintenance, especially since the fencing is likely to be subjected to breaches and other attempts to compromise it. Issues for Congress and policymakers include how best to allocate scarce border security resources while safeguarding homeland security, whether border fencing represents the best investment of border security funding, and what is the appropriate mix of border security resources.[126]

Fence Design

Many different fence designs that could be deployed to the border have their relative strengths and weaknesses. For instance, concrete panels are among the most cost-effective solutions. However, CBP agents cannot see through this type of fencing and prefer fencing that can be seen through, so as to identify the activity occurring on the Mexican side of the border and preserve their tactical advantage over potential border crossers, and to better avoid potential rockings or other violent incidents. Bollard fencing has been effective in its limited deployment and can also be seen through. However, it is expensive to install and to maintain. Chain link fencing is relatively economical, but more easily compromised. If fencing is to be constructed along the border, an issue concerns what kinds of fencing should be constructed in order to maximize its deterrent effect and its utility to the CBP while minimizing the costs associated with its construction and maintenance. If fencing is to be constructed along the border, an important question concerns what kinds of fencing should be constructed in order to maximize its deterrent effect and its utility to the CBP while minimizing the costs associated with its construction and maintenance.[127]

Fence Location

The CBP has testified that border fencing is most effective for its operational purposes when deployed along urban areas, where individuals crossing the border have a short distance to cover before they disappear into neighborhoods and become difficult to apprehend. From populated areas aliens can more easily find transportation into the interior. Hence, the CBP has chosen to construct border fencing in urban areas abutting the border, such as San Diego, Nogales, and El Paso.

The costs of construction in rural areas are much higher because of the need to bring the individuals and goods needed to build the fence to these areas for extended periods of time.

A practical issue concerns what areas of the border should be fenced. Should fencing be restricted to urban or semiurban areas so that the CBP will have a tactical advantage over border crossers, or should fencing be constructed along any geographical area of the border that features large numbers of unauthorized immigration? In rural areas, should fencing be limited to areas of high illegal entry in order to impede individuals from crossing the border, or should fencing be constructed as a deterrent in any area, even those with low levels of illegal entry? Should fencing be used in sectors where the distance between the nearest CBP station and the fence requires agents to spend most of their day commuting? Should fencing be deployed to the northern border as well as the southwest border? Will building fencing along more remote or environmentally harsher areas of the border increase the construction costs?

Land Acquisition

A number of issues concerning the acquisition of land must be considered for border fencing. Much of the land along the California and Arizona border is owned by the federal government. However, most of the land along the Texas border is owned by private individuals. What will the costs of acquiring the land to construct border fencing be, and have these costs been incorporated into estimates of border fencing costs? Will eminent domain be used to confiscate land from individuals who do not want to have fencing built on their lands?[128] A number of cases were prepared by the Bush administration against landowners along the border who had refused the government access to their land.[129]

Another issue may involve DHS's authority to build border fencing along tribal lands. The Arizona desert along the Tohono O'odham Reservation is one of the most heavily trafficked border areas in the country. The CBP is restricted in its operations in the reservation due to tribal concerns. The Tohono O'odham have vowed to fight the construction of fencing on tribal land due to environmental and cultural concerns.[130] Current law allows the Secretary of the Interior to grant rights-of-way over and across tribal land, provided the secretary receives prior written consent of the tribe.[131] If the tribe does not consent, DHS may look to its new waiver authority to construct a fence across tribal lands. However, it is not clear whether the expanded waiver that was given to the secretary of DHS would allow the department to override the statutory authority given to another federal agency. Ultimately, the U.S. federal government holds all Indian lands in trust. Congress may take such lands for public purposes, as long as it provides just compensation as required by the Fifth Amendment.[132]

Diplomatic Ramifications

The Mexican and Canadian governments both have expressed concern about the United States constructing barriers along the international border. Former Mexican President Vicente Fox strongly opposed the construction of border barriers on numerous occasions, arguing that these projects isolate the two countries, create frustration and misunderstandings, and do not solve the underlying problems that lead individuals to enter the United States illegally. The Mexican government has sent numerous diplomatic notes to the White House registering its complaints against the possible expansion of border fencing. The Canadian government has expressed concern over bills discussing proposed studies of fencing along the northern border. Canada cited the impracticality of fencing the northern border and the fact that the U.S. government has never discussed such a plan with Canadian authorities.[133]

Congress and policymakers may want to consider the potential diplomatic ramifications of constructing barriers along the border and whether the gains in border security outweigh the risk of alienating Mexico and Canada. Should the Mexican or Canadian government's opinions or wishes be considered where border fencing is concerned? Due to the need to coordinate intelligence and law enforcement activities at the border, should maintaining cordial working relationships with Mexico and Canada take precedence over sealing the border with physical barriers?[134]

Environmental Considerations

The addition of fences along the southwest border has the potential to harm sensitive environment, adversely affect critical habitat for protected species, and block migratory patterns for animals. The California Conservation Commission expressed these concerns when it objected to the completion of the San Diego border fence. Some environmentalists say that a fence along the Arizona border could be especially destructive to endangered jaguar and Sonoran desert pronghorn populations that usually frequent this area because it would fragment native habitat and ultimately reduce gene pools.[135] Environmentalists say that the fencing will disrupt the habitat of pygmy owls and other sensitive fauna in the wildlife refuges (e.g., the Buenos Aires National Wildlife Refuge in southern Arizona) and encourage illegal immigrants to use more remote, ecologically delicate terrain.[136]

Three times, including twice in 2007, DHS Secretary Chertoff has exempted fence construction along the border from environmental reviews normally required for such projects because the waivers avoid legal delays that threaten speedy completion.[137]

The lack of a clear consensus on the environmental impacts of border fencing has resulted in calls for a study of the issue. The expansion of fencing along the southwest border, notwithstanding the waiver, may make Congress interested in environmentally sensitive alternatives to normal fencing and whether they can effectively limit illegitimate cross-border traffic. For instance, vehicle barriers may be less intrusive because they permit unimpeded wildlife movement but can limit damaging vehicular traffic.[138]

Legal Considerations

The construction of barriers along the international border has raised many legal issues, most arising from requirements posed by environmental laws. For instance, before the enactment of the REAL ID Act waiver provision, the Sierra Club and other environmental groups challenged, under the National Environmental Policy Act, the federal government's plan to complete the San Diego border fence.[139] The lawsuit alleged that the government's final environmental impact statement did not address the entire 14-mile border infrastructure system and insufficiently discussed the parts that were evaluated. Secretary Chertoff exercised the waiver authority, causing the court to dismiss the environmentalists' lawsuit in December 2005. The groups will reportedly file an entirely new lawsuit arguing that the government must still comply with certain laws, including the Clean Water Act and the Clean Air Act. They will contend that waiver extends beyond Congress's authority.[140]

Unintended Consequences

Unintended consequences have arisen from the CBP's historical strategy of "prevention through deterrence," whereby agents and resources including border fencing and other barriers have been concentrated along urban areas and areas traditionally featuring high levels of illegal entry. One unintended consequence of this enforcement policy and the shift in migration patterns has been an increase in the number of migrant deaths each year. On average, 200 migrants died each year in the early 1990s, compared with 472 migrant deaths in 2005. Another unintended consequence may have been a relative increase, compared to the national average, in crime along the border in these more remote regions. While crime rates in San Diego and El Paso have declined over the past 15 years, the reduction in crime rates along the more rural areas of the border has lagged behind the national trends. Another unintended consequence of the border fencing has been the proliferation of tunnels dug underneath the border. Some have been quite sophisticated (e.g., using reinforced concrete).

Given the rerouting of migration flows that have occurred, are DHS and the relevant border communities prepared to handle the increased flow of illegal migration to nonreinforced areas? Is DHS prepared to deal with an increase in the phenomenon of cross-border tunnels and other attempts to defeat the purpose of the fencing? What will the impact on crime rates be along the unreinforced areas of the border? Will CBP agents be required to spend some of their patrolling time guarding the fence?[141]

ANALYSIS

Need to Balance Security Concerns against Other Needs Given Finite Resource Levels

A strategic challenge facing the United States is to apply a risk management framework that requires, at the highest level, the balancing of security concerns against other needs, given a finite resource level. The framework is required in order to consider how much the United States can afford to spend for security improvements in light of other, competing demands for limited funds, such as increasing costs of health care, energy and climate problems, transportation, Social Security, and other domestic problems. In this regard, it is important to complete comprehensive national threat and risk assessments to guide and prioritize investment decisions, so that risk management can guide allocation of scarce resources. Care is required when decisions are made about how to allocate limited resources across a large number of programs in multiple agencies. The balancing process also requires careful trade-offs that balance security concerns against other needs.[142]

One strategic issue is whether the two major U.S. land borders should be treated differently, in recognition of the greater cross-border cooperation offered to U.S. border officials by their Canadian counterparts. The Bush administration, with the concurrence of the Martin (Canadian) and Fox (Mexican) administrations, formally linked with the Security and Prosperity Partnership of North America. Hence, Harper had to unlink the two in his policies and has had to continue to defend discrimination between the borders to skeptical U.S. policymakers concerned that doing so might be perceived as ethnically motivated and hence politically dangerous.[143]

The U.S. government, especially the executive and legislative branches, faces significant management and organizational transformation challenges as they work to protect the country from terrorism and implement effective risk management policies. For instance, DHS must continue to integrate approximately 180,000 employees from 22 originating agencies, consolidate multiple management systems and processes, and transform into a more effective organization with robust planning, management, and operations.[144]

Because of the large amount of tasks required, the amount of government reorganization required, and the limited resources, one can say that for many of the border security goals, such as transportation-related vulnerabilities, the CSI, and fortifying the border infrastructure, the glass is either half full or half empty. From the large overview one must realize that border security is only one set of measures, together with preventing the continued growth of Islamist terrorism through engaging the struggle of ideas and developing an agenda of opportunity for the Middle East, and turning a national strategy into a comprehensive coalition strategy, to combat ethnic based threats of terrorism to the United States.[145]

Need for Sustainable Paradigms

In the future three border paradigms are possible. One is a substantial hardening of U.S. border defenses with security prioritized over all other considerations. A second paradigm is multilateral policy harmonization and a pooling of sovereignty similar to the European Union. A third is a series of initiatives involving a mix of enhanced cross-border security collaborations and partial policy convergence. Until now the United States has mainly taken the first paradigm—making policy unilaterally.

To the extent the United States has cooperated with other countries in terms of advance air passenger information and the Containerized Security Initiative, it has done so usually after it has made its policy and it has required the cooperation of other countries. In other policies, such as the fortification and militarization of its southern border, the U.S. government has made its policy totally unilaterally and against the express protests of the highest levels of the Mexican government.[146] U.S. policies with its northern border have been made largely unilaterally although it has engaged to some extent the Canadian government. However, much of the engagement has depended on personal diplomacy and has not been institutionalized.

Until the U.S. government perceives the need for and invests in the construction of long-term counterterrorism border security regimes, it will not be able to effectively design and implement its goals and strategies. Border security is such a large subject that it requires endless resources. Similar to the war on drugs or the war of transnational organized crime, the effort to prioritize border security cannot be sustained unilaterally. Globalization will guarantee that terrorists and criminals can take advantage of technology and the mechanisms to move people, money, goods, and products instantaneously. Globalization enables such persons to plan and commit terrorist and other crimes against the United States.

Several options exist for cooperation on border security. One potential mechanism is the Organization of American States. It already has a number of mechanisms for criminal cooperation. One is the periodic Meetings of the Ministers of Justice or Attorneys General of the America, or the Reunión Extraordinaria de los Ministros de Justicia de las Américas (REMJA). The aim of the REMJA is "to consider issues contributing to enhanced legal and judicial cooperation in the Americas."[147] REMJA is neither a standing OAS agency or entity, such as the Inter-American Drug Abuse Control Commission, nor a treaty-based structure. REMJA's viability completely depends on OAS institutions, such as the Permanent Council. For instance, the Permanent Council's Committee on Political and Juridical Affairs prepares and approves REMJA's agenda, promotes and tracks its conclusions and recommendations, and directs and observes its components.[148]

Another OAS mechanism that works on counterterrorism is the Inter-American Committee Against Terrorism, which was established in 1999.[149] The Inter-American Convention Against Terrorism is also a mechanism that can serve to meet counterterrorism goals, including border security ones.[150]

Another potential mechanism that could be used for border security is the North American Free Trade Agreement (NAFTA). Already NAFTA contains provisions on criminal cooperation relating to intellectual property protection and customs. Indeed, one of the expectations and goals of NAFTA was to facilitate free trade in order to provide more jobs and economic opportunities throughout NAFTA, but especially the most developing parts, such as Mexico. It would be possible to expand NAFTA and specially deal with border security.

7

Civil Rights and Foreign Intelligence Surveillance in the United States

Edgar H. Brenner

In the United States, respect for civil rights is fundamental to our core beliefs and reflects a reliance on the rule of law. However, civil rights do not exist in isolation and must be balanced against the need of society to protect itself against foreign and domestic threats, including the threat of terrorism. Intrusive governmental power can jeopardize universally cherished rights, such as freedom of speech and association. On the other hand, an uncritical emphasis on civil rights creates vulnerabilities that terrorists are eager and able to exploit.

Foreign terrorist organizations operate in the United States using both their own agents and domestic recruits. Because of the openness of American society, it is particularly difficult to identify these agents prior to the time when they commit a violent act. If the terrorists limit their activities in the United States to supporting and financing terrorists abroad, it is even more difficult for law enforcement to disrupt their operations. Apprehending foreign terrorists and their domestic supporters, while at the same time protecting civil rights, is the great challenge facing U.S. intelligence, security, and law enforcement services.

Because of the threat that terrorists will resort to the use of weapons of mass destruction (chemical, biological, and nuclear), a failure to strike the correct balance between fighting terrorism, achieving effective law enforcement, and maintaining civil rights threatens the country's existence. The competing goals must be analyzed in relation to the most important policy objectives. One of the greatest challenges the United States now faces is transforming the FBI from an organization focused on the arrest and punishment of persons guilty of crimes that have been committed, into an organization that is also capable of preventing terrorism. This is, concededly, a difficult task, but its importance is well recognized. In testimony before a Senate committee on June 27, 2002, FBI Director Robert S. Mueller III stated:

> Simply put, our focus is now one of prevention. This simple notion reflects itself in new priorities, different resource deployments, a different structure, different hiring and training, different business practices, and a substantially different information architecture.[1]

A similar note was sounded by Senator Charles Grassley (R-IA), who stated (using the title of a book for emphasis), "If the FBI is to successfully transform itself from a crime-solving agency to a terrorism prevention force, it must learn from the mistakes described in *1000 Years for Revenge*."[2]

For years the FBI was precluded by legal rulings from making this transformation, in that criminal law enforcement was separated from the gathering of foreign intelligence. This artificial "wall" between crime-solving and intelligence-gathering contributed to the disaster of 9/11. The existence of the wall meant that the Criminal Division of the Department of Justice could not use information gathered by the FBI in the secret surveillance of suspected foreign terrorists in the United States to prosecute them for crimes they may have committed. Also, the Criminal Division of the Department of Justice could not target suspects for secret electronic surveillance if the Department of Justice contemplated criminal proceedings against the target.

The USA PATRIOT Act, enacted shortly after 9/11, was intended to break down the wall so as to permit effective coordination between intelligence-gathering and law enforcement to prevent terrorism. This was accomplished by authorizing the FBI and other criminal investigators to probe suspicious activity in situations in which a terrorist event had not yet taken place. Under such circumstances it was impossible to make a showing of probable cause that an identifiable person had already committed a crime, or was about to commit a crime; a prerequisite to securing a conventional criminal search warrant.

However, some—but certainly not all—persons claiming a concern for civil liberties commenced a campaign against the PATRIOT Act, and focused on those portions of the act that allows the FBI a chance to prevent terrorism. This attack created a crisis in the legal framework of the war on terrorism. How this situation came to exist requires a review of legal history going back to the time of the Lyndon Johnson administration (1963–1969).

In *Katz v. United States*, 389 U.S. 347 (1967), the Supreme Court of the United States held for the first time that wiretapping by the government is subject to the Fourth Amendment of the U.S. Constitution, which restricts the authority of the government to search for and seize private property.[3]

In 1968, Congress enacted the Omnibus Crime Control and Safe Streets Act,[4] which among other things regulates electronic surveillance by the government in federal criminal cases. To secure an order "approving interception of wire, oral or electronic communications,"[5] the applicant must convince a federal judge that "there is probable cause for belief that an individual is committing, has committed, or is about to commit a particular offense enumerated in Section 2516 of this chapter."[6]

Four years later, in *United States v. United States District Court (Keith)*, 407 U.S. 297 (1972), the Supreme Court recognized that domestic security investigations could require different standards from those applicable in traditional criminal cases. However, the difference in standards between traditional criminal law enforcement and security investigations did not justify the elimination of the warrant requirement. Indeed, the Court emphasized the importance of the warrant requirement, namely, that except in narrowly limited emergency situations, the executive branch must obtain judicial approval of "searches and seizures through the warrant procedure." Though the case involved only domestic security, the Court's reasoning was also applicable to foreign security investigations.

But while insisting on the warrant procedure in domestic security investigations, the Court explained the distinction between surveillance to prosecute ordinary crime and "security surveillance" as follows:

> We recognize that domestic security surveillance may involve different policy and practical considerations from the surveillance of "ordinary crime." The gathering of security intelligence is often long range and involves the interrelation of various sources and types of information. The exact targets of such surveillance may be more difficult to identify than in surveillance operations against many types of crime specified in Title III. Often, too, the emphasis on domestic intelligence gathering is on the prevention of unlawful activity or the enhancement of the Government's preparedness for some possible future crisis or emergency. Thus, the focus of domestic surveillance may be less precise than that directed against more conventional types of crime.... Different standards may be compatible with the Fourth Amendment if they are reasonable both in relation to the legitimate need of the Government for intelligence information and the protected rights of our citizens (407 U.S. at 322).

Though the Supreme Court went to great lengths to explain that it expressed no opinion as to the issue of foreign power and foreign intelligence surveillance, the Court's reasoning as to the importance of the warrant requirement, and the difference between traditional criminal law surveillance and intelligence surveillance, was also applicable to foreign intelligence surveillance. Congress seemed to accept this view.

In 1978, Congress enacted the Foreign Intelligence Surveillance Act
(FISA), 50 U.S.C. 1801–1862. Under this legislation, applications for an
order authorizing electronic surveillance are submitted *ex parte* to a FISA
court that conducts its proceedings in secret[7] (§1803). The application must
show that "the target of the electronic surveillance is a foreign power or an
agent of a foreign power" (§1804(a)(4)(A)), and that the place of surveillance is being used, or is about to be used "by a foreign power or an agent
of a foreign power" (§1804(a)(4)(B)). When FISA was enacted, to secure a
warrant, the government was also required to certify to the FISA court "that
the purpose of the surveillance is to obtain foreign intelligence information"
(§1804(a)(7)(B)).

In order to grant the surveillance order, the FISA trial court also had to be
satisfied that no U.S. person (a U.S. citizen or resident alien) was considered
to be a foreign power, or an agent of a foreign power, "solely on the basis of
activities protected by the First Amendment to the Constitution of the
United States" (§1805(a)(3)(A)).

The enactment of the FISA law, its interpretation, both before and after
9/11, the 2001 amendments to FISA in the PATRIOT Act, the 2006 amendments to the PATRIOT Act and to FISA, and the 2007 and 2008 amendments
to FISA were discussed and debated in the context of reconciling an ongoing
conflict between individual civil rights and the need of the government to
secure national security information.

THE FISA TRIAL COURT CREATES THE WALL

The strange way in which FISA was interpreted by the FISA trial court is
summarized in the decision of the U.S. Foreign Intelligence Surveillance
Court of Review ("Court of Review") *In re: Sealed Case*, 310 F.3rd 717
(FISA Court of Review 2002).

According to the Court of Review, the FISA trial court assumed that FISA
"constructed a barrier between counterintelligence/intelligence officials and
law enforcement officers in the Executive Branch" (id., 721). The word
"wall" was used to describe the barrier (Id). In 1995, the Attorney General
(AG), in an effort to comply with FISA trial court rulings, adopted procedures limiting "contacts between the FBI and the Criminal Division in cases
where FISA surveillance or searches were being conducted by the FBI for
foreign intelligence (FI) or foreign counterintelligence (FCI) purposes"
(id., 727). An objective of the procedures was to avoid the fact or appearance that the Criminal Division was "directing or controlling the FI or FCI
investigation toward law enforcement objectives" (id., 727–28). The wall
was so high that it prevented "FBI intelligence officials from communicating
with the Criminal Division regarding ongoing FI or FCI investigations"
(id., 728). "Once prosecution of the target was being considered, the

procedures ... prevented the Criminal Division from providing any meaningful advice to the FBI" (id.).

THE WALL AFTER THE TERRORIST ATTACKS OF 9/11

In the aftermath of the September 11, 2001, terrorist attacks, the Court of Review noted that congressional testimony suggested that the wall between criminal law enforcement and intelligence may have contributed "to the FBI missing opportunities to anticipate the ... attacks" (id., 744). The court also noted:

> An FBI agent recently testified that efforts to conduct a criminal investigation of two of the alleged hijackers were blocked by senior FBI officials—understandably concerned about prior FISA court criticism—who interpreted that court's decisions as precluding a criminal investigator role. One agent, frustrated at encountering the "wall," wrote to headquarters: "[S]omeday someone will die—and wall or not—the public will not understand why we were not more effective and throwing every resource we had at certain 'problems' " (id., 744n 28).

This conclusion was reinforced by the *Final Report of the Congressional Joint Inquiry into 9/11*, Finding 12, page 8 (December 10, 2002), which includes the following:

> During the summer of 2001, when the Intelligence Community was bracing for an imminent al-Qa'ida attack, difficulties with FBI applications for Foreign Intelligence Surveillance Act (FISA) surveillance and the FISA process led to a diminished level of coverage of suspected al-Qa'ida operatives in the United States. The effect of these difficulties was compounded by the perception that spread among FBI personnel at headquarters and the field that the FISA process was lengthy and fraught with peril.

The inability of criminal law enforcement personnel to work in partnership with those engaged in foreign agent surveillance to fight terrorism effectively was a deeply held and widely shared frustration at the Department of Justice both before and after the 9/11 attacks.

The Department of Justice responded promptly to 9/11 with a variety of legislative proposals that could be described as a legal audit: a list of changes in the law submitted by the administration to Congress with the objective of improving the government's ability to fight terrorism. The full and clumsy name of this legislation is "Uniting and Strengthening America by Providing Appropriate Tools Required to Intercept and Obstruct Terrorism (USA PATRIOT Act of 2001)." The proposed legislation dealt with subjects ranging from money laundering to protecting the country's northern border. The most important and far-reaching provisions concerned the sharing of foreign security and other information with criminal law enforcement personnel who could make use of it.

Congress passed the PATRIOT Act on an expedited basis. No committee hearings were held, but there were debates in the House of Representatives and the Senate. Only one senator voted against the act, and the House approved it by a vote of 337 to 79.

Section 218 of the PATRIOT Act changed the FISA requirement that the "purpose" of FISA surveillance is to "obtain foreign intelligence information." The new requirement was that obtaining foreign intelligence need only be "a significant purpose." In other words, there could now be two (or more) purposes for surveillance: one, criminal law enforcement and the other, gathering foreign intelligence.

On its face, the PATRIOT Act eliminated the previously existing restrictions on sharing among law enforcement personnel various types of criminal investigative information. Section 203(a) authorized the sharing of grand jury information. Specific authority was given to share foreign intelligence or counterintelligence information generated in grand jury proceedings with a law enforcement or intelligence official who could use this information "in the performance of his official duties" (203(a)(1)). Similarly, the act provides that the contents "of any wire, oral or electronic communication" containing national security information may be disclosed to any federal law enforcement or intelligence officials to assist the official "in the performance of his official duties" (203(b)). To complete the circle, 203(d) provides that "it shall be lawful for foreign intelligence or counterintelligence ... [information] ... to be disclosed to any federal law enforcement, intelligence, protective, immigration, national defense, or national security official in order to assist the official receiving that information in the performance of his official duties."

In addition, Section 504 provided that "federal officers who conduct electronic surveillance to acquire foreign intelligence information under this title may *consult with federal law enforcement officers to coordinate efforts* to investigate or protect against ... actual or potential attacks, sabotage, international terrorism and other threats and dangers" (emphasis supplied).

A fair-minded reader of the PATRIOT Act would conclude that the wall between criminal law enforcement and intelligence/counterintelligence had been demolished. The AG of the United States came to this conclusion. As described by the Court of Review:

> On March 6, 2002, the Attorney General approved new "Intelligence Sharing Procedures" to implement the Act's amendments to FISA. The 2002 Procedures superseded prior procedures and were designed to permit the complete exchange of information and advice between intelligence and law enforcement officials. They eliminated the "direction and control" test and allowed the exchange of advice between the FBI, the OIPR [The Department of Justice Office of Intelligence Policy Review], and the Criminal Division regarding "the initiation, operation, continuation, or expansion of FISA searches or surveillance" (*In re: Sealed Case, supra* at p. 729).

THE FISA TRIAL COURT MAINTAINS THE WALL

The FISA trial court did not accept the AG's interpretation of the PATRIOT Act or the rules he promulgated to give effect to his interpretation. The court ordered that the FISA trial court's existing procedures "be adopted, *with modifications*, as minimization procedures to apply in all cases" (id.). By using the term "minimization," the court was saying that its procedures could stand alone as requirements designed to minimize the likelihood that FISA surveillance authority could be misused, either in the acquisition or dissemination of information.

To achieve its objective, the FISA court ordered in part that "law enforcement officials shall not make recommendations to intelligence officials concerning the initiation, operation, continuation or expansion of FISA searches or surveillances" (id., 720).

The Court of Review, then, described as follows additional requirements imposed by the lower FISA court:

> To ensure the Justice Department followed these strictures the court also fashioned what the government refers to as a "chaperone requirement"; that a unit of the Justice Department, the Office of Intelligence Policy and Review (OIPR) (composed of 31 lawyers and 25 support staff), "be invited" to all meetings between the FBI and the Criminal Division involving consultations for the purpose of coordinating efforts "to investigate or protect against foreign attack or other grave hostile acts, sabotage, international terrorism, or clandestine activities by foreign powers or their agents." If representatives of OIPR were unable to attend such meetings, "OIPR shall be apprised of the substance of the meetings forthwith in writing so that the court may be notified at the earliest opportunity" (id., 720).

The FISA trial court also adopted a new Rule 11, "which provide[d] that '[a]ll FISA applications shall include informative descriptions of any on-going criminal investigations of FISA targets, as well as the substance of any consultations between the FBI and criminal prosecutors at the Department of Justice or a United States Attorney's Office' " (id., 729–30).

THE COURT OF REVIEW OVERRULES THE FISA TRIAL COURT

It was because of these various burdensome and harmful requirements that the Department of Justice appealed to the Court of Review (id., 720). The Court of Review, in its first and only decision, reversed the FISA trial court on several grounds. It held that "[t]he FISA court's decision and order not only misinterpreted and misapplied the minimization procedures it was entitled to impose, ... [but] the FISA court may well have exceeded the constitutional bounds that restrict an Article III court. The FISA court asserted authority to govern the internal organization and investigative procedures of the Department of Justice, which are the province of the Executive Branch (Article II) and the Congress (Article 1)" (id., 731). With respect to the PATRIOT Act the Court of Review stated: "We also think that the refusal by the FISA court to consider the legal significance of the PATRIOT Act's crucial amendments was [an] error" (id., 730). Accordingly, the Court of Review also reversed the FISA trial court's orders, vacated its Rule 11, and directed that the trial court proceed in accordance with the Court of Review's opinion (id., 746).

As a result of the Court of Review decision, as of November 18, 2002, the FBI was free to marshal its criminal law and information-gathering expertise to protect the country against international terrorism. Thus, the FBI was now in a much better position to transform itself into an organization capable of preventing terrorist acts, the number one objective of FBI Director Mueller (see footnotes 1 and 2, *supra* and related text).

A U.S. DISTRICT COURT REJECTS THE KEY HOLDING OF THE FISA COURT REVIEW *IN RE: SEALED CASE*

Following the November 2002 decision of the FISA Court of Review *In re: Sealed Case*, the administration of FISA was conducted under the premise that under the PATRIOT Act there could be two purposes for surveillance: gathering of foreign intelligence and criminal law enforcement. A key proviso was that obtaining foreign intelligence must be a significant purpose of the surveillance. Even with this limitation, the "wall" between intelligence gathering and law enforcement was taken down. As noted below, the decision of the FISA Court of Review had a significant effect on the conduct of counterterrorism activities.

This key principle was brought into question in a September 26, 2007, decision of a U.S. District Court in Oregon. *Mayfield v. United States*, D. Oregon, September 26, 2007, Civil No. 04-1427-AA. The Oregon court entered a declaratory judgment that the Fourth Amendment to the U.S. Constitution precludes the use of a FISA warrant to secure information as part of a criminal investigation (see pages 35 and 44). The court observed that the procedure it declared unconstitutional "allows the government to avoid traditional Fourth Amendment judicial oversight used to obtain a surveillance order" (page 36).

The court reasoned that "when criminal investigators cannot have access to FISA surveillance," they could seek a warrant under Title III of the Criminal Code and 18 U.S.C. Section 2516(1). However, warrants issued under the referenced section are governed by Section 2518(b)(i), which provides that the warrant application must provide "details as to the particular offence that has been, is being, or is about to be committed." This is a probable cause standard not practical in foreign intelligence investigations in which typically the government agents are attempting to acquire information, a circumstance very different from traditional criminal law enforcement. If not reversed by the Court of Appeals for the Ninth Circuit, or by the Supreme Court of the United States, counterterrorism investigations will again become ineffective as they were before the implementation of the PATRIOT Act and the decision of the FISA Court of Review *In re: Sealed Case, supra.*

WHO WAS AT FAULT?

Why was it that the wall ever existed and then remained in place, jeopardizing the security of the United States, for as long as it did? Major factors were FISA trial court decisions that were just plain wrong, administrative inertia at the Department of Justice, and ineffective congressional oversight.

Congress can be criticized for enacting legislation that was misinterpreted as creating a wall between criminal law enforcement and the gathering of foreign intelligence; and then not using its oversight powers to pass correcting legislation. The Department of Justice did little to bring down the wall until after 9/11 when the PATRIOT Act was introduced.

When the PATRIOT Act's clear objective of removing the wall was frustrated by the FISA trial court, the decision of the Department of Justice to appeal to the FISA Court of Review admirably served the public interest and deserves high praise.

THE 50-COUNT INDICTMENT

How did the FBI respond to the challenge of its new authority? On February 19, 2003, Sami Al-Arian and seven others (all but one were non-U.S. citizens) were indicted in the U.S. District Court for the Middle District of Florida on charges of racketeering, conspiracy to murder people abroad, and with providing material support to terrorists. The "Florida 8" (only four of whom were before the court), were alleged to be members of the Palestinian Islamic Jihad, a terrorist organization suspected of causing the death of more than 100 Israeli civilians. If convicted, they could have faced life imprisonment. This case has been referred to as the "50-Count Indictment." It did, indeed, contain 50 counts. It was also 118 pages long.

The size and complexity of the case was apparent from an order of the trial judge entered on June 12, 2003. The court noted that

> [N]o party disputes that depositions will likely have to be taken in foreign countries. No party disputes that it will likely take at least six months to a year to conduct the trial in this matter. The government and defendants . . . all agree that it will take at least eighteen months for the government to copy and for

defendants to review the telephone recordings and conduct other discovery in this case (June 12, 2003, Order, p. 3).

The judge also observed in the order that the "telephone recordings are among some 21,000 hours of telephone recordings that the government recorded under one hundred fifty-two wiretap applications obtained pursuant to the Foreign Intelligence Surveillance Act ('FISA')" (id., pp. 2–3).

This case was one of the first instances of intelligence gathered in foreign surveillance used in a domestic criminal prosecution. According to then-Attorney General John Ashcroft, the indictment was made possible by the removal of the wall between intelligence and law enforcement brought about by the PATRIOT Act and the Court of Review decision referred to above.

The significance of this case is considerable. The FBI was able to monitor the agents of a foreign terrorist organization operating in the United States through a U.S. academic think tank and a U.S. charity; first to find out what they were doing and then to build a case against them. The government believed that the alleged terrorists were using their presence in the United States to plan and finance terrorist attacks abroad, and in so doing they violated U.S. law and thus could be apprehended before they caused additional terrorist acts abroad, or a major violent act in the United States.

The outcome of the trial, however, was a disaster for the prosecution. After a trial that lasted more than five months, the jury deliberated for 13 days and returned a verdict in early December 2005. The principal defendant was acquitted on 8 of 17 counts. The jury deadlocked on nine counts. Two defendants were acquitted of all charges and a fourth defendant, the manager of a Muslim charity located in Illinois, was also acquitted on 25 counts (*Washington Post*, December 7, 2005).

The matter was resolved in April 2006 when Professor Sami Al-Arian pleaded guilty to one count of conspiracy to provide support to a Palestinian terrorist organization. As part of the plea agreement, Sami Al-Arian agreed to be deported from the United States. He had been in federal custody since 2003 (*Washington Post*, April 18, 2006). As *The Washington Times* noted on its editorial page, the plea agreement that Al-Arian signed recited that the "defendant is pleading guilty because defendant is in fact guilty" (*The Washington Times*, April 19, 2006). By virtue of that stipulation, the prosecution's theory of the case, that Al-Arian headed a resident terror cell, was vindicated. Clearly, the failure to secure a jury verdict of guilt was a disappointment to the government.

It is worth noting that the trial judge regarded Professor Sami Al-Arian as guilty and sentenced him to prison for a term of four years and nine months. With credit for the time he was in custody, Al-Arian was to serve an additional 18 months before being deported (*Guardian Unlimited*, May 2, 2006).

PATRIOT ACT SECTION 215

Section 215 of the PATRIOT Act amends part of Title V of the FISA, 50 U.S.C. 1861 et seq., by adding provisions concerning access by the FBI to business records in international terrorism investigations. Sections (a)(1) and (a)(2) provided that "[t]he Director of the Federal Bureau of Investigation or a designee . . . whose rank shall not be lower than an Assistant Special Agent in Charge . . . may make an application for an order requiring the production of any tangible things (including books, records, papers, documents . . .) for an investigation to protect against international terrorism or clandestine intelligence activities." An investigation of a U.S. person may "not be conducted solely upon the basis of activities protected by the First Amendment to the Constitution."

An additional restriction is that the investigation must be conducted under guidelines "approved by the Attorney General under Executive Order 12333." This provision has the effect of incorporating Executive Order 12333 into the statute. On August 27, 2004, the executive order was amended by Executive Order 13355. This executive order, as amended, 69 FR 53593 (2004), sets forth the duties of the various intelligence agencies, including the FBI. It specified that the director of Central Intelligence is the primary adviser to the president on national foreign intelligence.[8] It requires that violations of law by government employees be reported to the AG; it restricts the gathering of information concerning the activities of U.S. citizens or foreign nationals living in the United States. Under certain circumstances, the AG must approve the gathering of information abroad relating to persons residing in the United States. The CIA may not engage in electronic surveillance within the United States. There is also a prohibition against assassination.

Under the Section 215 amendments to FISA, an application is made to a FISA judge (or to a magistrate judge) which shall specify in part "that the records concerned are sought for an authorized investigation . . . to obtain foreign intelligence information" (subsections (b)(1) and (2)). If the judge finds that that application meets the statutory requirements, an *ex parte* order is issued that does not disclose that it is issued for the purposes specified in the application (subsections (c)(1) and (20)). Subsection (d) provides: "No person shall disclose to any other person (other than those persons necessary to produce the tangible things under this section) that the Federal Bureau of Investigation has sought or obtained tangible things under this section."

THE ATTACK ON SECTION 215

On March 6, 2003, Representative Bernard Sanders (I-VT) introduced H.R. 1157 in the House of Representatives. The purpose of the bill was "to amend the Foreign Intelligence Surveillance Act to exempt bookstores and libraries from orders requiring the production of any tangible things for certain foreign intelligence investigations." According to unsigned literature made available by the American Civil Liberties Union (ACLU), by July 21, 2003, the bill had 129 congressional sponsors.

This same ACLU literature set forth the following reasons to support H.R. 1157:

- Under Section 215 the FBI does not need to show probable cause, not even reasonable grounds, to believe that the persons whose records it seeks is engaged in criminal activity before the FBI is granted a secret warrant.
- Libraries and booksellers report that Section 215 is having a chilling effect on many patrons who are concerned that their reading habits will be scrutinized by the federal government.
- H.R. 1157 would reinstate legal standards for investigations of libraries and bookstores that were in place before the passage of Section 215 of the USA PATRIOT Act. Under H.R. 1157 the FBI could use all other legal authorities at its disposal, as they have in the past, including search warrants and criminal subpoenas, to get library and bookstore records.
- H.R. 1157 also would remove libraries and bookstores from Section 215's gag order, which prohibits library and bookstore personnel from even telling others that the federal government is investigating a particular library or bookstore.

EVALUATING H.R. 1157

H.R. 1157 was only one of several legislative efforts intended to weaken the PATRIOT Act and reflects the important issues involved. Were the reasoning underlying H.R. 1157 to be accepted by Congress, the objective of transforming the FBI from a criminal law enforcement agency into one that can also prevent international terrorism would have been hampered. The potential consequences are serious in light of the 9/11 attacks. Why are the assumptions underlying H.R. 1157 so significant in the war against terrorism?

WHAT WAS WRONG WITH H.R. 1157?

1. To prevent terrorism, the FBI should not be restricted to traditional criminal law search warrants that require a showing of probable cause that a crime has been committed or is about to be committed. FISA surveillance and searches properly require a different standard because their purpose is to acquire information that is not yet known.
2. Terrorists are known to use library computers to communicate with each other. This potential source of intelligence information should not be put out of bounds by statute; nor should terrorists be granted a privileged sanctuary.

3. The so-called gag order, precluding the notification of suspects and others that a warrant has been issued, is a well-established part of the criminal law, both preceding and independent of the PATRIOT Act. Grand Jury proceedings are secret in that they may not be revealed by grand jurors, or court or government personnel (Federal Rules of Criminal Procedure 6(e)(2), West 1998 ed.). Subpoenas relating to grand jury proceedings are kept under seal (id., Rule 6(e) (6)). Persons who provide information concerning a search warrant "to any person" are subject to a fine or five years imprisonment, or both (18 U.S.C. 2232(b), West 1998 ed.). Similar prohibitions and penalties apply to disclosure of application for production of documents and electronic surveillance, both under the general criminal law and under FISA (504 S.C. 1862(d)(2), 18 U.S.C. 2232(c), West 1998 ed.). By keeping an investigation secret, officials can both ensure the effectiveness of the investigation as well as safeguard the reputation of persons who may never be charged with illegal conduct.

4. The supporters of the proposed legislation did not point to a pattern of governmental abuse in the investigation of libraries and bookstores. No individuals came forward claiming that they were victims of the kind of governmental overreaching that the H.R. 1157 was intended to prevent. It seemed clear at the time that the proponents were attempting to rely on a hypothetical possibility of abuse. This later turned out to be the case. (The AG has not abused Section 215 since it was yet to be utilized.)

5. The sponsors of H.R. 1157, without any basis in fact, asked Congress and the public to assume that high-ranking officials of the FBI filed false applications with judges or magistrate judges and ignored the Section 215 requirement that investigations of "a United States person . . . not [be] conducted solely upon the activities protected by the First Amendment to the United Stated Constitution."

6. In support of H.R. 1157, the sponsors asserted that it would reinstate pre-PATRIOT Act standards for investigations of libraries and bookstores. These statements reflected a willingness to restore the harmful wall between criminal law and foreign intelligence that existed before the PATRIOT Act and Court of Review decision.

THE ATTORNEY GENERAL'S SURPRISE ANNOUNCEMENT

In August 2003, the AG commenced a nationwide speaking tour to justify and explain the importance of the PATRIOT Act to law enforcement groups.[9] He was quoted as saying that "the law had been essential in preventing another terrorist attack."[10]

To get out its message concerning the PATRIOT Act, the Department of Justice also opened a Web site at www.lifeandliberty.gov.[11] This site contains official explanations of the Act and an extensive collection of newspaper stories and articles praising and defending the PATRIOT Act. Considerable space is devoted to responding to criticisms of the PATRIOT Act advanced by the ACLU.

According to the *Washington Post*, in September 2003, the AG disclosed that Section 215 had never been used.[12] He was quoted as saying that PATRIOT Act critics "had constructed castles in the air built on misrepresentation; supported by unfounded fear; held aloft by hysteria." (In the same article, Senator Joseph R. Biden, Jr., (D-DE) referred to PATRIOT Act criticisms as "ill informed and overblown."[13] Senators Dianne Feinstein (D-CA) and Oren G. Hatch (R-UT) were said to have "mounted a strong defense of the Patriot Act.")[14]

It is not immediately apparent what was meant by saying that Section 215 had never been used. It could mean only that no Section 215 court order had been requested. That would not necessarily preclude FBI agents from seeking and securing voluntary production under Section 215 of "tangible things" on the ground that a court order would be sought in the absence of cooperation.

Alternatively, the Department of Justice and the FBI may have been able to secure the information they needed by using conventional criminal subpoenas, FISA subpoenas and National Security Letters, and *ex parte* subpoenas. For example, "a wire or electronic communication service provider" must produce "toll and billing information . . . demanded by the FBI director, or a high-level designee, in a counterintelligence investigation" (18 U.S.C. 2709, 2003 West Ed.). A significant limitation of such National Security Letters is that they "may be used to obtain transactional records . . . [but] may not be used to obtain content information" (*Federal Bureau of Investigation Comprehensive Guidance on National Security Letters*, p. 3, June 1, 2007). Similarly, the FBI can demand production of certain financial records (12 U.S.C. 3414(a)(5)(A)) and also consumer reports (15 U.S.C. 1681(u)). Court-ordered *ex parte* subpoenas are available to the AG, or his high-level designee, to secure "educational records" (20 U.S.C. 1232g) and national education statistics (20 U.S.C. 9007).

It is incumbent on the Department of Justice, in connection with any comprehensive review of the PATRIOT Act, to report publicly on whether or not law enforcement has, or does not have, the investigatory tools it needs to prevent terrorist attacks. In other words, it appears to be time for a follow-up legal audit of the PATRIOT Act and the government's other legal tools used in the fight against terrorism.

PATRIOT ACT 2—A TRIAL BALLOON

Lawyers at the Department of Justice may also have concluded that in light of the PATRIOT Act's many gaps and shortcomings, it was time for a legal audit: a comprehensive review, correction, and improvement of the act. In the first quarter of 2003, a document surfaced entitled "Domestic Security Enhancement Act of 2003 (Confidential—not for distribution—Draft—January 9, 2003)." It was soon referred to as "Patriot Act 2" although the

Department of Justice denied that the 87-page document was an official proposal of either the Bush administration or the Department of Justice.

The document gave the appearance of being an effort by Department of Justice lawyers concerned with the inadequacy of the hurriedly passed PATRIOT Act. PATRIOT Act 2 included both important substantive provisions and technical corrections.

One important and substantive section, 101, would have amended FISA to reach "lone-wolf" terrorists—persons not known at the time of the investigation to be acting as agents of a foreign power—at the time a FISA jurisdictional prerequisite. Zacarias Moussaoui, sometimes alleged to be the twentieth 9/11 hijacker, then awaiting a federal court trial in Alexandria, Virginia, was said to be in the lone-wolf category.[15]

If PATRIOT Act 2 was intended as a trial balloon, it did not fly very far. According to the *Washington Times*, PATRIOT Act 2, after being leaked by the Department of Justice, "met with widespread criticism from the right and the left."[16] House Judiciary Chairman F. James Sensenbrenner (R-WI) told the AG "that it would be 'extremely counter-productive' to pursue . . . PATRIOT Act 2 legislation."[17]

PREVENTING TERRORISM AND THE FUTURE OF THE PATRIOT ACT

Since nine of the provisions of the PATRIOT Act would have "sunset," or cease to have their previous effect, on December 31, 2005,[18] it became necessary for Congress to reevaluate the act.

As the December 31, 2005 deadline approached, some persons, not familiar with that act, referred to the imminent expiration of the PATRIOT Act. In reality, the effects of the sunset provisions were progressive, not immediate, and related to nine of the act's sections. The sunset provisions did not affect any particular foreign intelligence investigation commenced prior to the year 2006. Nor did the sunset provisions apply to offenses that began or occurred prior to 2006. If not amended, the sunset provisions over time would affect new investigations and the investigation and prosecution of new criminal acts.

Notwithstanding the progressive effect of a failure to renew the sunset provisions of the PATRIOT Act, the director of the FBI's National Security Branch was quoted as saying "[as] tools are removed or not provided to us . . . it does diminish our effectiveness at what we do."[19]

On December 9, 2005, it was reported that Republican negotiators "accepted a White House brokered deal," reflected in a Senate and House Conference Report, extending the PATRIOT Act in modified form for four years. The AG said that the compromise was a "win for the American people."[20]

However, in an acrimonious final session of Congress prior to adjournment, the PATRIOT Act was extended for only five weeks, until February 3, 2006.[21]

Consequently, as of the end of 2005, the crisis in law enforcement and counterterrorism policy continued. What was at issue was whether or not to continue the FBI's post-9/11 role as an agency with the mission of preventing terrorism. The AG indicated the concessions to civil liberties reflected in the Conference Report were acceptable to the administration. Congress, however, was slow to respond.

It was not until March 7, 2006, that the House of Representatives approved a reauthorization of the PATRIOT Act that had previously been passed by the Senate.[22] The measure was subsequently signed by the president on March 9. According to the Conference Report, the short title of the reauthorization is "USA PATRIOT Improvement and Reauthorization Act of 2005" (H.R. Report 109–333, 2005). The legislation deals with a variety of subjects unrelated to the PATRIOT Act itself. For example, Title II concerns "Terrorist Death Penalty Enhancement," Title III concerns crime at "America's Seaports," Title IV concerns "Terrorism Financing," Title VI deals with the "Secret Service," and Title VII is the "Combat Methamphetamine Epidemic Act of 2005."

Section 102 of the new legislation eliminated the previous sunset provisions and establishes new four-year sunset provisions only with respect to "roving" wiretaps and for business records sought under Section 215 of FISA.

Section 106 amends Section 215 of the PATRIOT Act to provide that tangible things sought under a Section 215 order must be "relevant" to an authorized preliminary or full investigation and be supported by a statement of facts (see the undated "Joint Explanatory Statement of the Committee Conference"). Only high officials of the FBI may apply for an "order requiring the production of library circulation records, library patrons' lists, book sales records, educational records, book customer lists, firearms sales records, tax return records, educational records, or medical records containing information that would identify a person."

In addition, a recipient of a Section 215 order may disclose the order to a lawyer and challenge the order in secret proceedings before a special panel of FISA court judges called a "Petition Review Pool." The FISA court is directed to publish procedures for in-camera hearings on such petitions (Section 106(f)). In addition, the AG is required to adopt stringent "minimization procedures" to prevent "dissemination of non-publicly available information concerning unconsenting United States persons..." (Section 106(g)).

Section 108 concerns roving wiretaps and provides that an application for an order must contain specific facts that the target may possibly thwart more traditional surveillance.

Sections 115–119 concerns National Security Letters. The most significant change is that a recipient of a National Security Letter may within one year challenge a nondisclosure requirement by filing a petition in the U.S. district court where he resides or does business. The district court must close any hearings, and keep all records under seal to "prevent unauthorized disclosure" (Section 115(d)). It is notable that Congress did not give judicial review authority over National Security Letters to the FISA trial court. Presumably, this was done both to spare litigants the burden of traveling to Washington, D.C., and to reflect the fact that under prior law the United States was the only party to appear before the FISA trial court. By contrast, with respect to Section 215 orders, for the production of business records, judicial review authority was conferred on a "Petition Review Pool" of the FISA court.

In sum, the PATRIOT Act was reauthorized with new judicial review and congressional oversight provisions. Common sense ultimately prevailed. The threat of nonrenewal, or fundamental changes in the act, did not materialize.

However, this did not mean that controversy over FISA was at an end—quite the contrary. On August 3, 2007, Congress enacted P.L. 110-55, an amendment to FISA titled "Protect America Act of 2007." This act, signed into law by the president on August 5, 2007, was temporary legislation to deal with a new crisis in intelligence gathering that arose on May 21, 2008 (see pp. __ *infra.*) in that the important provisions of the act were to be repealed 180 days after enactment, namely, February 1, 2008 (Public Law 110-55). Because of this sunset provision, by early 2008 Congress would have to revisit key aspects of FISA, if only to extend the sunset dates as it did in 2005 and 2006 in connection with previous amendments to FISA.

THE PROTECT AMERICA ACT OF 2007

The Protect America Act of 2007 amended FISA in a number of significant ways. In Section 105A, as a "clarification," the FISA definition of the term "electronic surveillance" provides that the term shall not be "construed to encompass surveillance directed at a person reasonably believed to be located outside of the United States." This provision excludes from the FISA warrant requirements the interception of communications of persons outside of the United States that for any reason pass through and are intercepted in the United States even if a person in the United States happens to be a party to the communication. Prior to the clarification, "electronic surveillance" was defined as the interception of communications "sent by or intended to be received by a particular, known United States person who is in the United States, if the contents are acquired by intentionally targeting that United States person" (Section 101(f)).

In Section 105B, additional procedures are specified for the surveillance of persons "reasonably believed to be outside of the United States."

The Director of National Intelligence (DNI) and the AG may, for a period of one year, authorize the "acquisition of foreign intelligence information concerning persons reasonably believed to be outside of the United States if they certify in writing and under oath that five conditions are met (if immediate action is required, the certification may be completed within 72 hours). The five conditions constitute signification restrictions on the conduct of the DNI and the AG."

They must certify that (1) "there are reasonable procedures in place for determining that the acquisition of foreign intelligence information . . . concerns persons reasonably believed to be located outside of the United States." The certification must be supported by affidavits of high officials in the national security field.

Additionally, (2) these procedures "will be subject to review" by the FISA trial court. The DNI and the AG are also required to certify that the acquisition of information "does not constitute electronic surveillance." In light of the definition of "electronic surveillance" in Section 105A, this means that the surveillance is directed at a person "reasonably believed to be located outside of the United States."

(3) That "the acquisition involves the obtaining of foreign intelligence information from or with the assistance of a communications service provider."

(4) That "a significant purpose of the acquisition is to obtain foreign intelligence information." This provision reinforces the PATRIOT Act's amendments to FISA making it clear that electronic surveillance could have more than one purpose and need not be only to secure foreign intelligence information as the FISA trial court had incorrectly concluded.

(5) That "minimization procedures will be used that comply with the pre-existing FISA provisions that minimize the acquisition and dissemination of information concerning United States persons.

Pursuant to Section 105B(b), the Section 105A certificate "is not required to identify the specific facilities, places, premises, or property at which the acquisition of foreign intelligence information will be directed."

Section 105B(c) requires the AG to promptly transmit the certification to the FISA trial court under seal.

Pursuant to Section 105B(d), the AG and DNI are required to report to designated congressional committees their assessment of the compliance with the procedures, which they established.

Subsequent provisions deal with the obligations and rights of persons receiving a directive to secretly assist in the electronic acquisition of foreign intelligence information (Sections 105B(e)—(m)).

The government is obligated to compensate such persons "at the prevailing rate" for "providing information . . . or assistance" (Section 105B(f)).

Persons receiving such a directive may challenge its legality in the FISA trial court (Section 105B(h)(1)(A)). The presiding FISA trial court shall assign the petition to a FISA trial judge who shall conduct an initial review of the petition within 48 hours. If the trial judge determines that the petition is frivolous, the petition shall be immediately denied and the directive affirmed. If the petition is determined not to be frivolous, within 72 hours the petition shall be considered and a written statement issued of the reasons for any determination (Section 105B(h)(1)(B)).

A FISA trial judge considering a petition to modify or set aside a directive may grant the petition only if the directive does not meet the requirements of Section 105B "or is otherwise unlawful." If the trial judge does not modify or set aside the directive, it shall be immediately affirmed and the court shall "order the recipient to comply with such directive" (Section 105B(h)(1)(B) (2) and (3)). Any directive not explicitly modified or set aside shall remain in effect (id.).

After FISA trial court review an aggrieved person may in seven days see review in the FISA Court of Review, and if dissatisfied with the Court of Review's decision may petition the Supreme Court of the United States for discretionary review (Section 105B(i)).

All judicial proceedings under Section 105B are to be concluded expeditiously and shall be filed under seal and at the government's request its submissions shall be reviewed "exparte and in camera" (Sections 105B(j) and (l)). (Under such circumstances the petitioner will not know from the pleadings what arguments the government has advanced).

One of the most controversial provisions of Section 105B is subsection (1), which grants prospective immunity to "any person providing any information, facilities or assistance in accordance with a directive" under Section 105B(e). No immunity is granted to persons who provided similar assistance to the government after September 11, 2001, and prior to the enactment of the Protect America Act of 2007 in August 2007.

The legislation also amends FISA to provide for trial court review of "the procedures by which the government determines that acquisition conducted pursuant to Section 105B does not constitute electronic surveillance." The procedures are required to be submitted by the government to the trial court within 120 days of the "effective date of the Act and annually thereafter" (Section 105C(a)).

Within 180 days after the effective date of the Act, the FISA trial court shall determine whether or not the government's determination concerning its procedures for deciding what constitutes "electronic surveillance" is "clearly erroneous" (Section 105C(b)). If the court concludes that the "determination is not clearly erroneous, it shall enter an order approving the continued use of such procedures." If the court concludes that the "determination is clearly erroneous" the government is required to submit new procedures in 30 days or cease acquisition of information by means that the court regards as improper (Section 105C(c)).

In lieu of submitting new procedures, the government may appeal the FISA trial court decision to the FISA Court of Review and may thereafter seek discretionary review in the Supreme Court of the United States. During the period of the appeal and discretionary review process, the government may continue to utilize the challenged foreign intelligence acquisition procedures (Section 105C(d)).

Under another amendment to FISA designated as Section 4, the AG shall report semiannually to designated congressional committees concerning incidents of noncompliance with directives by elements of the intelligence community with the guidelines for determining if a person is "reasonably [believed] to be outside of the United States"; noncompliance with directives issued to persons under Section 105B(e) and the number of Section 105B(d) certifications issued under Section 105B(a) during the reporting period.

Under Section 6C the major prospective provisions of the Protect America Act of 2007 were to expire in 180 days, namely, February 1, 2008, though outstanding directives would remain in effect. As the critical date neared, Congress and the administration could not agree on the terms of a permanent extension.

Under Section 105B(g) communication service providers are prospectively protected from civil liability if they furnish "information, facilities, or technical assistance pursuant to a [FISA] court order."

Though some of the reasons for these amendments to FISA are based on highly classified information, in an August 22, 2007, interview with Chris Roberts of the *El Paso Times* (El Paso, Texas), National Intelligence Director Mike McConnell partially lifted the security curtain in key respects to explain the purpose behind some of the new provisions. The transcript of this interview, which is available at www.elpasotimes.com/news/ci_6685679, is cited as herein "Roberts Tr." followed by the number of the answer. (The answers here are numbered sequentially as they appear in the transcript. The answer numbers do not appear in the transcript itself.)

McConnell explained that the difficulty arose in connection with wire communications between foreign persons that happened to be routed through the United States. (By contrast, the wireless communications are not regarded as subject to the FISA warrant requirement. Roberts Tr. 1.) Initially, a FISA court judge had ruled that in such circumstances a FISA warrant was not required. Roberts Tr. 2. Subsequently, a different FISA judge (there are 11 FISA judges), in a ruling that became effective May 31, 2007, held that a warrant was required. This complete change in the interpretation of the warrant requirement led to a third crisis in intelligence gathering.[23] As McConnell remarked in the interview, to explain his dilemma after the new interpretation went into effect, "the current threat is increasing ... our capability is decreasing." Roberts Tr. 2.

The DNI also explained that it was not practical to secure a warrant for all intercepted communications passing through the United States since it takes 200 man hours to secure a FISA warrant for just one phone number. Roberts Tr. 4.

Between May and August 3, 2007, McConnell talked to 260 senators and congressmen in an effort to secure corrective legislation.

McConnell's second concern was the possible civil liability of service providers, such as private phone companies, that might be bankrupted by civil suits based on the assistance they rendered to the National Security Agency. Roberts Tr. 5, 7. Section 105B(1) of the Protect America Act of 2007 provided prospective immunity only. McConnell was adamant that a grant of retroactive immunity should be considered by Congress and granted when it reconvened.

The third problem involved foreign persons calling to the United States. Since such calls originating overseas number in the thousands, a warrant requirement would not be practical. Roberts Tr. 13. Since the number of U.S. persons deemed to be targets as a result of overseas communications number less than 100, a Section 105 warrant requirement was, in his view, practical.

An interesting commentary on the FISA statutory amendment process was made in an August 19, 2007, *New York Times* article by James Risen and Eric Lichtblau. They wrote, "The measure, which President Bush signed into law on August 5, was written and pushed through both the House and Senate so quickly that few in Congress had time to absorb its full impact, some Congressional aides say."

How many members of Congress "absorbed" the legislation may be difficult to judge, but we do know from the McConnell interview that he talked to 260 members of Congress in a three-month period. This drawn-out and extensive consultative process has its own ominous aspects.

Instead of concentrating on coordinating and guiding national intelligence efforts, during a period of several months the DNI briefed 260 members of Congress in an effort to undo an errant ruling by one judge sitting on the error-prone FISA court. By virtue of the large number of persons McConnell felt it necessary to meet with to forge a consensus for remedial legislation, intelligence sources and methods were compromised. This is not a mere matter of technical or academic concern. In the interview, McConnell made it clear that as a result of the expanded congressional consultative process "Americans are going to die." Roberts Tr. 14, 15.

AMERICANS ARE GOING TO DIE

So that there is no confusion as to this important consideration, the relevant portions of the Roberts Transcript are reproduced below:

Q. You have to do public relations, I assume.

A. Well, one of the things you do is you talk to reporters. And you give them the facts the best you can. Now part of this is a classified world. *The fact we're doing it this way means that some Americans are going to die*, because we do this mission unknown to the bad guys because they're using a process that we can exploit and the more we talk about it, the more they will go with an alternative means and when they go to alternative means, remember what I said, a significant portion of what we do, this is not just threats against the United States, this is war in Afghanistan and Iraq.

Q. So you're saying that the reporting and the debate in Congress means that some Americans are going to die?[24]

A. That's what I mean. Because we have made it so public. We used to do these things very differently, but for whatever reason, you know, it's a democratic process and sunshine's a good thing. We need to have the debate...

Q. So you don't think there was an alternative way to do this?

A. There may have been an alternative way, but we are where we are....

Q. A better way, I should say.

A. All of my briefs initially were classified. But it became apparent that we were not going to be able to carry the day if we don't talk to more people.

Q. Some might say that's the price you pay for living in a free society. Do you think that this is necessary that these Americans die?

A. We could have gotten there a different way. We conducted intelligence since World War II and we've maintained a sensitivity as far as sources and methods. It's basically a sources and methods argument. If you don't protect sources and methods then those you target will choose alternative means, different paths...

Roberts Tr. 14–18. (emphasis supplied)

THE FAILURE OF CONGRESS TO IMPLEMENT 9/11 COMMISSION RECOMMENDATIONS

Nowhere are the failures of Congress to implement 9/11 Commission recommendations more egregious than with respect to intelligence (and Homeland Security) oversight. *The 9/11 Commission Report*, while conceding the difficulty of changing congressional committee jurisdiction, characterized congressional oversight for "intelligence and counter terrorism" as "dysfunctional" (Report at p. 420).

In one of its most important recommendations, the commission stated, "We have considered various alternatives: A joint committee on the old model of the Joint Committee on Atomic Energy is one. A single committee in each house of Congress, combining authorizing and approaching authorities, is another" (id.). The commission urged that the "committees should be smaller—perhaps seven or nine members in each house" (id., 421).

Congress ignored the commission's recommendations with respect to reforming congressional oversight of intelligence until January 2007 when the House of Representatives took steps to implement the 9/11

Commission's recommendation, which urged the "creation of smaller committees responsible for both authorization and appropriation of intelligence funding, thereby limiting the numbers of lawmakers involved in the process and improving oversight" (Res. 35 (110th Congress) History). The House reorganization process was hampered by the fact, as noted in the official explanation:

> The House Appropriations Committee has been reluctant to give up its long-standing prerogatives related to the appropriations process to a separate committee. The Defense Subcommittee already has jurisdiction over military intelligence spending, and is reluctant to give up jurisdiction over the entire intelligence budget.

As a "compromise" the House created an additional committee called a "Select Intelligence Oversight Panel of the Committee on Appropriations." The 13-member panel is made up of 10 House Appropriations Committee members ("including the Chairman and Ranking Members of the full committee and Defense Appropriations Subcommittee"). Three members were selected from the Permanent Select Committee on Intelligence. All appointments were made by the Speaker of the House.

Representative Rush Holt (D-NJ), chairman of the Select Intelligence Oversight Panel, writing in *Defense News* (August 6, 2007) described the panel's three functions: continuing the study of budget requests for "and execution of intelligence activities"; to "make recommendations to relevant Appropriations subcommittees"; and to "prepare an annual report to the Appropriations Defense subcommittee."

Holt noted that "[c]reation of the panel increased fourfold the number of hearings on intelligence matters" compared with the previous year and that "controversial and high profile" issues such as "electronic surveillance activities" were examined in depth. Notwithstanding this apparent improvement in the House's intelligence oversight, the handling of the 2007 FISA amendments by both houses of Congress was irresponsible. The Senate, unlike the House of Representatives, did not even restructure its intelligence oversight and appropriation functions.

Theoretically, the amendment process could have been very different from what actually occurred. Instead of participating in 260 interviews with members of Congress during a three-month period, the DNI could have appeared twice: before one Senate and one House committee. The two committees could have promptly approved remedial legislation for congressional action, saving the country from the two-month period of diminished intelligence-gathering capability, which the existing system permitted.

Even more important, if there had been only two intelligence committees, both with small membership, as the 9/11 Commission advised, the risk of exposing "sources and methods" would have been greatly reduced. Disclosing classified information to 260 members of Congress increases the chance that sources and methods will be compromised. Yet the DNI regretfully came to the conclusion that the needed corrective legislation would not pass unless he increased significantly the number of his briefings. NoDNI should be faced with such a dilemma. Congress should take seriously the DNI's warning that diffusion of congressional decision-making authority relating to intelligence contributes to the unfortunate reality that "Americans will die."

Restricting the number of committees and persons involved in intelligence matters should not preclude full and vigorous debate of all relevant policy issues. To insure that this objective is achieved, the selections of committee members should be structured to include a broad spectrum of viewpoints.

THE CONTINUING DISPUTE OVER THE PROTECT AMERICA ACT

As noted above, key provisions of the Protect America Act were to "sunset" on February 1, 2008, but Congress was unable to agree on the terms of a permanent extension. Accordingly, a 15-day extension of the act was passed and signed by the president.

As the end of the 15-day period approached, there was still no agreement between the House of Representatives and the Senate. The *Washington Post*, February 13, 2008, reported that the Senate approved permanent legislation containing retroactive immunity to communications providers that had assisted the government. The same story noted that some House Democrats objected to the immunity provision passed by the Senate. In order to bring the dispute to a conclusion, a White House spokesperson announced that the president would not sign another extension of the Protect America Act. "It is increasingly clear Congress will not act until it has to, and a second extension will only lead to a third," the spokesperson was quoted as saying (id.).

However, no agreement between the House and Senate versions could be reached and the Protect America Act of 2007 sunset provision went in to effect at midnight on February 16, 2008. Congress declared a week-long recess precluding any legislation during that period (*Washington Post*, February 16, 2008). Two House Republicans, writing in the Commentary section of *The Washington Times* (February 28, 2008), charged that House leaders refused to submit the Senate-passed version to a floor vote in the House "because they knew it would pass with bipartisan support." Under the sunset provisions, previously authorized surveillance directives could continue until August 2008, but new surveillance activities would be governed by the law as it existed prior to the effective date of the Protect America Act on August 5, 2007. Congressional Democrats and McConnell sharply disputed the significance of this change.

In the op ed column of the February 15, 2008, edition of the *Washington Post*, McConnell explained the importance of retroactive immunity and stressed that without it intelligence-gathering capability would be significantly decreased. Robert D. Novak in a *Washington Post* column (February 18, 2008) characterized the House opposition to retroactive immunity as a sellout to trial lawyers who had provided generous financial support to the Democratic Party.

The *New York Times* reported that House Democrats sought to minimize the significance of the lapsed authority. The National Edition of February 16, 2008, contains the following:

> House Democrats, in turn, accused the president of needlessly frightening the American people and insisted that intelligence agencies would still have the ability to monitor suspected terrorists if temporary surveillance authority lapsed at midnight Saturday. The Democrats noted that the underlying law, the Foreign Intelligence Surveillance Act, would remain in force.

This argument is obviously disingenuous. With the failure to extend the Protect America Act, the law reverted to the FISA law as it existed between May 31, 2007, and August 5, 2007. As previously noted, this was a crisis period in intelligence gathering. As a result of a FISA court judge's ruling imposing a new and impractical warrant requirement concerning communications that happened to be routed through the United States, the ability to gather intelligence, according to McConnell, was decreased. In addition, the warrant requirement was being applied to overseas calls to persons in the United States prior to the time such U.S. persons were targeted for surveillance. The Protect America Act was enacted in part to remedy this serious situation. The failure of Congress to act has the effect of reimposing a dangerous restriction on gathering foreign intelligence, corrected by the Protect America Act of 2007.

To respond to Republican criticism of the failure of the House of Representatives to renew the Protect America Act of 2007, a distinguished group of Congressional Democrats submitted an article to the *Washington Post*, February 25, 2008. The authors were Senators Jay Rockefeller, chairman of the Senate Select Committee on Intelligence, Patrick Leahy, chairman of the Senate Judiciary Committee, Congressmen Silvestre Reyes, chairman of the House Permanent Select Committee on Intelligence, and John Conyers, chairman of the House Judiciary Committee. They argued that intelligence-gathering did not "go dark" on February 16 when the Protect America Act expired because if "a new member of a known group, a new phone number or a new email address is identified, U.S. intelligence can add it to existing orders, and surveillance can begin immediately." A problem with this argument is that it had previously been reported that some telecommunications companies had "delayed or refused compliance with requests to add surveillance targets to general orders that were approved before the law expired" (*Washington Post*, February 23, 2008). With the immunity issue unresolved, their reluctance is understandable. The four authors contended that in an emergency, surveillance can begin immediately and that FISA court orders do not have to be obtained for three days. This is in effect an argument that a failure of Congress to pass legislation constitutes an "emergency" justifying surveillance.

Significantly, the article did not mention the issue of retroactive immunity for telecommunication companies that had assisted the government after 9/11. Clearly, the authors displayed no sense of urgency. They mentioned reconciling House and Senate differences "in coming weeks."

Nor do the four authors acknowledge that in light of a new FISA trial court ruling that became effective on May 31, 2007, the surveillance of communications between persons outside the United States became subject to FISA warrant requirements if the electronic impulses containing the communication passed through switches located in the United States. As McConnell explained, this placed an unworkable burden on those involved in covert surveillance and diminished intelligence-gathering capability.

In addition, the FISA trial court was insisting that warrants be secured for surveillance of communications originating abroad but directed to the U.S. persons even prior to the time that a U.S. person became an investigation target.

It was to deal with the crisis these interpretations created that the Protect America Act of 2007 was enacted. The failure of Congress to extend the act recreated the unworkable situation that led to its enactment except to the extent that additional "names and numbers" could be added to existing directives, which could continue in effect for a year from their date of issuance. Notably, no one has publicly contended that the intelligence community regards the "supplementing directive" approach as both legal and workable.

H.R. 3773

On March 13, 2008, the House of Representatives went into a rare secret session, only the fifth since 1825, to consider the FISA legislation. "After a two-hour security sweep of the House Chamber, the session convened at 10:00 PM." The secret session was not productive. According to the Democrats, nothing compelling was presented. The Republicans contended that the Democrats were unwilling to listen (see *Washington Post*, March 15, 2008).

The next day, Friday, March 14, 2008, the House of Representatives on a party line vote, passed comprehensive FISA amendments greatly at variance with the bipartisan version passed by the Senate (*Los Angeles Times*, March 15, 2008).

The House of Representatives "FISA Amendments of 2008" H.R. 3773 is lengthy (46 pages), complicated, and strewn with questionable policy judgments.

Section 702(b)(3) provides in part that without prior FISA court approval the intelligence community "may not intentionally target a United States person reasonably believed to be *located outside the United States*" (emphasis supplied). This is a radical change from the original FISA provision, Section 1801(f)(1), in which the meaning of the term "electronic surveillance" is made applicable to "a particular known United States person, *who is in the United States*" (emphasis supplied).

Section 703 specifies in considerable detail the procedures to be followed to secure FISA court approval for targeting "a United States person believed to be located outside the United States."

Under Section 704(a)(2), absent a FISA court order, a U.S. person located outside the United States shall not be targeted where such person "has a reasonable expectation of privacy and a warrant would be required if the acquisition were conducted in the United States for law enforcement purposes." This is a standard previously applicable to targeting a U.S. person in the United States (see Section 1801(f)(1)).

Under the House amendments, except for emergency authorizations, surveillance shall be preceded by a written certification under oath to the FISA court signed by the AG and the DNI (Section 702(g)(1) and (2)).

Section 110 directs that inspector generals in the intelligence community shall conduct an investigation and report to Congress concerning the "president's surveillance program" conducted during the period beginning September 11, 2001, and ending January 17, 2007.

The significance of the January 17, 2007, date is that by a letter of that date the AG of the United States advised key congressional leaders that "a Judge of the Foreign Intelligence Surveillance Court issued orders authorizing the Government to target for collection international communications into or out of the United States where there is probable cause to believe that one of the communicants is a member or agent of al Qaeda or an associated terrorist organization." As a consequence, the Terrorist Surveillance Program that had previously been conducted without a FISA warrant was terminated when the current authorizations expired. After the date of the AG's letter, the surveillance was to be "conducted subject to the approval of the [FISA] Court" (letter from the Attorney General of the United States to Congressional leaders, dated January 17, 2007, www.fas.ord/irp/agency/doj/fisa/ag011707.pdf [accessed March 24, 2008]).

The House proposals in Title VIII regulate litigation by private parties against electronic communication service providers who furnished assistance to the intelligence community. By contrast, the Senate version granted such providers retroactive immunity. The government is permitted to intervene in pending litigation and provides classified information to the court.

Title III establishes in the Legislative Branch of government a "commission on warrantless electronic surveillance" to investigate and report "on electronic surveillance activities conducted without a warrant between September 11, 2001, and January 17, 2007."

The guidelines and procedures mandated by the House-passed legislation are so complicated that the DNI is directed to "establish a training program for appropriate personnel of the intelligence community to ensure that the guidelines ... are properly implemented" (Section 702(f)(3)).

In an editorial on March 16, 2008, the *Washington Post* seemed to accept the fact that reconciling the Senate and House versions would be a difficult and time-consuming task. It was suggested that a realistic goal would be to reconcile them before the current set of surveillance directions began to expire in August 2008 (*Washington Post*, March 16, 2008).

THE FIRST AMENDMENT ACT OF 2008

The prediction as to the amount of time it would take to resolve the House/Senate differences turned out to be remarkably accurate. H.R. 6304, the FISA Amendments Act of 2008, was passed by the House on June 20 and by the Senate on June 25, 2008. The president signed the bill in a Rose Garden ceremony on July 10, 2008.

The "Legislative History" consists primarily of a 23-page "Section-by-Section Analysis and Explanation by Senator John D. Rockefeller IV, Chairman of the (Senate) Select Committee on Intelligence," prepared prior to passage of the legislation by the Senate. Hereinafter, this document is cited as "FISA Analysis" followed by the page number.

Previously, the Senate and the House had reached an impasse. H.R. 3773 was passed by the House on November 15, 2007, and the significantly different FISA amendments passed the Senate as S.2248 on February 12, 2008. As Rockefeller explained, "No formal conference was convened to resolve the difference between the two Houses on H.R. 3773 and S.2248. Instead, following an agreement reached without a formal conference, the House passed a new bill, H.R. 6304, which contains a complete compromise of the difference on H.R. 3773" (FISA Analysis, p. 1).

The most significant aspects of the FISA Amendments Act of 2008 are as follows:

1. Electronic Communications Service Providers are given retroactive immunity in Section 802 for assistance rendered to the government between September 11, 2001, and January 17, 2007, when the warrantless surveillance program came to an end. In order for a provider to receive this immunity the AG must furnish a certification to the U.S. District Court in which the action against the provider is pending, substantiating the government's request for assistance. The court can reject the certification if it "is not supported by substantial evidence" (Section 802(b), FISA Analysis, p. 18–21). This Title of the Act should achieve the objective sought by the DNI to protect providers cooperating with the government after 9/11 to promote national security.

2. Section 102(a) amends FISA to provide that it is the exclusive means by which electronic surveillance and interception of certain communications may be

conducted (FISA Analysis, p. 12–14). Congress rejected the contention by the government that the Authorization for the Use of Military Force, Pub. L. 107-40 (September 18, 2001) was an additional statutory basis for electronic surveillance. Henceforth, express statutory authorizations will be required (id., 13).

3. Section 109(b) allows "the FISA court [by a majority vote of its judges] to hold a hearing, or rehearing, of a matter *en banc*, which is by all the judges who constitute the FISA court sitting together" (FISA Analysis, p. 17). This traditional power of trial courts was previously unavailable to the FISA court. The *en banc* authority will make it possible for the court on its own, or on application of a party, to correct erroneous rulings by a single judge. This is a welcome development.

4. Title I of the Act establishes a new FISA Title VII and makes significant changes in the targeting of the communications of persons outside the United States.

5. Section 702 deals with the surveillance of non-U.S. persons "reasonably believed to be located outside the United States." Such acquisitions "may be conducted only in accordance with targeting and minimization procedures approved at least annually by the FISA court and a certification of the Attorney General and the DNI" that the statutory requirements have been met or that "exigent circumstances" require targeting for a limited time without prior court order (FISA Analysis, pp. 4–6). The certification "is not required to identify the specific facilities, places, premises, or property at which the acquisition . . . will be directed or conducted" (Section 702(g)(4)).

6. Section 703 deals with the acquisition within the United States of foreign intelligence concerning U.S. persons located outside the United States. Such surveillance requires a FISA Court order and a finding by the court, *inter alia*, that there is a probable cause to believe that the U.S. person is "a foreign power, an agent of a foreign power, or an officer or employee of a foreign power" (Section 703(c)(1), FISA Analysis, pp. 9–10).

7. Section 704 governs "the physical search of a home, office, or business of a U.S. person by an element of the United States intelligence community, outside of the United States." The court must determine that there is probable cause to believe that the target "is a foreign power, or an agent, officer or employee of a foreign power" (FISA Analysis, pp. 10–11). The analysis goes on to explain that "because an acquisition under section 704 is conducted outside the United States, or is otherwise not covered by FISA, the FISA court is expressly not given jurisdiction to review the means by which an acquisition under this section may be accomplished" (id., p. 11. Section 704(c)(3)(A)).

CONCLUSION

What stands out in the history of FISA is the extent to which national security was prejudiced by the errors and poor judgment of the FISA trial court. Prior to 9/11, the wall it created between intelligence and law enforcement was, according to the FISA Court of Review, not required by statute or permitted by the U.S. Constitution. The unnecessary wall contributed to the disaster of 9/11.

Though it deserves most of the blame, the FISA trial court was not the only culpable party. Both the Department of Justice, under several administrations, and Congress, must share a degree of responsibility.

After 9/11, with the enactment of the PATRIOT Act, it should have been clear to the FISA trial court that Congress had "taken down the wall." However, the FISA trial court perversely maintained the wall for almost a year until reversed by the FISA Court of Review on November 18, 2002. This period of time was the second crisis in intelligence gathering attributable to the FISA trial court.

During 2005 and 2006, the drawn-out process of renewing and modifying the PATRIOT Act put at risk the effective gathering of foreign intelligence and counterintelligence. Ultimately, common sense prevailed, and the PATRIOT Act was renewed with significant but acceptable changes.

The third crisis in intelligence gathering took place in 2007 when one of the 11 FISA trial court judges changed a long-standing rule of interpretation that a FISA warrant was not required to intercept communications between parties, neither of whom were located in the United States, merely because the interception took place domestically. This strained interpretation adversely affected the gathering of needed intelligence. This unfortunate situation led in part to the 2007 FISA amendments in the Protect America Act, an objective of which was to undo one FISA judge's impractical interpretation of the warrant requirement.

The fourth crisis was not created by the FISA court but rather by the inaction of the House of Representatives that permitted portions of the Protect America Act of 2007 to sunset on February 16, 2008, creating unfortunate uncertainty concerning the surveillance of new targets. There was little justification for taking this chance with national security.

The failure to act in a timely fashion was compounded by the House of Representatives enacting comprehensive FISA amendments greatly at variance from the bipartisan Senate version, which was supported by the intelligence community and the president. This created an impasse, which was difficult and predictably time-consuming for Congress to resolve. It did not do so until July 2008 when amendments to FISA were enacted.

What is also disappointing about the congressional amendment process is that Congress did not implement the 9/11 Commission recommendation that oversight of intelligence activities be by one joint committee of Congress, or one House and one Senate committee. Instead, the DNI, in order to ensure the passage of essential correcting legislation, found it necessary to meet with 260 members of Congress and to appear before various committees. This inevitably led to compromising intelligence sources and methods, a matter so serious that McConnell concluded that as a result "Americans will die."

Any hope that when the 2007 FISA amendment came up for renewal in 2008, Congress would have reformed its procedures for safeguarding classified information by reducing the number of committees and persons involved in considering intelligence matters was not realized.

Postscript

It is fair to assume that comrades-in-scholarship improve knowledge particularly when the subject studied is as perplexed as the quest for security at home and abroad. It is hoped that *Terrorists in Our Midst*, a multi-authored work, can shed some collective insights on this challenge facing the United States with serious international implications for the remainder of the twenty-first century.

Since the manuscript was completed in the fall of 2009, the editor and some of his colleagues have decided to prepare a postscript. It contains several aspects omitted, clarifies previous interpretations, supplements noteworthy developments, and offers some general observations and preliminary recommendations. Each contributor to the postscript is solely responsible for his identified section.

THE ROLE OF INTELLIGENCE IN AFFINITY TERRORISM

Raymond Tanter and Stephen Kersting

In reflecting on the role of intelligence in foreign-affinity terrorism, it is critical for successive American administrations to build on institutions and policies created by their predecessors, while making incremental adjustments as new threats appear on the horizon. Recall German strategist Helmut von Moltke's famous dictum, "No [war] plan survives contact with the enemy." Likewise, Daniel Benjamin, Coordinator for Counterterrorism at the Department of State holds that, "One of the critical tests of an administration's counterterrorism policies is to see how they emerge from contact with a genuine terrorist event."[1]

To determine how policies and institutions from the Bush administration survived from contact with terrorist events during the Obama presidency and add a postscript to the cases discussed in this study, consider several incidents that closed out the first decade of the twenty-first century.

In the most successful affinity terrorist attack to date in the United States, Nidal Malik Hasan, a U.S. Army major serving as a psychiatrist, killed 13 of his comrades and wounded 30 more during a November 2009 shooting spree at Fort Hood, in Texas. The attack was of the same type but of an order of magnitude greater than the shooting of a Little Rock Army recruiter that June by Abdulhakim Mujahid Muhammad. Based on the available information, Major Hasan is the prototypical affinity terrorist. Born and raised in the United States, he had no formal relationship with a terrorist organization. Yet, for reasons that remain obscure, Major Hasan came to identify with radical Islamists fighting U.S. forces in Iraq and Afghanistan. His disillusionment led Hasan to make statements that intelligence agencies could have used to question his loyalty to the United States; such statements along with the fact that he initiated contact with a radical cleric based in Yemen—Anwar al-Awlaki—should have rung alarm bells at the Bureau (FBI) as well as at the Central Intelligence Agency (CIA) and within U.S. military intelligence.[2]

Regarding the role of intelligence in affinity terrorism, there does not seem to have been an intelligence sharing problem in the mold of pre-9/11 failures. Instead, the FBI appears to have been reluctant to act on the intelligence it had. The CIA and FBI reportedly knew of Major Hasan's electronic communications with al-Awlaki, who was a spiritual advisor to two 9/11 highjackers, months before the attack at Fort Hood. Press reports indicate that it was surveillance of al-Awlaki's communications in Yemen that revealed the connection to Major Hasan; the emails were most likely uncovered by the NSA and referred to the FBI via the National Counterterrorism Center—the location for fusion of terrorism related intelligence, both foreign and domestic. Key institutions of the Bush administration were in place for use by the Obama administration.

The FBI claims that the content of the messages between Hasan and al-Awlaki in no way indicated terrorist intent and could have been explained at the time as innocuous research into Muslim attitudes, within Major Hasan's research field.[3] The seemingly harmless content of the emails draws into sharp relief the challenges of preventing affinity terrorism. In terms of getting the information into the hands of the intelligence community component that should make decisions, in this case the FBI, the intelligence system worked. However, the key policy question arising from the Fort Hood incident is identifying the red line at which an individual should come under serious investigation for terrorist suspicions. The seemingly harmless nature of the content of Hasan's messages with al-Awlaki illustrates the difficulty of stopping affinity terrorists who have no need to communicate their specific intent to do harm.

Another affinity case is that of five Muslim men from Alexandria, Virginia: Umar Chaudhry, Waqar Khan, Ahmad A. Minni, Aman Hassan Yemer, and Ramy Zamzam. They contacted two al Qaeda-linked terrorist groups and traveled to Pakistan to undergo terrorist training. Because the men contacted Jaish-e-Mohammed and Lashkar-e-Jangvi via email, the U.S. intelligence community should have known of their terrorist intentions. Yet, the men were only arrested once they had traveled to Pakistan, by that nation's authorities.[4] As in the Fort Hood case, the bar was set too high in terms of evidence meriting further investigation and possible arrest.

One affinity terrorist caught after committing his crimes is David Headley, who trained with Lashkar e-Taiba during 2002 and 2003 and helped plan the Mumbai bombing of 2008. While "innocently" coming and going from Chicago, Headley was also supporting a terrorist organization in December 2009.[5]

A rare intelligence coup against an impending foreign-affinity attack was the arrest of Najibullah Zazi, a citizen of Afghanistan and U.S. resident. Zazi had received instructions from an al Qaeda operative in Pakistan over the Internet. He was arrested with bomb designs on his laptop, batteries, and scales for measuring explosive materials. Again, it was email messages that touched off concern about Zazi; the British government alerted the FBI of an email intercepted by Scotland Yard that led to Zazi's eventual arrest.[6] At issue is why Zazi's messages warranted an arrest while those of Major Hasan and the five Virginia men did not. The FBI clearly needs to reevaluate its threshold for such investigations and develop more consistent standards for gathering intelligence and apprehending suspects.

Other successful preventions of foreign-affinity terrorism include the arrests of six individuals in 2007 for planning to attack Fort Dix, four individuals in May 2009 for planning to bomb a Bronx synagogue and shoot down military airplanes, and seven North Carolina men in July 2009 for planning to attack Quantico Marine base.[7]

Though not a foreign-affinity attack, on Christmas Day 2009, America received a severe wake-up call from what this study calls a "satellite terrorist," who attempted to detonate explosives onboard a flight from Amsterdam to Detroit. Abdul Farouk Abdulmutallab, a Nigerian, studied in Yemen for several months and associated with the same radical cleric that Major Hasan had emailed, al-Awlaki; the father of Abdulmutallab warned the U.S. embassy in Nigeria that he feared his son had been radicalized. As in the Fort Hood case, the intelligence community seems to have shared the information among its constituent parts, but that information was not used to add Abdulmutallab to an appropriate watchlist in time. Customs and Border Protection officials only learned of the threat when the flight was already en route.[8]

The National Counterterrorism Center (NCTC) is tasked with taking intelligence collected on terrorist threats by constituent members of the intelligence community and analyzing it to provide warnings of impending threats. The Terrorist Identities Datamart Environment (TIDE), a product of the Intelligence Reform Act of 2004, is a database maintained by NCTC to record identities of individuals for which there is some intelligence but not enough to subject them to additional scrutiny at airports or keep them from boarding aircraft bound for the United States.

At issue is why intelligence collected at the U.S. embassy in Nigeria and elsewhere never resulted in Abdulmutallab's graduation from TIDE to the "Selectees" list. It is a smaller database than TIDE, requiring greater scrutiny of persons with Abdulmutallab's profile, which in turn could have permitted inspectors to detect his explosives.

The Fort Hood and Christmas attacks of 2009 call not so much for a reevaluation of the intelligence bureaucracy as they do an incremental adjustment of institutional tripwires. These thresholds initiate an investigation or addition to terrorist watchlists in accord with the threat profile of certain individuals. As President Obama said following the Christmas bombing attempt, "It was a failure to integrate and understand the intelligence we already had." [9] There is too much emphasis on explosive detection technology at airport check-in facilities and not enough on the person with the reservation. Technology and intelligence should work in tandem to prevent potential terrorists from boarding aircraft. The watchlist system is a step in the right direction, but it has to give increased attention to threat profiles.

Al Qaeda is clearly adapting to the post-9/11 pressure it faces, employing satellites like Abdulmutallab, double agents like the Jordanian CIA informant who killed seven CIA personnel in Afghanistan, and benefiting from affinity terrorists like Major Hasan, the Virginia Five, and Najibullah Zazi. As Bruce Hoffman notes, "Al-Qaeda has become increasingly adept at using the Internet to locate these would-be terrorists and to feed them propaganda." [10]

From an intelligence perspective going forward, it will be as important for U.S. officials to recognize and disrupt radicalization at home as it will be to seek and destroy al Qaeda members abroad. One affinity terrorist, with little more than email messages and his father indicating a turn toward radicalization can do as much damage as a hardened al Qaeda member.

In view of this discussion of terrorist incidents during the Obama administration, some critics accuse President Obama of being more lax on terrorism than his predecessor, George W. Bush.

On one hand, President Obama was slow to acknowledge that the country was at war, e.g., when he seemed reluctant to use the phrase "War on Terrorism."[11] He also was a bit uncertain in response to the Fort Hood and Christmas Day incidents that occurred during his first term in the Oval Office.

On the other hand, President Obama left the Bush administration's Terrorist Surveillance Program and other intelligence institutions and policies of the Bush presidency largely intact. He also expanded drone attacks against al Qaeda targets along the Afghanistan-Pakistan border and embraced the powers afforded the executive branch by the USA PATRIOT Act. The bottom line is that institutional and policy continuity more than change characterizes President Obama's approach to affinity terrorism.

INTELLIGENCE: AN ENDANGERED SPECIES

William H. Lewis

Late December 2009 awakened the Obama administration to the many failings of its intelligence community. Al Qaeda launched two separate attacks less than a week apart—one failed, the second was successful—triggering a wide-ranging review of the intrinsic weaknesses of our intelligence programs and procedures. In the immediate wake of the Christmas Day attempt to bring down a U.S. plane over Detroit, the president declared that the U.S. government had sufficient information to have uncovered the plot and potentially disrupt the attacks, but our intelligence community failed to connect the dots. (The killing of seven CIA operatives in Afghanistan several days later was not immediately addressed by the White House.) The president charged that the failure was "systematic" in nature.

In reality, the failures are endemic and reflect the basic flaws that exist within the sprawling community. Post-mortems are being conducted by the administration, individual agencies, and by congressional communities. But several deficiencies are glaringly evident. The vaunted stove-piper of institutional compartmentation has not been dislodged; synchronicity of effort has been weakened by bureaucratic obstructionism and culture rigidities; data proliferation has overloaded a capacity for analysis. As the administration's early 2010 report on community weaknesses amply demonstrates, the dots are fundamentally of our making—these reflect bureaucratic disconnectivity, a confederacy of isolates.

What bureaucratic cross-pollination occurs represents a means-ends inversion that focuses on power-turf rather than shared value and the national interest. An internal administration excavation searching for reasons for failure to prevent the attempted downing of Delta flight 253 reported the following on January 2010:

- Intelligence systems technology is not up to the task of sorting, making sense, and prioritizing the avalanche of data accumulating on a daily basis;

- "There was not a comprehensive or functioning process for tracking terrorist threat reporting and actions taken such that departments and agencies are held accountable for running down all leads";
- "The Central Intelligence Agency should issue guidance aimed to ensure the timely distribution of intelligence reports" (a clear reflection of a lack of clear lines of responsibility).
- The Director of National Intelligence "should take steps to enhance the rigor and raise the standard of trade craft intelligence analysis, especially analysis designed to uneven and prevent terrorist plots."

The president, in his assessment, appeared primarily concerned with sorting out missions and assigning clear-cut roles. In his own words: "I'm directing that our intelligence community immediately assign specific responsibility for investigating all leads on high propriety threats so that these leads are pursued upon actively and aggressively—not just most of the time, but all of the time." This is but the initial phase on the administration's assessment of the community's basic deficiencies. There is reason to anticipate a greater, more intense examination of the architecture and a need for some downsizing and restructuring. Certainly, the prospect of congressional reviews will help to focus the Obama administration's efforts to generate reforms within the existing, poorly performing constellation of intelligence agencies.

THE ROLE OF LAW ENFORCEMENT AGENCIES IN COMBATING TERRORISM

Oliver (Buck) Revell

It has been almost four years since I discussed the concept of this book with Professor Yonah Alexander of the Potomac Institute. We are friends and professional colleagues who have over the past 25 years participated in trying to educate the public about the dangers facing our nation from the threat of terrorism from within and from hostile nation states and international terrorist organizations. I agreed to submit a chapter to his book and to specifically examine both the history of and challenges facing law enforcement and security agencies dealing with the terrorist phenomena. Terrorism is, as I have stated in the chapter I wrote, a tactic used by nations, organizations, and even individuals to use force and violence or the threat of these actions to intimidate, coerce, and attempt to compel a nation or smaller group to react to the terrorist act or threat in ways which are not in the best interests of those who are the target or focus of the entity using the terrorist tactics. I submitted my final draft for this chapter in January 2009, but due to outside factors the final text is just now being completed. Given the lapse of time, Professor Alexander asked me to write a postscript to my chapter to give the reader a more timely presentation on new and evolving issues involving the use of terrorism and on the problems, issues, and progress of agencies that are charged with meeting the terrorist threat. That is the purpose of this follow-up to my chapter. As Professor Alexander gave a comprehensive review of the majority of terrorist acts that have occurred over the past two years, I will concentrate on a few of the events that have the most impact on our nation's effort to protect itself from those who would cause it harm by the use of terrorist tactics.

Perhaps the most significant terrorist act in the past two years was the swarm attack on various locations in the Indian city of Mumbai. On November 26, 2008 a group of 10 Pakistani terrorists attacked multiple targets in Mumbai, the center of Indian finance and commerce. Attacks were launched against two five-star hotels that cater to Western business executives, the Taj Mahal Palace and the Oberoi; a Jewish religious center, and the Mumbai railroad station. During the three-day siege, attacks were carried out by use of automatic rifles, pistols, hand grenades, and remote detonating devices; several fires were set to obscure the target areas. One hundred eighty-eight persons were killed including several police officers, nine of the ten terrorist attackers, and twenty-eight foreigners of which six were Americans and eight were Israelis. The captured terrorist, Mohammed Ajmal Kasab, confessed that he was recruited by the Pakistani terrorist group Lashkar e-Taiba (LeT) and was trained for approximately one year to carry out a jihadist suicide attack. He claims not to have known the final target until shortly before his team of 10 terrorists set out by ship from the Pakistani city of Karachi.

The U.S. government immediately reacted by providing support from the U.S. embassy in New Delhi including, CIA, FBI, and Diplomatic Security personnel, and by sending then Secretary of State Condoleezza Rice to meet with the Indian Prime Minister Manmohan Singh and his senior officials to ensure the Indian government that the U.S. government would provide all of the aid and assistance possible. As six of the victims killed and many of the wounded were Americans, the FBI had concurrent criminal jurisdiction with India in the investigation of the crimes committed against American citizens. Of course, this jurisdiction was only asserted in India with the approval of the Indian government.

The findings in this massive attack are significant for American law enforcement and security services in several ways. The mission, although carried out with low-tech weapons, guns, and explosives, was highly planned and sophisticated in execution. Both satellite and physical surveillance were extensively utilized in the planning process. The use of a seaborne assault reduced significantly the chances of being intercepted by Indian authorities.

Each site to be attacked had been carefully chosen for its symbolic and commercial impact on India and the Western elements within India. Satellite images, GPS navigation, and satellite telephones, as well as untraceable cell phones, were used during the attacks. The terrorist attack teams maintained communications with their controllers during the ongoing attacks and changed targets on orders from their superiors. The intention was to kill and wound as many victims as possible before they were killed by the Indian authorities. Each of the terrorists knew that this was a suicide attack and that each would likely not survive and should not strive to do so. They were told that they would be greatly honored and their families rewarded. To understand this kind of motivation one should examine the use of suicide attackers, such as those who carried out the September 11, 2001, attacks in the United States. A leading Islamist authority, Sheikh Yusuf Qaradawi, recently explained the distinction this way: attacks on enemies are not suicide operations, but "heroic martyrdom operations" in which the kamikazes act not "out of hopelessness and despair, but are driven by an overwhelming desire to cast terror and fear into the hearts of the oppressors." In other words, Islamists find suicide for personal reasons abominable, suicide for jihad admirable.

The Mumbai attacks had significant unintended consequences for both the LeT and the Pakistani government. The close relationship between the LeT and former ranking members of the Pakistani All Services Intelligence Services was firmly established. The ongoing coordination and relationship between the LeT, al Qaeda and the Taliban was determined, and the investigation brought U.S. law enforcement (primarily the FBI) into a direct investigative and coordination role with and between Indian and Pakistani police. The New York City Police Department sent a team to study the swarm attack tactics used by the LeT assault team to determine the potential use of such tactics against New York City, and the Department of Homeland Security also used the horrific attack as a lessons-learned assessment. On February 24, 2010, FBI Director Mueller visited India to confer directly on the progress of the investigation and to explore the ramifications of the newly discovered evidence that an American citizen, David Coleman Headley, had been a significant co-conspirator in the Mumbai attacks and had provided intelligence and material support to the attackers. Headley has been indicted in Federal Court in Chicago for his part in the Mumbai attacks, along with a Canadian associate Tahawwur Rana.

The Mumbai attacks illustrate that the jihadist network is global, that it is capable of very sophisticated planning and operations, and that it can inflect terrible damage with low-tech weapons.

Another case of very significant magnitude is the somewhat convoluted conspiracy involving Najibullah Zazi, a 24-year-old Afghan who lived in Queens before moving to Denver. Zazi apparently became radicalized while living in the United States and made several trips to Pakistan, and possibly one to Afghanistan. Zazi pled guilty in federal court in Brooklyn, New York on February 22, 2010, to conspiracy to use weapons of mass destruction, to conspiracy to commit murder overseas, and to providing material support for a terrorist organization. Zazi confessed that he was recruited and trained by al Qaeda operatives during his trips to Pakistan. Zazi's guilty plea was followed on February 25 with federal indictments (on the same charges) of two of his high school classmates, Adis Medunjanin and Zarein Ahmedzay. The three defendants face life in prison if convicted. Zazi apparently was the ring leader and his guilty plea came after he cooperated with authorities in exposing the details of the plots, which included multiple bombings of New York subway Stations and aiding the Taliban in their fight to regain control of Afghanistan. This case involved months of highly sensitive investigation in New York, Colorado, and Pakistan. The only negative development known to date is the unilateral action by the NYPD Intelligence Division to make inquires with their sources without coordinating the action with the NYPD Counter-Terrorism Bureau, which is the interface between the NYPD and the NYJTTF. These premature actions by the NYPD Intelligence Division apparently led to the conspirators being warned and calling off their immediate plans. Hopefully, Commissioner Ray Kelley of the NYPD will close the loop on this gap in operational security. As this commentary is being written there are reports of additional members of this cell being sought in the United States and internationally.

Another area of new concern for the law enforcement and intelligence communities is the large number of Somali youth that has migrated to the United States and has now returned to Somalia to engage in jihad. More than 20 young Somali immigrants to the United States who settled in the Minneapolis area have been reported to have become radicalized while in the United States and to have returned to Somalia and joined the Al Shabaab, a militant Islamist group with ties to al Qaeda. One of these Somali youths, Shirwa Ahmed, became the first-known American suicide bomber when he blew himself up in a suicide attack in Somalia. Although there has been no known attempt by these young refugees to return to America to commit terrorist acts, FBI Director Robert Mueller has stated that Ahmed was "radicalized in his hometown in Minnesota." If the current military action taking place in Afghanistan and Pakistan is successful against the Taliban and al Qaeda, it is likely that elements of al Qaeda will return to Somalia, and the presence of these radicalized refugees may offer al Qaeda another means by which to attack America.

One of the ways that Muslims living in the United States are radicalized is through jihadist Web sites that give access to hate-filled rhetoric, vicious propaganda, and even training in how to commit acts of terrorism. According to the authoritative Middle East Media Research Institute (MEMRI), over 3,000 jihadist Web sites are hosted on American Web site providers (ISPs). It was from these Web sites that a young 19-year-old Jordanian illegal immigrant living in Italy, Texas decided to commit jihad while staying in the United States illegally. Hosam Maher Husein Smadi communicated with a number of jihadist Web sites and conveyed his desire to commit an act of jihad in the spring of 2009. Smadi's desire to commit a violent act of jihad was intercepted by the FBI, and a slowly and carefully developed scenario was put in place. An undercover Dallas JTTF agent became the front for a fictitious al Qaeda terrorist cell living covertly in the United States. Carefully following legal protocols that avoid the issue of entrapment, the undercover agent went through a list of potential targets that Smadi was interested in attacking; they included a major Dallas National Guard facility and the Dallas/Fort Worth International Airport. Smadi decided that these facilities were too well guarded and settled on the iconic Fountain Place Tower in downtown Dallas. Fountain Place is a green glass monolith some 60 floors high and is immediately identifiable with Dallas from the television series *Dallas* and from aerial shots from TV coverage of Dallas Cowboys football games. Smadi liked the symbolism of the building and the fact that it was the Dallas home of the Wells Fargo Bank. Smadi decided that he wanted to use a truck bomb like in the first New York Trade Center bombing and to detonate the bomb mid-day himself to cause the highest number of casualties. He told the agent what he wanted to do and how he wanted to do it. In its press release, the FBI made the following statement:

> The Special Agent in Charge for the Dallas Office of the FBI, announced today (9/24/09) that Hosam Maher Husein Smadi, 19, has been arrested and charged in a federal criminal complaint with attempting to use a weapon of mass destruction. Smadi, who was under continuous surveillance by the FBI, was arrested today near Fountain Place, a 60-story glass office tower located at 1445 Ross Avenue in downtown Dallas, after he placed an inert/inactive car bomb at the location. Smadi, a Jordanian citizen in the U.S. illegally, lived and worked in Italy, Texas. He has repeatedly espoused his desire to commit violent jihad and has been the focus of an undercover FBI investigation.

In an affidavit presented to the magistrate judge during his first court hearing, it was revealed that Smadi dialed in the cell phone number that was supposed to set off the bomb and refused a set of ear plugs because he wanted to hear the explosion. Smadi appears to be a "lone wolf" acting entirely out of hatred he developed viewing jihadist Web sites while in the United States. The U.S. attorney and FBI SAC both highly praised the members of the JTTF and their parent agencies for their support and assistance in developing this case.

There are two cases prominently in the news at the time of this commentary that I will only mention because of their importance. Judgments on actions taken or not taken are currently being investigated and will be the subject of Congressional hearings, so I will just comment on the law enforcement and intelligence issues that each of these cases raises. I am referring specifically to the Fort Hood massacre on November 15, 2009, and the attempted bombing of the Northwest flight from Holland to Detroit on Christmas Day 2009. In both of these cases the subjects are in custody, and criminal investigations and prosecutions are moving forward. What is clear is that there were warning signs in both cases that were not acted upon with the intensity and speed required. It is also of major concern that Major Nidal Malik Hasan, M.D., an Army psychiatrist assigned to Fort Hood, Texas, who is now charged with 13 counts of murder and 38 counts of attempted murder, was a misfit for the position he was assigned and gave many indications that he should not be in the Army, much less assigned to treat returning soldiers who could well be suffering post-traumatic stress syndrome. And, he certainly was not fit for overseas duty with our forces in Afghanistan. Whether his email correspondence amounted to a basis for referral from the National Counterterrorism Center to Army Criminal Investigation Command or FBI field operations remains to be seen, but the fact that he was in touch with an American-born radical al Qaeda cleric Anwar Al-Awlaki operating out of Yemen should have raised sufficient concern for there to have been additional scrutiny. The Department of Defense has indicated that at least six officers and perhaps more will be disciplined for failure to take appropriate action in dealing with Hasan's conduct and performance issues. FBI Director Mueller has asked former FBI and CIA Director, William Webster, to conduct an inquiry into whether the FBI supervisor at the NCTC took appropriate notice and action on the email intercepts between Hasan and Al-Awlaki.

Regarding the Christmas Day bombing attempt, both House and Senate committees have begun hearings and have already stated that the failure to detain Umar Farouk Abdulmutallab, a known threat according to his own family, who was known to have been in Yemen and in contact with the al Qaeda in the Arabian Peninsula (AQAP), and possibly with radical cleric Al-Awlaki, constitutes a systematic failure to analyze, connect, and act upon gathered intelligence. There is no doubt that additional issues will be raised at the conclusion of internal reviews and Congressional hearings.

With the increased use of cybercrime to support their networks and increased interaction with organized crime groups and drug cartels, international terrorists, including groups from the United States who have adopted the cause of international terrorist organizations, will continue to present the law enforcement and security agencies of the United States and our international partners with unprecedented challenges in protecting our societies. These challenges will require a mature and responsible Congress that recognizes that the first duty of government is to protect its people.

COMBATING THE FINANCING OF THE INTERNATIONAL TERRORISM NETWORK IN THE UNITED STATES

Bruce Zagaris

U.S. Technical and Financial Assistance

The Office of Overseas Prosecutorial Development, Assistance and Training (OPDAT), the Counter-Terrorism Section (CTS), and the Asset Forfeiture and Money Laundering Section (AFMLS), with the assistance of the Department of Justice (DOJ), play a central role in providing technical assistance to foreign counterparts, both to attack the financial underpinnings of terrorism and to develop legal infrastructures to combat. In this regard, OPDAT, CTS, and AFMLS work as integral parts of the interagency U.S. Terrorist Financing Working Group (TFWG), co-chaired by the state department's INL Bureau and the Office of the Coordinator for Counterterrorism (S/CT).

The TFWG supports seven Resident Legal Advisors (RLAs) assigned overseas, located in Bangladesh, Indonesia, Kenya, Pakistan, Paraguay, Turkey, and the United Arab Emirates. Working in countries where governments are vulnerable to terrorist financing, RLAs focus on money laundering and financial crimes and on developing counterterrorism legislation that criminalizes terrorist acts, terrorist financing, and the provision of material support or resources to terrorist organizations. The RLAs also develop technical assistance programs for prosecutors, judges, and, in collaboration with DOJ's International Criminal Investigative Training Assistance Program (ICITAP), police investigators to assist in the implementation of new money laundering and terrorist financing procedures.

U.S. Law Enforcement Case Developments

In 2008, Lloyds TSB Bank, a U.K. corporation headquartered in London, agreed to forfeit $350 million to the United States and the New York County District Attorney's Office in connection with violations of the International Emergency Economic Powers Act (IEEPA). The violations relate to transactions Lloyds illegally conducted on behalf of customers from Iran, Sudan, and other countries sanctioned in programs administered by the Office of Foreign Assets Controls (OFAC).

On November 24, 2008, in the Northern District of Texas, a jury found all defendants in *U.S. v. Holy Land Foundation* guilty of all counts charged. HLF was a Hamas front organization that received start-up assistance from Mousa Abu Marzook—a leader of Hamas and a specially designated terrorist—and raised millions of dollars for Hamas over a 13-year record. The new trial resulted from a mistrial declared on October 22, 2007, when a jury found defendant Mohammed El-Mezican not guilty on most charges, but failed to reach a verdict on a material support count against him, and deadlocked on the remaining counts against the other defendants. HLF was the largest Muslim charity in the United States until it was declared a specially designated terrorist organization in 2001 and was shut down. HLF raised millions of dollars for Hamas over a 13-year period.

On August 18, 2009, U.S. District Judge James Carr issued a sweeping order, declaring that in 2006 OFAC wrongly froze the assets of an Ohio-based charity it suspected of having links to the Islamic group Hamas because it acted without giving the organization proper notice either before or after the freeze and deprived it of due process.[12]

Judge Carr granted KindHearts' motion for partial summary judgment with regard to three of its claims: (1) that OFAC violated the Fourth Amendment when it seized KindHearts' assets without probable cause and prior judicial review and issuance of a warrant; (2) OFAC's failure to provide notice, and an opportunity to be heard, and its restrictions on plaintiff's access to its documents violated its fundamental procedural due process rights; and (3) OFAC's limitation on the extent to which KindHearts' blocked funds are available to it to compensate its counsel was arbitrary and capricious and violated the Administrative Procedure Act.

On January 19, 2010, a Saudi bank filed a Memorandum of Points and Authorities in Support of its Motion to Quash a USA PATRIOT Act Subpoena.[13] The case raises interesting and important issues of extraterritorial jurisdiction, diplomatic controversies, and constitutional issues.

The statute in question is the PATRIOT Act subpoena under 31 U.S.C. § 5318(k)(3), which allows the executive branch the authority to compel a foreign bank to produce documents located outside the U.S. without a court order. The statute establishes a self-enforcing subpoena power that allows the government to punish noncompliance by depriving the Al Rajhi Bank of valuable correspondent relationships with U.S. banks, without any prior judicial authorization.

Al Rajhi Bank's pleading argues that the statute limits the information that may be sought in a PATRIOT Act subpoena to records related to a foreign bank's correspondent accounts with U.S. banks. The motion observes that the subpoena at issue is not so limited. Instead, it seeks documents that are located in Saudi Arabia and that relate to a Saudi customer's account with the Bank—which have no apparent relationship to any correspondent account. The government does not assert that any relationship exists between those records and any of the bank's U.S. correspondent accounts. The pleading argues that, as a result, the subpoena is invalid because it was not issued for any purpose authorized by the statute. The litigation should be worthwhile to monitor for potential developments on counterterrorism financial enforcement.

International Developments

The effort to curtail the financing of terrorism, especially the deprivation of funding to al Qaeda and the Taliban, has not been successful. Both al Qaeda and the Taliban have experienced a resurgence in recent years. The new regulatory regime *has* reduced the risk of banks and money transmitting businesses being used to facilitate terrorist financing. Additionally, the economic sanctions regime developed by the United States and the international community for designating and freezing the assets of suspected terrorists and their associates has disrupted the ability of corrupt Islamic charitable organizations to raise millions of dollars to finance terrorist activities.

The UN asset freeze program has not worked well. Each year states are submitting fewer and fewer names of suspected terrorists for designation to freeze their assets. Even when names are submitted for designation, states are not freezing terrorist-related assets. Hence, the cumulative amount of frozen assets has declined over the last few years. On December 17, 2009, the United Nations Security adopted a resolution on blacklisting al Qaeda and persons suspected of terrorist acts. On the one hand, it offers enhanced rights to persons who are blacklisted. On the other hand, it seeks strengthened application and enforcement of the existing sanctions.[14]

National and regional courts have held that governments need not honor the UN freeze program on the basis that the program violated fundamental human rights law. For instance, on June 4, 2009, Justice Russel W. Zinn ruled that the Canadian government had to comply with the right to enter Canada under the *Canadian Charter of Rights and Freedoms* (the Charter) notwithstanding the fact that the UN Security Council 1267 Committee plaintiff and Sudanese citizen Abousfian Abdelrazik as an associate of al Qaeda.[15] Mr. Abdelrazik lived in Sudan, but wanted to return to Canada, where he is also a citizen. His immediate family, including his young children, are in Montreal. He brought a suit because of his inability to return to Canada, claiming that the Canadian government had improperly thwarted his return to Canada, thereby breaching his right as a citizen of Canada pursuant to section 6 of the Charter.

The opinion, along with those of the European Court of Justice and the United Kingdom, exemplifies judicial difficulties in applying the UN counterterrorism sanctions. All the opinions cite the lack of transparency and fairness with the 1267 Committee's regulations in their decisions that national governments, or regional organizations in the case of the European Union, need not enforce the regulations. Indeed, the perceived problems with the operations of the listing and delisting of the 1267 Committee also explain why the listing of new persons has slowed significantly. Each year, states are submitting fewer and fewer names for inclusion on the

Consolidated List for asset freeze. The amount of terrorist assets frozen over the last several years has stalled. There has been no increase in terrorist assets frozen since 2004.

On June 23, 2009, the Financial Action Task Force (FATF) issued an "International Best Practices on Freezing of Terrorist Assets." The paper provides nonbinding guidance based on updates in relevant UN Security Council resolutions relating to the prevention and suppression of the financing of terrorist acts—UNSCR 1267, and its successor resolutions and UNSCR 1373 and any successor resolutions related to the freezing, or, if appropriate, seizure of terrorist assets. Efforts to combat terrorist financing are significantly undermined if jurisdictions do not freeze the funds or other assets of designated persons quickly and effectively. In determining the limits of or promoting widespread support for an effective counterterrorist financing regime, however, jurisdictions must respect human rights, respect the rule of law, and recognize the rights of innocent third parties. The guidance helps implement FATF Special Recommendation III on freezing or seizing terrorist-related funds or assets.[16]

On February 11, 2010, at a meeting in Strasbourg, France, the European Parliament voted 378 to 196 to reject an agreement between the United States and European Union that would have enabled U.S. authorities to have access for the next nine months to portions of vast databases of financial transactions maintained by Society for Worldwide Interbank Financial Transactions (SWIFT), the company that conducts almost all international bank transfers.[17]

Data from SWIFT has been at the core of the U.S. Treasury's Terrorist Finance Tracking Program, established in the aftermath of the September 2001 attacks. The controversy about the use of the SWIFT data started in 2006 when the media reported that the treasury had been secretly using SWIFT data for counterterrorism purposes.[18]

The failure of the European Parliament to approve the new proposed agreement shows the gap between the European Union and the United States on data privacy. In Europe data privacy rights are fundamental law, whereas in the United States no fundamental protections exist on data privacy, except under the First and Fourth Amendments of the Constitution. The United States has major gateways to data privacy where counterterrorism enforcement is concerned. In recent times the European Union and EU courts have also decided that international counterterrorism financial sanctions require better due process.

Another disappointment is that the Department of Justice has failed to successfully prosecute networks of deep-pocket donors and financial facilitators responsible for financing al Qaeda, Hamas, and affiliated terrorist networks. An exception is the conviction in November 24, 2008, of the Holy Land Foundation (HLF), mentioned above.

BORDER SECURITY

Bruce Zagaris

At the end of 2009, the United States aims to establish and maintain effective control of its borders through five goals: 1) establish substantial probability of apprehending terrorists trying to illegally enter between ports of entry; 2) deter illegal entries through improved enforcement; 3) detect, apprehend, and deter smugglers of humans, drugs, and other contraband; 4) leverage "Smart Border" technology to multiply the effect of enforcement personnel; and 5) reduce crime in border communities and consequently improve quality of life and economic vitality of targeted areas. The national strategy remains increasing deployment of personnel, equipment, intelligence, support, technology, and infrastructure. Reducing U.S. vulnerability to the entry of terrorists, illegal aliens, and drugs by increasing personnel and resources remains the key goal.

CBP requested an additional 2,200 new CBP agent positions in FY2009. By the end of 2009, CBP had more than double the workforce it had in 2001.

CBP's approach to border security strikes a balance among personnel and force multiplier tools such as fencing, the use of intelligence, other tactical infrastructure, technology, and air assets.

The CBP Construction Program addresses requirements on the northern and southern borders for new and enhanced facilities to fulfill immediate operational needs; to accommodate increasing capacity demands associated with new agent, officer, pilot, and asset deployments; to modify or correct deficiencies within existing structures; and to replace temporary structures with permanent solutions.

DHS has made substantial progress in securing U.S. borders between the ports of entry. In 2009, 100 percent of Other Than Mexican (OTM) aliens apprehended along the southwest and norther borders were subject to detention pending removal and were otherwise ineligible for release from custody under U.S. immigration law. This contrasts to 2005, when only 34 percent were detained. The success of this effort has been primarily based on DHS enhancements in additional bed space and a streamlined process for removal of aliens, or "Expedited Removal."

The Secure Border Initiative (SBI) continues. The SBInet Tactical Infrastructure program continues to rely on completing 370 miles of pedestrian fencing and 300 miles of vehicle fencing along the southwest border. To address known as well as potential threats at the northern border, the CBP is creating a stronger, more proactive presence at and between ports of entry. Eight border patrol sectors encompassing 12 states stretch from the Pacific, across the Rocky Mountains, Great Plains, the Great Lakes, to the Atlantic. To support efforts, CBP Air and Marine has developed a plan to increase security along the northern border through the accelerated start up of operations at five locations. By the spring of 2008, Air and Marine established the following five air wings on the northern border: Bellingham, Washington; Plattsburgh, New York; Great Falls, Montana; Grand Forks, North Dakota; and Detroit, Michigan.

An important part of security extends beyond U.S. physical borders. The Immigration Advisory Program (IAP) is an important element in this strategy, enhancing security by preventing terrorists and other high-risk passengers from boarding aircraft destined for the United States. The goal of the IAP is to protect air travel and improve national security by reducing suspected overseas threats prior to a flight's departure, thereby avoiding delaying, canceling, or diverting flights. However, on December 25, 2009, a Nigerian national boarded a Northwest airliner in Amsterdam and right before the plane landed in Detroit, tried unsuccessfully to ignite a bomb. The fact that he was not put on a "no-fly" list, even though his father reported suspicions about his son's radicalization to U.S. authorities in Nigeria, has ignited a reassessment of the IAP and the intelligence cooperation within the United States and between the United States and other governments.

The Western Hemisphere Travel Initiative (WHTI) started in 2010 and ensures that travelers to the United States possess standardized, secure documents to allow CBP to quickly and accurately identify travelers and their citizenship while shortening the inspection process. With funds requested in FY2009, CBP has completed the deployment of the radio-frequency identification (RFID) sensor and license plate reader technologies started in 2008 and added in 2009 89 new CBP officers to the U.S. land border ports of entry.

In 2008–9, DHS developed the Border Enforcement Security Task Force (BEST) concept to coordinate the efforts of ICE, CBP, and DHS intelligence personnel working cooperatively with foreign, federal, state, and local law enforcement agencies to take a comprehensive approach to disrupt and dismantle criminal organizations.

The CBP is continuing to improve and expand its trusted traveler programs, which expedite the processing of known, low-risk travelers so that it can better focus its attention on higher-risk, unknown travelers. Global Entry is another program to expedite processing of travelers—in this case, U.S. citizens and Lawful Permanent Residents, The program is a pilot that CBP is testing in select airports. It provides automated kiosks to validate identification by matching travel documents with biometrics.

Since his election, President Barack Obama has reiterated his support from comprehensive immigration reform. However, preoccupation with health care reform and falling support for his policies makes prospects of such reform remote.

In 2009, a key and growing area of emphasis involves DHS's role in interdicting the illegal flow of weapons and currency into Mexico. The increased surge of violence on the southwest border and the interior of Mexico is a serious concern. CBP is working with its partners in the DEA and High Intensity Drug Trafficking Area focuses on expanding the National License Plate Reader (LPR) initiative to use intelligence on drug traffickers and drug trafficking organizations. The LPR initiative uses established locations to gather information concerning travel patterns and border nexus on drug traffickers to enable intelligence-driven operations and interdictions. The program will be expanded in 2010 to encompass the northern border and other areas throughout the United States. Its capabilities can be used to help other law enforcement entities in their investigations of their high value targets, by combining existing DEA and other law enforcement database capabilities with new technology to identify and interdict conveyances being utilized to transport bulk cash, drugs, weapons, and other illegal contraband.

In 2009, the Importer Security Filing interim final rule, also known as "10 + 2," went into effect. It provides CBP timely information about cargo shipments that will improve CBP's ability to detect and interdict high-risk shipments. The initiative will improve CBP's efforts to review 100 percent of all cargo before it arrives in the United States, using advanced cargo data, automated targeting and risk assessment systems, intelligence, and cutting-edge inspection technologies, such as large-scale X-ray, gamma ray machines, and radiation detection devices. Shipments determined by CBP to be high risk are examined either overseas as part of its Container Security Initiative or upon arrival at a U.S. port. In addition, over 98 percent of all arriving maritime containerized cargo is presently scanned for radiation through radiation portal monitors.

The Obama administration's 2010 budget calls for a 6 percent increase for DHS and 11 percent for ICE. In addition, DOJ is playing an increasing role in border control and immigration. It has a central role in the administration's Border Security Initiative and the new policy initiatives criminalizing illegal border crossing. For instance, after the September 2001 terrorist incidents, DOJ started an Office of the Federal Detention Trustee (OFDT), which was designed to coordinate and avoid duplication for all federal detention under DOJ. After the creation of DHS in March 2003, DHS refused to have its immigrant detention program coordinated by DOJ, creating resentment within OFDT and leading to an uncoordinated cross-departmental federal detention complex.

OFTD requested an 11 percent increase in its $1.4 billion budget for 2010. In September 2008, immigrants composed 44 percent of all U.S. Marshals Service (USMS) pre-trial detainees. Soon, given the Bush-Obama continuity in immigration enforcement, more than half of the detainees handled by USMS will be immigrants.

GENERAL OBSERVATIONS AND PRELIMINARY RECOMMENDATIONS

Yonah Alexander

As this manuscript went to press, one of the most powerful earthquakes on record struck Chile on February 27, 2010, and unleashed tsunami waves across the Pacific, prompting emergency alerts in dozens of countries. This unpredictable disaster, whose tragic consequences will last for years, followed up an earlier sudden quake this year in Haiti, causing 200,000 deaths and enormous social and economic costs.

These misfortunes and other calamities wrought by "Mother Nature," as well as the ongoing global economic crisis, have evoked extreme fear of future unexpected dangers.

Nonetheless, "man-made" extremism and violence such as terrorism will also continue to challenge humanity for generations to come. Now, nearly nine years after the September 11, 2001, catastrophe, the world still girds for the grim fear of terrorism.

The academic community, as always, has had the intellectual and practical responsibility for learning the historical lessons of this threat, among the multitude of other challenges facing the world; identifying future signal warnings wherever possible; and recommending strategies to reduce risks on both conventional and unconventional levels.

It is with this sense of mission in mind that the International Center for Terrorism Studies (ICTS) at the Potomac Institute for Policy Studies organized its 11th annual seminar, "Terrorism: Review of 2009 and Outlook for 2010" on January 29, 2010, held at the Brookings Institution.[19] More specifically, following President Barack Obama's State of the Union pledge on January 20, 2010, to "take the fight to al Qaeda," the panel at the event reported that while bin Laden's international network has been damaged by recent attacks on its hideouts in Pakistan, it remains the single most dangerous terrorist threat to the United States. in 2010 and beyond. With al Qaeda continuing to recruit new followers, acquiring new ways to attack, and spreading to new regions of the world, the panel warned further attacks on the United States and Europe are almost certain to occur.

"The good news is we're taking the attack to al Qaeda," said Ambassador Robert Godec, Office of Coordinator for Counterterrorism, Department of State, speaking for the Obama administration. He cited reports that recent strikes in the mountainous border region of Pakistan exacted a toll on al Qaeda leaders. "Despite this success," he said, "al Qaeda remains our most serious threat. A new development is that al Qaeda affiliates in other parts of the world are now seeking to attack the United States, no longer focusing just on regional targets." The panel pointed to the Christmas Day bomb attempt on NW flight 253 over Detroit, organized by al Qaeda in Yemen, which highlighted "terrorists finding new ways to attack," said Michael Swetnam, CEO and Chairman, Potomac Institute. "The so-called underwear bomb didn't succeed, but it did create great public attention and concern."

"Al Qaeda is damaged, but still dangerous," said Charles Allen, former Assistant Director, Central Intelligence Agency (CIA) and Undersecretary for Intelligence, Department of Homeland Security. He said that "in 2006 al Qaeda changed strategy to recruit foreign nationals, creating a home-grown problem" evidenced in the deadly shootout at Fort Hood Army base in Texas. Allen added that a proliferation of radicalized Islamic Web sites targets immigrants not yet fully assimilated into U.S. society and "can have a profound affect on youth."

"Tragically, the worst is yet to come," said Yonah Alexander. "Terrorism is going to confront us the remainder of the twenty-first century," he said, citing potential new threats from nuclear, radiological, chemical, and bio-terrorism. "It is a fight we must win. We can't be blinded by the most recent attack in anticipating the next one. Yemen is clearly a new terrorist breeding ground. But it isn't the only one. Since 9/11, attacks by al Qaeda and other terrorists have risen 550 percent in North and West/Central Africa—only a short plane ride from Europe and the U.S."

He cited a special report released at the panel, "Maghreb & Sahel Terrorism: Addressing the Rising Threat from al-Qaeda & other Terrorists in North & West/Central Africa," which documents the surge in activity from al Qaeda in the Islamic Maghreb and from other terrorists in the region.[20]

The panel also addressed a question by moderator Michelle van Cleave, former National Counterintelligence Executive: "Are these criminal acts, or are they in the nature of war?" Brig. Gen. David Reist, U.S. Marine Corps (retired) said, "terrorism is the most severe threat to our security on both sides of the Atlantic," and "we must not lower our guard, despite public fatigue." However "terrorism" is categorized, the panel agreed that meeting its threat required many elements of national power and international cooperation, for the long term.

Indeed, numerous reports in early 2010 underscore the escalating nature of the terrorist threats to all societies. The following recent international media coverage, selected at random, characterizes the concern and magnitude of the multifaceted challenges and responses by governmental and intergovernmental bodies:[21]

- Abu Sayyaf radical Islamists rebels kill 11 Filipinos
- A homicide car bomb attacked NATO forces in Kandahar, Afghanistan
- Anarchists targeted police, banks, and property in Thessaloniki, Greece
- Venezuela provided support to both ETA (Basque terrorist group in Spain) and FARC (Revolutionary Armed Forces of Columbia) in an assassination plot against Colombia's President Alvaro Uribe

- Northern Ireland could become al Qaeda's potential target
- President Mahmoud Ahmadinejad of Iran urges Sayyed Hassan Nasrallah, Hezbollah's Secretary General, to annihilate Israel if it attacks Lebanon
- A bomb blast at a mosque in Pakistan's northwestern tribal belt killed 29 people and wounded some 50 others
- A suicide attacker driving a minibus killed 20 Shiite pilgrims, including women and children, near the shrine city Karbala in Iraq
- Taliban extremists are increasingly using civilians as human shields as they battle against Afghan-NATO forces
- Lashkar-e-Taiba al-Alwi (a previously unknown jihadist group that had splintered from a larger Pakistan-based organization) claimed responsibility for an attack at a German bakery restaurant in Pune, India, killing 11 and injuring 60
- Britain bans Somali terrorist group al-Shabbab
- Israel is vigilant in the face of multiple threats (e.g., Hamas, Hezbollah, Iran)
- India and Saudi Arabia sign extradition treaty and pledge to fight terror
- A key ETA leader was arrested in France
- South Africa seized North Korean weapons shipped to the Congo
- The Pakistani Rapid Action Battalion arrested Rezwan Ahmed, who coordinated the operations of Jaish-e-Mohammed (JeM, a Pakistan-based anti-Indian group) in Bangladesh
- Turkey's Parliament created the Undersecretariat of Public Order and Security, a new unit to combat terrorism, functioning under the auspices of the Internal Ministry
- The Financial Action Task Force (representing 34 nations) called on additional states to take steps to block Iran's terrorist financing and money laundering
- Three British citizens, who plotted to carry out violent jihad in the United Kingdom, are facing trial in Manchester

In the United States, new security concerns were recorded again in early 2010. Selected examples include these items:[22]

- Conspiracy theories against the United States are expanding, including the charge that America "artificially" caused the Haiti earthquake, according to Hassan Hamada, a Lebanese journalist.
- Abu Yahya Al-Libi, a senior al Qaeda commander, in an article warned that all U.S. measures in the battle against terrorism will never bring security for which it yearns and that today after a series of failures in Somalia, Afghanistan, and Iraq, it realizes that its end as a super power is certain.
- Al Qaeda in the Arabian Peninsula (AQAP)'s top military commander, Qasian al-Raimi, threatened new terror attacks against the United States and warned Americans that the group "will blow up the earth from below your feet."

- The growing perceptions of threats from biological terrorism have led to the increase of security businesses dealing with devices capable of detecting dangerous substances.

- Howard Schmidt, White House cybersecurity chief, asserted that the major economic threat facing this country is the cybersecurity problem.

- The United States and Mexico signed a Declaration of Principles and Cooperation on joint efforts to secure the U.S.-Mexico border and share information about transnational threats.

As the foregoing developments in the recent "terrorist weather" reports indicate, the United States is facing expanding security threats at home and abroad. This book focused mostly on those American citizens (either born or naturalized), as well as permanent residents, who consider themselves members of a specific "diaspora" grouping whose loyalty is linked to "foreign affinity" causes rather than to the national interests of the United States. While attachments to foreign culture, legacies, and aspirations have been the hallmark of American pluralism and are protected by the Constitution, terrorists are legally accountable for their criminal actions.

An early case in point is the assassination of Robert F. Kennedy (who sought the nomination of the Democratic Party for the presidency of the United States) on June 5, 1968, at the Ambassador Hotel in Los Angeles. His attacker, Sirhan Bishara Sirhan, was a permanent resident who held Jordanian citizenship. In justifying his act, Sirhan explained that he killed Kennedy because of his pro-Israel views on the Palestinian problem. Sirhan was convicted and sentenced to life in prison.[23]

It is not surprising, therefore, that one of the most important tools developed in the aftermath of 9/11 is the USA PATRIOT Act. On February 27, 2010, President Obama signed into law the bill H.R. 3961, which provides a one-year extension of several terrorist provisions that were included in the Act and the Intelligence Reform and Terrorism Prevention Act of 2004.[24]

Indeed, this legal measure is a step in the right direction. After all, domestic extremism and terrorism is a top American concern. Summarizing the nature of this threat, Homeland Security Secretary Janet Napolitano stated on February 21, 2010, that citizens who resort to terrorism and plot against the United States are now as big a challenge as international terrorism. She further observed that the government is just starting to confront this reality and does not have a good handle on how to prevent someone from becoming a violent extremist.[25]

Despite the above misgiving, it appears that the current administration is making some important policy shifts regarding security concerns in general. A latest example is Washington's classified review of nuclear weapons policy which will, for the first time, make preventing nuclear-armed terrorists a central aim of American strategic planning. It is expected, therefore, that when the Nuclear Posture Review will be completed in 2011, it will require the U.S. government to focus on countering nuclear terrorists.[26]

This developing strategic trend is indeed encouraging in light of the pre-9/11 record when many government officials and members of Congress did not consider terrorism to pose a major threat to the United States. Increasingly, terrorism is no longer viewed in this country as a minor nuisance or irritant but rather as a serious challenge to all contemporary societies and perhaps even to the very survival of civilization itself.

On the basis of this academic work, as well as other studies during the past four decades, it can be generally concluded that the "best practices" approaches to combat terrorism—nationally, regionally, and globally—are founded on a broad range of actions, including apprehension or elimination of operatives and their leadership; destruction of command, control, and communications; disruption of infrastructures and sanctuaries; denial of material support and funding; and infliction of severe punishment on state sponsors and collaborators.

Also, the following counterterrorism policies need to be adopted or strengthened by the United States and other countries:

- Develop coherent governmental and intergovernmental policies;
- Establish efficient organizational structures to conduct, coordinate, and implement policies;
- Introduce new legal instruments to close gaps in domestic and international law;
- Produce quality human and technological intelligence and enhance sharing within and among nations;
- Strengthen law enforcement capabilities at all levels and encourage regional and global cooperation;
- Wage an intensified campaign to disrupt the flow of funds to terrorist movements in concert with financial and economic institutions worldwide;
- Prevent the proliferation of weapons of mass destruction to rogue states and terrorist groups;
- Initiate new concepts, doctrines, training, and missions for military forces tasked to combat terrorism in different environments such as urban insurgencies;
- Increase cooperative relationships and alliances with like-minded nations through diplomatic efforts and provide counterterrorism technical assistance to those states in need of support;
- Expand the involvement of civic societies, such as religious, professional, and educational bodies, in participating in the battle against terrorism.

To be sure, the implementation of the foregoing approaches guarantees neither a prompt defeat nor an achievable total victory over terrorism.

The challenge facing the international community must be constructed on a long-term, realistic, and integrated strategy of both weapons and ideas not dissimilar to the twentieth century experiences fighting Fascism, Nazism, and Communism. It would be, however, presumptuous for me and my colleagues on this project to offer definitive recommendations on response strategies in confronting terrorism. One of the main reasons for our reluctance to assume such a role is the recognition that developing effective counterterrorism measures requires continuous and rigorous analysis by both public and private bodies. Nevertheless, there are three specific areas of concern that are critical for implementing more effectively a comprehensive strategy. The first is combating radicalization and extreme violence, particularly involving teenagers who constitute potential recruits for terrorist groups such as al Qaeda. The following road map is suggested for the consideration of the United States and its friends and allies:

- Build an international consensus on radicalization as a threat;
- Engage governments on formulating and enhancing effectiveness of policies to combat radicalization;
- Identify methodologies for gathering and formulating data on radicalization;
- Select influential actors and stakeholders, support their efforts, and facilitate their networking where appropriate;
- Provide "out-of-the-box" approach to counter radical messages and movements within diverse cultural and ideological contexts;
- Develop model programs to counter radicalization process/efforts with an ongoing eye to evaluating their effectiveness;
- Assess de-radicalization efforts on individuals and target populations and their effects on future terrorist activity;
- Ensure that educational programs within foreign governments do not promote intolerance, bigotry, discrimination, victimization, or stereotyping to the extent that such efforts promote extremist views and actions.

The second area that requires continued attention is related to cyberterrorist threats to our modern societies. Some of the principal measures that will reduce the exposure to "nonexplosive" attacks and bring them to a tolerable level include:

- A broad program of awareness and education;
- Infrastructure protection through industry cooperation and information sharing;
- Immediate actions prior to the completion of a formal risk assessment:
  - Isolate critical control systems from insecure networks by disconnection or adequate firewalls;

- Adopt best practices for password control and protection, or install more modern authentication mechanisms;
- Provide for individual accountability through protected action logs or the equivalent
- Reconsideration of laws related to infrastructure protection;
- A revised program of research and development;
- A national organization structure.

The third area of "added value" is the contribution of the civic society to the counterterrorism strategy, such as the media's contribution to such efforts. Among the selected academic views on the media's role are the following observations:

- Terrorism may be viewed as a crime and is not to be considered an act of war. Terrorists are to be treated as criminals rather than prisoners of war.
- Both censorship and self-regulation are proposed by different groups as the only legitimate method of regulating media involvement with terrorism. Those who deal with terrorism directly tend to favor some form of government direction or censorship; the media generally favor self-regulation.
- A balance is required between guaranteeing the public's right to security and its right to be informed. The freedom of the press to report is not, therefore, absolute.
- Terrorism includes a significant propaganda dimension and therefore the media should not assist terrorists in their effort to secure positive publicity.
- Terrorists exhibit psychological traits that the authorities seek to exploit in incident resolution; media coverage should be consistent with and supportive of those efforts.
- The media should act in a manner consistent with and supportive of the democratic system within which they function. Associated ethics should be central to media coverage and override competitive or commercial factors.
- The media have on occasion reported terrorism irresponsibly, and a negative attitude on the part of authorities dealing with incidents has resulted.
- The role played by the media differs in various countries because it is influenced by relevant legal provisions, the structure of the media industry in a given country, and the nature of government-media relations derived from past experience with terrorist incidents.
- In spite of differences, efforts to improve government-media cooperation, for the benefit of victims in particular, are occurring. Establishing a clear framework for cooperation, including respect for the independence and integrity of both parties, offers a positive method of resolving these contentious issues.

In sum, the aforementioned observations and preliminary recommendations, and the analysis and reflections provided previously by members of our research project, are intended to represent another academic effort in this important field of security concerns. Combating this challenge effectively requires heeding the advice of King Solomon's dictum: "Be not afraid of sudden terror,"[27] as well as Sir Winston Churchill's vow to the House of Commons on June 4, 1940: "We shall never surrender."[28]

Notes

PREFACE

1. In spite of the absence of a global definition of "terrorism," the element of fear is most commonly incorporated in numerous governmental and nongovernmental sources. See, for example, Anser Institute for Homeland Security's preferred definition: "the calculated use of violence or threat of unlawful violence to inculcate fear; intended to coerce or intimidate governments or societies in pursuit of goals that are generally political, religious or ideological" in "A Primer on Homeland Security," http://www.homelandsecurity.org, p. 7.

2. Assessment of all costs must consider not only the nearly 3,000 people killed and thousands more wounded, but also the psychological, economic, political, and strategic consequences. See, for instance, Dean C. Alexander and Yonah Alexander, *Terrorism and Business: The Impact of September 11, 2001* (Ardsley, New York: Transnational Publications, 2002). It has been reported that the cost of the war on terrorism by the end of 2009, over eight years after the 9/11 attacks, is $944 billion. See http://www.fas.org/sgp/crs/natsec/rc33110.pdf. Also, Michael R. Bloomberg, mayor of New York City, asserted on January 7, 2010, that providing security for the trials of Khalid Shaikh Mohammed and other terrorism suspects connected with 9/11 will cost his administration more than $200 million a year, http://www.nytimes.com/2010/01/07/ny region/07terror.html.

3. A release by the White House, January 27, 2010.

4. See "Annual Threat Assessment of U.S. Intelligence Committee for the Senate Select Committee on Intelligence," February 2, 2010, and press reports such as the *New York Times, Washington Post* and *Washington Times*, dated February 3, 2010.

5. In addition to Denis C. Blair, the panel included Robert S. Mueller III, director of the Federal Bureau of Investigation (FBI); Leon E. Panetta, director of the

Central Intelligence Agency (CIA); Lt. Gen. Ronald S. Burgess, Jr., director of the Defense Intelligence Agency (DIA); and John Dinger, the acting assistant secretary of state for intelligence and research.

6. See, for example, http://www.huffingonpost.com/jeff-stein/top-spies-terror -warningb447220.html.

7. See, for instance, http://www.upi.com/top-news/US/2009/11/06/Fort-Hood -mourns-shooting-victims/UPI-82601257502739/, and several press reports such as the *New York Times*, November 13, 2009, and the *Washington Post*, November 14, 15, 18, 21, 24, and 27, 2009.

8. See, for example, http://www.upi.com/top-news/US/2010/01/03/kean -terrorist-suspect-did-us -a-favor/UPI-8742262558585.

9. It has been reported that two Saudi nationals, Muhamad Attik-al-Harbi (prisoner #333) and Said Ali Shari (prisoner #372), who were released from Guantanamo on November 9, 2007 and sent to Saudi Arabia and then joined AQAP, were behind the Christmas Day operation. See "National Security Brief" (Washington, D.C.: Center for Security Policy, December 29, 2009) and the *New York Times*, December 20, 2009. On a related issue, Abdulmutallab disclosed during his interrogation that there are other operatives like him and that additional attacks against the United States are being planned: see http://news.oneindia.in/2010/02/04/ intelligencechiefs-warn-of-more-qaeda-terror-plots-against.html. More recently, several of the developments connected with AQAP and al Qaeda should be noted. First, Sheik Abu-Syfan Al-Azadi (also known as Ali al-Shinri), the group's Saudi deputy commander, in an audio recording titled "A Response to the Crusader Aggression" and produced by AQAP media company Al-Malahim dated February 8, 2010, called on Muslims to strike at American interests in the region (see MEMRI Special Dispatch No. 2798, February 8, 2010, and http:/www.memrijttm.org/ content/en/report.html?report=3961+param=APT and *New York Times*, February 9, 2010). And second, the Shabad (fighting the weak Saudi government) and Raskamboni Rebel Group (that previously cooperated with the Hizbul Islam terrorist movement and currently controls territory near the Kenyan frontier) have declared that they have joined the "International Jihad of al Qaeda" (*New York Times*, February 2, 2010).

10. The released statement titled "The Operation of Brother Mujahid Umar Farouk the Nigerian in Response to the American Attack in Yemen" appeared on the jihadist Web site Shumukh Al-Islam. See MEMRI Special Dispatch No. 27/47, December 28, 2009. Interestingly, in an audio message by al Qaeda's Osama bin Laden that was aired by Al-Jazeera TV on January 24, 2010, he also claimed credit for the Christmas operation. Bin Laden declared that the message of that attack was the same message "conveyed to you by the heroes of 9/11," that "America will not even dream of security, until security becomes a reality in Palestine." MEMRI Special Dispatch No. 2765, January 24, 2010. Also visit http://www.memritv.org/ clip/en/0/0/0/0/0/0/2357.htm. See also CNN, January 24, 2010.

11. It has also been reported that while Awlaki preached at a local mosque in San Diego, he met with two of the 9/11 operatives, Khalid al-Mihdhar and Nawaf al-Hamzi, who hijacked the plane that crashed into the Pentagon. See *Washington Times*, February 3, 2010.

12. Awlaki's online activities have also inspired Canadian and British Muslims. Thus, his Web site and videos included the July 7, 2005 London transportation bomber. See, for instance, *The Telegraph* (U.K.), November 23, 2009.

13. See, for example, http://www.nydailynews.com/news/national/2010/02/03/2010-02-03_american_jihadi_alert_terror_pros_say_yemen_qaeda_to_send_yank_recruits.html.

14. U.S. policy provides for killing American citizens abroad if they present a direct threat to national security. See, for instance, http://www.edition.cnn.com/2010/politics/02/04/killing.americans/. See also *New York Times*, December 26, 2009.

15. See, for example, http://www.boston.com/news/nation/washington/articles/2010/01/18/number_of_terror_suspects_spikes_in_past_year/.

16. See, for instance, *New York Times*, December 14, 2009.

17. See, for example, *New York Times*, November 19, 2009, www.upi.com January 3, 2010, and www.ww4report.com/node/8210.

18. See, for instance, CBS News, December 9, 2009 and *Washington Times*, December 21, 2009.

19. See, for example, *Washington Post*, November 23, 2009.

20. See, for instance, "Terror Chatter Increasing on the Internet," The National Terror Alert Response Center's posting, February 12, 2010, http://www.nationalterroralert.com/updates/2010/02/12/terror-chatter-increasing-on-the-internet/.

21. See *New York Times* and *Washington Post*, November 25, 2009.

22. Eric Rozenman, "News Media's Unreliable Muslim Source," *Washington Jewish Week*, January 28, 2010.

23. See, for instance, Andrea Elliott, "The Jihadist Next Door," *New York Times Magazine*, January 31, 2010, 26–35, 42.

24. See, for example, Shaun Waterman, "Terror Reviews Avoid Word 'Islamist'," *Washington Times*, February 12, 2010.

25. On April 19, 1995, Timothy James McVeigh and Terry Lynn Nichols detonated a homemade incendiary device in protest of the government on the second anniversary of the infamous Waco Seige in Waco, Texas. The two men were American right-wing extremists who sought to disrupt what they considered a tyrannical government establishment and punish those involved in the system. The explosion destroyed the Alfred P. Murrah Federal Building, killing 168 people and wounding 450 others. For further information, please see http://www.washingtonpost.com/wp-srv/national/longterm/oklahoma/bg/mcveigh.htm.

26. The full transcript of President Franklin Delano Roosevelt's First Inaugural Address can be found at http://www.nationalcenter.org/FRooseveltFirstInaugural.html.

CHAPTER 1

1. Research for this book was initiated in 2002 and completed in fall 2009. The first chapter, however, is also based on some material gathered by the author prior to 9/11. Each contributor is solely responsible for the content and interpretation of his own chapter. It should be noted that several earlier drafts of the work were reviewed by external reviewers. Their suggestions were considered by the contributors.

2. Baoz Ganor, "Defining Terrorism: Is One Man's Terrorist Another Man's Freedom Fighter?" *International Policy Institute for Counter-Terrorism* 4 (1998).

3. http://terrorism.about.com/od/whatisterroris1/ss/DefineTerrorism.htm.

4. United Nations, "Definitions of Terrorism," 2006, web.archive.org/web/20070129121539, www.unodc.org/unodc/terrorism_definitions.html.

5. United Nations General Assembly, GARes. 51/210, 1999.

6. See, for example, *British Parliament Report (2007)*, surveying legal definitions of terrorism. www.tamilnation.org/terrorism/uk/070317carli.htm.

7. UN Security Council Resolutions, www.un.org/Docs/sc/unsc_resolutions04.html, 2004.

8. www.decisions.fct-cf.gc.ca/en/2007/2007fc568.2007fc.568.html.

9. North Atlantic Trade Organization, "NATO and the Fight against Terrorism," www.nato.int/cps/en/natolive/topics_48801.htm.

10. North Atlantic Trade Organization, "News Conference by NATO Secretary General Jaap de Hoop Scheffer at the Informal Meeting of NATO Defence Ministers and the Meeting of the NATO-Russia Council," February 9, 2007, www.nato.int/cps/en/natolive/opinions_8087.htm.

11. North Atlantic Treaty Organization, "Invocation of Article 5: Five Years On," Summer 2006, www.nato.int/docu/review/2006/issue2/english/art2.html.

12. U.S. Code. Title 22 §2656f (d).

13. See also http://caselaw.lp.findlaw.com/casecode/uscodes/18/parts/i/chapters/113b/sections/section_2331.html.

14. Reported in the *Washington Post*, March 21, 2009.

15. Speech delivered by John Brennan at the Centre for Strategy and International Studies, as reported in the *Washington Times*, September 1, 2009.

16. "Truth, Honesty, and Justice. The Alternative to Wars, Terrorism and Politics," *Definition of Terrorism*, July 14, 2002, www.worldjustice.org/taj/defterror.html.

17. Merriam-Webster Dictionary, www.merriamwebster.com/dictionary/diaspora. See also Ethno-Nationalist Terrorism, www.apsu.edu/oconnort/3400/3400lect03.htm and International Institute for Diaspora Studies, http://diasporastudies.org?Whatis/Whatis.html.

18. William Safran, "Diasporas in Modern Societies: Myths of Homeland and Return," *Diaspora: A Journal of Transnational Studies* 1, no. 1 (1991): 83–84, http://diasporastudies.org?Whatis/Whatis.html.

19. Reported in the *Washington Times*, September 3, 2009.

20. *Webster's International Dictionary of the English Language* (Springfield, MA: G. & C. Merriam Company, 1900), 583, 584.

21. Ibid.

22. This definition was crafted by a special task force of experts that was established in connection with the project on foreign-ability terrorism. It was adopted by the group at a February 11, 2003, meeting held at the Potomac Institute for Policy Studies in Arlington, Virginia.

23. See FBI, *Five Year Report* (Washington, DC: Government Printing Office, 1995), 7.

24. For some general overviews see, for example, Yonah Alexander, ed., *International Terrorism: National, Regional and Global Perspectives* (New York: Praeger Pubishers, 1976); Tunde Adeniran and Yonah Alexander, eds., *International Violence* (New York: Praeger Publishers, 1983); Walter Laqueur and Yonah Alexander, eds., *The Terrorism Reader: A Historical Anthology*, rev. ed. (New York: New American Library, 1987); and Yonah Alexander ed., *Combating Terrorism: Strategies of Ten Countries* (Ann Arbor, MI: University of Michigan Press, 2007).

25. See, for instance, Yonah Alexander and Michael S. Swetnam, *Usama bin Laden's al Qaida: Profile of a Terrorist Network* (Ardsley, NY: Transnational Publications, 2001).

26. See, for example, bin Laden's audiotape attacking the United States that was aired on Al-Jazeera TV on June 3, 2009, and his audio message that was posted on Islamic Web sites on September 13, 2009. Also Ayman al-Zawahiri, al Qaeda's second in command, appeared on a video marking the eighth anniversary of the September 11, 2009, attack on the United States (reported by Reuters in Dubai), www.reuters.com/article/worldnews/idUSTRE58L.STX20090922.

27. See, for instance, Ray S. Cline and Yonah Alexander, *Terrorism as State-Sponsored Covert Warfare* (Fairfax, VA: Hero Books, 1986).

28. See, for example, Ray S. Cline and Yonah Alexander, *Terrorism: The Soviet Connection* (New York: Crane Russak, 1984).

29. For an overview of Iran's case study, see, for instance, Yonah Alexander and Milton Hoenig, *The New Iranian Leadership: Ahmadinejad, Terrorism, Nuclear Ambition and the Middle East* (Westport, CT: Praeger Security International, 2008).

30. For recent reports on Tehran's deception regarding building a secret facility near the city of Qom, see, for example, *Washington Post*, September 26, 2009.

31. This information is drawn from the database developed and maintained by the Inter-University Center for Terrorism Studies based in Washington, DC, and Arlington, VA.

32. For a comprehensive study, see *The 9/11 Commission Report*, Final Report of the National Commission on Terrorist Attacks upon the United States (New York: W. W. Norton, 2003).

33. See, for example, Paul Leventhal and Yonah Alexander, eds., *Preventing Nuclear Terrorism* (Lexington, MA: Lexington Books, 1987); and Yonah Alexander and Milton Hoenig, *Super Terrorism: Biological, Chemical, Nuclear* (Ardsley, NY: Transnational Publications, 2001).

34. Cited in American Bar Association (Standing Committee on Law and National Security), *National Security Law Report* 29, no. 3 (August 2007): 1–2.

35. Ibid.

36. Mathhew Bunn, "Thwarting Terrorists: More to Be Done," *Washington Post*, September 26, 2007.

37. See, for instance, Yonah Alexander and Michael S. Swetnam, eds., *Cyber Terrorism and Information Warfare: Threats and Responses* (Ardsley, NY: Transnational Publications, 2001).

38. See, for example, Michael F. Noone and Yonah Alexander, eds., *Cases and Materials on Terrorism: Three Nations' Response* (The Hague: Kluwer Law International, 1997); Yonah Alexander, ed., *Counterterrorism Strategies: Successes*

and Failures of Six Nations (Washington, DC: Potomac Books, 2006); Yonah Alexander, Edgar H. Brenner, and Serhat Tutuncuoglu, eds., *Turkey: Terrorism, Civil Rights and the European Union* (London: Cavendish, 2008); and Yonah Alexander and Tyler B. Richardson, eds., *Terror on the High Seas: From Piracy to Strategic Challenge* (Santa Barbara, CA: Praeger Security International, an Imprint of ABC-CLIO, LLC, 2009).

39. See, for instance, Brian M. Jenkins, "Terrorism in the United States," *TVI Journal 5*, no. 1 (1984); and FBI, *Terrorism in the United States* (Washington, DC: Government Printing Office, 1988).

40. See, for example, FBI, *Terrorism in the United States* (Washington, DC: Government Printing Office, 1999).

41. One of the plotters, Oussama Kassir, a Lebanese-Swede, was sentenced to life in prison some 10 years later. Reported in the *New York Times*, September 16, 2009.

42. See, for instance, City of Oklahoma, *Final Report*, 1996.

43. *Terror from the Right*, A Special Report from the Southern Poverty Law Center's Intelligence Project, 2009.

44. *Intelligence Report*, Fall 2009, Issue 135.

45. Ibid.

46. The following are some of the sources related to American citizens' terrorist activities in the United States. A number of these actors and their specific plots are mentioned in this chapter:

- Adam Yahiye Gadahn 2006: www.globalsecurity.org/security/profiles/adam_gadahn.htm
- Ahmed Omar Abu Ali 2005: www.washingtonpost.com/wp-dyn/articles/A43940-2005Feb22.html
- Atlanta 2006: www.heritage.org/research/HomelandDefense/bg2085.cfm
- Bryant Neal Vinas 2009: www.nytimes.com/2009/07/24/nyregion/24terror.html?pagewanted=2
- Christopher Paul 2009: www.msnbc.msn.com/id/29413551/
- Dirty Bomb Plot 2002: www.heritage.org/research/HomelandDefense/bg2085.cfm
- Fort Dix Plot 2007: www.washingtonpost.com/wpdyn/content/article/2007/05/08/AR2007050800465_2.html
- Gale William Nettles 2004: www.foxnews.com/story/0,2933,128156,00.html
- Iyman Faris 2003: www.heritage.org/research/HomelandDefense/bg2085.cfm
- JFK Plot 2007: www.npr.org/templates/story/story.php?storyId=10672115
- LA Cell 2005 (Jam'iyyat Ul-Saheeh): www.adl.org/main_Terrorism/los_angeles_sentenced.htm
- Lackawanna Six (Buffalo, NY) 2002: www.heritage.org/research/HomelandDefense/bg2085.cfm
- Mahmud Faruq Brent 2005: www.atimes.com/atimes/South_Asia/IH10Df01.html

- Michael Reynolds 2005: www.foxnews.com/story/0,2933,335500,00.html
- New York Plot 2009: www.chicagodefender.com/article-4616-terror-plot
  -suspects-have-lengthy-criminal-records.html
- New York Subway/RNC Convention 2004: www.heritage.org/research/
  HomelandDefense/bg2085.cfm
- Ohio Plot 2006: www.heritage.org/research/HomelandDefense/bg2085.cfm
- Pakistan connections 2005: www.adl.org/NR/exeres/F2BE5059-644D
  -448B-B5DF-2C12E1289C2E,8C8C250F-DA79-405F-B716-
  D4409CAB5396,frameless.htm
- Portland Cell 2002: http://community.seattletimes.nwsource.com/archive/?
  date=20031017&slug=portlandseven17m
- Ronald Allen Grecula 2006: www.nefafoundation.org/miscellaneous/
  FeaturedDocs/US_v_Grecula_DOJPRGuiltyPlea.pdf
- Saifullah Anjum Ranjha 2008: www.ice.gov/pi/nr/0808/080822baltimore.htm
- Sears Tower/Miami Plot 2006: www.heritage.org/research/HomelandDefense/
  bg2085.cfm
- Thanksgiving 2008 NYC: www.nytimes.com/2009/07/24/nyregion/24terror
  .html?_r=1
- Umer and Hamid Hayat 2005: www.foxnews.com/story/0,2933,335500,00
  .html
- Virginia Jihad 2004: www.cnn.com/2004/US/South/03/04/paintball.terror/
  index.html
- Yassin Aref and Mohammed Hossain: www.foxnews.com/story/
  0,2933,335500,00.html

47. See, for example, *Washington Post* and *New York Times*, September 24, 2009, and CNN.com/crime, September 25, 2009. For a detailed study, see National Consortium for the Study of Terrorism and Responses to Terrorism (START), *2009 Research Review*, www.start.umd.edu.

48. See, for instance, Yonah Alexander and Edgar H. Brenner, eds., *U.S. Federal Legal Responses to Terrorism* (Ardsley, NY: Transnational Publications, 2007); Yonah Alexander and Donald Musch, eds., *Terrorism: Documents of Local and International Control*, vols. 15–35 (Dobbs Ferry, NY: Oceana, 1999–2007); and Yonah Alexander and Michael Kraft, eds., *Evolution of US Counterterrorism Policy*, 3 vols. (Westport, CT: Praeger Security International, 2008).

49. Reported by UPI, September 23, 2009.

50. For security developments in Iraq, see, for example, Reuters fact box, September 12, 2009.

51. ACLU, "Even Bigger, Even Weaker: The Emerging Surveillance Society: Where Are We Now?" (an update to the ACLU report "Bigger Monster, Weaker Chains," published in January 2003; September 2007).

52. George Santayana, *The Life of Reason* (Amherst, NY: Prometheus Books, 1998).

CHAPTER 2

1. Robert Leiken, "Bearers of Global Jihad? Immigration and National Security after 9/11," *The Nixon Center*, March 2004, www.nixoncenter.org/publications/monographs/Leiken_Bearers_of_Global_Jihad.pdf.

2. Ibid.

3. Section 411 of the USA PATRIOT Act of 2001 (8 U.S.C. § 1182) authorized by the Secretary of State, in consultation with or upon the request of the Attorney General, to designate terrorist organizations for immigration purposes.

4. Allegedly, there are bases operating in remote areas of Kashmir and Pakistan that train terrorists specifically to infiltrate the West. As many as 400 had been trained by early February 2004. "One veteran U.S. law-enforcement official with an extensive history in counterterrorism said many of the training camps in the Pakistan-controlled regions of Kashmir are operated by the Harakat ul-Ansar, an Islamic militant group tied to bin Laden." Jerry Seper, "Islamic Extremists Invade U.S., Join Sleeper Cells," *Washington Times*, February 10, 2004.

5. " 'The estimate is that there are 100 or more al Qaeda operatives inside the United States, some who have been here for a considerable period of time, all of whom went through a training process to prepare them to carry out terrorist plots when they were called upon to do so,' U.S. Sen. Bob Graham, D-Florida, said Friday on CNN's 'Novak, Hunt and Shields.' 'That probably is the most immediate threat of a terrorist attack against the United States. . . . In addition, there are perhaps a dozen or more other international terrorist organizations that also have agents inside the United States,' he said." "Senator: Al Qaeda Cells Inside United States," *CNN*, February 23, 2002, www.cnn.com/2002/US/02/23/gen.terror.graham/.

6. Statement for the Record of Larry A. Mefford, assistant director, Counterterrorism Division, Federal Bureau of Investigation, on "The State of the Terrorist Threat Facing the United States," before the U.S. Senate Terrorism, Technology and Homeland Security Subcommittee, Washington, D.C., June 27, 2003, www.fbi.gov/congress/congress03/mefford062703.htm.

7. Mohammed Rauf was from Pakistan-Occupied Kashmir.

8. David Johnston, "Somali Is Accused of Planning a Terror Attack at a Shopping Center in Ohio," *New York Times*, June 15, 2004, www.nytimes.com/2004/06/15/national/15terror.html?pagewanted=print&position=.

9. Testimony of Robert S. Mueller, III, director, FBI before the House Appropriations Committee, Subcommittee on the Departments of Commerce, Justice, and State, the Judiciary and Related Agencies, March 27, 2003, "FBI's Fiscal Year (FY) 2004 Budget," www.fbi.gov/congress/congress03/mueller032703.htm.

10. "Ahmed Ressam's Millennium Plot," *PBS Frontline*, 2001, www.pbs.org/wgbh/pages/frontline/shows/trail/inside/cron.html.

11. Leiken, "Bearers of Global Jihad?"

12. Chicago Crime Commission, "Gangs: Public Enemy No. 1," 1995, https://www.chicagocrimecommission.org.

13. *Patterns of Global Terrorism, 2002*, U.S. Department of State, April 2003, http://www.state.gov/s/ct/rls/crt/2002/html/index.htm.

14. For more information, see International Policy Institute for Counter-Terrorism, "International Terrorism: Terrorist Organization Profiles," www.ict .org.il.

15. Also, see Keith B. Richburg and Fred Barbash, "Madrid Bombings Kill at Least 190: Al Qaeda-Linked Group Claims Responsibility," *Washington Post*, March 11, 2003, www.washingtonpost.com/wp-dyn/articles/A48577-2004Mar11.html.

16. The important unit regarding foreign-affinity terrorism is the sleeper group, because they employ the local Muslim population to infiltrate a Western nation undetected. However, both sleepers and satellites pose threats to Western countries. Their sympathetic coreligionists can hide those who infiltrate the domestic Muslim community, while those who avoid the Diaspora community are like needles in a haystack for authorities to monitor. In the European context, an example of an affiliate group might be Sheikh Omar Bakri Muhammad's, Al Muhajiroun in the United Kingdom. He presents himself as spokesman of the political wing of The International Islamic Front for Jihad against Jews and Crusaders, established by Osama bin Laden in 1996. But the Sheikh denied any organizational connection with bin Laden. "We have no direct links with Osama bin Laden," he declared. " [But] we have ideological links with the world Islamic movement, including Osama bin Laden." Middle East Media Research Institute (MEMRI), "Radical Islamist Profiles: Sheikh Omar Bakri Muhammad," London, Inquiry and Analysis Series, No. 73, October 24, 2001, http://memri.org/bin/articles.cgi?Page=archives &Area=ia&ID=IA7301. See also Patrick E. Tyler and Don Van Natta Jr., "Militants in Europe Openly Call for Jihad and the Rule of Islam," *New York Times*, April 26, 2004, www.nytimes.com/2004/04/26/international/europe/26 EURO.html?hp=&pagewanted=print&position=.

17. Tom W. Smith, "Estimating the Muslim Population in the United States," The American Jewish Committee, www.ajc.org/InTheMedia/PubIntergroupRelations.asp? did=356&pid=818. Also see Tom Smith, "Counting Flocks and Lost Sheep: Trends in Religious Preference since World War II," GSS Social Change Report No. 26. (Chicago: NORC, 1991). In contrast to Smith, see M. M. Ali, "Muslims in America: The Nation's Fastest Growing Religion," *Washington Report on Middle East Affairs* 15 (May/June 1996): 13, 107; Council on American Islamic Relations, "About Islam and American Muslims," www.cair-net.org; Yvonne Yazbeck Haddad, ed., *The Muslims of America* (New York: Oxford University Press, 1991); and Carol L. Stone, "Estimate of Muslims Living in America," in *The Muslims of America*, ed. Yvonne Yazbeck Haddad (New York: Oxford University Press, 1991).

18. "About Islam and American Muslims," *The Council on American Islamic Relations*, 2000, http://sun.cair.com/AboutIslam/IslamBasics.aspx.

19. Ihsan Bagby, Paul M. Perl, and Bryan T. Froehle, *The Mosque in America: A National Portrait: A Report from the Mosque Study Project* (Washington, DC: Council on American Islamic Relations, April 26, 2001).

20. Ibid, 3.

21. Ibid.

22. Ibid.

23. Robert S. Leiken, "Al Qaeda's New Soldiers," *The New Republic*, April 26, 2004, https://ssl.tnr.com/p/docsub.mhtml?i=20040426&s=leiken042604.

24. *United States of America v. John Phillip Walker Lindh*, in the U.S. District Court for the Eastern District of Virginia, Alexandria Division, Grand Jury Indictment, February 2002, www.usdoj.gov/ag/2ndindictment.htm. Also see, Testimony of Robert S. Mueller, III, director, FBI before the House Appropriations Committee, Subcommittee on the Departments of Commerce, Justice, and State, the Judiciary and Related Agencies, March 27, 2003, "FBI's Fiscal Year (FY) 2004 Budget," www.fbi.gov/congress/congress03/mueller032703.htm.

25. Testimony of Robert S. Mueller, III, director, FBI, before the Select Committee on Intelligence of the U.S. Senate, February 11, 2003, "War on Terrorism," www.fbi.gov/congress/congress03/mueller021103.htm.

26. Statement of John S. Pistole, executive assistant director, Counterterrorism/Counterintelligence, FBI, before the National Commission on Terrorist Attacks Upon the United States, April 14, 2004, www.fbi.gov/congress/congress04/pistole041404 .htm.Also an 11-count indictment of May 27, 2004, charged Abu Hamza al-Masri with attempts in late 1999 and early 2000 to set up the camp for "violent jihad" in Oregon about which authorities also charged James Ujaama, Alan Cowell, "Britain Arrests Radical Cleric Who Faces U.S. Terror Charges," *New York Times*, May 27, 2004, www.nytimes.com/2004/05/27/national/27CND-CLER.html?hp=&pagewanted =print&position=.

27. Testimony of Robert S. Mueller, III, director, FBI, before the Senate Select Committee on Intelligence and the House Permanent Select Committee on Intelligence, October 17, 2002, "Joint Intelligence Committee Inquiry," www.fbi.gov/congress/congress02/mueller101702.htm.

28. http://www.fbi.gov/wanted/terrorists/gadahn_a.htm.

29. Ibid, 4.

30. William Peters and Michael J. Bandler, Interview with Yvonne Haddad, "Islam in the United States: A Tentative Ascent," *U.S. Society and Values: The Religious Landscape of the United States* 2, no. 1 (March 1997): 20, http://www.islamfortoday .com/usahaddad.htm.

31. Craig Smith, "France Struggles to Curb Extremist Muslim Clerics," *New York Times*, April 30, 2004, http://nytimes.com/2004/04/30/international/europe/ 30FRAN.html?pagewanted=print&position=.

32. Leiken, "Bearers of Global Jihad?"

33. Rounding and categories that are not mutually exclusive causes figures in the text to sum greater than 100%. *Islam in America: The Official Facts*, The Institute of Islamic Information and Education, http://www.ilaam.net/Opinions/Islam InUSFactSheet.html.

34. U.S. Department of Commerce, Bureau of the Census, "Report on Arab Population Released by Census Bureau," December 3, 2003, www.census.gov/ Press-Release/www/releases/archives/census_2000/001576.html.

35. Ibid, 3.

36. "Converts: Converts in U.S. Prisons," *The Media Guide to Islam: A Journalist's Guide to Covering Islam*, San Francisco State University, modified August 20, 2003, http://mediaguidetoislam.sfsu.edu/intheus/06c_converts.htm.

37. Daniel Pipes estimates that Muslim converts in general in the United States total about one million, white Americans constitute only some 50,000. Hence, the

African American converts to Islam total some 950,000 as of the late 1990s, according to Pipes.

38. Department of Justice, Office of the Inspector General, "A Review of the Bureau of Prisons' Selection of Muslim Religious Services Providers," April 2004, www.usdoj.gov/oig/special/0404/index.htm.

39. Steve Emerson "infiltrated" Islamist meetings to gather information for his book, *American Jihad: The Terrorists Living among Us* (New York: Free Press, 2002), 5–41.

40. This is not to assert that al Qaeda will try to use gangs or criminal organizations in their operations. Al Qaeda has in the past been "highly selective in its recruitment, allowing only the most capable and committed operatives to become fully-fledged members." "In the Spotlight: Al Qaeda (the Base)," *Center for Defense Information: Terrorism Project*, December 30, 2002, www.cdi.org/terrorism/alqaeda-pr.cfm. Moreover, al Qaeda does not have a history of cooperating with non-Muslims in its operations. Rhonda Roumani and Marianne Stigset, "Al-Qaeda Link to Madrid Blasts May Alter EU Policies," *Daily Star*, available at *Lebanonwire*, March 13, 2004, www .lebanonwire.com/0403/04031326DS.asp. However, al Qaeda might benefit from ease with acquiring weapons that could come from close association of criminal organizations in prison with incarcerated gang members, some of whom may convert to Islam.

41. Seper, "Islamic Extremists Invade U.S."

42. Peter Skerry, "Political Islam in the United States and Europe," in *Political Islam: Challenges for US Policy*, edited by Dick Clark (Aspen Institute Congressional Program, 2003), 39, http://www.brookings.edu/gs/skerry_islam.pdf.

43. Ibid., 40–41.

44. Ibid., 42.

45. Persian World Outreach, "The Persian Diaspora," www.farsinet.com/pwo/ diaspora.html. In addition, "The Iranian Revolution and ascent to power of Imam Khomeini in 1979, followed by nearly a decade of debilitating war between Iran and Iraq, brought some Iranians westward. Many have settled in America, with significant numbers relocating in California." Jane Smith, "Patterns of Muslim Immigration," http://infousa.state.gov/education/overview/muslimlife/immigrat.htm.

46. Raymond Tanter, *Rogue Regimes: Terrorism and Proliferation*, updated edition (New York: St. Martin's Griffin, 1999), 37–38.

47. Acknowledgments to Grey Terry for the fire metaphor.

48. Rogue regimes acting as state sponsors of international terrorism might contract to terrorist groups and provide funds to carry out operations. But when terrorist groups act independently of rogue states, such groups may rely on "hawala." In contrast to formal banking, hawala is an alternative or parallel remittance system, which operates outside of, or parallel to, traditional financial channels. "Like any other remittance system, hawala can, and does, play a role in money laundering." Patrick M. Jost, U.S. Department of the Treasury and Harjit Singh Sandhu, Interpol, "The Hawala Alternative Remittance System and Its Role in Money Laundering," Interpol General Secretariat, Lyon, January 2000, www.interpol.int/Public/FinancialCrime/ MoneyLaundering/hawala/default.asp#1. Built on trust among dealers, hawalas engage in financial transactions that often leave no paper trail. Hawala dealers are familiar fixtures in the Middle East and now operate in the United States. Hamas and Hezbollah use hawalas to move their money around the world. Council on

Foreign Relations, "The Money: Drying Up the Funds for Terror," *Terrorism: Questions and Answers*, 2004, http://cfrterrorism.org/responses/money.html.

49. "Ansar al-Islam in Iraqi Kurdistan," *Human Rights Watch*, 2004, www.hrw.org/backgrounder/mena/ansarbk020503.htm.

50. Jonathan Schanzer, "Saddam's Ambassador to al Qaeda," *Weekly Standard*, The Washington Institute for Near East Policy, March 1, 2004, www.washingtoninstitute.org.

51. Information Division, Israeli Foreign Ministry, www.fas.org/irp/world/para/docs/960411.htm.

52. Iran's "Islamic Revolutionary Guard Corps (IRGC) and Ministry of Intelligence and Security (MOIS) were directly involved in the planning and support of terrorist acts and continued to exhort a variety of groups, especially Palestinian groups with leadership cadres in Syria and Lebanese Hezbollah, to use terrorism in pursuit of their goals. In addition, the IRGC was increasingly involved in supplying lethal assistance to Iraqi militant groups, which destabilizes Iraq." *Country Report on Terrorism*, April 28, 2006.

53. *Patterns of Global Terrorism, 2002.*

54. Raymond Tanter, "Iran's Threat to Coalition Forces in Iraq," *PolicyWatch*, no. 827, The Washington Institute of Near East Policy, January 15, 2004, http://www.washingtoninstitute.org/templateC05.php?CID=1705.

55. Ibid.

56. Eli Lake, "Iran Advocacy Group Said to Skirt Lobby Rules," *Washington Times*, November 13, 2009; available at http://www.washingtontimes.com/news/2009/nov/13/exclusive-did-iranian-advocacy-group-violate-laws//print/.

57. For an example of how the Muslim Brotherhood exhorts youths to join formal terrorist organizations, see the Muslim Brotherhood Movement homepage, "Allah is our objective. The messenger is our leader. Quran is our law. Jihad is our way. Dying in the way of Allah is our highest hope." http://www.ikhwanweb.com/.

58. "The Muslim Brotherhood in Egypt," *Encyclopedia of the Orient Online*, http://i-cias.com/e.o/mus_br_egypt.htm.

59. Ibid.

60. Richard P. Mitchell and John O. Voll, *The Society of the Muslim Brothers* (New York: Oxford University Press, 1969, 1993). Writing in the 1960s, Mitchell dismisses the common view of the movement as revolutionary and terrorist because its leadership, according to him, had no wish to seize power.

61. The Muslim Brotherhood is a very diverse affiliation of groups. The Brotherhood initiated branches in neighboring countries soon after its founding in Egypt and has local offices in over 70 countries. The movement is intentionally decentralized, stemming from its suppression at the hands of security forces and preoccupation with maintaining its existence in the face of such pressure. The group itself acknowledges: "The movement is flexible enough to allow working under the 'Ikhwan' name, under other names, or working according to every countr[y's] circumstances." The group's goals are also relevant to this discussion:

1- Building the Muslim individual: brother or sister with a strong body, high manners, cultured thought, ability to earn, strong faith, correct worship, conscious of time, of benefit to others, organized, and self-struggling character.

2- Building the Muslim family: choosing a good wife (husband), educating children Islamicaly [sic], and inviting other families.

3- Building the Muslim society (thru building individuals and families) and addressing the problems of the society realistically.

4- Building the Muslim state.

5- Building the Khilafa (basically a shape of unity between the Islamic states).

6- Mastering the world with Islam.The Muslim Brotherhood homepage, http://www.ikhwanweb.com/.

62. Paul M. Barrett, "The Brotherhood: A Student Journeys into a Secret Circle of Extremism," *Wall Street Journal*, December 22, 2003. All references in the text to the story about Mustafa Saied are from the Barrett article.

63. For an example of a verse from the Koran that is interpreted by some to be intolerant of other religions, consider [5.51] "O you who believe! Do not take the Jews and the Christians for friends; they are friends of each other; and whoever amongst you takes them for a friend, then surely he is one of them; surely Allah does not guide the unjust people." *The Koran*, www.hti.umich.edu/k/koran/bool.html.

64. Although Youssef Al Qaradawi condemned the 9/11 attacks as terrorism, he also excuses assaults against Israel by Hamas, Islamic Jihad, and al-Aqsa Martyrs Brigades, stating that, "they are not murderers, they are not killers and it's a transgression against them to call them so and label them so. They are people who are defending their homeland and their holy rights, which were attacked and transgressed against." "Martyrs or Murderers? Terrorism and Suicide Bombing," The Brookings Institution Conference, October 20, 2002, www.scholarofthehouse.org/shabelfaands.html.

65. Barrett, "A Student Journeys into a Secret Circle."

66. "Muslim Brotherhood—Syria," *Encyclopedia of the Orient*, http://i-cias.com/e.o/mus_br_syria.htm.

67. "The Muslim Brotherhood has given rise to a number of more militant and violent organizations, such as Hamas, Gama'a al-Islamiya, and Islamic Jihad," "Muslim Brotherhood," *The Columbia Encyclopedia*, 6th ed., 2001. www.bartleby.com/65/mu/MuslimBr.html.

68. Thanks to Stacie Dotson for her insight in understanding the evolution of the Brotherhood and its spinoffs. Acknowledgments also to Clare Lopez for her ideas on how formal organizations relate to Islamic movements.

69. The word madrassa in the Arabic language means school. The word can also appear transliterated as madrassa, as madrash, or as madressa. Typically it refers to an Islamic school for Muslims. It resembles a parochial school or a yeshiva, but with the purpose of teaching children about the religion of Islam. Both males and females attend madrassas: they sit in separate classes to learn in an Islamic context. A madrassa typically offers two courses of study, a "hifz" course to memorize the Koran and become a hafiz, and an Alim course to become a scholar or mullah. A regular curriculum includes learning Arabic, Koran memorization and interpretation, Islamic law, hadith, and the history of Islam. Depending on the individual madrassa, it may teach

additional courses like Arabic literature, English, science and history. http://en
.wikipedia.org/wiki/Madrassa.

70. "Palestinian Islamic Jihad: Harakat al-Jihad al-Islami al-Filastini,"
International Policy Institute for Counter-Terrorism, http://middleeastfacts.com/
middle-east/palestinian-islamic-jihad-islami.php.

71. Daniel Pipes and Steven Emerson, "Why Won't the US Government Close
Down Terrorist Groups on These Shores!?" *Jewish World Review*, August 14,
2001.

72. Ibid.

73. Ibid.

74. "Hamas," *International Policy Institute for Counter-Terrorism*, www.ict
.org.il/.

75. Hamas has recently undergone a transition due to the Israeli assassination of
its spiritual leader and founder Sheik Yassin, which has thrown the group's policy
toward the United States into a period of flux. Before his own assassination, Abdel
Aziz al-Rantissi criticized and blamed the United States for the assassination of Sheik
Yassin, asserting that Israel would not have acted without U.S. approval. Barbara
Plett, "Yassin Killing Brings Call for Islamic Unity," *BBC*, March 24, 2004, http://
news.bbc.co.uk/1/hi/world/middle_east/3564957.stm. Although Hamas backed
away from assertions speculations that it would target the United States and has
not targeted Americans in the past, the possibility does exist for Hamas under new
leadership to change its strategic goals.

76. John Mintz, "FBI Focus Increases on Hamas, Hizballah; Ruling Enables
Intensified Probes," *Washington Post*, May 8, 2003.

77. Matthew Levitt, "Hamas from Cradle to Grave," *Middle East Quarterly* 11,
no. 1 (Winter 2004), www.meforum.org/article/582.

78. Ibid.

79. Testimony of Robert S. Mueller, III, director, FBI, before the Select
Committee on Intelligence of the U.S. Senate, February 24, 2004, www.fbi.gov/
congress/congress04/mueller022404.htm, www.fbi.gov/page2/feb04/threats
022404.htm.

80. *Patterns of Global Terrorism, 2002*, U.S. Department of State, April 30,
2003, http://www.state.gov/s/ct/rls/crt/2002/html/index.htm. Also see Matthew
Levitt, "Navigating the U.S. Government's Terrorist Lists," *PolicyWatch*, no. 585,
The Washington Institute for Near East Policy, November 30, 2001, www.washington
institute.org.

81. *Patterns of Global Terrorism, 2003*, "Overview of State Sponsored Terrorism,"
http://www.state.gov/s/ct/rls/crt/2003/c12108.htm.

82. *Patterns of Global Terrorism, 2002*.

83. The overview of FTOs in the text is from Department of State, *Patterns of
Global Terrorism, 2002*. Released by the Office of the Coordinator for Counterter-
rorism, April 30, 2003, Appendix B: Background Information on Designated Foreign
Terrorist Organizations, http://www.state.gov/s/ct/rls/crt/2002/html/19991.htm.

84. FTO designations are to expire automatically after two years. But the Secretary of State may redesignate an organization for additional two-year period(s),
upon a finding that the statutory criteria continue to be met. The procedural

requirements for designating an organization as an FTO also apply to any redesignation of that organization.

85. The Secretary of State redesignated 25 groups as FTOs on October 2, 2003. The initial designations of these groups in 1997 and 1999 were to expire on October 3, 2003. By recertifying them as FTOs and publishing that decision in the Federal Register, the U.S. government stated that it preserved the ability to take action against them in accordance with the provisions of the Immigration and Nationality Act, as amended. This act makes it illegal for persons in the United States or subject to U.S. jurisdiction to provide material support to such terrorist groups. The act requires U.S. financial institutions to block assets held by them; and it enables visa denial to representatives of these groups. "The Secretary [of State] made this decision in consultation with the Attorney General and the Secretary of the Treasury after a thorough review of these groups' terrorist activities over the past two years." Richard Boucher, Spokesman, Press Statement (Revised), Redesignation of Foreign Terrorist Organizations, 2003, Washington, D.C., October 2, 2003, http:// www.america.gov/st/washfile-english/2003/December/20031223171637rethcirj0 .1411859.html. Whether the number of Islamist groups is 17 or 18 depends on the classification of Al-Aqsa Martyrs Brigade. This group has attempted to gain support and recruits by employing the religious rhetoric of Hamas, including its martyrdom terminology. However, the group is an offshoot of Fatah, which is an avowedly secular unit within the Palestine Liberation Organization. As a result of leading the fight against Israel from September 2000, Hamas has "swallowed" traditional PLO organizations, such as Fatah, Tanzim, and even al Aksa Martyrs Brigade.

86. Ibid.For a complete list, see http://www.ustreas.gov/offices/enforcement/ofac/ sdn/index.shtml.

87. Office of the Coordinator for Counterterrorism, U.S. Department of State, "Terrorist Exclusion List," Washington, DC, November 15, 2002, http://www .state.gov/s/ct/rls/other/des/123086.htm.

88. Bruce Bueno de Mesquita, "What Motivates Terrorists? Which Regimes Are Most Likely to Spawn Terrorist Groups? How Can the Scourge of Terrorism Be Stopped?" *Hoover Digest*, no. 1, 2002, http://www.hoover.org/publications/digest/ 4471321.html.

89. *Los Angeles Times*, October 9, 1997.

90. *Newsweek on Web*, September 26, 2002. Also Reuters of October 13, 1997 states that, "A U.S. decision branding Iran's main rebel group 'terrorists' is being seen in Tehran as the first positive sign of American goodwill towards the new government of moderate President Mohammad Khatami."

91. Philip Reeker, Deputy Spokesman, Department of State, Foreign Press Center Briefing, Washington, DC, October 25, 2001, http://2002-2009-fpc.state.gov/ 7515.htm.

92. William Branigin, "Bush Nominates Negroponte to New Intel Post," *Washington Post*, February 17, 2005.

93. Richard A. Posner, "The Reorganized U.S. Intelligence System after One Year," *American Enterprise Institute* (AEI), National Security Outlook Special Edition, May 2006.

94. Charles Babington, "Hayden Confirmed as CIA Chief," *Washington Post*, May 27, 2006.

95. Federation of American Scientists Web site, www.fas.org/irp/agency/ttic/.
96. Posner, "Reorganized U.S. Intelligence System," 3.
97. Letter from Senator Patrick Leahy (D-VT) to Attorney General John Ashcroft, January 1, 2003, www.eff.org/Privacy/TIA/leahy-letter.php.
98. Department of Justice Fact Sheet for the Terrorist Screening Center.
99. Posner, "Reorganized U.S. Intelligence System," 3.

CHAPTER 3

1. See *Making Intelligence Smarter: The Future of U.S. Intelligence* (New York: Council on Foreign Relations, 1996); *The Future of U.S. Intelligence* (Washington, D.C.: Consortium for the Study of Intelligence, 1996); *In from the Cold War: The Report of the Twentieth Century Fund Task Force on the Future of U.S. Intelligence* (New York: The Twentieth Century Fund Press, 1996); *IC 21: Intelligence in the 21st Century*, staff study, House Permanent Select Committee on Intelligence, House of Representatives, 104th Cong. (Washington, DC: US Government Printing Office, 1996).
2. Commissions established in 2000–2001 to examine the capabilities of the National Reconnaissance Office and the National Imagery Agency proved equally disappointing in achieving their agreed remit goals.
3. For decades, the Irish-American community had been an avid supporter of the Irish Republican Army's efforts to liberate Northern Ireland from British colonial domination. The Royal Hibernians were key role players. Counterparts could be found within the German-American community prior to the entrance of the United States into World War II. Armenian and Polish diaspora communities were long-standing supporters of their motherland brethren, as has been true of diaspora Jews.
4. The U.S. Code Section 2656(f) calls terrorism "premeditated, politically motivated violence perpetuated against noncombatant targets by subnational groups or clandestine agents, usually intended to influence an audience." See William H. Lewis, "The War on Terrorism: A Retrospective," *Mediterranean Quarterly* 13, no. 4 (Fall 2002): 21–37.
5. Fouad Ajami, "The Sentry's Solitude," *Foreign Affairs* 80, no. 6 (November/December 2001): 2–16; Gilles Keppel, *Jihad: The Trail of Political Islam* (Boston, MA: Harvard University Press, 2002); and Raphael Patai, *The Arab Mind* (New York: Hatherleigh Press, 2001).
6. Rouleau notes that bin Laden's mutation from freedom fighter into revolutionary began with his return to Saudi Arabia in 1990 and his growing frustration at his government's refusal to permit him to organize a group of freedom fighters to drive Iraqi forces out of Kuwait and topple the Saddam Hussein regime. He was further outraged when the Saudi government participated in Operation Desert Storm during which it leased military facilities to U.S. forces. In 1991, bin Laden directed his outrage against the United States declaring a jihad against the United States. See Eric Rouleau, "Trouble in the Kingdom," *Foreign Affairs* 81, no. 4 (July/August 2002): 75–89.
7. See the Ellen Laipson review, "While America Slept: Understanding Terrorism and Counterterrorism," *Foreign Affairs*, January 2003; see also Daniel Benjamin and Steven Simon, *The Age of Terror* (New York: Random House, 2002), 490.

8. Hundreds of foreigners, primarily Muslims, were rounded up after September 11 and held without charge. Tens of thousands more were called in for questioning and fingerprinting. Not a single terrorist was found. (See *The Economist*, *Special Report*, September 2, 2006.)

9. The Supreme Court in mid-2006 urged congress to engender effective oversight to control the president's claim of wartime powers. The court majority vouchsafed that customary and international law and the "Law of War," including the Geneva Conventions dealing with humane treatment of prisoners (read: Combatants) should guide policies and practices. By late 2006, the White House continued its reservations regarding the Court's decision.

10. Eugene Robinson, "Values We Have to Hide Abroad," *Washington Post*, September 8, 2006.

11. Bob Woodward, *Bush at War* (New York: Simon & Schuster, 2002), 36.

12. "Former Aide Takes Aim at War on Terror," *Washington Post*, June 16, 2003.

13. However, dissention and allegations of misconduct and corruption have risen within the office of the Special Inspector General of Iraq (SIGI) which are currently being investigated by the FBI, the Department of the Army, and other interested agencies. A creature of the Congress created in 2004–2005, SIGI may experience an abbreviated existence of charges of fraud, misallocation of funds, and "sustained pattern of inappropriate behavior" are proven.

14. Intelligence agencies continue to revise provisions of recorded data and information on three antiterrorism activities. For example, in December 2007, CIA Director Michael Hayden acknowledged that his agency had destroyed videotapes of harsh interrogations of high profile Al-Qaeda figures (Abu Zubnida and Abd al-Rhim al-Nashiri) undertaken in 2002. The destruction occurred in 2005 without proper authorization.

15. "Former Aide Takes Aim at War on Terror," *Washington Post*, June 16, 2003.

16. The author had personal experience of such "combat operations" over more than a decade of intelligence community service.

17. Ibid.

18. Woodward, *Bush at War*, 90.

19. Ibid., 116–17.

20. *Washington Post*, August 18, 2006.

21. In 2006, the Initial DNI, Ambassador John Negroponte, in an effort to enhance the analytical capabilities of the intelligence "community," appointed Thomas Fingar his deputy director for analysis. A veteran officer with more than two decades of intelligence experience, Fingar is expected to insure that the intelligence analyses received are identified. Underscoring the importance of transparency were "revelations" that a major source concerning Iraq's productions of chemical and biological weapons was an Iraqi unearthed by German agencies. Nicknamed "Curveball" by the latter, he was not directly questioned by U.S. officials before preparation of the 2002 NIE on Iraq's WMD, but was subsequently found to be lacking in reliability.

22. John D. Negroponte, "Yes, We are Better Prepared," *Washington Post*, September 10, 2006.

23. Ibid.

24. John Lehman, "We're Not Winning This War," *Washington Post*, August 31, 2006.

25. George Packer, *The Assassin's Gate: America In Iraq* (New York: Farrar, Straus and Giroux, 2005), 107. A wide range of other studies tend to confirm the actions to construct a separate conduit (read: stove pipe) into a receptive White House staff. Particularly helpful: Bob Woodward, *Plan of Attack: The Definitive Account of the Decision to Invade Iraq* (New York: Simon & Schuster, 2004); James Mann, *Rise of the Vulcans: The History of Bush's War Cabinet* (New York: Penguin Group, 2004); Thomas P. M. Barnett, *The Pentagon's New Map: War and Peace in the Twenty-First Century* (New York: Penguin Group, 2004); Hans Blix, *Disarming Iraq: The Search for Weapons of Mass Destruction* (London: Bloomsbury, 2004); Thomas L. Friedman, *The World Is Flat: A Brief History of the Twenty-first Century* (New York: Farrar, Straus and Giroux, 2005; and *The 9/11 Commission Report, National Commission on Terrorist Attacks*.

26. The interrogation of two detainees was videotaped in 2003 for "training purpose" but destroyed in 2005, despite urgings to the contrary by members of congress and the courts. Revelation of the destruction occurred in 2007. By early 2008, the justice department had launched a criminal investigation. Congress also conducted its own investigation of the issue in 2008 and 2009.

27. Of more than passing interests, in Britain renditions have been outlawed since a Court of Appeals ruling in 1999 overturned the conviction of an Irish Republican, Peter Mullen, who had been seized in Zimbabwe and spirited back for trial. His abduction was criticized by the court as a "blatant and extremely serious failure to adhere to the rule of law."

28. The Army Field Manual also proscribes the following: forcing detainees to be naked, perform sexual acts, or pose in a sexual manner; placing hoods or sacks over detainees' heads; beating, shocking, or burning detainees; exposing detainees to extreme heat or cold; threatening detainees with dogs; depriving detainees food, water, or medical care.

29. The key detainee cases were *Rasul v. Bush*, *Padilla v. Rumsfeld*, and *Hamdi v. Rumsfeld*, in which the administration interpretation of executive power and no federal jurisdiction was rejected by the Supreme Court, which outlined the basic requirements of "due process" but left to congress discretion on needed legislative guidance. Congress responded with the Detainee Treatment Act (2005) and the Military Commission Act (2006). The administration continues to resist, however, broader legislative and judicial oversight of its policies and practices with relation to presidential authority in pursuing the "war on terror."

30. Academicians are also divided on the subject. For example, Richard Betts concludes in his book, *Enemies of Intelligence* (2007) that exigent circumstances such as a threatened repeat of 9/11 may warrant extreme surveillance and interrogation measures. Others argue for restricted rules of engagement. See David Roberge's review of James Olsen's *Fair Play: The Moral Dimensions of Spying* in *Studies in Intelligence* 51, no. 1 (2007).

31. In June 2004, the Supreme Court ruled that habeas corpus should remain available to everyone detained on U.S. territory, unless explicitly suspended. In 2006, the same court ruled that the basic protections accorded all wartime detainees under the Geneva Convention applied to all, including unlawful enemy combatants

outside the United States. The president, however, secured the 2006 Military Commissions Act stripping Guantanamo detainees of any vestige of habeus corpus rights. In 2007, the Supreme Court returned to the issue and agreed to hear a detainee petition for review of rights accorded him under habeus corpus jurisprudence in the United States.

CHAPTER 4

1. FBI, *Terrorism in the United States* (Washington, DC: Government Printing Office, 1993), 1–2.

2. *The Vice President's Task Force on Terrorism* (Washington, DC: Government Printing Office, 1986), Summary of Findings and Recommendations.

3. Robert Kupperman and Jeff Kamen, *Final Warning: Averting Disaster in the New Age of Terrorism.* Bob Kuppermann was a renowned physicist who did a vast amount of research on the potential use of weapons of mass destruction by terrorist organizations. he and Jeff Kaman, a well-known investigative journalist, forced the government to take the WMD threat seriously with this compelling book.

4. Oliver B. Revell testimony before U.S. House of Representatives Committee on International Relations. *Hearings on Al Qaeda and the Global Reach of Terrorism*, 107th Cong., 1st sess., Serial No. 107–50 (Washington, DC: Government Printing Office, 2001).

5. Ibid.

6. Oliver Revell, "Law Enforcement Views Radical Islam: Protecting America," *Middle East Quarterly*, March 1995.

7. Oliver Revell, "Counterterrorism and Democratic Values: An American Practioner's Experience," in *Close Calls: Intervention, Terrorism, Missile Defense and "Just War" Today*, edited by Elliott Abrams (Washington, DC: Ethics and Public Policy Center, 1998), 237–50.

8. Ibid.

9. Revell, "Law Enforcement Views Radical Islam."

10. Emerson has been vilified by many in the Muslim community as being anti-Islamic, and yet he goes to great lengths to separate the Jihadist from the general Muslim community. Emerson's latest book, *Jihad Incorporated*, continues to expose the penetration of our society by skilled and dedicated Jihadists.

11. Oliver "Buck" Revell and Dwight Arnan Williams, *A G-Man's Journal: A Legendary Career Inside the FBI* (New York: Pocket Books, 1998), 471–81.

12. *Vice President's Task Force on Terrorism Report*, 1986.

13. Revell testimony op cite.

14. INTERPOL Web site, http:www.interpol.int/Public/Terrorism.

15. Revell, *A G-Man's Journal*, 245.

16. Ibid., 247.

17. Craig S. Smith, "Europe's Chief on Terrorism to Reassure U.S. on Efforts," *New York Times*, May 10, 2004.

18. Revell, *A G-Man's Journal*, 245.

19. Ibid.

20. Ibid., 111–12.

21. Ibid.

22. Ibid., 296.

23. Ibid., 297.

24. Andrew C. McCarthy, *Willful Blindness: A Memoir of the Jihad* (New York: Encounter Books, 2008), 307–18. Andy McCarthy not only successfully prosecuted the most difficult and complex trial of Jihadist ever tried in America, but he has also become an outstanding commentator and analyst of the terrorist assault on our society and the weaknesses in our system to combat them.

25. Remarks of FBI Executive Assistant Director Arthur Cummings, chairman of the IACP Committee on Terrorism at a COT conference, Dublin, Ireland, May 2008.

26. Ibid.

27. In his book, *The Terror Watch: Inside the Desperate Race to Stop the Next Attack*, published in 2007, author and columnist Ron Kessler graphically depicts the extraordinary efforts that are ongoing to prevent major terrorist attacks against America by the law enforcement, intelligence, and military services of the United States and our allies.

CHAPTER 5

1. See, for example, Audrey Kurth Cronin, "Behind the Curve: Globalization and International Terrorism," *International Security* 27 (Winter 2002/2003): 30.

2. Lee Wolosky and Stephen Heifetz, "Regulating Terrorism," *Law and Policy in International Business* 34 (2002): 1, 3.

3. For a discussion of different typologies for financing transnational terrorism, see U.S. Department of State, International Narcotics Control Strategy Report, Vol. II, March 2005; Financial Action Task Force, Typologies Report 2004–2005; Financial Action Task Force, information on semiannual meeting held on January 30–February 1, 2002. For a summary of the meeting, see www.fatf.org; Lawrence J. Speer, "FATF Vows Unity in Curbing Terrorist Financing, Criminal Money Laundering," *Daily Report for Executives*, February 4, 2002, A2; and Bruce Zagaris, "FATF Makes No Change in Non-cooperative Countries and Begins Compliance with Counterterrorism Financial Enforcement," *International Enforcement Law Reporter* 18 (April 2002): 134–36.

4. Philip B. Heymann, "Dealing with Terrorism," *International Security* 26 (2001): 24, 31.

5. U.S. Department of State, International Narcotics Control Strategy Report, March 2003, XII-24.

6. Ibid., 25.

7. 50 U.S.C. App. 5(b). See also, Act Oct 6, 1917, Ch. 106, 40 Stat. 411.

8. 5 U.S.C. § 1701 *et seq.*

9. OFAC maintains the SDN List at Appendix A to 31 C.F.R. Chap. V. Additions or changes to the SDN List are announced via OFAC's Web site (www.treas.gov/ofac) and the Federal Register.

10. For background on international economic sanctions, see Barry E. Carter, *International Economic Sanctions: Improving the Haphazard U.S. Legal Regime* (Cambridge: Cambridge University Press, 1988) and Gary Clyde Hufbauer, Jeffrey J. Schott, and Kimberly Ann Elliott, *Economic Sanctions Reconsidered: History and Current Policy*, 2nd ed. (Washington, DC: Institute for International Economics, 1990).

11. For a discussion of the U.S. law and policy of export controls, see *Law and Policy of Export Controls: Recent Essays on Key Export Issues*, edited by Homer E. Moyer, Jr., Robert C. Cassidy, Jr., Michael T. Buckley, and J. Clifford Frazier (American Bar Association, Section of International Law & Policy, 1993).

12. See generally, Peter L. Flanagan and Les P Carnegie, "Key Elements of an Effective U.S. Foreign Trade Control Compliance Program," in *Coping with U.S. Export Controls 2009*, edited by Evan R. Berlack, Peter L. Flanagan, and Christopher R. Wall (New York: Practising Law Institute, 2009), 447–70.

13. Philip K. Ankel and Glenn H. Kaminstky, *Exporting to Special Destinations and Persons: Terrorist-Supporting and Embargoed Countries, Designated Terrorists and Sanctioned Persons* (Washington, DC: Bureau of Industry and Security, U.S. Department of Commerce); *Coping with U.S. Export Controls 2009.*

14. This section is essentially a reprint of Bruce Zagaris's, "U.S. Initiates Sanctions against bin Laden and Associates," *International Enforcement Law Reporter* 17 (November 2001): 480–85.

15. U.S. statutory law provides for a broad framework within which the president and Executive Branch have the authority to promulgate sanctions and blocking orders, especially in times of emergencies. See, for example, Benjamin H. Flowe, Jr., and Ray Gold, "The Legality of U.S. Sanctions," *Global Dialogue* 2 (2000): 95–109.

16. Executive Order No. 13, 224, 3 C.F.R. 768 (2002), reprinted in 50 U.S.C.A. § 1701 (West 2002). For the September 24 list, see Office of Foreign Assets Control, *Executive Order 13224* (www.ustreas.gov/offices/enforcement/ofac/sanctions/t11ter.pdf); President Freezes Terrorists' Assets, remarks by the president, Secretary of the Treasury O'Neill and Secretary of State Powell on Executive Order, The Rose Garden, Office of the Press Secretary, September 24, 2001 (www.whitehouse.gov/news/releases/2001/09/20010924-html). The most recent updates to the OFAC Bulletin can be found at www.treasury.gov/offices/enforcement/ofac/bulletin.txt.

17. 50 U.S.C. § 1701 *et seq.*

18. 22 U.S.C. § 287c.

19. President George W. Bush, Remarks by President Bush, Secretary of the Treasury O'Neill and Secretary of State Powell on Executive Order (September 24, 2001), www.usnewsiwre.com/topnews/search3/0924-110.html.

20. Ben H. Flowe, Jr., and Ray Gold, *President Bush Waives Glenn Amendment Sanctions against India and Pakistan and Imposes Additional Sanctions against Terrorists, Export Licensing Client Memo*, September 24, 2001 (available by subscription from RayGold@bcr-dc.com).

21. Ibid.

22. Joseph M. Myers, "Disrupting Terrorist Networks: The New U.S. and International Regime for Halting Terrorist Funding," *Law and Policy in International Business* 34 (2002): 17, 18.

23. Flowe and Gold, *President Bush Waives Glenn Amendment Sanctions*.

24. This and the following section is based on the article by Bruce Zagaris, "U.S. and Other Countries Attack against Additional List of Terrorist Supporters," *International Enforcement Law Reporter* 17 (December 2001): 19–51.

25. For the complete list, see www.treasury.gov/offices/enforcement/ofac/sdn/; for background, see Joseph Kahn with Judith Miller, "U.S. Freezes More Accounts; Saudi and Pakistani Assets Cited for Ties to Bin Laden," *New York Times*, October 13, 2001.

26. Assistant Secretary for Economic and Business Affairs E. Anthony Wayne (State Dept.), Testimony before the Senate Committee on Banking, Housing, and Urban Affairs, July 13, 2005.

27. David S. Hilzenbath and John Mintz, "More Assets on Hold in Anti-terror Effort," *Washington Post*, October 13, 2001; see also Jeff Gerth and Judith Miller, "Philanthropist, or Fount of Funds for Terrorists?" *New York Times*, October 13, 2001.

28. Kahn and Miller, "U.S. Freezes More Accounts."

29. Hilzenbath and Mintz, "More Assets on Hold in Anti-terror Effort."

30. Richard Wolffe, "U.S. Treasury Adds More Names to 'Frozen Assets' List," *Financial Times*, October 12, 2001.

31. Richard Wolffe, "U.S. Probe Takes Close Look at Trail of 'Honey Money,'" *Financial Times*, October 12, 2001.

32. Ibid.

33. Joseph Kahn and Patrick E. Tyler, "U.S. Widens Net to Snare Terror Assets; Expands List," *New York Times*, November 3, 2001.

34. Ibid.

35. Alan Sipress, "Crackdown Expanded to All Groups in Terror List," *Washington Post*, November 3, 2001.

36. Ali Waked, "France and Spain Bid to 'Legalize' Hamas," *Ynet News*, March 6, 2005.

37. The U.S. SDN List is available at www.treas.gov/offices/enforcement/ofac/sdn/.

38. Information on the European Union lists can be found at http://europa.eu.

39. The UN List regarding al Qaeda is available at www.un.org/sc/committees/1267/consolist.shtml.

40. See 70 Fed. Reg. 38567.

41. U.S. Department of Treasury, OFAC, Nonproliferation, *What You Need to Know about Treasury Restrictions*, www.treasury.gov/offices/enforcement/ofac/programs/wmd/wmd.pdf.

42. Ibid.

43. See www.state.gov/t/isn/c22080.htm.

44. This section is adopted and updated from an article by Bruce Zagaris, "U.S. Forms New Investigative Team to Target Terrorist Financial Networks," *International Enforcement Law Reporter* 17 (December 2001): 519–20.

45. Peter Spiegel, "U.S. Team Created to Target al-Qaeda Finances," *Financial Times*, October 26, 2001.

46. For additional background on Operation Green Quest, see U.S. Department of State, International Narcotics Control Strategy Report, March 2003, XII–12.

47. Ibid.

48. U.S. Department of State, International Narcotics Control Strategy Report, March 2003, XII–11.

49. Ibid.

50. U.S. Department of Treasury, Office of Terrorism and Financial Intelligence.

51. U.S. Department of Treasury, *U.S. Treasury Department Announces New Executive Office for Terrorist Financing and Financial Crimes*, March 3, 2003.

52. FinCEN, *Strategic Plan FY2006–2008*, 8.

53. This section is a revision of part of the article by Bruce Zagaris, "U.S. Enacts Counter Terrorism Act with Significant New International Provisions," *International Enforcement Law Reporter* 17 (December 2001): 522–26.

54. "US Money Laundering Accusation Ignites Resentment in Macao," *Asia Pulse via Yahoo!*, September 19, 2005, see also "Macau Bank's Customers Withdraw," *CNN.com*, September 19, 2005.

55. See 18 U.S.C. [sec] 983(i) (2002). However, property owners can contest IEEPA actions under other provisions of law. See, for example, *Holy Land Foundation v. Ashcroft*, 2002 U.S. Dist. LEXIS 14641 (D.D.C. August 8, 2002) (challenging a blocking order issued by the U.S. Attorney General, which blocked a Muslim foundation from its assets, on the grounds that the order violated the Administrative Procedure Act, various constitutional rights, and the Religious Freedom Restoration Act).

56. For a useful discussion of the operation of Sec. 319(b), the new summons and subpoena power from a perspective of foreign banks, see Joseph Tompkins, *The Impact of the USA PATRIOT Act on Non-US Banks*, Prepared in Connection with the International Monetary Fund Seminar on Current Developments in Monetary and Financial Law Held on May 7–17, 2002, in Washington, DC, 14–15, http://imf.org/external/np/leg/sem/2002/cdmfl/eng/tompki.pdf. This discussion is based largely on Tompkins's discussion.

57. 31 U.S.C. § 5318(k)(3)(C)(i).

58. Id., 31 U.S.C. § 5318(k)(3)(C)(iii).

59. Id., 31 U.S.C. § 5318(k)(3)(A)(i).

60. See Rest. 3rd, Restatement of the Foreign Relations Law of the United States § 442 (2002).

61. See Stefan D. Cassella, "Forfeiture of Terrorist Assets under the USA PATRIOT Act of 2001," *Law and Policy in International Business* 34 (2002): 7, 15.

62. Expanded Overview—Concentration Accounts, Federal Financial Institutions Examination Council (FFIEC) Bank Secrecy Act (BSA)/Anti-Money Laundering (AML) Examination Manual.

63. See, for example, Anti-Money Laundering Programs for Unregistered Investment Companies, 67 F.R. 60617 (September 26, 2002).

64. Secretary of the Treasury, *A Report to Congress in Accordance with §359*, November 2002.

65. Berliner Corcoran & Rowe LLP, ELC Memo on Five Fold IEEPA Penalty.

66. A copy of the Executive Order can be accessed on the OFAC Web site at www.treas.gov/offices/enforcement/ofac/actions/20060426.shtml.

67. Ibid.

68. *Holy Land Foundation for Relief and Development v. John Ashcroft et al.*, 219 F. Supp. 2d 67 (D.D.C. 2002); 333 F. 2d 156 (D.C. Cir. 2003).

69. *Boim v. Quanic Literacy Institute*, 340 F.Supp. 2d 885 (N.D. Ill 2004).

70. Leslie Eaton, "U.S. Prosecution of Muslim Group Ends in Mistrial," *New York Times*, October 23, 207.

71. Peter Whoriskey, "Mistrial Declared in Islamic Charity Case," *Washington Post*, October 23, 2007.

72. Eaton, "U.S. Prosecution of Muslim Group."

73. Id, quoting Cole. See also David Cole, "Anti-terrorism on Trial," *Washington Post*, October 24, 2007. Cole correctly notes that "material support" laws criminalize giving anything of value, including humanitarian aid or one's own volunteer services, to an organization the government has labeled a "terrorist" group. Since the government argues that it is no defense that the supported did not intend to further any terrorist conduct or even that the support in fact furthered no terrorism, the law practically imposes guilty by association. Cole, "Anti-terrorism on Trial."

74. *Benevolence Int'l Found., Inc. v. Ashcroft*, No. 02 C 763 (N.D. Ill. January 30, 2002).

75. 200 F. Supp. 2d 935 (D.Ill. 2002).

76. For information on the three charities, see OMB Watch, *Part 2: Status of Charities Shut Down by Treasury, Muslim Charities and the War on Terror: Top Ten Concerns and Status Update*, March 2006, 8.

77. Ibid., 11–14.

78. Treasury has explained that the promotion of both faith-based and secular charitable giving is a central goal of the Bush administration. The Arab American and American Muslim communities share this goal. President Bush has expressed a strong interest in ensuring that Arab Americans and American Muslims feel comfortable maintaining their tradition of charitable giving. Accordingly, in response to requests for guidance, Treasury has developed a voluntary set of best practices guidelines for U.S.-based charities intended to reduce the likelihood that charitable funds will be diverted for violent ends. U.S. Department of Treasury, *Response to Inquiries from Arab American and American Muslim Communities for Guidance on Charitable Best Practices*, November 7, 200,2 PO-3607.

79. For a copy of the guidelines, see U.S. Department of the Treasury, *Anti-terrorist Financing Guidelines: Voluntary Best Practices for U.S. Based Charities*, www.treas.gov/offices/enforcement/key-issues/protecting/charities-intro.shtml (accessed June 1, 2006).

80. Ibid.

81. Ibid.

82. Ibid.

83. U.S. Department of the Treasury, *Anti-terrorist Financing Guidelines: Voluntary Best Practices for U.S. Based Charities*, Sec. III Governance Accountability and Transparency, 4.

84. *Annotated Version: Reflecting Comments by OMB Watch and Others*, Submitted to Treasury, February 1, 2006, on the Anti-terrorist Financing Guidelines;

OMB Watch, "Nonprofits Call for Withdrawal of Anti-terror Financing Guidelines," 7 *OMB Watcher*, February 7, 2006, www.ombwatch.org/article/article/print/3277/-1/420; OMB Watch, *Muslim Charities and the War on Terror: Top Ten Concerns and Status Update*, March 2006.

85. Available at www.usig.org/PDFs/Principles_Final.pdf. These principles provide alternatives that are more flexible and recognize the inherently diverse nature of charitable organizations and simultaneously effectively minimize the risk of diversion of charitable assets.

86. Serge Schmemann, "U.N. Requires Members to Act against Terror," *New York Times*, September 29, 2001. For the text and report of the resolution, see *Security Council Unanimously Adopts Wide-Ranging Anti-terrorism Resolution; Calls for Suppressing Financing, Improving International Cooperation; Resolution 1373 (2001) Also Creates Committee to Monitor Implementation*, Security Council 4385th Meeting SC/7158, September 28, 2001, www.un.org/News/Press/docs/2001/sc7158.doc.htm.

87. FATF, *FATF Cracks Down on Terrorist Financing*, Press Release, October 31, 2001.

88. FATF, *Nine Special Recommendations on Terrorist Financing*, October 22, 2004.

89. FATF, *Special Recommendation IX: Cash Couriers Detecting and Preventing the Cross-Border Transportation of Cash by Terrorists and Other Criminals, International Best Practices*, October 11, 2002.

90. Coincidentally on the day preceding FATF announced its WMD initiative, the U.S. government announced a national initiative that will target the counterproliferation assets of U.S. law enforcement, licensing, and intelligence agencies to combat the growing national security threat posed by illegal exports of restricted U.S. military and dual-use technology to foreign countries and terrorist organizations. See U.S. Department of Justice, *Justice Department and Partner Agencies Launch National Counter-Proliferation Initiative*, October 11, 2007.

91. FATF, Guidance regarding the implementation of activity-based financial prohibitions of UN Security Council Resolution 1737 (October 12, 2007) (The October Activity-Based Proliferation Guidance).

92. See Guidance on implementing financial provisions of UNSC Resolutions to counterproliferation of weapons of mass destruction, www.fatf-gafi.org/dataoecd/28/62/38902632.pdf (The June 2007 Proliferation Financing Guidance).

93. See Bruce Zagaris, "U.S. Announces Counter-Proliferation Initiative," *International Enforcement Law Reporter* 23 (December 2007).

94. Wayne, Testimony before the Senate Committee on Banking.

95. For a discussion of the criticism and call for a higher level and centralized office to direct, coordinate, and reaffirm domestic agencies and international policies of the United States on counterterrorism financial enforcement, *see* Bruce Zagaris, "Bush Administration Embarks on New Initiative to Combat Terrorism Financing amid Broad Criticisms," *International Enforcement Law Reporter* 18 (December 2002): 491, 492, discussing Independent Task Force Report, *Terrorist Financing*, October 16, 2002 (Council on Foreign Relations) (www.cfr.org).

96. See, for example, UN List at www.un.org/docs/sc/committees/1267/1267 ListEng.htm; and the EU List at http://ec.europa.eu/comm/external_relations/cfsp/ sanctions/list/consol-list.htm.

97. Nikos Passos, "Fighting Terror with Error: The Counter-productive Regulation of Informal Value Transfers," *Crime Law and Social Change* 45 (November 11, 2006): 315, 321.

98. 31 C.F.R. Part 598.

99. Federal Reserve System, 12 CFR Part 233, Regulation GG; Docket No. R-1298; Department of the Treasury 31 CFR Part 132 RIN 1505-AB78 Prohibition on Funding of Unlawful Internet Gambling, Notice of Joint Proposed Rulemaking, October 12, 2007.

100. For example, a report has found that private contractors employed by U.S. agencies in order to assist other countries in drafting laws meeting international standards "did not result in laws meeting FATF standards" or "had substantial deficiencies." U.S. Government Accountability Office (2005). *Terrorist Financing: Better Strategic Planning Needed to Coordinate U.S. Efforts to Deliver Counterterrorism Financing Training and Technical Assistance Abroad* (Washington, DC: Government Accountability Office), 17.

101. Independent Task Force Report, *Terrorist Financing*, October 16, 2002 (Council on Foreign Relations) (www.cfr.org).

102. See Peter Reuter and Edwin M. Truman, *Chasing Dirty Money: The Fight against Money Laundering* (Washington, DC: Institute for International Economics, November 2004) (many of their comments, although directed at the anti-money -laundering enforcement regime, apply equally to CTFE).

103. See Tom Viles, "Hawala, Hysteria and Hegemony," *Journal of Money Laundering Control* 11, no. 1 (2008): 25–33.

CHAPTER 6

1. The author of Chapter 6, Bruce Zagaris, is Partner, Berliner Corcoran & Rowe LLP (BCR), Washington, D.C. The author is grateful for the assistance of Elena Papangelopoulou, a legal intern at BCR.

2. Peter Andreas and Ethan Nadelmann, *Policing the Globe: Criminalization and Crime Control in International Relations* (Oxford: Oxford University Press, 2006), 116–17.

3. National Commission on Terrorist Attacks Upon the United States, *The Final Report of the National Commission on Terrorist Attacks Upon the United States (The 9/11 Commission Report)* (New York: W. W. Norton, 2004), 390–91.

4. U.S. Government Accountability Office (GAO), *Homeland Security Progress Has Been Made to Address the Vulnerabilities Exposed by 9/11, but Continued Federal Action Is Needed to Further Mitigate Security Risks*, GAO-07-375, January 2007, 1.

5. Pub. L. No. 107-71, 115 Stat. 597 (2001).

6. The Homeland Security Act of 2002, signed into law on November 25, 2002, transferred TSA from the Department of Transportation to the new Department of Homeland Security. Pub. L. No. 107-296, §403, 116 Stat. 2135, 2178.

7. GAO, *Homeland Security Progress Has Been Made*, 14.

8. Ibid.

9. Ibid.

10. Pub. L. No. 108-458, 118 Stat. 3638.

11. GAO, *Homeland Security Progress Has Been Made*, 16.

12. Ibid., 6.

13. Ibid.

14. Ibid., 7.

15. Ibid., 51.

16. Ibid., 52.

17. Ibid., 52–53.

18. Ibid., 54.

19. Ibid.

20. Ibid., 53.

21. Ibid., 55–56.

22. Eben Kaplan, *Flynn: Homeland Security 'Report Card'*, October 25, 2007 (Excerpt from an Interview with Stephen E. Flynn) (www.CFT.org).

23. *Strengthening Enforcement and Border Security: The 9/11 Commission Staff Report on Terrorist Travel, Joint Hearing before the Subcommittee on Immigration, Border Security and Citizenship and Subcommittee on Terrorism, Technology and Homeland Security of the Committee on the Judiciary*, U.S. Senate, 109th Cong., 1st sess., March 14, 2005, S. Hrg. 109-71, Opening statement of Hon. John Cornyn (R-TX).

24. Ibid., Opening statement of Senator John Kyl (R-AZ).

25. Ibid.

26. GAO, *Homeland Security Progress Has Been Made*, 8.

27. Ibid., 9.

28. Ibid.

29. *Strengthening Enforcement and Border Security: The 9/11 Commission Staff Report on Terrorist Travel*, Testimony of Elaine Dezenski, acting Assistant Secretary for Border and Transportation Security Policy and Planning, Department of Homeland Security.

30. Ibid., Opening statement of Senator Edward M. Kennedy.

31. Ibid.

32. *Strengthening Enforcement and Border Security: The 9/11 Commission Staff Report on Terrorist Travel*, Testimony of Thomas J. Walters, assistant commissioner for the Office of Training and Development, Customs and Border Protection, DHS.

33. GAO, *Homeland Security Progress Has Been Made*, 10.

34. Ibid., 11.

35. *Strengthening Enforcement and Border Security: The 9/11 Commission Staff Report on Terrorist Travel*, Opening statement of Senator Edward M. Kennedy.

36. Pub. L. No. 107-567, 115 Stat. 272 (2001).

37. Pub. L. No. 107-173, 116 Stat. 543 (2002).

38. GAO, *Homeland Security Progress Has Been Made*, 15. For additional information on legislative requirements related to US-VISIT, see GAO, *Border Security:*

US-VISIT Faces Strategic, Technological, and Operational Challenges at Land Ports of Entry, GEO-07-248 (Washington, DC, December 2006).

39. Ibid., 16.

40. *Strengthening Enforcement and Border Security: The 9/11 Commission Staff Report on Terrorist Travel*, Opening statement of Hon. John Cornyn (R-TX).

41. S. 2611, 109th Cong. (2006).

42. S. 1348, 110th Cong. (2007).

43. *See* Manuel-Roig Franzia, *Washington Post*, January 8, 2008.

44. S. 2294, 110th Cong. (2007).

45. *Sources and Methods of Foreign Nationals Engaged in Economic and Military Espionage*: Hearing before the Subcommittee on Immigration, Border Security and Claims, 109th Cong. 30 (2005) (statement of William A. Wulf, PhD, president, National Academy of Engineering, The National Academies), http://frwebgate.access.gpo.gov/cgi-bin/getdoc.cgi?dbname=109_house_hearings&docid=f:23433.pdf (accessed January 3, 2008).

46. Gerald L. Epstein and David Heyman, *Security Controls on the Access of Foreign Scientists and Engineers to the United States, a White Paper of the Commission on Scientific Communication and National Security*, Center for Strategic and International Studies, October 2005, 2, www.csis.org/media/csis/pubs/051005_whitepaper.pdf (accessed January 3, 2008).

47. U.S. General Accounting Office, *Border Security: Improvements Needed to Reduce Time Taken to Adjudicate Visas for Science Students and Scholars*, GAO-04-371, February 2004, 42.

48. Ibid., 24.

49. Epstein and Heyman, *Security Controls on the Access of Foreign Scientists and Engineers*, note 2.

50. National Science Foundation, *Info Brief* (*Science Resource Statistics*), July 2006, 1, www.nsf.gov/statistics/infbrief/nsf06321/nsf06321.pdf (accessed January 3, 2008).

51. Ibid.

52. Epstein and Heyman, *Security Controls on the Access of Foreign Scientists and Engineers*.

53. *Sources and Methods of Foreign Nationals Engaged in Economic and Military Espionage*, 30, 31.

54. Epstein and Heyman, *Security Controls on the Access of Foreign Scientists and Engineers*, note 2.

55. Ibid., notes 2, 11.

56. Ibid.

57. *Container Security Initiative*, Wikipedia, http://en.wikipedia.org (accessed December 31, 2007).

58. U.S. Customs and Border Protection, *CSI in Brief*, www.cbp.gov/linkhandler/cgov/border_secuirty/international_activities/csi/csi_strategic_plan.ctt/csi_strategic_plan.pdf.

59. Ibid.

60. Ibid.

61. U.S. Government Accountability Office, *Container Security: A Flexible Staffing Model and Minimum Equipment Requirements Would Improve Overseas Targeting and Inspection Efforts*, overview AGO-05-557.

62. Ibid., 24–25.

63. Ibid., 26–29.

64. Ibid., overview and 2–3.

65. Kaplan, *Homeland Security 'Report Card'*; Flynn, "The Neglected Home Front," *Foreign Affairs*, September/October 2004, www.foreignaffairs.org.

66. National Commission on Terrorist Attacks Upon the United States, *Final Report of the National Commission on Terrorist Attacks Upon the United States*, 390.

67. Ibid.

68. DHS, *Fact Sheet: Securing Our Nation's Borders*, June 29, 2006, www .dhs.gov/xnews/releases/press_release_0938.shtm.

69. Ibid.

70. Ibid.

71. Ibid.

72. Ibid.

73. Ben Rowswell, *Ogdensburg Revisited: Adapting Canada-US Security Cooperation to the New International Era*, CSIS, Policy Papers on the Americas, Vol. XV, Study 5, at 2, May 2004.

74. Andre Belelieu, "Canada Alert, the Smart Process at Two: Losing Momentum," *CSIS Hemisphere Focus*, 11 (December 10, 2003).

75. Rowswell, *Ogdensburg Revisited*, 2–3.

76. Ibid., 3.

77. Ibid., 5.

78. Ibid.

79. Tanya Primiani and Christopher Sands, *Terrorists in Toronto: Is Canada Secure? Are We?*, CSIS Commentary, June 20, 2006, www.csis.org.

80. Department of Justice Canada, *The Anti-terrorism Act*, www.justice.gc.ca/en/anti_terr/fact_sheets/imp_us.html (accessed November 14, 2007).

81. Ibid.

82. Rowswell, *Ogdensburg Revisited*, 5.

83. Ibid.

84. Primiani and Sands, *Terrorists in Toronto*.

85. Tanya Primiani and Christopher Sands, *Canada Changes the Tone on Passports*, CSIS Commentary, June 9, 2006, www.csis.org.

86. Rowswell, *Ogdensburg Revisited*, 14.

87. Ibid.

88. Ibid., 15.

89. Ibid., 15–16.

90. Ibid., 17.

91. Ibid.

92. 8 U.S.C. §1103(a)(5). The authorities granted by this section now are with the secretary of DHS. See The Homeland Security Act of 2002, P.L. 104-208, §§102(a), 441, 1512(d), and 1517.

93. Blas NuZez-Neto and Stephen ViZa, Congressional Research Service, *Border Security: Barriers along the U.S. International Border*, CRS Report for Congress, Code RL33658 CRS-1, December 12, 2006.

94. Randall C. Archibold, "Border Fence Project Raises Environmental Concerns," *New York Times*, November 21, 2007.

95. For more information on the San Diego border fence, please refer to Blas NuZez, *Border Security: The San Diego Fence*, CRS Report RS22026.

96. For an expanded discussion of the USBP, see Blas NuZez-Neto, *Border Security: The Role of the U.S. Border Patrol*, CRS Report RL32562.

97. U.S. Government Accountability Office, *Border Control—Revised Strategy Is Showing Some Positive Results*, GAO/GGD-95-30, January 31, 1995.

98. NuZez-Neto and ViZa, *Barriers along the U.S. International Border*, CRS-1-2.

99. See P.L. 104-208, Div. C. Congress enacted the IIRIRA as part of the Omnibus Consolidated Appropriations Act of 1997.

100. P.L. 109-13.

101. NuZez-Neto and ViZa, *Barriers along the U.S. International Border*, CRS-2.

102. U.S. Department of Justice, Office of the Inspector General, *Operation Gatekeeper: An Investigation into Allegations of Fraud and Misconduct*, July 1998, www.usdoj.gov/oig/special/9807/gk01.htm#P160_18689.

103. GAO Report 95-30.

104. U.S. Department of Justice, Office of the Inspector General, *Operation Gatekeeper: An Investigation into Allegations of Fraud and Misconduct*, July 1998, www.usdoj.gov/oig/special/9807/index.htm (hereafter the DOJ-OIG Gatekeeper Report).

105. U.S. Department of Justice, Immigration and Naturalization Service, *Operation Gatekeeper Fact Sheet*, July 14, 1998.

106. NuZez-Neto and ViZa, *Barriers along the U.S. International Border*, CRS-4, citing the DOJ-OIG Gatekeeper Report.

107. Ibid., citing GAO 95-30, at 13.

108. Ibid.

109. NuZez-Neto and ViZa, *Barriers along the U.S. International Border*, CRS-4, citing Peter Andreas, "The Escalation of U.S. Immigration Control in the Post-NAFTA Era," *Political Science Quarterly* 113 (1998–1999): 595.

110. P.L. 109-13; for more information on the REAL ID Act, see Michael John Garcia, Margaret Mikyung Lee, and Todd Tatelman, *Immigration: Analysis of the Major Provisions of the REAL ID Act of 2005*, CRS Report RL 32754.

111. NuZez-Neto and ViZa, *Barriers along the U.S. International Border*, CRS-8.

112. 151 Cong. Rec. H557 (daily ed., February 10, 2005).

113. Department of Homeland Security, "Determination Pursuant to Section 102 of the Illegal Immigration Reform and Immigrant Responsibility Act of 12996 as

Amended by Section 102 of the REAL ID Act of 2005," 70 Federal Register 55622 -02, September 22, 2005.

114. NuZez-Neto and ViZa, *Barriers along the U.S. International Border*, CRS-9, citing Interview with CBP Congressional Affairs, September 13, 2006.

115. Ibid.

116. Ibid.

117. Ibid., CRS-14.

118. Ibid., CRS-21.

119. Ibid., CRS-22.

120. Mexican Plan Nacional de Desarollo (National Development Plan), 69.

121. Ibid., 70.

122. Ibid., 70 (Strategy 14.2).

123. Ibid.

124. NuZez-Neto and ViZa, *Barriers along the U.S. International Border*, CRS-22–23.

125. Ibid., CRS-24–25.

126. Ibid., CRS-25–26.

127. Ibid., CRS-26–27.

128. Ibid., CRS-28.

129. Associated Press, "Border Fence Cases Appear Court-Bound," *Washington Post*, January 10, 2008.

130. Ibid., CRS-29, citing Randal Archibold, "Border Fence Must Skirt Objections from Arizona Tribe," *New York Times*, September 20, 2006.

131. 25 U.S.C. §324.

132. *United States v. Sioux Nation of Indians*, 448 U.S. 371 (1980).

133. Ibid., CRS-29–30.

134. Ibid.

135. Eline Zimmerman, SFGate.com, *Border Protections Imperil Environment— Last Wilderness Area South of San Diego Could Be Damaged*, February 27, 2006, www.sfgate.com/cgi-bin/article.cgi?file=/c/a/2006/02/27/MNG2GHFBFL1.DTL type=printable.

136. Randall C. Archibold, "Border Fence Project Raises Environmental Concerns," *New York Times*, November 21, 2007.

137. Ibid.

138. NuZez-Neto and ViZa, *Barriers along the U.S. International Border*, CRS-30–31.

139. *Sierra Club v. Ashcroft*, No. 04-CV-272 (S.D. Cal. February 10, 2004).

140. NuZez-Neto and ViZa, *Barriers along the U.S. International Border*, CRS-32.

141. Ibid., CRS-32–33.

142. U.S. Government Accountability Office, *Homeland Security Progress Has Been Made to Address the Vulnerabilities Exposed by 9/11*, GAO-07-375, 11–12.

143. Primiani and Sands, *Canada Changes the Tone on Passports*.

144. U.S. Government Accountability Office, *Homeland Security Progress Has Been Made*, 12.

145. National Commission on Terrorist Attacks Upon the United States, *Final Report of the National Commission on Terrorist Attacks*, 374–83.

146. See http://news.bbc.co.uk/2/hi/americas/4488624.stm; and www.washington post.com/wp-dyn/content/article/2007/11/15/AR2007111502272.html (accessed January 4, 2008).

147. See OAS, Resolution of Meeting of Ministers of Justice, AG/RES. 1482 (XXXVII-O/97), June 5, 1997, http//www.oas.org.

148. David P. Warner, "Law Enforcement Cooperation the Organization of American States: A Focus on REMJA," *University of Miami Inter-American Law Review* 27 (2006): 387, 411–12.

149. See OAS, General Assembly AG/RES. 1650 (XX(X-O/99), June 7, 1999.

150. See, for example, Konstantinos D. Magliveras, "The Inter-American Convention against Terrorism: Do Such Instruments Contribute to the Effective Combat of Terrorism?" *International Enforcement Law Reporter* 19 (2003): 52; and Bruce Zagaris, "Developments in the International Architecture and Framework of International Criminal and Enforcement Cooperation in the Western Hemisphere," *University of Miami Inter-American Law Review* 37 (2006): 421, 491–92.

CHAPTER 7

1. Yonah Alexander and Donald J. Musch, eds. *Terrorism: Documents of International and Local Control*, vol. 35 (Dobbs Ferry, NY: Oceana, 2002), 434.

2. *Washington Post*, September 10, 2003.

3. Amendment IV provides: "The right of the people to be secure in their persons, houses, papers, and effects, against unreasonable searches and seizures, shall not be violated, and no Warrant shall issue, but upon probable clause, supported by Oath or affirmation, and particularly describing the place to be searched, and the persons or things to be seized."

4. Pub. L. 90-351.

5. 18 U.S.C. 2518(3) (West Federal Criminal Code and Rules, 1998 ed.).

6. 18 U.S.C. 2518(1)(3)(A). Id.

7. In 1994, the Act was amended to include physical searches. Pub. L. 103-359, 108 Stat. 3444 (October 14, 1994).

8. The Final Report of the "9/11 Commission" (Norton & Company 2004) included a recommendation that "(t)he current position of Director of Central Intelligence should be limited in authority by the creation of a National Intelligence Director with two main areas of responsibility: (1) to oversee national intelligence centers of specific subjects of interest across the U.S. government and (2) to manage the national intelligence program and oversee the agencies that contribute to it." Final Report p. 411. P.L. 108-458 created the new position of Director of National Intelligence.

9. *New York Times*, August 20, 2003.

10. Ibid.

11. The site is divided into the following subjects: Home, Major Speeches, Dispelling the Myths, Passed by Congress, Congress Speaks, Stories and Articles, Responding to Congress, Text of the Patriot Act, and Anti-Terror Record.

12. *Washington Post*, October 22, 2003.

13. Ibid.

14. Ibid.

15. PATRIOT Act 2 proposed to include the lone-wolf terrorist in the FISA definition of "foreign power" in 50 U.S.C. 1801(a)(4) by covering not only "a group engaged in international terrorism, or activities in preparation therefore," but also an "individual" engaged in similar activities but not known to be affiliated with other persons. S. 113, introduced in the Senate by Jon Kyl (R-AZ) on January 9, 2003, sought, among other things, to accomplish the same result by different means. S. 113 proposed to expand the FISA definition of "agent of a foreign power" in 50 U.S.C. 1801(b)(1) by adding a new section "C" to cover any non-U.S. person who "engages in international terrorism or activities in preparation therefore." The "lone wolf" problem was taken care of in section 6001 of the Intelligence Reform and Terrorism Prevention Act of 2004. Now, a non-U.S. person who engages in international terrorism or *activities in preparation for international terrorism* is deemed to be an "agent of a foreign power" under FISA. On May 3, 2006, the jury declined to recommend the death penalty for Zacarias Moussaoui, opting instead for life in prison without the possibility of parole. The jury did not believe that Moussaoui's actions "resulted in the death of approximately 3,000 people." Three jurors concluded that Moussaoui had only "limited knowledge of the 9/11 attack plans." *Washington Post*, May 4, 2006.

16. *Washington Times*, September 12, 2003.

17. *Washington Post*, September 11, 2003.

18. PATRIOT Act, Section 224.

19. *Washington Post*, December 19, 2005.

20. *Washington Post*, December 9, 2005.

21. *Washington Post*, December 23, 2005.

22. *New York Times*, March 8, 2006.

23. The first was when the FISA court without statutory or constitutional justification created a "wall" between intelligence-gathering and law enforcement. The second was when the FISA court after the enactment of the PATRIOT Act refused to "take down the wall"; see http://fas.org/irp/agency/doj/fisa/mayfield2007.pdf, court ruling in *Mayfield v. United States*, District of Oregon, September 26, 2007 (vacated on appeal, December 10, 2009).

24. This comment is said to have annoyed unnamed congressional Democrats. *Washington Post*, September 29, 2007.

POSTSCRIPT

1. Daniel Benjamin, "Obama Administration's Counterterrorism Policy at One Year," Keynote Address at the CATO Institute, January 13, 2010; available at http://www.cato.org/event.php?eventid=6807.

2. Giles Whittell, "Fort Hood Gunman Major Nidal Malik Hasan 'tried to contact al-Qaeda'," *The Times*, November 10, 2009; available at http://www.times online.co.uk/tol/news/world/us_and_americas/article6910273.ece.

3. Bobby Ghosh, "FBI Fights Claims It Ignored Intel on Hasan," *Time Magazine*, November 11, 2009; available at http://www.time.com/time/nation/article/0,8599,1937574,00.html.

4. Jerry Markon and Shaiq Hussain, "N. Va. Men Allegedly Tried to Join Jihadists," *Washington Post*, December 11, 2009; available at http://www.washingtonpost.com/wp-dyn/content/article/2009/12/10/AR2009121000919.html.

5. Laura Fitzpatrick, Dan Fletcher, and Randy James, "Alleged Terrorism Plotter David Headley," *Time Magazine*, December 9, 2009; available at http://www.time.com/time/nation/article/0,8599,1946462,00.html.

6. "British Spies Help Prevent al Qaeda-Inspired Attack on New York Subway," *Telegraph*, November 9, 2009; available at http://www.telegraph.co.uk/news/world news/northamerica/usa/6529436/British-spies-help-prevent-al-Qaeda-inspired -attack-on-New-York-subway.html.

7. "Introspection, Not Rationalization, Needed in Wake of Fort Hood Slaughter," *IPT News*, November 6, 2009; available at http://www.investigativeproject.org/1500/introspection-not-rationalization-needed-in-wake.

8. Sebastian Rotella, "U.S. Learned Intelligence on Airline Attack Suspect While He Was En Route," *Los Angeles Times*, January 7, 2010; available at http://www.latimes.com/news/nation-and-world/la-na-airline-terror7-2010jan07,0,2520443, print.story.

9. Michael A. Fletcher and William Branigin, "Obama Sharply Criticizes Intelligence Agencies over Bungled Bomb Plot," *Washington Post*, January 5, 2010.

10. Bruce Hoffman, "Al-Qaeda Has a New Strategy. Obama Needs One, Too." *Washington Post*, January 10, 2010; available at http://www.washingtonpost.com/wp-dyn/content/article/2010/01/08/AR2010010803555_pf.html.

11. Peter Baker, "Obama's War over Terror," *New York Times Magazine*, January 4, 2010; available at http://www.nytimes.com/2010/01/17/magazine/17Terror-t .html.

12. *KindHearts for Charitable Humanitarian Development, Inc. v. Timothy Geithner, et al.*, U.S. Dist. Court, N.D. Ohio, W.D., Case No.: 3:08CV2400, Order (hereafter "KindHearts Order"). "Judge Rules Against Freeze on Assets," *New York Times*, August 19, 2009.

13. *Al Rajhi Banking & Investment Corporation v. Eric H. Holder, Jr., et al.*, U.S. Dist. Ct. For D.C., Case 1:10-mc-00055-ESH, Memorandum of Points and Authorities in Support of Petitioner's Motion to Quash USA PATRIOT Act Subpoena, January 19, 2010.

14. UN Security Council Resolution 1904, S/RES/1904 (2009), December 18, 2009.

15. *Abousfian Abdelrazik and Minister Of Foreign Affairs and Attorney General of Canada*, 2009 FC 580, T-727-08, June 4, 2009.

16. Financial Action Task Forces, "International Best Practices—Freezing of Terrorist Assets," June 23, 2009. For a discussion of the development, see Bruce Zagaris, "FATF Issues Best Practices on Freezing of Terrorist Assets," 25 Int'l Enforcement L. Rep. 368 (September 2009).

17. Ellen Nakashima, "U.S. Blasts E.U. Rejection of Deal to Share Bank Data," *Washington Post*, February 14, 2010, A18.

18. Stanley Pignal, "European Parliament Rejects U.S. Data Swap Deal," *Financial Times*, February 11, 2010. James Kanter, "Europe Rejects Sharing of Bank Data with U.S.," *New York Times*, February 12, 2010, B6.

19. For details, visit http://www.potomacinstitute.org,

20. For a special report, "Maghreb & Sahel Terrorism," authored by Yonah Alexander, visit http://www.potomacinstitute.org/index.php?option=com _content&view=article&id=525:icts-reports-on-maghreb-and-shael-terrorism- &catid=42:studies&Itemid=64.

21. Media reports are drawn from the IUCTS database. See, for example, http:// news.smh.com.au/breaking-news-world/attack-on-pilgrims-kills-20-in-iraq-20100203-ndjk.html; MEMRI Special Dispatch, No. 2828, February 26, 2010; and Stephen Tankel, "The Long Arm of Lashkar-e-Taiba," *Policy Watch*, no. 1631 (February 17, 2010).

22. Media reports are drawn from the IUCTS database.

23. For an Arab perspective on the case, see, for example, M. T. Mehdi, *Kennedy and Sirhan: Why?* (New York: New World Press, 1968).

24. See H.R. 3961, visit http://thomas.loc.gov/cgi-bin/bdquery/z?d111: HR03961:. For additional information, see also JINSA Report #965, "White House Steps Up to Protect Americans," February 25, 2010 and JINSA Report #967, "February Wrap-Up: Elections in Iraq A Failure to Understand Syria and Kadhafi Calls for Jihad," February 26, 2010.

25. See the National Terror Alert Response Center, February 22, 2010; visit Newsalert at http://www.nationalterroralert.com.

26. Ibid, December 19, 2009.

27. Proverbs 3, 25.

28. Quoted Robert Debs Heinl, *Dictionary of Military and Naval Quotations* (Annapolis, Maryland: United States Naval Institute, 1966), 318.

Selected Bibliography

"About Islam and American Muslims." *Council on American Islamic Relations*. www.cair-net.org.

Alexander, Yonah, Edgar H. Brenner, and Serhat Tutuncuoglu Krause, eds. *Turkey Terrorism, Civil Rights and the European Union*. New York: Routledge, 2008.

Alexander, Yonah, and Donald J. Musch, eds. *Terrorism, Documents of International and Local Control*. Vol. 35. Dobbs Ferry, New York: Oceana, 2002.

Ali, M. M. *Muslims in America: The Nation's Fastest Growing Religion*. Rep. no. 15. Washington Report on Middle East Affairs, 1996.

Alison, Miranda. *Women and Political Violence Female Combatants in Ethno-National Conflict (Contemporary Security Studies)*. New York: Routledge, 2008.

The Al-Qaida and Taliban Sanctions Committee—1267. www.un.org/sc/committees/1267/consolist.shtml.

The Al-Qaida and Taliban Sanctions Committee. United Nations. www.un.org/docs/sc/committees/1267/1267ListEng.htm.

American Law Institute. "Third Restatement of the Foreign Relations Law of the United States"; sec. 442. Washington, DC: American Law Institute, 2002.

Amoore, Louise. *Risk and the War on Terror*. New York: Routledge, 2008.

Andreas, Peter, and Ethan Nadelmann. *Policing the Globe: Criminalization and Crime Control in International Relations*. Oxford: Oxford University Press, 2006.

Ansar al-Islam in Iraqi Kurdistan. 2004. Human Rights Watch. www.hrw.org/backgrounder/mena/ansarbk020503.ht.

Archibold, Randall C. "Border Fence Project Raises Environmental Concerns." *New York Times*, November 21, 2007.

Ashour, Omar. *Deradicalization of Armed Islamist Movements*. New York: Routledge, 2009.

Associated Press. "Border Fence Cases Appear Court-Bound." *Washington Post*, January 10, 2008.

Babington, Charles. "Hayden Confirmed as CIA Chief." *Washington Post*, May 27, 2006.

Babington, Charles, and Dan Eggen. "GOP Leaders Reach Deal on Patriot Act." *Washington Post*, December 9, 2005.

Bagby, Ihsan, Paul M. Perl, and Bryan T. Froehle. *The Mosque in America, a National Portrait: A Report from the Mosque Study Project*. Washington, DC: Council on American Islamic Relations, 2001.

Barnett, Thomas. *The Pentagon's New Map: War and Peace in the Twenty-First Century*. New York: Penguin Group, 2004.

Barrett, Paul M. "The Brotherhood: A Student Journeys into a Secret Circle of Extremism." *Wall Street Journal*, December 22, 2003.

Belelieu, Andre. "Canada Alert, the Smart Process at Two: Losing Momentum." *CSIS Hemisphere Focus* XI, December 10, 2003.

Benjamin, Daniel, and Steven Simon. *The Age of Terror*. New York: Random House, 2002.

Bergesen, Albert. *The Sayyid Qutb Reader*. New York: Routledge, 2007.

Bigo, Didier, and Anastassia Tsoukala, eds. *Terror, Insecurity and Liberty*. New York: Routledge, 2008.

Blakeley, Ruth. *State Terrorism in the Global South*. New York: Routledge, 2009.

Blix, Hans. *Disarming Iraq: The Search for Weapons of Mass Destruction*. London: Bloomsbury, 2004.

Brachman, Jarret. *Global Jihadism: Theory and Practice* (Cass Series on Political Violence). New York: Routledge, 2008.

Branigin, William. "Bush Calls Blockage of Patriot Act 'Inexcusable.' " *Washington Post*, December 19, 2005.

———. "Bush Nominates Negroponte to New Intel Post." *Washington Post*, February 17, 2005.

Brecher, Bob, Mark Devenney, and Aaron Winter, eds. *Discourses and Practices of Terrorism*. New York: Routledge, 2009.

Bush, President George W. "Remarks by President Bush, Secretary of the Treasury O'Neill and Secretary of State Powell on Executive Order." Press release. September 24, 2001. www.usnewsiwre.com/topnews/search3/0924-110.html.

Carey, Sabine C. *Protest, Repression and Political Regimes. An Empirical Investigation (Routledge Research in Comparative Politics)*. New York: Routledge, 2008.

Carter, Barry E. *International Economic Sanctions: Improving the Haphazard U.S. Legal Regime*. Cambridge: Cambridge University Press, 1988.

Cassella, Stefan D. "Forfeiture of Terrorist Assets under the USA PATRIOT Act of 2001." *Law and Policy in International Business* 34 (2002): 15.

Cavelty, Myriam Dunn. *The Politics of Securing the Homeland: Critical Infrastructure, Risk and Securitisation* (CSS Studies in Security and International Relations). New York: Routledge, 2008.

Cesari, Jocelyne. *Muslims in the West after 9/11*. New York: Routledge, 2009.

Cole, David. "Anti-terrorism on Trial." *Washington Post*, October 24, 2007.

Common Foreign and Security Policy (CFSP)—Consolidated List of Persons. European Commission. http://ec.europa.eu/comm/external_relations/cfsp/sanctions/list/consol-list.htm.

Converts: Converts in US Prisons. The Media Guide to Islam: A Journalist's Guide to Covering Islam. San Francisco, CA: San Francisco State University, August 20, 2003.

Couch, Cameron. *Managing Terrorism and Insurgency.* New York: Routledge, 2009.

Council on Foreign Relations. *Terrorist Financing.* Independent Task Force Report. October 16, 2002. www.cfr.org.

Court order issued in the case of Sami al-Arian, June 12, 2003. http://www.flmd.uscourts.gov/Al-Arian/8-03-cr-00077-JSM-TBM/docs/290883/0.pdf.

Cowell, Alan. "Britain Arrests Radical Cleric Who Faces U.S. Terror Charges." *New York Times,* May 27, 2004.

Cronin, Audrey Kurth. "Behind the Curve: Globalization and International Terrorism." *International Security* 27 (Winter 2002/2003): 30.

———. *Ending Terrorism Lessons for Policymakers from the Decline and Demise of Terrorist Groups* (Adelphi Papers). New York: Routledge, 2007.

Cummings, Arthur. "Remarks of FBI Executive Assistant Director Arthur Cummings, chairman of the IACP Committee on Terrorism at a COT conference." Ireland, Dublin. May 2008.

Dahlburg, John-Thor. "Ex-Professor Acquitted in Patriot Act Test Case." *Washington Post,* December 7, 2005.

De Mesquita, Bruce Bueno. "What Motivates Terrorists? Which Regimes Are Most Likely to Spawn Terrorist Groups? How Can the Scourge of Terrorism Be Stopped?" *Hoover Digest,* November 1, 2002. www-hoover.stanford.edu/publications/digest/021/bdm.html.

Department of Justice Canada, The Anti-terrorism Act. www.justice.gc.ca/en/anti_terr/fact_sheets/imp_us.html (accessed November 14, 2007).

Devetak, Richard, and Christopher W. Hughes, eds. *Globalization and Political Violence: Globalization's Shadow* (Warwick Studies in Globalisation). New York: Routledge, 2008.

Dingley, James. *Combating Terrorism in Northern Ireland* (Cass Series on Political Violence). New York: Routledge, 2008.

Dutta, Suchitra. *Political Assassinations and International Politics* (Cass Series on Political Violence). New York: Routledge, 2008.

Eaton, Leslie. "U.S. Prosecution of Muslim Group Ends in Mistrial." *New York Times,* October 23, 2007.

Eggen, Dan, and Ellen Nakashima. "Spy Law Lapse Blamed for Lost Information." *Washington Post,* February 23, 2008.

Emerson, Steven. *American Jihad: The Terrorists Living among Us.* New York: Free Press, 2002.

Epstein, Gerald L., and David Heyman. *Security Controls on the Access of Foreign Scientists and Engineers to the United States: A White Paper of the Commission on Scientific Communication and National Security.* Washington, DC: Center for Strategic and International Studies, 2005.

Federal Bureau of Investigation. *Comprehensive Guidance on National Security Letters*, June 1, 2007.

———. *FBI's Fiscal Year 2004 Budget*, House Appropriations Committee, Subcommittee on the Departments of Commerce, Justice, and State, the Judiciary and Related Agencies Cong. (2003) (testimony of S. Mueller, III, director, FBI).

———. *Terrorism in the United States*. Washington, DC: Government Printing Office, 1993.

Ferná, Natividad. *Perceptions and Policy in Transatlantic Relations: Prospective Visions from the US and Europe*. New York: Routledge, 2008.

Financial Action Task Force. *Detecting and Preventing the Cross-Border Transportation of Cash by Terrorists and Other Criminals: International Best Practices.* February 12, 2005. www.fatf-gafi.org/dataoecd/50/63/34424128.pdf.

———. "FATF Cracks Down on Terrorist Financing." Press release. October 31, 2001. www.fatf-gafi.org/dataoecd/45/48/34269864.pdf.

———. *Guidance on Implementing Financial Provisions of UNSC Resolutions to Counter Proliferation of Weapons of Mass Destruction*. September 5, 2007. www.fatf-gafi.org/dataoecd/23/16/39318680.pdf.

———. *Guidance Regarding the Implementation of Activity-Based Financial Prohibitions of United Nations Security Council Resolution 1737*. October 12, 2007. www.fatf-gafi.org/dataoecd/43/17/39494050.pdf.

———. *Information on Semi-annual Meeting Held on Jan. 30–Feb. 1, 2002*. Rep.

———. *Nine Special Recommendations on Terrorist Financing*. Rep. no. 22. October 2004. www.fatf-gafi.org/document/9/0,3343,en_32250379_32236920 _34032073_1_1_1,00.html.

———. *Typologies Report 2004–2005*.

Financial Crimes Enforcement Network. *Strategic Plan FY 2006–2008: Safeguarding the Financial System from the Abuse of Financial Crime*, February 2005. http://www.fincen.gov/news_room/rp/files/strategic_plan_2006.pdf.

FISA Court of Review. *In re: Sealed Case*, 310 F.3rd 717 (2002).

Flowe, Ben H., Jr., and Ray Gold. *President Bush Waives Glenn Amendment Sanctions against India and Pakistan and Imposes Additional Sanctions against Terrorists, Export Licensing Client Memo*. September 24, 2001.

Flowe, Benjamin H., Jr., and Ray Gold. "The Legality of U.S. Sanctions." *Global Dialogue* 2 (2000): 95–109.

Flynn, Stephen E. "Flynn: Homeland Security 'Report Card.' " Interview by Eben Kaplan, August 10, 2006. www.cft.org.

———. "The Neglected Home Front." *Foreign Affairs*, September–October 2004.

"Former Aide Takes Aim at War on Terror." *Washington Post*, June 16, 2003.

Fossella, Vito, and Peter King. "A Big Bouquet for al Qaeda." *Washington Times*, February 28, 2008.

"Freezing Funds: List of Terrorists and Terrorist Groups." *Europa—the European Union On-Line*. http://europa.eu/scadplus/leg/en/lvb/l33208.htm.

Friedman, Thomas L. *The World Is Flat: A Brief History of the Twenty-first Century*. New York: Farrar, Straus and Giroux, 2005.

"Frontline: Trail of a Terrorist: The Millennium Plot: Ahmed Ressam's Millennium Plot." *PBS*, July 1, 2009. www.pbs.org/wgbh/pages/frontline/shows/trail/inside/cron.html.

Gonzales, Alberto R. *Letter to Sens. Patrick Leahy and Arlen Specter*, January 17, 2007. Federation of American Scientists. www.fas.org/irp/agency/doj/fisa/ag011707.pdf.

Gonzalez-Perez, Margaret. *Women and Terrorism*. New York: Routledge, 2008.

Grenfell, Damian. *Rethinking Security and Violence: Savage Globalization (Rethinking Globalizations)*. New York: Routledge, 2008.

"The Guilt of Sami al-Arian." *Washington Times*, April 19, 2006.

Gupta, Dipak. *Understanding Terrorism and Political Violence* (Cass Series on Political Violence). New York: Routledge, 2008.

Haddad, Yvonne Yazbeck, ed. *The Muslims of America*. New York: Oxford University Press, 1991.

"Hamas." *International Policy Institute for Counter Terrorism*. www.ict.org.il.

Harmon, Christop. *Terrorism Today* (Cass Series on Political Violence). 2nd ed. New York: Routledge, 2007.

Harrison, John. *International Aviation and Terrorism*. Routledge: New York, 2009.

Harvey, Frank P. *The Homeland Security Dilemma*. New York: Routledge, 2008.

Heifetz, Stephen, and Lee Wolosky. "Regulating Terrorism." *Law and Policy in International Business* 34 (2002): 1, 3.

Herszenhorn, David M. "Sharp Exchanges over Surveillance Law." *New York Times*, February 16, 2008.

Heymann, Philip B. "Dealing with Terrorism." *International Security* 26 (2001): 24, 31.

Hilzenbath, David S., and John Mintz. "More Assets on Hold in Anti-terror Effort." *Washington Post*, October 13, 2001.

Holt, Rush. *Jane's Defense News* (Bracknell, United Kingdom), August 6, 2007.

Horgan, John. *Leaving Terrorism behind Individual and Collective Disengagement*, edited by Tore Bjorgo. Milton Park, Abingdon, Oxon: Routledge, 2009.

———. *Terrorism Studies: A Reader*. New York: Routledge, 2008.

———. *Walking Away from Terrorism* (Cass Series on Political Violence). New York: Routledge, 2008.

Hsu, Spencer S. "Former Fla. Professor to Be Deported." *Washington Post*, April 18, 2006.

Hufbauer, Gary Clyde, Jeffrey J. Schott, and Kimberly Ann Elliot. *Economic Sanctions Reconsidered: History and Current Policy*. 2nd ed. Washington, DC: Institute for International Economics, 1990.

"In the Spotlight: Al Qaeda (The Base)." *Center for Defense Information: Terrorism Project*. December 30, 2002. www.cdi.org/terrorism/alqaeda-pr.cfm.

Inalcik, Halil. *Learning, the Medrese, and the Ulema*. New York: Praeger, 1973.

Inbar, Efraim, and Hillil Frisch, eds. *Radical Islam and International Security*. New York: Routledge, 2007.

"International Terrorism: Terrorist Organization Profiles." Herzliah, Israel: International Policy Institute for Counter-Terrorism, 2009.

"Islam in America: The Official Facts." Institute of Islamic Information and Education. www.iiie.net/Opinions/IslamInUSFactSheet.html.

Israeli Foreign Ministry. *Information Division*. www.fas.org/irp/world/para/docs/960411.htm.

Jackson, Richard, Marie Breen Smythe, and Jeroen Gunning, eds. *Critical Terrorism Studies*. New York: Routledge, 2009.

Johnston, David. "Somali Is Accused of Planning a Terror Attack at a Shopping Center in Ohio." *New York Times*, June 15, 2004.

Jost, Patrick M., and Harjit Singh Sandhu. "The Hawala Alternative Remittance System and Its Role in Money Laundering." *INTERPOL*, January 2000. www.interpol.int/Public/FinancialCrime/MoneyLaundering/hawala/default.asp#1.

Kahn, Joseph, and Judith Miller. "U.S. Freezes More Accounts; Saudi and Pakistani Assets Cited for Ties to Bin Laden." *New York Times*, October 13, 2001.

Kahn, Joseph, and Patrick E. Tyler. "U.S. Widens Net to Snare Terror Assets; Expands List." *New York Times*, November 3, 2001.

Kane, Paul. "Senate Authorizes Broad Expansion of Surveillance Act." *Washington Post*, February 13, 2008.

Kaplan, Jeffrey. *Terrorist Groups and the New Tribalism: The Fifth Wave of Terrorism* (Cass Series on Political Violence). New York: Routledge, 2009.

Katona, Peter. *Global Biosecurity Threats and Responses* (Contemporary Security Studies). New York: Routledge, 2008.

Katzenstein, Pet. *Rethinking Japanese Security* (Security and Governance). New York: Routledge, 2008.

Keppel, Gilles. *Jihad: The Trail of Political Islam*. Cambridge: Harvard University Press, 2002.

Kessler, Ronald. *The Terrorist Watch: Inside the Desperate Race to Stop the Next Attack*. New York: Crown Forum, 2007.

Kjeilen, Tore. "Muslim Brotherhood—Syria." *Encyclopedia of the Orient*. http://i-cias.com/e.o/mus_br_syria.htm.

———. "The Muslim Brotherhood in Egypt." *Encyclopedia of the Orient Online*. http://i-cias.com/e.o/mus_br_egypt.htm.

"The Koran—Boolean Search." *DLPS List of All Collections*. http://quod.lib.umich.edu/k/koran/bool.html.

Kupperman, Robert, and Jeff Kamen. *Final Warning: Averting Disaster in the New Age of Terrorism*. New York: Doubleday, 1989.

Laipson, Ellen. "While America Slept: Understanding Terrorism and Counterterrorism." *Foreign Affairs*, January 2003.

Lang, Anthony F., Jr, and Amanda Russell Beattie, eds. *War, Torture, and Terrorism*. New York: Routledge, 2008.

Lehman, John. "We're Not Winning This War." *Washington Post*, August 31, 2006.

Leiken, Robert S. "Al Qaeda's New Soldiers." *New Republic*, April 26, 2004. https://ssl.tnr.com/p/docsub.mhtml?i=20040426&s=leiken042604.

———. *Bearers of Global Jihad? Immigration and National Security after 9/11*. Report. March 2004. The Nixon Center. www.nixoncenter.org/publications/monographs/Leiken_Bearers_of_Global_Jihad.pdf.

"Letter from Senator Patrick Leahy (D-VT) to Attorney General John Ashcroft." January 1, 2003. www.eff.org/Privacy/TIA/leahy-letter.php.

Levitt, Matthew. "Hamas from Cradle to Grave." *Middle East Quarterly* 11 (Winter 2004). www.meforum.org/article/582.

———. "Navigating the U.S. Government's Terrorist Lists." *PolicyWatch*, November 30, 2001, 585. The Washington Institute for Near East Policy. www.washingtoninstitute.org.

Lewis, William H. "The War on Terrorism: A Retrospective." *Mediterranean Quarterly* 13 (Fall 2002): 21–37.

Lichtblau, Eric. "Ashcroft Says Efforts to Weaken Terrorism Law Will Place Americans at Greater Risk." *New York Times*, August 20, 2003.

Lutz, Brenda. *Global Terrorism*. New York: Routledge, 2008.

"Macau Bank's Customers Withdraw." *CNN.com*, September 19, 2005.

Mandaville, Peter. *Global Political Islam*. New York: Routledge, 2007.

Mann, James. *Rise of the Vulcans: The History of Bush's War Cabinet*. New York: Penguin Group, 2004.

Markon, Jerry, and Timothy Dwyer. "Jurors Reject Death Penalty for Moussaoui." *Washington Post*, May 4, 2006.

"Martyrs or Murderers? Terrorism and Suicide Bombing." Proceedings of The Brookings Institution Conference. October 20, 2002. www.scholarofthehouse.org/shabelfaands.html.

McCarthy, Andrew C. *Willful Blindness: A Memoir of the Jihad*. New York: Encounter Books, 2008.

McConnell, Mike. "Debate on the Foreign Intelligence Surveillance Act." Interview by Chris Roberts. *Transcript: Debate on the Foreign Intelligence Surveillance Act—El Paso Times*. August 22, 2007. www.elpasotimes.com/news/ci_6685679.

———. "A Key Gap in Fighting Terrorism." *Washington Post*, February 15, 2008.

Mexico. Gobierno de los Estados Unidos Mexicanos. Presidencia de la Republica. *Plan Nacional de Desarollo, 2007–2012*. 2007.

Milbank, Dana. "President Asks for Expanded Patriot Act." *Washington Post*, September 11, 2003.

Miller, Judith, and Jeff Gerth. "Philanthropist, or Fount of Funds for Terrorists?" *New York Times*, October 13, 2001.

Mintz, John. "FBI Focus Increases on Hamas, Hizballah; Ruling Enables Intensified Probes." *Washington Post*, May 8, 2003.

Mitchell, Robert P., and John O. Voll. *The Society of the Muslim Brothers*. 2nd ed. New York: Oxford University Press, 1993.

"The Money: Drying Up the Funds for Terror." *Terrorism: Questions and Answers*, 2004. Council on Foreign Relations. http://cfrterrorism.org/responses/money.html.

Moyer, Homer E., Jr., Robert C. Cassidy Jr., Michael T. Buckley, and J. CLifford Frazier, eds. *Law and Policy of Export Controls: Recent Essays on Key Export Issues*. American Bar Association Section of International Law and Policy, 1993.

"Muslim Brotherhood." *Columbia Encyclopedia*. 6th ed. New York: Columbia University Press, 2001. www.bartleby.com/65/mu/MuslimBr.html.

Muslim Brotherhood Movement Homepage, December 2007. www.ummah.org.uk/ikhwan/.

Myers, Joseph M. "Disrupting Terrorist Networks: The New U.S. and International Regime for Halting Terrorist Funding." *Law and Policy in International Business* 34 (2002): 17–18.

National Commission on Terrorist Attacks. *The 9/11 Commission Report: Final Report of the National Commission on Terrorist Attacks upon the United States.* Boston: W. W. Norton, 2004.

National Science Foundation. *Info Brief* (Science Resource Statistics). Arlington, VA: National Science Foundation, July 2006.

Neal, Andrew. *Exceptionalism and the War on Terror: The Politics of Liberty and Security after 9/11* (Routledge Studies in Liberty and Security). New York: Routledge, 2008.

Negroponte, John D. "Yes, We Are Better Prepared." *Washington Post*, September 10, 2006.

Ness, Cindy D., ed. *Female Terrorism and Militancy.* New York: Routledge, 2007.

Normack, Magnus. *Unconventional Weapons and International Terrorism*, edited by Magnus Ranstorp. New York: Routledge, 2009.

Norman, Paul. *Understanding Contemporary Terrorism and the Global Response.* New York: UCL Press, 2006.

Novak, Robert D. "Why Torts Trumped Terrorism." *Washington Post*, February 18, 2008.

Nuñez-Neto, Blas. Congressional Research Service. *Border Security: The San Diego Fence*, CRS Report for Congress, Code RS22026, January 13, 2005.

———. *Border Security: The Role of the U.S. Border Patrol*, CRS Report for Congress, Code RL32562, November 20, 2008.

Nuñez-Neto, Blas, and Stephen Viña. *Congressional Research Service, Border Security: Barriers along the U.S. International Border*, CRS Report for Congress, Code RL33658 CRS-1, December 12, 2006.

Office of Management and Budget Watch. "Nonprofits Call for Withdrawal of Anti-terror Financing Guidelines." *OMB Watcher*, February 7, 2006. www.ombwatch.org/article/article/print/3277/-1/420.

Organization of American States, General Assembly AG/RES.1650 (XXIX-O/99), June 7, 1999.

Organization of American States, Resolution of Meeting of Ministers of Justice, AG/RES. 1482 (XXXVII-O/97), June 5, 1997.

———. *Part 2: Status of Charities Shut Down by Treasury.* March 2006.

Operation Gatekeeper: An Investigation into Allegations of Fraud and Misconduct. July 1998. U.S. Department of Justice, Office of the Inspector General. www.usdoj.gov/oig/special/9807/gk01.htm#P160_18689.

Packer, George. *The Assassin's Gate: America in Iraq.* New York: Farrar, Straus and Giroux, 2005.

Palestinian Islamic Jihad: Harakat al-Jihad al-Islami al-Filastini. International Policy Institute for Counter Terrorism. www.ict.org.il/inter_ter/orgdet.cfm?orgid=28.

Passos, Nikos. "Fighting Terror with Error: The Counter-Productive Regulation of Informal Value Transfers." *Crime, Law, and Social Change* 45 (November 11, 2006): 315–21.

Patai, Raphael. *The Arab Mind*. New York: Hatherleigh, 2001.

"The Persian Diaspora, List of Persians and Farsi Speaking Peoples Living Outside of Iran, Worldwide Outreach to Persians, Outreach to Muslims around the Globe." *FarsiNet, Iranian Persian Global eCommunity for Farsi Speaking People, Persian Website, Free Farsi Books, Free farsi Injil, Persian Iranian Repository—Persian Farsi eCommunity—Persian Muslim Articles—Iranian Muslim Art—Farsi Muslim Poetry—What Is Islam for Irnians—What Is Holy War in Islam?—Jihad in Islam—Conflict between Islam and Israel—Why Muslims Hate America*. July 1, 2009. www.farsinet.com/pwo/diaspora.html.

Peters, William, and Michael J. Bandler. "Islam in the United States: A Tentative Ascent—A Conversation with Yvonne Haddad." *U.S. Society and Values*, USIA Electronic Journal, Vol. 2, No. 1. March 1997. Available at http://www.au.af.mil/au/awc/awcgate/documents/haddad.htm.

Pipes, Daniel, and Steven Emerson. "Why Won't the US Government Close Down Terrorist Groups on These Shores!?" *Jewish World Review*, August 14, 2004.

Plett, Barbara. "Yassin Killing Brings Call for Islamic Unity." *BBC News*, March 24, 2004. http://news.bbc.co.uk/1/hi/world/middle_east/3564957.stm.

Posner, Richard A. "The Reorganized U.S. Intelligence System after One Year." *American Enterprise Institute: National Security Outlook Special Edition*. AEI Online, April 2006. www.aei.org/outlook/24213.

Primiani, Tanya, and Christopher Sands. "Canada Changes the Tone on Passports." *CSIS Commentary*, June 9, 2006.

———. "Terrorists in Toronto: Is Canada Secure? Are We?" *CSIS Commentary*, June 20, 2006.

Public Safety and Terrorism. INTERPOL. www.interpol.int/public/terrorism.

Radical Islamist Profiles: Sheikh Omar Bakri Muhammad. Rep. no. 73. Washington, DC: Middle East Media Research Institute, 2001.

Reuter, Peter, and Edwin M. Truman. *Chasing Dirty Money: The Fight against Money Laundering*. Washington, DC: Institute for International Economics, November 2004.

Revell, Oliver. "Counterterrorism and Democratic Values: An American Practitioner's Experience." In *Close Calls: Intervention, Terrorism, Missile Defense and 'Just War' Today*, edited by Elliot Abrams, 237–50. Washington, DC: Ethics and Public Policy Center, 1998.

———. "Law Enforcement Views Radical Islam: Protecting America." *Middle East Quarterly*, March 1995.

Revell, Oliver "Buck", and Dwight Arnan Williams. *A G-Man's Journal: A Legendary Career Inside the FBI*. New York: Pocket Books, 1998.

Richburg, Keith B., and Fred Barbash. "Madrid Bombings Kill at Least 190: Al Qaeda-Linked Group Claims Responsibility." *Washington Post*. March 11, 2004. http://www.washingtonpost.com/wp-dyn/articles/A48577-2004Mar11.html.

Risen, James, and Eric Lichtblau. "Concerns Raised on Wider Spying Under New Law." *New York Times*, August 19, 2007.

Robarge, David. Review of *Fair Play: The Moral Dimensions of Spying* by James M. Olson. Washington, DC: Potomac Books, 2006. https://www.cia.gov/library/center-for-the-study-of-intelligence/csi-publications/csi-studies/studies/vol51no1/fair-play-the-moral-dilemmas-of-spying.html.

Robinson, Eugene. "Values We Have to Hide Abroad." *Washington Post*, September 8, 2006.

Rockefeller, Jay, Patrick Leahy, Silvestre Reyes, and John Conyers. "Scare Tactics and Our Surveillance Bill." *Washington Post*, February 25, 2008.

Roig-Franzia, Manuel. "Mexico Rebukes U.S. Candidates on Migrant Issues." *Washington Post*, January 8, 2008.

Rouleau, Eric. "Trouble in the Kingdom." *Foreign Affairs* 81, no. 4 (July/August 2002): 75–89.

Roumani, Rhonda, and Marianne Stigset. "Al-Qaeda Link to Madrid Blasts May Alter EU Policies." *Daily Star. Lebanonwire*, March 13, 2004. www.lebanonwire.com /0403/04031326DS.asp.

Roumaniuk, Peter. *Global Counterterrorism*. New York: Routledge, 2009.

Rowswell, Ben. *Ogdensburg Revisited: Adapting Canada-US Security Cooperation to the New International Era*. Washington, DC: Center for Strategic and International Studies, 2004.

"Rules for Spying." *Washington Post*, March 16, 2008.

"Saddam's Ambassador to al Qaeda." *Weekly Standard*, March 1, 2004.

Schmemann, Serge. "U.N. Requires Members to Act against Terror." *New York Times*, September 29, 2001. www.nytimes.com/2001/09/29/international/29 NATI.html?scp=2&sq=U.N.%20Requires%20Members%20to%20Act% 20against%20Terror&st=cse.

Schmid, Alex, Albert J. Jongman, and Eric Price, eds. *Handbook of Terrorism Research: Research, Theories and Concepts*. New York: Routledge, 2008.

Schmidt, Susan. "Patriot Act Misunderstood, Senators Say; Complaints about Civil Liberties Go Beyond Legislation's Reach, Some Insist." *Washington Post*, October 22, 2003.

Security Council Unanimously Adopts Wide-Ranging Anti-terrorism Resolution; Calls for Suppressing Financing, Improving International Cooperation; Resolution 1373 (2001) Also Creates Committee to Monitor Implementation, Security Council 4385th Meeting SC/7158, September 28, 2001.

"Senator: Al Qaeda Cells Inside United States." *CNN*, February 23, 2002. www.cnn.com/2002/US/02/23/gen.terror.graham.

"The Sentry's Solitude." *Foreign Affairs* 80, no. 6 (November/December 2001): 2–16.

Seper, Jerry. "Islamic Extremists Invade U.S., Join Sleeper Cells." *Washington Times*, February 10, 2004.

Sheppard, Ben. *The Psychology of Strategic Terrorism*. New York: Routledge, 2008.

Sipress, Alan. "Crackdown Expanded to All Groups in Terror List." *Washington Post*, November 3, 2001.

Skerry, Peter. "Political Islam in the United States and Europe." *Political Islam: Challenges for US Policy*. 2003. Aspen Institute Congressional Program.

www.aspeninstitute.org/AspenInstitute/files/CCLIBRARYFILES/FILENAME/
0000000559/islamintheus.pdf.

Smith, Craig S. "Europe's Chief on Terrorism to Reassure U.S. on Efforts." *New York Times*, May 10, 2004.

———. "France Struggles to Curb Extremist Muslim Clerics." *New York Times*, April 30, 2004. http://nytimes.com/2004/04/30/international/europe/30FRAN.html?pagewanted=print&position=.

Smith, Tom W. *Counting Flocks and Lost Sheep: Trends in Religious Preference since World War II*. Rep. no. 26. Chicago: GSS Social Change Report, 1991.

———. "Estimating the Muslim Population in the United States." *Home-American Jewish Committee*, July 1, 2009. www.ajc.org/InTheMedia/PubIntergroup Relations.asp?did=356&pid=818.

"Special Report." *The Economist*, September 2, 2006.

Speer, Lawrence J. "FATF Vows Unity in Curbing Terrorist Financing, Criminal Money Laundering." *Daily Report for Executives*, February 4, 2002.

Spiegel, Peter. "U.S. Team Created to Target al-Qaeda Finances." *Financial Times*, October 26, 2001.

Stephens, Closs. *Terrorism and the Politics of Response: London in a Time of Terror* (Routledge Critical Terrorism Studies). New York: Routledge, 2008.

Stolberg, Sheryl Gay. "Senate Passes Legislation to Renew Patriot Act." *New York Times*, March 8, 2006.

Stone, Carol L. "Estimate of Muslims Living in America." *The Muslims of America*. New York: Oxford University Press, 1991.

Tanter, Raymond. "PolicyWatch: Iran's Threat to Coalition Forces in Iraq." *Analysis of Near East Policy from the Scholars and Associates of The Washington Institute* 827. January 15, 2004. http://www.washingtoninstitute.org/distribution/POL827.doc.

———. *Rogue Regimes: Terrorism and Proliferation*. New York: St. Martin's Griffin, 1999.

Terrorist Threat Integration Center. *Federation of American Scientists*. www.fas.org/irp/agency/ttic/.

Tompkins, Joseph B., Jr. *The Impact of the USA PATRIOT Act on Non-US Banks: Prepared in Connection with the International Monetary Fund Seminar on Current Developments in Monetary and Financial Law Held on May 7–17, 2002, in Washington, DC*. http://imf.org/external/np/leg/sem/2002/cdmfl/eng/tompki.pdf.

Treasury Guidelines Working Group of Charitable Sector Organizations and Advisors. *Principles of International Charity*. March 2005. www.usig.org/PDFs/Principles_Final.pdf.

Tyler, Patrick E., and Don Van Natta Jr. "Militants in Europe Openly Call for Jihad and the Rule of Islam." *New York Times*, April 26, 2004.

U.S. Code. 5 U.S.C. 1701 *et seq.*

———. 8 U.S.C. §1103(a)(5). "Secretary of Homeland Security."

———. 15 U.S.C. 1681(u).

———. 18 U.S.C. [sec] 983(i) (2002).

———. 18 U.S.C. 2232 (b-c)

———. 18 U.S.C. 2518(3) (West Federal Criminal Code and Rules, 1998 ed.).

———. 18 U.S.C. 2709.

———. U.S. Code. 20 U.S.C. 1232(g).

———. 20 U.S.C. 3414(a)(5)(A).

———. 20 U.S.C. 9007.

———. 22 U.S.C. 287(c)

———. 25 U.S.C. §324. "Consent of Certain Tribes; Consent of Individual Indians,"

———. 31 U.S.C. § 5318(k)(3)(C)(i).

———. 31 U.S.C. 5318(A)

———. 50 U.S.C. App. 5(b).

———. 50 U.S.C. 1801–1862

———. 50 U.S.C. 1701 *et seq.*

———. Pub. L. 110-55. "Protect America Act of 2007." August 3, 2007.

———. Pub. L. 90-351.

———. Pub. L. No. 108-458, 118 Stat. 3638.

———. Pub. L. No. 107-567, 115 Stat. 272 (2001).

———. Pub. L. No. 107-173, 116 Stat. 543 (2002).

———. Pub. L. No. 107-296, §403, 116 Stat. 2135, 2178.

———. Pub. L. No. 107-71, 115 Stat. 597 (2001).

———. Pub. L. 103-359, 108 Stat. 3444 (October 14, 1994)

———. Pub. L. 104-208, Div. C. *The Homeland Security Act of 2002*

———. Pub. L. 107-56. USA PATRIOT Act. 2001.

———. Pub. L. 107-40. September 18, 2001.

———. Pub. L. 109-13.*The Emergency Supplemental Appropriations Act for Defense, the Global War on Terror, and Tsunami Relief, 2005,* 109th Cong.

U.S. Congress. House. H.R. Res. 1157, 108th Cong. (2003). "To amend the Foreign Intelligence Surveillance Act to exempt bookstores and libraries from orders requiring the production of any tangible things for certain foreign intelligence investigations, and for other purposes."

———. H.R. 3162, 107 Cong. (2001) (enacted).

———. H.R. Res. 3199, 109th Cong. (enacted).

———. H.R. Res. 3773, 110th Cong. (enacted).

———. H.R. Res. 6304, 110th Cong. (enacted).

———. H.R. Res. 35, 110th Cong. (enacted).

———. Committee on International Relations. *Hearings on Al Qaeda and the Global Reach of Terrorism.* 107th Cong. 1st sess., 107–50 (2001) (testimony of Oliver "Buck" Revell).

U.S. Congress. Senate. *Comprehensive Immigration Reform Act of 2006,* S. 2611, 109th Cong.

———. *Comprehensive Immigration Reform Act of 2007,* S. 1348, 110th Cong.

———. *Domestic Security Enhancement Act of 2003,* January 9, 2003. 108th Congress.

———. *Immigration Enforcement and Border Security Act of 2007,* S. 2294, 110th Cong.

————. National Commission on Terrorist Attacks upon the U.S. (testimony of John S. Pistole, executive assistant director, Counterterrorism/Counterintelligence, FBI) (2004).

————. Select Committee on Intelligence of the U.S. Senate (February 24, 2004) (testimony of Robert S. Mueller, III, director, FBI).

————. Select Committee on Intelligence of the U.S. Senate (February 11, 2003) (testimony of Robert S. Mueller, III, director, FBI).

————. Senate Committee on Banking, Housing, and Urban Affairs (July 13, 2005) (testimony of Assistant Secretary for Economic and Business Affairs E. Anthony Wayne [State Dept.]).

————. Senate Judiciary Committee, Subcommittee on Immigration, Border Security, and Citizenship, and Subcommittee on Terrorism, Technology, and Homeland Security. *Strengthening Enforcement and Border Security: The 9/11 Commission Staff Report on Terrorist Travel.* 109th Cong., 1st sess. S. Rep. 109–71.

————. Senate Select Committee on Intelligence and the House Permanent Select Committee on Intelligence. *Joint Intelligence Committee Inquiry.* 107th Cong. (2002) (testimony of Robert S. Mueller, III, director, FBI).

————. Subcommittee on Immigration, Border Security and Claims. *Sources and Methods of Foreign Nationals Engaged in Economic and Military Espionage* hearing. 109th Cong. (2005) (testimony of William A. Wulf).

————. "To exclude United States persons from the definition of 'foreign power' under the Foreign Intelligence Surveillance Act of 1978 relating to international terrorism," S. 113, 108th Cong.

————. U.S. Senate Terrorism, Technology and Homeland Security Subcommittee. *The State of the Terrorist Threat Facing the United States.* 108th Cong. (2003) (testimony of Larry A. Mefford, assistant director Counterterrorism Division FBI).

U.S. Department of Commerce. Bureau of the Census. December 3, 2003. www.census.gov/Press-Release/www/releases/archives/census_2000/001576.html.

————. Bureau of Industry and Security. *Exporting to Special Destinations and Persons: Terrorist-Support and Embargoed Countries, Designated Terrorists and Sanctioned Persons.* Phillip K. Ankel and Glenn H. Kaminstky.

————. Determination Pursuant to Section 102 of the Illegal Immigration Reform and Immigrant Responsibility Act of 12996 as Amended by Section 102 of the REAL ID Act of 2005. 70 Federal Register 55622-02, September 22, 2005.

————. "Fact Sheet: Securing Our Nation's Borders." Press release. June 29, 2006. www.dhs.gov/xnews/releases/press_release_0938.shtm.

————. *Fact Sheet: The Terrorist Screening Center.* www.dhs.gov/xnews/releases/press_release_0246.shtm.

U.S. Department of Justice. *Department and Partner Agencies Launch National Counter-Proliferation Initiative.* October 11, 2007.

————. Immigration and Nationalization Service. "Operation Gatekeeper Fact Sheet." Press release. July 14, 1998.

————. *Patterns of Muslim Immigration.* Jane Smith. http://usinfo.state.gov/products/pubs/muslimlife/immigrat.htm.

U.S. Department of State. "Country Reports on Terrorism 2006." April 28, 2006. www.state.gov/s/ct/rls/crt/2006/.

———. Exec. Order 13224, 3 C.F.R. 768 (2002).

———. Exec. Order 13355, 3 C.F.R. (2004).

———. Exec. Order 13382. www.state.gov/t/isn/c22080.htm.

———. *Foreign Press Center Briefing.* Deputy Spokesman, Philip Reeker, October 25, 2001. http://fpc.state.gov/7515.htm.

———. *International Narcotics Control Strategy* Rep. XII–24. March 2003.

———. *International Narcotics Control Strategy Report.* Vol. 2. March 2005.

———. Office of the Coordinator for Counterterrorism. *Patterns of Global Terrorism.* November 15, 2002. www.state.gov/s/ct/rls/fs/2002/15222.htm.

———. "Patterns of Global Terrorism 2002." April 30, 2002. www.state.gov/s/ct/rls/crt/2002/html/index.htm.

———. "Patterns of Global Terrorism 2003." April 2002. www.state.gov/s/ct/rls/pgtrpt/2003/31644.htm.

———. "Richard Boucher, Spokesman, Press Statement (Revised), Redesignation of Foreign Terrorist Organizations 2003/1000." October 2, 2003. www.state.gov/r/pa/prs/ps/2003/24851.htm.

U.S. Department of the Treasury. *Anti-terrorist Financing Guidelines: Voluntary Best Practices for U.S. Based Charities.* June 1, 2006. www.treas.gov/offices/enforcement/key issues/protecting/charitiesintro.shtml.

———. Federal Reserve System, 12 CFR Part 233, Regulation GG; Docket No. R-1298.

———. Office of Foreign Assets Control. *Nonproliferation: What You Need to Know about Treasury Restrictions.* www.treasury.gov/offices/enforcement/ofac/programs/wmd/wmd.pdf.

———. Office of Public Affairs. "Response to Inquiries from Arab American and American Muslim Communities." Press release. November 2007. http://www.treas.gov/press/releases/po3607.htm.

———. U.S. Secretary of the Treasury. *A Report to Congress in Accordance with §359, 2002.*

———. 31 C.F.R. 103.11(z).

———. 31 CFR Part 132 RIN 1505-AB78. Prohibition on Funding of Unlawful Internet Gambling, Notice of Joint Proposed Rulemaking, October 12, 2007.

———. 31 C.F.R. Part 598.

———. *U.S. Treasury Department Announces New Executive Office for Terrorist Financing and Financial Crimes.* March 3, 2003.

———. *U.S. Treasury: Office of Terrorism and Financial Intelligence (TFI).* U.S. Department of the Treasury. http://www.treas.gov/offices/enforcement/.

———. *U.S. Treasury SDN List.* www.treas.gov/offices/enforcement/ofac/sdn.

U.S. District Court for the District of Columbia. *Holy Land Foundation for Relief and Development v. John Ashcroft et al.,* 333 F. 2d 156 (2003).

———. *Holy Land Foundation v. Ashcroft,* 2002 U.S. Dist. LEXIS 14641 (August 8, 2002).

U.S. District Court for the Eastern District of Virginia, Alexandria Division. *United States of America v. John Phillip Walker Lindh*, February 2002.

U.S. District Court for the Northern District of Illinois, Eastern Division. *Benevolence International Foundation, Inc. v. John Ashcroft, et al.*, No. 02 C 763 (January 30, 2002).

———. *Boim v. Quranic Literacy Institute, et al.*, 340 F.Supp. 2d 885 (2004).

U.S. District Court. Oregon. *Mayfield v. United States*, September 26, 2007, Civil No. 04-1427-AA.

U.S. District Court for the Southern District of California. *Sierra Club v. Ashcroft*, No. 04-CV-272, February 10, 2004.

U.S. Government Accountability Office. *Border Control—Revised Strategy Is Showing Some Positive Results*, GAO/GGD-95-30, January 31, 1995.

———. *Border Security: US-VISIT Faces Strategic, Technological, and Operational Challenges at Land Ports of Entry*, GEO-07-248, December 2006.

———. *Border Security: Improvements Needed to Reduce Time Taken to Adjudicate Visas for Science Students and Scholars*, GAO-04-371, February 2004.

———. *Container Security: A Flexible Staffing Model and Minimum Equipment Requirements Would Improve Overseas Targeting and Inspection Efforts*, overview AGO-05-557, April 2005.

———. *Homeland Security Progress Has Been Made to Address the Vulnerabilities Exposed by 9/11, but Continued Federal Action Is Needed to Further Mitigate Security Risks*, GAO-07-375, January 2007.

———. *Terrorist Financing: Better Strategic Planning Needed to Coordinate U.S. Efforts to Deliver Counter-Terrorism Financing Training and Technical Assistance Abroad*. 2005.

U.S. Supreme Court. *Katz v. United States*, 389 U.S. 347 (1967).

———. *United States v. Sioux Nation of Indians*. No. 79-639. June 30, 1980.

———. *United States v. United States District Court (Keith)*, 407 U.S. 297 (1972).

"US Money Laundering Accusation Ignites Resentment in Macao." *Asia Pulse via Yahoo!* September 19, 2005.

VandeHei, Jim. "Past Votes Dog Some Presidential Candidates; Democrats Defend Siding with Bush." *Washington Post*, September 12, 2003.

The Vice President's Task Force on Terrorism. *Summary of Findings and Recommendations*. Washington, DC: Government Printing Office, 1986.

Viles, Tom. "Hawala, Hysteria, and Hegemony." *Journal of Money Laundering Control* 11, no. 1 (2008).

Vinci, Anthony. *Armed Groups and the Balance of Power*. New York: Routledge, 2008.

Waked, Ali. "France and Spain Bid to 'Legalize' Hamas." *Ynet News*, March 6, 2005.

Warner, David P. "Law Enforcement Cooperation the Organization of American States: A Focus on REMJA." *University of Miami Inter-American Law Review* 27 (2006): 387+.

Weinberg, Leonar. *Democracy and the War on Terror: Civil Liberties and the Fight against Terrorism* (Cass Series on Political Violence). New York: Routledge, 2008.

———. *Democratic Responses to Terrorism (Democracy and Terrorism)*. New York: Routledge, 2007.

Weinberg, Leonar, Ami Pedahzur, and Arie Perliger, eds. *Political Parties and Terrorist Groups*. 2nd ed. New York: Routledge, 2008.

Weisman, Jonathan. "House Passes a Surveillance Bill Not to Bush's Liking." *Washington Post*, March 15, 2008.

———. "Patriot Act Extension Is Reduced to a Month." *Washington Post*, December 23, 2005.

Weisman, Jonathan, and Dan Eggen. "Warrantless Surveillance to Expire." *Washington Post*, February 16, 2008.

The White House. Office of the Press Secretary. "President Freezes Terrorists? Assets, Remarks by the President, Secretary of the Treasury O'Neill and Secretary of State Powell on Executive Order, The Rose Garden." Press release. September 24, 2001. www.whitehouse.gov/news/releases/2001/09/20010924- html.

Whoriskey, Peter. "Mistrial Declared in Islamic Charity Case." *Washington Post*, October 23, 2007.

Wilkinson, Paul. *Homeland Security in the UK*. New York: Routledge, 2007.

———. *State Terrorism and Human Rights*. New York: Routledge, 2010.

Wolffe, Richard. "U.S. Probe Takes Close Look at Trail of 'Honey Money.' " *Financial Times*, October 12, 2001. www.ft.com/home/us.

———. "U.S. Treasury Adds More Names to 'Frozen Assets' List." *Financial Times*, October 12, 2001. www.ft.com/home/us.

Woodward, Bob. *Bush at War*. New York: Simon & Schuster, 2002.

———. *Plan of Attack*. New York: Simon & Schuster, 2004.

Zagaris, Bruce. "Bush Administration Embarks on New Initiative to Combat Terrorism Financing Amid Broad Criticisms." *International Enforcement Law Reporter* 18 (December 2002): 491–92.

———. "FATF Makes No Change in Non-cooperative Countries and Begins Compliance with Counterterrorism Financial Enforcement." *International Enforcement Law Reporter* 18 (April 2002): 134–36.

———. "U.S. and Other Countries Attack against Additional List of Terrorist Supporters." *International Enforcement Law Reporter* 19th ser. 17 (December 2001).

———. "U.S. Announces Counter-Proliferation Initiative." *International Enforcement Law Reporter* 23 (December 2007).

———. "U.S. Enacts Counter Terrorism Act with Significant New International Provisions." *International Enforcement Law Reporter* 17 (December 2001): 522–26.

———. "U.S. Forms New Investigative Team to Target Terrorist Financial Networks." *International Enforcement Law Reporter* 17 (December 2001): 519–20.

Zimmerman, Eline. "Border Protections Imperil Environment? Last Wilderness Area South of San Diego Could Be Damaged." *San Francisco Chronicle*, February 27, 2006.

Index

Hussain, Tahawwur, xviii
Hussein, Saddam, 25, 42, 50, 56, 109

Illegal Immigration Reform and
    Immigrant Responsibility Act
    (IIRIRA), 174, 176
Immigration Advisory Program
    (IAP), 235
Immigration and Customs
    Enforcement (ICE), 58, 165, 169
Immigration and Nationality Act,
    152, 161
Immigration and Naturalization Service
    (INS), 103, 146, 157, 175–176
Immigration Enforcement and Border
    Security Act of 2007 (IEBSA), 163
Importer Security Filing interim final
    rule, 236
In re: Sealed Case, 190, 192, 194–195
India, xviii, 34, 40, 44–45, 96, 99, 226
Indonesia, 230
Indyk, Martin, 56
Inkster, Norman D., 95–96
Inspector General (of the NSA), 70–71,
    114–115, 158
Integrated Border Enforcement Teams
    (IBETs), 172
intelligence community, x, xiii, xx, 15,
    27, 29–30, 50, 57, 59–60, 61, 64, 72,
    74, 76, 113, 115, 117, 191, 206,
    212–216, 220–224
Intelligence Oversight Act, 70
Intelligence Reform and Terrorism
    Prevention Act of 2004, 27, 57, 77,
    114, 153, 160–161, 222
Intelligence Sharing Procedures, 192
Interagency Intelligence Subcommittee,
    91
Inter-American Drug Abuse Control
    Commission (CICAD), 186
Inter-American Committee Against
    Terrorism (CICTE), 186
Inter-American Convention Against
    Terrorism, 186
Interdepartmental Group on
    Terrorism, 90
intermestic terrorism, 30, 32, 51

Internal Revenue Service (IRS), 128
International Association of Chiefs of
    Police (IACP), 95–97, 115
"International Best Practices on
    Freezing Terrorist Assets," 233
International Committee of the Red
    Cross, 66
International Convention Against the
    Taking of Hostages, 90
International Convention for the
    Suppression of Terrorism Bombings
    (1997), 171
International Convention for the
    Suppression of the Financing of
    Terrorism, 3, 171
International Criminal Investigative
    Training Assistance Program
    (ICITAP), 230
International Emergency Economic
    Powers Act (IEEPA), 121–122, 132,
    138–140, 230
International Joint Commission, 171
International Terrorist Group
    (subdivision of Interpol), 94
Internet Service Provider (ISP), 228
Interpol, 94–96, 159
Intifada, 49
Iran, xvi, xix, 13–16, 19–20, 23,
    40–44, 47–48, 51, 53–54, 56, 83,
    85–86, 116, 121, 127, 144
Iraq, xvi, xviii, 9, 12, 15, 19, 21, 25,
    42–44, 50, 56, 67, 68, 71, 78, 114,
    168, 208, 220
Iraq War, 50
Islamic American Relief Agency, 140
Islamic charitable organizations, 232
Islamic Cultural Institute, Milan, 125
Islamic Front of Syria, 46
Islamic Jihad, 22, 40, 46–47, 48–49,
    63, 85, 88, 125, 195
Islamist, 25, 31–42, 44–48, 52–53, 64,
    74, 88, 185
Islamist Affinity Terrorism, 31, 32
Israel, 9, 15–16, 42, 45, 48–49, 55, 86,
    90, 96, 101, 118, 139
Italy, 64, 79, 88–89, 95
Italy, Texas, 228

About the Editor and Contributors

YONAH ALEXANDER is Professor Emeritus of international studies and Director of the Institute for Studies in International Terrorism at the State University of New York. Formerly, he was affiliated with Columbia University Graduate School of Journalism; a senior staff member at the Georgetown University Center for Strategic and International Studies; and Professor and Director of Terrorism Studies Program at George Washington University. Currently, he is Senior Fellow and Director of the International Center for Terrorism Studies at the Potomac Institute for Policy Studies, Director of the Inter-University Center for Terrorism Studies, and Co-director of the Inter-University Center for Legal Studies. He founded and served as editor-in-chief of three international journals: *Terrorism, Political Communication and Persuasion*, and *Minority and Group Rights*. He has published nearly 100 books, including the 2008–2009 works: *The New Iranian Leadership: Ahmadinejad, Nuclear Ambition and the Middle East; Evolution of U.S. Counterterrorism Policy: A Documentary Collection* (3 Vols); *Turkey: Terrorism, Civil Rights, and the European Union*; and *Terror on the High Seas: From Piracy to Strategic Challenge* (2 Vols). His works have been published in two dozen languages.

M. E. (SPIKE) BOWMAN was, most recently, Deputy, National Counterintelligence Executive. Previously he was Senior Research Fellow at the Center for Technology and National Security Policy. He is retired from the Senior Executive Service, Federal Bureau of Investigation, where he served successively as Deputy General Counsel (National Security Law), Senior Counsel for National Security Law, and Director, Intelligence Issues and

Policy Group (National Security Branch). He is a former intelligence officer, an international lawyer, and a specialist in national security law with extensive experience in espionage and terrorism investigations. In addition to national security experience, he is a retired U.S. Navy Captain who served as Head of International Law at the Naval War College, as a diplomat at the U.S. Embassy in Rome, and as Chief of Litigation for the U.S. Navy. Mr. Bowman is a graduate of Willamette University (B.A.), the University of Wisconsin (M.A.), the University of Idaho (J.D., *Cum Laude*), and George Washington University (LL.M., International and Comparative Law, *With Highest Honors*).

EDGAR H. BRENNER is Co-director of the Inter-University Center for Legal Studies at the International Law Institute in Washington, D.C., as well as Senior Advisor and Legal Counsel to the Inter-University Center for Terrorism Studies. He is a graduate of Carleton College and of Yale Law School, and he has an Honorary Doctor of Humane Letters (EC: IBR 1988). He is a member of the District of Columbia Bar, the Bar of various U.S. Courts of Appeal, and the Bar of the Supreme Court of the United States. He has lectured on various aspects of counterterrorism law and policy at such venues as George Washington University, Tel Aviv University, University of Bahcesehir Law School, Marmara University Law School, University of Michigan Law School, Carleton College, and Wilton Park (U.K.).

He is co-editor (with Yonah Alexander) of *Legal Aspects of Terrorism in the United States* (4 Vols) (Oceana Publishers, 2000), *Terrorism and the Law* (Transnational, 2001), *U.S. Federal Legal Responses to Terrorism* (Transnational, 2002), *The United Kingdom's Legal Responses To Terrorism* (Transnational and Cavendish, 2003), and *Turkey: Terrorism, Civil Rights, and the European Union* (Routledge, 2008).

Mr. Brenner is a Carleton College Alumni Award Recipient and is a Trustee Emeritus of the Institutes of Behavior Resources.

STEPHEN KERSTING received his B.S. in international politics from Georgetown University and his M.A. in security studies from the Security Studies Program at Georgetown University. He conducts research on security issues in the Middle East, with particular attention to intelligence, terrorism, and U.S.-Iran relations.

WILLIAM H. LEWIS has served in the Office of National Estimates under its renowned founder, Sherman Kent. In the State and Defense Departments, he has been appointed to presidential commissions, study groups on the Middle East, and special missions to Morocco, Libya, Sudan, and Kenya. His academic career includes professorships with the University of Michigan, Johns Hopkins University, and George Washington University. He has authored numerous books and articles relating to national security and Middle East policy issues.

DAVID G. REIST, BGen, USMC (Ret), is a Senior Research Fellow at the Potomac Institute for Policy Studies. He most recently served as the Assistant Deputy Commandant, Installations and Logistics Department (LP), Headquarters, U.S. Marine Corps, Washington, D.C.

Brigadier General Reist's command assignments include: CO Company A, 2nd Landing Support Battalion (1981–1982); CO Company A, Marine Barracks 8th & I (1985–1986); CO Beach & Port Company, 2nd Landing Support Battalion (1989–1990); CO 1st Landing Support Battalion (1997–1998); CO 1st Transportation Support Battalion (2002–2004) (redesignated Transportation Support Group during Operation Iraqi Freedom); Combat Service Support Group-11 during Operation Iraqi Freedom-II; and CG 1st Force Service Support Group (redesignated 1st Marine Logistics Group) (2005–2007).

Brigadier General Reist's staff assignments include: Division G-4, 3rd Marine Division (1982–1983); Head, Motor Transport, Engineer, and Utilities Writer Section, Marine Corps Institute (1983–1984); Registrar, Marine Corps Institute (1984–1985); Operations Officer, MSSG-22 for LF6F 4-87 and 1-89 (1987–1989); Executive Officer, 2nd Landing Support Battalion (1990); Ground Prepositioning Program Sponsor (1990–1992) and Maritime Prepositioning Program Sponsor (1992–1993), Plans, Policies, and Operations, Headquarters Marine Corps; Current Operations Officer, U.S. Central Command J-4/7 (1994–1997); Deputy G-3, 1st FSSG (2000); Faculty Advisor (2000–2001) and Deputy Director (2001–2002), Marine Corps Command and Staff College; Chief of Staff, 1st FSSG (2004–2005) and Deputy CG (Support), I Marine Expeditionary Force Forward (2006–2007).

Brigadier General Reist graduated from the State University of New York at Geneseo in 1978 with a B.S. in biology. He also holds a Master of Strategic Studies from the Marine Corps War College and a Master of Arts in National Security and Strategic Studies from the Naval War College.

OLIVER (BUCK) REVELL is President of Revell Group International, Inc., Rowlett, Dallas County, Texas; the Chairman, Board of Directors, Middle East Media Research Institute (MEMRI) Washington, D.C.; Senior Advisor to Synfuels International of Dallas, Texas; a director of Vance Security USA, Inc., Oakton, Virginia, and EMThrax, LLC of Augusta, Georgia; he is also a Trustee of the Center for American & International Law, Plano, Texas.

He served for five years as an Officer and Aviator in the U.S. Marine Corps, leaving active duty in 1964 as a Captain. He then served 30 years as a Special Agent and Senior Executive of the Federal Bureau of Investigation (1964–1994). From 1980 until 1991 he served in FBI Headquarters first as Assistant Director in charge of Criminal Investigations (including terrorism);

then as Associate Deputy Director he was in charge of the Investigative, Intelligence, Counter-Terrorism, Training, Laboratory and International programs of the Bureau (1985–91). He served as a member of the President's Council on Integrity and Efficiency (1980–91), the National Foreign Intelligence Board (1987–91), and the Senior Review Group, Vice President's Task Force on Terrorism (1985–1986). Mr. Revell also served as Vice Chairman of the Interagency Group for Counter-Intelligence (1985–91) and on the Terrorist Crisis Management Committee of the National Security Council. In September 1987, Mr. Revell was placed in charge of a joint FBI/CIA/U.S. military operation (Operation Goldenrod) which led to the first apprehension overseas of an international terrorist. President Reagan commended him for his leadership of this endeavor. On May 1, 1992, the Attorney General ordered Mr. Revell to Los Angeles placing him in command of joint Federal law enforcement efforts to suppress the riots and civil disorder; he also coordinated the law enforcement activities of the assigned Military Forces. He received the Attorney General's Special Commendation Award for this endeavor. He was Special Agent in Charge (SAC) of the Dallas Division of the FBI at the time of his retirement in September 1994. He retired with the restored rank of Associate Deputy Director.

In 1989, President George H. W. Bush awarded Mr. Revell the Presidential Distinguished Senior Executive Award and in 1990 the Presidential Meritorious Senior Executive Award. In 1991 he was awarded The FBI Medal for Meritorious Achievement and the National Intelligence Distinguished Service Medal and a Commendation from the Secretary of Defense for his efforts to protect the Homeland during the Desert Storm Operation. In October 1994, Mr. Revell was awarded the Albert J. Wood Public Affairs Award by the Middle East Forum for his "efforts in the fight against International Terrorism."

Mr. Revell attended the University of Georgia, is a graduate of East Tennessee State University, and holds a Masters degree in Government & Public Administration from Temple University; he is graduate of Senior Executive Programs in National and International Security and Senior Executives in Government of the Kennedy School, Harvard University.

RAYMOND TANTER served at the White House as a senior member on the National Security Council staff from 1981 to 1982. In 1983–1984, he was personal representative of the Secretary of Defense to arms control talks in Madrid, Helsinki, Stockholm, and Vienna. In 1967, Professor Tanter was Deputy Director of Behavioral Sciences at the Advanced Research Projects Agency of the U.S. Department of Defense and a member of the Civilian Executive Panel, Chief of Naval Operations, 1980–1981. In 2005, he helped found the Iran Policy Committee and serves as its President. He is a member of the Council on Foreign Relations and the Committee on the Present Danger. Professor Tanter teaches courses on terrorism and proliferation at

Georgetown University. He is also professor emeritus at the University of Michigan and adjunct scholar at The Washington Institute for Near East Policy.

BRUCE ZAGARIS is a partner with the Washington, D.C. law firm of Berliner Corcoran & Rowe LLP. Since 1975, much of Mr. Zagaris's work has involved counseling on international financial sector matters and the regulation of money movement. Much of his practice involves counseling and participating in international enforcement initiatives of a regulatory and white-collar-crime nature concerning money movement.

He advises individuals and businesses on compliance policy and implementation. His work has included advising governments and representing them in treaty negotiations, preparation of legislation, and designing regulatory mechanisms. He has served as a consultant for international organizations, such as the IMF, the Asian Development Bank, the UN Crime Branch, and Caribbean FATF. He has participated in internal investigations and in civil, criminal, and administrative litigation, representing defendants, third parties, and serving as an expert witness. He is a regular teacher and trainer for law schools and a host of organizations on anti-money-laundering and financial regulatory matters.

In 1985, he founded the International Enforcement Law Reporter (www .ielr.com), a monthly journal for which he is editor. He has been an expert witness in a number of trials concerning money laundering and related matters.